Administrative Assistant's and Secretary's Handbook

FIFTH EDITION

Administrative Assistant's and Secretary's Handbook

FIFTH EDITION

James Stroman ■ **Kevin Wilson** ■ **Jennifer Wauson**

AMACOM

American Management Association

New York • Atlanta • Brussels • Chicago • Mexico City • San Francisco
Shanghai • Tokyo • Toronto • Washington, D. C.

Administrative assistant's
and secretary's handbook

Bulk discounts available. For details visit:
www.amacombooks.org/go/specialsales
Or contact special sales:
Phone: 800-250-5308
Email: specialsls@amanet.org
View all the AMACOM titles at: www.amacombooks.org
American Management Association: www.amanet.org

This publication is designed to provide accurate and authoritative information in regard to the subject matter covered. It is sold with the understanding that the publisher is not engaged in rendering legal, accounting, or other professional service. If legal advice or other expert assistance is required, the services of a competent professional person should be sought.

Library of Congress Cataloging-in-Publication Data

Stroman, James.
    Administrative assistant's and secretary's handbook / by James Stroman, Kevin Wilson, Jennifer Wauson. — Fifth edition.
        pages cm
    Includes bibliographical references and index.
    ISBN 978-0-8144-3352-2 — ISBN 0-8144-3352-9 1. Secretaries—Handbooks, manuals, etc.
2. Office practice—Handbooks, manuals, etc. I. Wilson, K. (Kevin), 1958– II. Wauson, Jennifer. III. Title.
    HF5547.5.S8163   2014
    651.3—dc23   2013045476

About AMA
American Management Association (www.amanet.org) is a world leader in talent development, advancing the skills of individuals to drive business success. Our mission is to support the goals of individuals and organizations through a complete range of products and services, including classroom and virtual seminars, webcasts, webinars, podcasts, conferences, corporate and government solutions, business books, and research. AMA's approach to improving performance combines experiential learning—learning through doing—with opportunities for ongoing professional growth at every step of one's career journey.

Printing number
10 9 8 7 6 5 4 3 2 1

Dedicated to the people who have shaped our lives in magnificent ways

John Wilson

Ruth Wilson

Horace Wauson

Evelyn Wauson

Bob Brueck

Pat Brueck

Contents

SECTION TWO   OFFICE EQUIPMENT AND COMPUTERS

SECTION THREE **OFFICE PRODUCTIVITY SOFTWARE**

SECTION FIVE   LANGUAGE USAGE

41 Business Math   468

SECTION SEVEN **CAREER ADVANCEMENT**

42 Your Future   479

43 Presentation Skills   486

44 Communications Skills   491

45 Office Management and Supervision   498

Preface

One of the most important positions in any company is that of administrative assistant, also referred to as executive secretary, private secretary, personal secretary, or office administrator. The job requires versatility, skill, precision, efficiency, and a constant willingness to increase one's knowledge.

Being a top-notch administrative assistant in the business or the professional world is a satisfying and rewarding career in itself. It also provides, for those who want it, an excellent opportunity for advancement.

This handbook covers the many aspects of an administrative assistant's job—from opening the mail to scheduling meeting, from making travel arrangements to operating computers. It's both an ideal how-to book for newcomers and a handy reminder for veterans: a compact, yet comprehensive, all-purpose business reference that provides the information you need quickly and concisely.

This latest edition includes up-to-date information on Microsoft Office, Microsoft Windows, as well as online resources like Google Gmail and Google Documents. There is also new content on using tablets and smartphones on the job.

We hope that the *Administrative Assistant's and Secretary's Handbook* will sharpen your interpretation of this exciting vocation and provide you with everything you need to become a valued, competent, and indispensable assistant on your way up the wonderful ladder of success.

Administrative Assistant's and Secretary's Handbook

FIFTH EDITION

General Procedures

1

Overview for the New Administrative Assistant

Why Are You Needed?

As an administrative assistant, you are hired to relieve your busy employer of a great deal of work, especially the details of office procedure and other matters that do not require your employer's personal involvement. You'll act as a liaison between your boss and the rest of the company. Sometimes you'll act as a buffer. Depending on the size of the company, you may also be called on to perform tasks normally outside the secretarial role in sales, banking, billing, payroll, accounting, advertising, public relations, purchasing, and more. Everything you do for your employer must duplicate as closely as possible what he or she would do if not absorbed in work that couldn't be delegated.

Every businessperson dreams of having the perfect administrative assistant, and every administrative assistant dreams of having the perfect boss. We hope you and your boss will become so well adjusted to each other that you'll work as a team, each trusting the other to carry part of the load in harmony.

What Do Employers Want?

It's helpful to know what an employer expects of a "perfect administrative assistant" so that you can present yourself at your best during both the job interview and those critical first weeks on the job. Here are a few of the most important qualities:

■ *Punctuality.* An employer wants an administrative assistant who is consistently punctual and always on hand during office hours. An administrative assistant who continually arrives even a few minutes late or who frequently misses work can cause havoc in a busy office. The employer knows from experience that such an administrative assistant may not be truly interested in the work. This person will be passed over or terminated in favor of someone with greater respect for the job—an administrative assistant who is always punctual and always there when needed.

■ *Dependability.* An employer considers the applicant's disposition and personality, trying to judge whether he or she is dependable. For example, would the candidate rush home at precisely five o'clock despite an office crisis, or would he or she take enough responsibility to volunteer to remain after hours if an emergency arises?

- *Ability to learn.* An employer wants to know the extent of the applicant's education—not only formal programs and degrees but also self-instruction and single courses. This information indicates the applicant's willingness and capacity for learning. For example, an employer may hope that you know the specific computer software the company already uses but not be too concerned if you aren't familiar with it if you show the potential to learn quickly.

- *Willingness to follow instructions.* An employer wants a candidate who follows instructions carefully and willingly. Of course, a good administrative assistant will soon take initiative and perform certain tasks differently to save time or improve results. But the administrative assistant who always demands complete control may ultimately become unwilling to follow instructions, debating or questioning every one of the boss's directives. Though intelligent input from an administrative assistant is prized, an employer usually prefers not to argue points that he or she has already decided. The employer is concerned with more important matters than explaining all the reasons for pursuing a particular policy. Therefore, the employer looks for an administrative assistant who will execute a decision no matter how many alternatives may seem obvious, or no matter what a former boss did in the same situation. In other words, the employer wants someone whose personality will be an asset rather than a handicap.

- *Loyalty and confidentiality.* Although these qualities are impossible to discover during an interview alone, every boss wants his or her administrative assistant to possess them. In an office, there is nothing more unwelcome than the "human sieve" who constantly chatters about every conversation heard, spreads idle rumors like wildfire, and must constantly be screened from confidential projects and information. No matter how efficient, how educated, and how experienced that administrative assistant is, his or her employment will be short-lived.

- *And something else.* A keen employer wants more in a prospective administrative assistant than these general qualifications. During an extended interview, the employer will be looking for quick-wittedness, flexibility, commitment to work, a certain quality and level of conversation, and a sense of courtesy. This last attribute is essential in establishing cordial relations with clients and fellow employees.

Interview Tips

During your interview, it is wise to be as relaxed as possible despite a natural tendency to be nervous. Arrive on time, of course, and be well groomed and neatly dressed; otherwise, the appointment may be canceled at the receptionist's desk.

If you try too hard to sell yourself, you'll make a poor impression. Allow the employer to form his or her own first impression. After all, he or she knows what kind of administrative assistant is needed and, in addition, may prefer to work with a certain type of person. If you're not what the employer wants, it's better for both of you that another applicant be chosen.

During an interview, the employer may try to see where your attention is focused, asking such questions as how many sick days you used on your previous jobs and how many outside activities you engage in. Previous sick days can and will be checked, so don't lie. If you have many outside interests, mention only those that in some way contribute to your job, such as night courses or professional associations. You don't want to give the impression that you're "too busy" to work.

If you receive a job offer, the salary may be less than what you think you're worth. There's often a discrepancy between what we'd like to make and what we can make. Job applicants fresh from school, in particular, may feel this way until they become more familiar with what the market is actually paying. Before refusing a position on the basis of salary alone, first be sure you know what the salaries are for comparable secretarial and administrative assistant positions in your area and for someone with your education and experience. Then find out whether you'll be eligible for a raise after a short period of probation. Finally, consider whether the position has opportunities for increased responsibility and advancement. While it may not seem true to you right now as a job applicant, a big salary is rarely more important than professional satisfaction.

Your Apprenticeship

Even if you are already well experienced, once you have a new position, you must be prepared to serve an apprenticeship with your new employer. Your past experience may be useful only in that it has taught you to learn quickly and to evaluate new situations. At your new office, there may be a different method for almost every daily procedure, even for distributing and opening the mail. No doubt, there will be a filing system you haven't used elsewhere. You may be asked to use letter formats, paragraphing, punctuation, and abbreviations that were vetoed by a previous employer.

You may also discover that your new boss has an extensive vocabulary with many words you'll need to learn, or just the reverse—a poor vocabulary that needs your assistance. Will your new boss wish you to type a letter exactly as dictated, or do you have permission to "add to and take from"? Or will the boss furnish only the essentials of what he or she wishes to convey and request that you put the letter together in proper form yourself?

Your need to be flexible extends to the computer system in the new office. You may find many differences between the hardware and software you used in school or at a past job and what you must use now. Even an updated version of the same software package may have a different user interface and functions. You need to familiarize yourself with the new computer and software, even if it means staying after work to read the manual and to experiment.

Stimulated by your brand-new environment and your past experience, you may find yourself coming up with dozens of ideas and suggestions within your first few weeks on the job. When you have a suggestion to offer, remember that it may very well have been made before and rejected for excellent reasons. When one of your ideas is refused, don't take it personally. Soon, after you're more familiar with the company and its operations, you'll be able to make a better suggestion. At the same time, don't be reluctant to give input freely when the boss asks for it.

A new employee's overeagerness to offer advice, recommend changes, and carry over methods from old jobs may just disguise a need to be recognized for his or her capability. In this situation, the best way to prove yourself is to do your best, learn quickly, follow instructions accurately and intelligently, and cooperate with fellow employees. Show consideration for others beyond the call of duty. A little extra giving will cost you absolutely nothing and will bring huge dividends in trust and friendship among your coworkers and with your employer.

2

Daily Routine

Your Office

Office conditions for administrative assistants vary. Your employer may be an entrepreneur working from a small office or even from home. You may find yourself in a law firm, a doctor's office, a sales office, a warehouse front office, a retail business, or a service business. Your company may have branches in several states or even several countries. The general activity of the business—selling, servicing, or perhaps manufacturing—may be located in the same area where you're expected to perform your job, or it may be far removed from where you work. All these conditions may change over time as the company does.

Your Workstation

The location and conditions of where you do your day-to-day work can be critical to how effectively you perform. Look first at how your workstation is placed physically within the entire office setup. Is there a reason your desk is where it is? Analyze the traffic patterns around and through your workspace. Do coworkers have to pass through it to get from one operation to another? Study your own work patterns. How often do you go back and forth to the filing cabinets each day? How far away from your desk are they? Do other workers share these files? Is there a more efficient way to organize the office?

You may find it helpful to draw a sketch of your office and try out alternative arrangements on paper before you make suggestions to your employer. Each proposed change must consider two questions: (1) Will you work more effectively in a different office layout? (2) Will your proposed changes affect another worker's effectiveness?

Whether or not you have input on the physical placement of your workstation, your desk and immediate workspace are yours to organize in a way that makes you comfortable and allows you to be as productive as possible. Your immediate workspace may include a desk, chairs, files, bookshelves, credenza, and portable tables. As you arrange these items, plan a layout that considers your work habits as well as the traffic patterns for yourself, other employees, and clients.

Here are just a few factors to consider:

- *Desk chair.* Your chair should help promote good posture and back support, and it should be adjustable so you will not tire quickly. If possible, try to obtain an ergonomically designed chair.

- *Lighting.* Proper lighting is highly important in any office. Your work area should have sufficient lighting to avoid causing you eyestrain and headaches yet be positioned to minimize glare on your computer monitor.

- *Desk.* Your desk should be large enough to hold the office supplies and equipment you work with most often and to provide a clear area on which to work. Keep your most often used supplies and equipment (such as your telephone, memo pad, in-and-out box, and stapler) within easy reach when you are seated at your desk. Any reference books that you use frequently should also be easy to reach, as well as a desk reference organizer. A desk organizer with slots is useful to store various work-in-progress folders so they can be quickly found when needed.

- *Supplies.* In your own desk, keep enough frequently used supplies to last for a week. At the beginning of each week, restock your supply. Neatly arrange these materials in drawer organizers, small boxes, or other containers. Store ink pads upside down.

- *Computer.* Your computer should be on a surface apart from your desk, preferably its own desk or table. In any case, you should be able to fit your legs under this surface comfortably as you work. Power cords should be kept out of the way so you will not inadvertently disconnect them with your feet. Multiple power cables can be connected together with twist-ties.

Besides a computer, keyboard, monitor, and printer, your computer workstation will most likely also be equipped with a mouse, a good-quality mouse pad for extra traction, a network card for communications and file sharing, a hard disk drive, a DVD-ROM storage system, a printer, and software. Other useful accessories to help organize and protect this equipment include plastic dust covers for both the computer and keyboard when they are not in use, along with an antiglare monitor cover to reduce eyestrain. All expensive office equipment such as computers, monitors, and printers should be plugged into a surge protector.

If you work for a small company, you may have to arrange all these elements so they can also be used by fellow employees without interfering with your other work.

Office Supplies

Depending on the size of the company and your own responsibilities, you may have to order office supplies for yourself, your department, or the entire business. You can purchase supplies at an office supply store, in person or by ordering over the phone, by fax, or by mail from an office supply catalog. You can also use office supply websites such as Staples.com, Officemax.com, or OfficeDepot.com to order online. Purchases can be shipped or delivered.

When preparing an order, do not overestimate your needs. A multiple-item discount is not always useful because certain items (such as beverages and snacks) cannot be stored too long. Keep an inventory of your supplies and when you use them. A logbook is a useful way to keep a record of supply use.

In addition to everyday supplies like pens, pencils, staples, paper clips, and file folders, some items may need special consideration. For example, printer and copier paper, computer printer toner or ink cartridges, and copier replacement cartridges or toner, must be ordered with your exact office equipment in mind. Add the replacement model numbers for these items to your logbook for easy future reference.

Office supplies should be kept in a supply cabinet, shelf, or file cabinet. If coworkers have access to these supplies, consider labeling the shelves to keep them organized. Keep the supply storage area orderly and clean. Items that you use most often should be stored at eye level, where they will be easy to see and reach. Liquids that might spill should be kept on the bottom shelf. Try to keep the label from the original packaging attached to the supplies; the information will be helpful when reordering the item. For the same reason, keep opened reams of copier and office paper inside the wrapper, leaving the label on one end. There are many different types and weights of office paper, and some are better suited for certain applications than others. For example, most copiers work best with 20-pound uncoated paper stock. Saving the label will help ensure that you have the right product for the job.

Reference Works

Every office should have a minimum number of reference works and other sources of information. These are invaluable in writing, taking dictation, and transcribing, and will help you improve your work by enlarging your knowledge of the subjects covered in correspondence or reports.

The book you are likely to consult most often will be an abridged dictionary, and it should be on your desk. There are a number of good dictionaries. The one we recommend is *Merriam-Webster's Collegiate Dictionary* because it contains most of the information an administrative assistant requires for daily work: spelling, syllabication, pronunciation, meaning, usage, derivation, and even synonyms in many cases. Occasionally, *Roget's Thesaurus* may also be of value, though in a busy office there is seldom time to consult it.

If you do most of your work on a computer, you may elect to use a software-based dictionary. These programs can be installed on your computer and allow you to look up word spellings, definitions, synonyms, and antonyms with the click of a mouse. You can use an online dictionary such as Dictionary.com.

Work Planning

The first thing to do when you arrive at the office every day should be to air the rooms and regulate the heat or air conditioning (unless it's set on a permanent basis by building maintenance). Then arrange your desk for maximum efficiency, and replenish your supplies. Prepare your notebook and pencils for taking phone messages or to be ready if your employer gives you a task that requires taking notes.

Consult your calendar book or your computer's calendar to be sure you're aware of all you must do during the day. Check your list of recurring matters: appointments, meetings, payroll dates, bill payments, and tax or insurance deadlines. Give your employer a reminder list of appointments and other activities, and prepare any material from the files he or she will need.

As part of your normal daily routine, try to order your activities in the most productive way. When you have to leave your desk to run an errand, for example, do other errands at the same time. Whenever possible, use the telephone instead of delivering a message in person (unless, of course, your employer asks you to do so). You may also use email.

If you have tasks that involve mailing or shipping, plan them with pickup and delivery times in mind. Maintain a daily to-do list on paper or in your computer, and check off each item as it is accomplished. When new projects come in, try to complete them as quickly as possible. Prioritize your work. If you have several ongoing projects and a new one comes in, ask your employer which one has the highest priority.

Each evening before you leave the office, make a list of what you need to do the following workday. Then put away all of your work and work-in-progress files, either in your desk drawers or in a filing cabinet. Work that is especially sensitive, such as client lists or accounting records, should be put away in a locked file cabinet.

Your regular routine includes keeping your work area clean. Clean out your desk drawers periodically. Your computer and other office equipment should be cleaned using a slightly damp towel. Compressed air in a can is useful for blowing dust off your computer keyboard and monitor screen. Disk-drive cleaning kits use a special diskette to clean the internal working parts.

In addition to maintaining your immediate area, schedule regular servicing for all office equipment as part of a preventive maintenance program. You do not want to wait for equipment to break down in the middle of a big project with a firm deadline. Here, the old adage is so important: An ounce of prevention is worth a pound of cure.

Finally, always be thinking of ways you can improve your own performance and the efficiency of the office. Look for problems and try to find ways to solve them. An orderly, smoothly running business has a greater chance for success, and your company's success will help ensure your own.

Dictation and Transcription

Besides storing notebooks and pens in your own desk, keep a notebook, pencil, and pen in an inconspicuous place in your boss's office so you'll always be ready to take dictation, even if you've just looked in to announce a caller or deliver a message. You will save your boss valuable time, since you won't have to retreat to your own desk for supplies.

Each day, when you begin dictation, first write the date at the top of the notebook page. When the dictation is over, write the date once more at the end, and draw a line across the page. Though there may be several dictation periods each day, you will find this notation helpful, if only in times of emergency; you will be able to refer to your notes rapidly should questions arise.

If you take dictation from more than one person, keep separate notebooks with the name of each person on the outside in a prominent place. If you are asked a question about one of the letters, you will be able to reply without hesitation, especially if you've remembered to write the date before and after each session of dictation.

During regular dictation, your employer will often include faxes, emails, or other communications that should be sent out promptly, though he or she may continue dictating for an hour or more before you can take care of them. In such an event, immediately after taking the dictation of the fax, email, or urgent letter, turn down the corner of the page in your notebook so that you can find the material as soon as you reach your desk. Occasionally, your employer may dictate a remark that you cannot hear distinctly. It's imperative that you ask your boss to repeat the statement before continuing.

Accuracy is more important than an unwillingness to interrupt, and your employer will respect you all the more.

When the dictation contains names of correspondents, companies, and products that are unfamiliar to you, ask if these names are in the files or whether there are explanatory papers you should have. Ask this before you close that bit of dictation, and plan to refer to those papers before transcribing your notes.

Dictation Equipment

In many offices, administrative assistants do not take dictation or use shorthand. Instead, the employer uses a digital recorder. These machines save you the job of taking dictation before transcribing the letter. While your employer is dictating into the recorder, you can finish other tasks that would otherwise have to be neglected. In addition, some employers have difficulty dictating to another person but can speak into a machine with ease; therefore, their dictation is actually easier to comprehend this way.

The digital recorders connect to a computer in order to transfer the audio file for transcription. Specialized software is available that allows an administrative assistant to listen to the audio files on the computer for transcription. Some systems include a foot pedal that connects to the computer for pausing the audio playback. Digital recorders typically include built-in memory for storing several hours of audio.

Voice messages can be attached to an email message and listened to using speakers or headphones connected to your computer. Your boss may leave voice messages or forward voice messages from other callers that need to be transcribed. Integrated messaging allows for telephone voice messages to be forwarded to your email system. To listen to the message, simply open the email and press the play button. Figure 2-1 shows an email containing a voice message.

FIGURE 2-1   Email message containing a voice message.

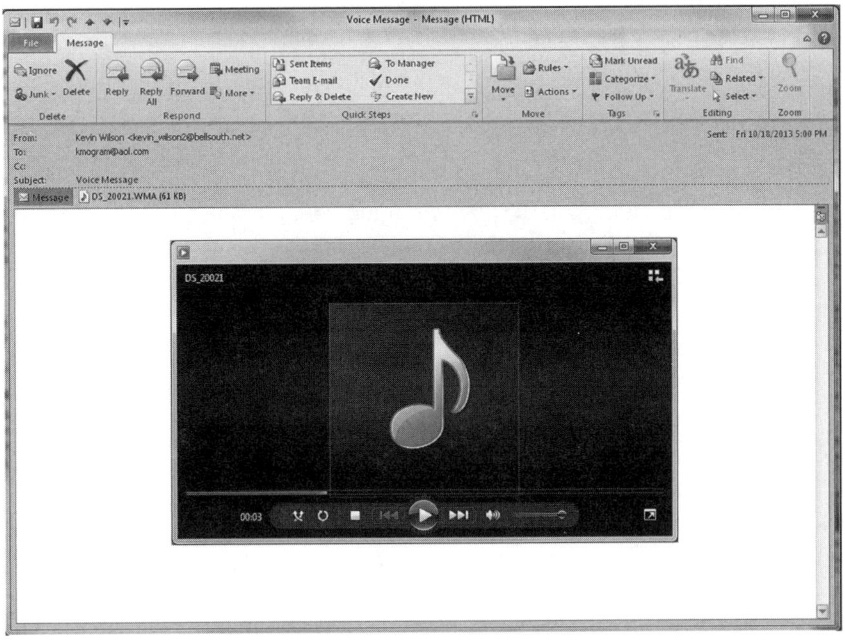

Screen shot used with permission of Microsoft.

Transcription

Transcription involves good typing skills, knowledge of grammar and punctuation, mastery of word-processing software, and familiarity with transcription software, as well as good formatting, proofreading, and listening skills.

If you find that your skills are weak in any of these areas, try to improve them. Be sure you have the right equipment that will make the job easier. For example, purchase a foot pedal so you don't have to start and stop the recording by pressing a button or clicking your mouse. This takes your attention away from the transcription document and makes the process more tedious. Always use effective English and sentence structure, even if the speaker on the recording didn't follow the usage rules.

After transcription of your notes, be sure to read over what you've typed. If there is even one error, it's better that you find it rather than another person. As you proof your work, check to make sure the transcription makes sense. Are there any inconsistencies to references? Is the grammar, punctuation, and formatting correct? Have you used the correct words? And, of course, run a spell-checker and proof the document for typos.

Your Employer's Office

Some employers consider their offices sacred ground that is not to be touched; others appreciate having their assistants dust and straighten up. You'll soon learn your own boss's preferences. If he or she doesn't mind, start by stacking the files being consulted and replacing those already consulted in the cabinet. Ask, however, before removing papers or documents from your boss's desk, especially those you have noticed there for quite some time. Discretion is always necessary. You must not overstep your role by touching or mentioning papers that your employer considers personal or private. In addition, many employers maintain their own unique filing system atop their desks and will advise their administrative assistant not to touch those stacks unless absolutely necessary. One such necessity may be if the boss telephones from out of the office and asks you to retrieve a letter or document from atop the desk. If this happens, turn the stack to the side at the point you found the letter, so that you can later replace it exactly where it was.

When you make appointments for your employer, record them on both your boss's calendar and your own. Be sure to remind your employer of these appointments—even though they're clearly on the calendar—so that he or she won't schedule too much work, for example, on the morning of a conference.

The Intangibles

Besides performing the usual office duties, all administrative assistants encounter many situations that are a test of character, judgment, and memory. The administrative assistant must know exactly what the employer wants kept confidential. In some instances, your employer may frankly explain when something is not for public consumption, but do not assume otherwise if he or she says nothing. When someone asks you about a confidential matter, it should never be necessary to lie. A graceful "I couldn't say" is sufficient, especially in response to those who understand and respect your position.

An administrative assistant must exercise self-control every moment, even when courtesy is strained. While on the job, you are not living your personal life but, rather, representing your employer. Because of this, you cannot succumb to mood swings or to criticism of those around you. You must always think before speaking and keep yourself open like an impersonal channel for the fulfillment of your role as administrative assistant. Think of how a diplomat must act while representing his or her country in a foreign land.

A great many little matters between an administrative assistant and his or her boss will be left unmentioned by both of them. In a good working relationship, a type of telepathy develops between employer and administrative assistant. Their understanding of each other contributes to their mutual success.

3

Telephone Usage

Telephone Manners

Administrative assistants must have a pleasing telephone personality and a well-modulated voice that conveys dignity and courtesy. Because you are not seen by the person at the other end of the line, you are judged—and more important, your employer is judged—by your telephone manners. Show interest in what is being said. Reply in clear tones, never raising your voice. Be a good listener, and know what the person at the other end of the line is saying to you.

When the telephone rings, answer it as quickly as possible. At all times, have a memo pad and pen near the telephone. If it's necessary to delay for some reason, make a polite request such as, "Please wait a moment while I check the record for you." If you must spend some time finding the desired information, offer to call back. If the caller prefers to stay on the line, put the line on hold rather than setting the telephone receiver down on your desktop.

For the sake of out-of-town visitors who may call to ask directions, keep a map of the area on a nearby wall or in a desk drawer. You can provide extra courtesy by plotting their trip from the airport or freeway.

Taking and Transferring Calls

State the name of your company and your own name when answering an incoming call: "The Brown Company, Ms. Robertson speaking." If the business is large enough to have several departments and the operator has already answered the call before ringing your extension, state your department and your name: "Accounting Department, Ms. Robertson speaking." If there is no department and a call is referred to you, give only your name: "Ms. Robertson speaking."

Answering a Colleague's Telephone

When answering a colleague's extension, state the colleague's name and your own: "Ms. Scott's office, Ms. Robertson speaking." If the person called is unavailable, ask if the caller wishes to hold the line, leave a message, or call back. If the preference is to hold, go back on the line at short intervals to explain the delay, asking if the caller wishes to leave a message. (See the next section on taking messages.) If the caller decides to leave a message, be sure that the person called receives the message as soon as he or she returns.

Transferring a Call

If you can take care of the matter yourself, do not transfer the call. If you must transfer the call, first tell the caller: "Mr. Jack Phillips is in charge of insurance, and I am sure he will advise you promptly. I'll transfer you." If the transfer must be made through an operator, always provide full information so that the caller doesn't need to be questioned again: "I have Mr. Black on the line. Please connect him with Mr. Phillips in the insurance department." If the caller has not identified himself, say: "Please transfer this call to Mr. Phillips in the insurance department." If you do not know to whom the call should be directed, advise the caller: "I'll have the proper person call you back in just a few minutes."

Taking Messages

When a caller has a message to leave for your employer or another employee, take the message verbatim. Write it exactly as stated, taking time and being patient with the caller. If you don't understand what the caller is saying, ask to have the message repeated. The message may be very important to your employer, and a single word omitted or out of place could make a significant difference in the meaning. If you are unfamiliar with the caller's name, ask for the spelling. Make sure you note whom the message is for.

A major advantage of using printed telephone message slips rather than blank scraps of paper is that you are more likely to take a complete message by filling in the printed form. A telephone message slip has lines for the name of the person being called, the date and time of the incoming call, the name of the person calling, the name of that person's company or organization (if given), the caller's telephone number, and the message (if any). The last line on the slip is for your initials as the taker of the message. By placing your initials at the end, you will be assuring yourself as well as your employer that the information is complete and accurate.

Screening Calls

Although many employees answer their own telephone, you'll be expected at one time or another to screen your boss's incoming calls. In this case, you become the judge as to whether your boss should be disturbed.

When screening calls, be extremely tactful so that the caller will not be affronted. You want to be able to meet the caller face-to-face the next day without feeling embarrassed about the way you treated him or her over the telephone. A simple question—"May I tell Mr. Jones who's calling?"—should encourage the caller to give a name without hesitation. If the caller refuses, explain that your employer is unable to accept a call without knowing whom it's from, and suggest that a letter be written.

Many callers will ask for your employer by name and will tell you the question they need answered. You then need to confer with your boss to know if screening should be done or if you should put the call put through immediately.

Protecting Your Employer

Don't be overly zealous in trying to "protect" your employer by screening calls when not specifically asked to do so. When a business is just getting under way, for example, many executives welcome all calls and don't want the administrative assistant to screen any potential clients. If that is the case, then simply say to the caller: "Thank you. I will connect you with Mr. Jones."

If you answer the telephone for all of the employees in the company and a caller does not request a specific person, inquire as to the nature of the call so that you can transfer it to the proper department or employee. When you realize what the caller's needs are, you could say: "Ms. Johnson in our accounting department should be able to assist you with this. I will transfer your call to her."

Courtesy

All callers should be treated with great respect and a patient tone of voice. If another call comes in while you're speaking, ask the first caller to hold the line, answer the second call, ask if the second caller can hold for a moment, saying you are on another line, and then return to the first caller. Never keep a caller waiting or on hold for any length of time. When you return to the line, thank the caller for holding. Keep in mind that his or her time is valuable.

Never put one line on hold without informing the caller, not even when two or more incoming calls arrive simultaneously and two or more lines are ringing. Many callers will hang up when this happens, and your employer could very well miss a much-needed business call. You've no doubt experienced this yourself as a caller and will always retain negative thoughts concerning that company. Always have the courtesy to say, "Hello. Can you hold a moment, please?" Then wait until the caller answers yes or no. It is frustrating for a caller to be asked, "Can you hold a moment, please?" and then be cut off before he or she has had a chance to say no.

Telephone Etiquette Tips

The following checklist will assist you in practicing good telephone etiquette and performing your telephone answering responsibilities in a professional manner.

1. When you take a call, turn away from your computer, desk, and other work. Don't allow distractions to take your attention away from the caller.
2. Always have something available to write with.
3. Answer calls by the second or third ring.
4. Smile when you answer your calls. Even though the caller can't see it, he or she will hear the smile in your voice.
5. Use a "telephone voice" where you control your volume and speed. Speak clearly.
6. Be enthusiastic and respectful.
7. Greet the caller and identify yourself, your business, and your department.
8. Ask the caller, "To whom am I speaking?"
9. Then ask the caller, "How may I help you?"
10. Avoid unnecessary jargon and acronyms in your conversations.
11. Use the caller's name in your conversation.

12. Practice good listening skills.

13. If there is a problem, be concerned, empathetic, and apologetic.

14. Thank the caller for calling. Ask the caller to call again.

15. Never eat, drink, or chew gum while you are on a call.

Often-Used Numbers

Your employer no doubt will use certain personal telephone numbers regularly. You will soon memorize many of them without effort, but it's useful to keep a short alphabetical list of these numbers close to the telephone for quick consultation. The list might include numbers for the boss's spouse's workplace, the schools his or her children attend, and the stores the boss and his or her family frequent, as well as their country or health clubs and the boss's physician, dentist, mechanic, accountant, and personal friends. Most office telephones can be programmed to dial frequently called numbers automatically, saving you time and effort. You could also store the list of frequently used phone numbers in a file on your computer's desktop.

Domestic Information

For telephone number information within your area code, dial 411. For long-distance information, dial 1 - area code - 555-1212.

International Long-Distance Calls

You can place 1 + area code + seven-digit number direct-dial calls to the United States, Canada, Bermuda, Puerto Rico, and most of the Caribbean islands. Other international calls may be dialed directly by dialing the following:

- International call dial prefix 011
- Country code—every country has a two- or three-digit country code; search the Internet for the correct country code
- City code—most major international cities have a one- to five-digit city code
- Local telephone number—local numbers vary in length

Voice-Mail Etiquette

The goal of voice-mail etiquette is to improve communications without being inconsiderate. With voice mail, there are two sides to the communication: callers and the person being called. Each should follow certain guidelines.

Callers frequently become upset with "bad" voice-mail systems; however, they fail to pay attention to the fact that sometimes they are "bad" callers. The following are some things for callers to consider when encountering voice mail:

- Leave a clear, concise message with a phone number.
- Provide a good time for the call to be returned.

■ Unless you have indicated it is an emergency or a problem with an extreme time deadline, do not assume the person checks voice mail regularly—you should assume a call back will not be immediate.

■ Remember that sometimes voice messages are lost somewhere in the system. A person may accidentally delete a message.

■ Use voice mail as a way of informing a person that other communications are waiting or coming, since voice-mail users frequently check voice mail more often than email or the fax machine.

■ Never leave confidential, inflammatory, or embarrassing messages on a voice-mail message.

If your office has voice mail available, you should observe the following guidelines:

■ When recording your message, keep your greeting short.

■ Tell people how and when they can reach you.

■ Update your message frequently to inform people of your schedule, especially if you cannot return messages quickly.

■ Keep your message friendly, but don't forget professionalism.

■ If you use voice mail to receive messages, check it frequently throughout the day.

■ Return calls in a timely manner—don't use voice mail as a way to avoid interaction.

■ Encourage your callers to leave detailed messages—you may be able to leave the answer on their voice mail without a two-way conversation.

■ Respect the confidentiality of any messages you receive. Treat all voice-mail messages the same way you would treat any private conversation.

Answering Services

If your company uses an answering service, always let the service know when you come into the office in the morning and when you are leaving in the evening. Many services will allow you to forward your telephone calls to the service, or they will answer your calls automatically if you do not pick up after a set number of rings. Always leave the answering service a number where your employer can be reached in case of an emergency.

Telephone Usage

4

Mail Services and Shipping

The Office Mail

Mail is an important method of communication between a company and the outside business world. The administrative assistant usually handles the daily processing of mail. This may include sorting the mail and distributing it to the proper departments or individuals. It may also include opening the employer's mail, prioritizing it, and gathering the necessary preliminary information needed to answer specific requests or solve problems.

Sending out business mail involves much more than a letter and a stamp, even when those letters are sent by the hundreds of thousands. There are larger documents and packages to be mailed, varying timetables to be met, and destinations ranging from next door to around the world. Dozens of work-saving, timesaving, and money-saving strategies can help move the mail more efficiently

A competent assistant should become acquainted with these profit-boosting moves, from the best physical ways to prepare the mail to the advantages of one mail service over another. He or she should also keep abreast of U.S. Postal Service (USPS) rules and regulations and methods of moving the mail. Neither you nor the company may need all this information at present, but companies constantly change and grow. The assistant who can fulfill a company's new mailing needs—or who knows where to get the information quickly—is invaluable.

Addressing for Success

A company is judged by the way its letters are composed and spaced on the pages, and even by the manner in which its envelopes are addressed. All of this does more than simply create a good impression; it affects whether the mail is delivered in a timely fashion.

The USPS relies on computerized mail-processing machines—optical character readers (OCRs) and bar-code sorters (BCSs)—designed to increase the speed, efficiency, and accuracy of processing mail while keeping postal operating costs down. Consistently accurate delivery, faster mail turnaround, and greater profits are just some of the ways your company can benefit from this state-of-the-art system.

This high-speed equipment is programmed to "read" and sort up to 36,000 pieces of mail per hour. That's ten pieces every second. But if your company's mail is not technically compatible, these sophisticated machines will not be able to sort it. Your mail will have to be sorted by hand, and the company will miss the related benefits of the equipment.

Two factors determine whether mail is considered technically compatible: (1) mail that is "machinable" or, in other words, the right size and shape to speed with ease through the equipment; and (2) mail that is electronically "readable," or capable of being read, coded, and sorted by the equipment.

The following is a list of the most common addressing problems:

- Not enough contrast
- Script-type font used
- Address not visible through window in envelope
- Address slants
- Serif-type font used
- Not all capital letters
- Characters touch
- Logo behind delivery address line
- Information below delivery address line

How to Make Sure Your Mail Gets Through

There are a variety of issues related to successful mail delivery, such as the size of your letters, address information and location, bar-code area, the use of windowed envelopes, and print quality.

Size

Begin by making sure that your letter mail is the proper size. The maximum size for a first-class letter is 12 inches by 15 inches by ¾ inches thick. Items of the proper size will speed through the machines without a hitch.

Letter mail larger than the maximum may be mailed, but it must bypass the OCR and be processed through slower and less efficient manual or mechanized methods. It may also be subject to a surcharge even though the postage is correct for the weight.

Address Location

The OCR looks for the address within an imaginary rectangle on each piece of mail called the OCR read area. Make some quick measurements of your company's envelope stationery. The OCR will not have trouble finding the delivery address if it's located within the following boundaries:

Sides of the rectangle:	½ inch in from the right and left edges
Bottom of the rectangle:	⅝ inch up from the bottom edge
Top of the rectangle:	2¾ inches up from the bottom edge

To provide the OCR with the information needed for the finest sort, put all the lines of the address within the above area. If that is not possible, it will still help to place as many address lines in the OCR read area as you can. *A word of caution:* Make sure no portion of the return address appears in the read area.

Mail Services

Lines of the Address

The OCR cannot rearrange address information that is out of proper sequence. Make sure addresses are complete, including apartment or suite numbers and proper delivery designations (e.g., street, road, avenue). Often there will be, in a single city, streets with the same name—for example, Hanford Street, Hanford Court, Hanford Lane, and Hanford Avenue—so always use the proper designation.

Two-letter state abbreviations (listed in Table 4-1) should always be used because the OCR recognizes them at a glance. Do not place a period after each initial of the abbreviation—that is, use AR instead of A.R.

Table 4-2 shows common abbreviations that may be used with addresses. Do not use periods at the end of the abbreviation; instead use all uppercase letters.

Foreign Addresses

Foreign mailings should have the country name printed in capital letters as the only information on the bottom line. The postal delivery zone, if any, should be included with the city, not after the country. For example:

Mr. Thomas Clark
117 Russell Drive
London WIP6HQ
ENGLAND

Non-Address Information

Extraneous (non-address) printing that appears in or near the OCR read area could cause the piece of mail to be rejected. To ensure that the equipment locates and reads only the delivery address, non-address information (advertising copy, company logos, etc.) that must appear in the read area should be positioned above the delivery address line. In other words, the space below and on either side of the delivery address line within the read area should be clear of all printing and other markings, not actually part of the address. Positioning such information as far away from the address as possible also helps.

Bar-Code Area

After reading an address, the OCR will print the appropriate bar code on the bottom of the piece of mail. Then, by reading the code, BCSs quickly route each envelope and card to its destination. But BCSs recognize only bar codes and reject mail that has some other type of printing where the bar code goes. Make sure the bar code area remains free of all markings.

Window Envelopes

If your company uses window envelopes, be certain that the entire address is always visible, even during full movement of the insert. If part of the address is hidden, the OCR will reject the envelope and send it off for manual or mechanized processing.

Address Characters

The OCR will read most computer-printed addresses. It cannot read type styles such as script, italic, and highly stylized characters. Among the best typeface designs to choose from are those known as sans serif.

Mail Services

TABLE 4-1   Two-Letter Postal Abbreviations for States, Territories, and the District of Columbia

Abbr.	Name	Abbr.	Name
AL	Alabama	NE	Nebraska
AK	Alaska	NV	Nevada
AS	American Samoa	NH	New Hampshire
AZ	Arizona	NJ	New Jersey
AR	Arkansas	NM	New Mexico
CA	California	NY	New York
CO	Colorado	NC	North Carolina
CT	Connecticut	ND	North Dakota
DE	Delaware	MP	Northern Mariana Islands
DC	District of Columbia	OH	Ohio
FM	Federated States of Micronesia	OK	Oklahoma
FL	Florida	OR	Oregon
GA	Georgia	PA	Pennsylvania
GU	Guam	PR	Puerto Rico
HI	Hawaii	RI	Rhode Island
ID	Idaho	SC	South Carolina
IL	Illinois	SD	South Dakota
IN	Indiana	TN	Tennessee
IA	Iowa	TX	Texas
KS	Kansas	UT	Utah
KY	Kentucky	VT	Vermont
LA	Louisiana	VA	Virginia
ME	Maine	VI	Virgin Islands, U.S.
MH	Marshall Islands	WA	Washington
MD	Maryland	WV	West Virginia
MA	Massachusetts	WI	Wisconsin
MI	Michigan	WY	Wyoming
MN	Minnesota	AA	Armed Forces, the Americas
MS	Mississippi	AE	Armed Forces, Europe
MO	Missouri	AP	Armed Forces, Pacific
MT	Montana		

Mail Services

TABLE 4-2   Common Abbreviations Used with Addresses

Abbr.	Word	Abbr.	Word
AVE	Avenue	SQ	Square
BLVD	Boulevard	ST	Street
CTR	Center	STA	Station
CIR	Circle	TER	Terrace
CT	Court	TRL	Trail
DR	Drive	TPKE	Turnpike
EXPY	Expressway	VLY	Valley
HTS	Heights	WAY	Way
HWY	Highway	APT	Apartment
IS	Island	RM	Room
JCT	Junction	STE	Suite
LK	Lake	N	North
LN	Lane	E	East
MTN	Mountain	S	South
PKWY	Parkway	W	West
PL	Place	NE	Northeast
PLZ	Plaza	NW	Northwest
RDG	Ridge	SE	Southeast
RD	Road	SW	Southwest

Print Quality and Color

Print quality is of great importance to the OCR. It quickly reads clear, sharp print but may not be able to distinguish characters that are faded, broken, or smudged. Black ink on a white background is best. Although certain color combinations are acceptable, the OCR cannot read the address if there is not enough contrast between the ink and paper. Keep the ink as dark as possible and the background as light as possible.

Spacing

Spacing between characters, words, and address lines is equally important. The OCR must see a clear vertical space between each character and each word, or it will not know where one ends and the next one begins. For similar reasons, it needs a clear horizontal space between each line of the address.

Postal Automation: Encoding for Business Mailers

Even if an address is sharply imprinted and speeds through the OCR, the letter itself won't be deliverable if the information in the address is incorrect. If you maintain a computer-based address list, the Postal Business Center for your area may be able to help you clean up your list and add valuable ZIP + 4 (5-digit zip code plus 4-digit addendum) and carrier route information. This is accomplished using downloadable software tools available from the USPS website at www.usps.com.

The Postal Service provides this service for your company because the benefits are mutual: for your company, more accurate and readable addresses, which provides faster sorting of mail and fewer undeliverable pieces (undeliverable third-class mail is money thrown away), and for the USPS, more efficient moving of the mail, saving it money, which can then be passed onto customers by holding the line on rates.

To clean up your list, here is what you can do:

1. Standardize your address list, making sure cities match the zip codes on the list.

2. Change all characters to uppercase for increased readability by automation equipment.

3. Correct minor misspellings and add missing directions and suffixes.

4. Validate or correct each five-digit zip code.

5. Add the extra digits of ZIP + 4 codes.

6. Ask the USPS to give you a report on any address that cannot be coded. For example, you'll discover which address needs an apartment or suite number to be complete or which address does not exist as given.

Postage Meters

What's the next step after addressing your company's mail with the most accurate address information? Putting on postage, of course, so you can get the mail on its way. Many small companies stamp their short letters and save longer correspondence and packages for a trip to the post office. Your company can save both time and money by instead investing in its own postage meter.

A postage meter offers savings for every office, not just larger ones with a heavy flow of outgoing mail. A postage meter ensures that your office does not overpay postage or underestimate it. It takes much less time to put metered postage on mail than it does to apply stamps, helping make more efficient use of staff time. In addition, your business correspondence moves more quickly once it leaves your office since the post office does not have to spend time canceling and postmarking the mail.

A postage meter prints postage directly onto your mail pieces (or onto a meter tape, which you apply to your mail piece). Postage meters are a very convenient way to pay for postage and track postage costs for your business or organization.

A postage meter is also great to have around the office for all of your mailing needs. You can send out any class of mail (except periodicals) in any quantity at any rate with the same postage meter.

Postage meters come in all sizes. Very large mailers have big, specialized meters that fold, stuff, weigh, and meter postage onto envelopes. Some meters are small and

TABLE 4-3   USPS-Authorized Postage Meter and PC Postage System Providers

Company	Telephone Number	Web Address
Data-Pac Mailing Systems Corp.	800-355-1775	www.data-pac.com
FP Mailing Solutions	800-341-6052	www.fp-usa.com
Hasler, Inc.	800-995-2035	www.haslerinc.com
Neopost	800-636-7678	www.neopostinc.com
Pitney Bowes Inc.	800-322-8000	www.pb.com

require each mail piece to be hand-fed, which can take time. A meter manufacturer can help you decide which meter is right for your mailing needs.

If you already have a postage meter and you're starting to do bulk mailing, using your meter is a smart choice. Although you can use the same postage meter for all of your mail, you must apply for a permit to use the meter for bulk mailings. Also, there are special markings required for bulk mailings that can be applied with your meter stamp. That saves you an extra step.

Table 4-3 lists the USPS-authorized postage meter and computer or online postage system providers.

Printing Postage Online

There are a variety of web-based solutions available for printing postage using your computer. For example, the USPS has the Click-N-Ship service, which allows you to print a label and postage for Express Mail and Priority Mail and schedule a free package pickup. There is no monthly fee and no special software, hardware, or paper needed.

Other online postage printing providers include the following:

- Ebay.com
- Stamps.com
- Endicia.com
- PB.com

Packaging

Much of the mail you'll be asked to send out as an administrative assistant will consist of letters and documents. But even with a mailroom on the premises, you may have to prepare and send out the occasional package yourself.

For a package to arrive in good condition at its destination, it's important to observe four basic principles in packaging your shipments:

1. *Use a corrugated container.* These "cardboard boxes" come in a variety of strengths and weights.

Mail Services

Select a box that is large enough to allow some room around the contents in every direction. This will protect the contents from punctures, tears, or rips on the corners or side of the box when turning in transit.

Boxes are available from many shipping supply companies, as well as mailing and packaging chain stores. Make sure that the box will support the weight of your shipment. Every box has a stamp printed on it specifying the maximum weight it will support. It is not a good idea to reuse shipping containers unless they are in good shape and will not be supporting much weight. Moisture and other shipping conditions tend to lessen the strength of corrugated containers.

To see whether a box is strong enough for mailing your item, look for the manufacturer's strength certification on the bottom of the box. The first and last measurements are the most important to you. "Bursting test" shows you (in pounds per square inch) how well the fiberboard can resist rupture or breaking. "Gross Wt LT [load type]" shows you (in pounds) how much weight the box can hold. Once you know the load type, weight, and size of your item, you can use Table 4-4 to choose a box by grade if necessary.

2. *Protect the contents.* Use wadded-up newspaper, crumpled brown grocery bags, air bubble pack, foam peanuts, or shredded paper. Depending on the contents of the package, it may be a good idea to wrap them in plastic as well to keep the packing material from sticking to them or getting inside. The packing material should be placed on the bottom, on all four sides, and on the top to provide several inches of protection between the contents and the sides of the box.

3. *Close the box securely.* Most shipping companies, including the USPS, will not accept boxes tied with string. Nor should you use masking tape or regular cellophane tape; neither has enough strength to keep the box closed. Instead, use carton sealing tape, pressure-sensitive tape, water-activated paper tape, or water-activated reinforced tape. In general, you should apply three strips of tape to the top and the bottom. One strip should seal the box, and the other two strips should seal the sides.

4. *Use the proper labeling.* Make sure you include a zip code; as an added precaution, you may want to include the addressee's telephone number. Your company's

TABLE 4-4 Box Grade Requirements

Maximum Weight of Box and Contents			
Easy and Average Loads (pounds)	Difficult Loads (pounds)	Maximum Length Plus Girth (inches)	Box Grade
20	–	67	125
40	20	100	175
65	40	108	200
70	65	108	275
–	70	108	350
–	70	130	350

Mail Services

return address is also important. You never know if the recipient has moved or is out of town and cannot receive your shipment. In some cases, your shipment can be held at the destination, but there are time limits on this. It's also a good idea to pack a copy of the label with all of the identifying information inside the box so if the outside label is damaged or removed, the shipper can determine the destination by opening the box. When applying your labels to the package, always place them on the top, away from seams or box edges. Then apply several strips of clear carton sealing tape over the label to prevent it from falling off.

You should write both addresses in waterproof ink (or type them on a label), using letters that can be easily read from thirty inches away (arm's length). Ten- to twelve-point type is a good size for computer-printed labels.

The address format preferred by the USPS uses uppercase letters and has a uniform left margin in the address block. For example:

LUIS ENSOR
23 MAPLE CT APT 4
ANYTOWN, CA 99887-7665

On the outside of your parcel, you should put special markings like those listed below. They let postal employees know the nature of the parcel's contents. But do not assume that the markings in themselves will keep your parcel from getting damaged.

- Mark "Fragile" on parcels that contain breakable items.

- Mark "Perishable" on parcels that contain food or other items that can decay or spoil.

- Mark "Do Not Bend" on parcels that contain photographs, artwork, or similar items, but only if they are protected with a stiffener like fiberboard.

You should put these special markings in three places: above the address, below the postage, and on the back or bottom of your parcel. If you prefer, ask a post office window clerk to rubber stamp your parcel with these markings.

For odd-shaped or extremely fragile objects, it's best to check with the shipping service for advice on how to package the item and the best way to send it.

Certain potentially harmful or dangerous articles and substances may be mailed if special packaging and labeling requirements are met. Contact your local postmaster for details and ask for Publication 2, *Packaging for Mailing,* or visit the USPS website at www.usps.com.

U.S. Postal Service Mail Services

Most of your company's mail probably goes out and comes in via the USPS. The following information only touches the high points of the many services it offers so you'll know they are there when needed. A complete and separate brochure is available from the USPS on each subject mentioned. USPS services change from time to time so it's useful to call or visit a local post office occasionally. In addition, the USPS maintains a Marketing and Communications Office in large metropolitan areas to advise the public of such services and answer questions by telephone or in person.

Mail Services

Express Mail

Express Mail is the USPS's fastest service. It offers guaranteed delivery service 365 days a year, including weekends and holidays. The USPS also offers Global Express Mail to some 200 countries and territories, and is the only company to offer Express Mail Military Service at domestic prices to select Army Post Office (APO) and Fleet Post Office (FPO) addresses.

Important letters, documents, and merchandise may be sent via Express Mail. A full postage refund is made for all domestic shipments delivered later than the guaranteed commitment for that particular service.

To use Express Mail Next-Day Service, you can take your shipment to any designated Express Mail post office, generally by 5 p.m.; deposit it in an Express Mail collection box; call for on-demand pickup; or hand it to your letter carrier. Your local post office can give you specific Express Mail acceptance times for your area. Depending on the destination, your mailing will be delivered to the addressee either by noon or by 3 p.m. the next day. Express Mail post office–to–post office service can also be picked up at the destination post office by 10 a.m. the next day. If you require expedited delivery but are not sure that your correspondents will be physically at the delivery address to accept and sign for the mail, you may exercise the Waiver of Signature option at the time of mailing.

The USPS may not be able to reach some destinations overnight and, in this case, they provide guaranteed second-day delivery service. You can get on-demand pickup and information on the delivery status of your mailing by calling 800-222-1811.

Express Mail is convenient to use. The USPS provides you with mailing containers (envelopes, boxes, and tubes) and the necessary mailing labels at no charge. Customers find the two-pound flat-rate envelope convenient to use. Any amount of material that fits into it may be mailed in this special flat-rate envelope. The postage is the rate charged for a two-pound piece of Express Mail, regardless of the weight of the material in the envelope.

Priority Mail

When the overnight speed of Express Mail is not needed but preferential handling is desired, use Priority Mail. Priority Mail offers expedited delivery at the least expensive rate in the industry. The maximum weight for Priority Mail is seventy pounds, and the maximum size is 108 inches in length and girth combined. You also have the option of sending mail weighing less than thirteen ounces as Priority Mail.

For proper handling, Priority Mail should be well identified. Your local post office will provide Priority Mail stickers, labels, envelopes, and boxes at no extra charge. For larger quantities (usually fifty), you can also order over the phone (800-610-8734) or via the Internet (supplies.usps.gov). You will find the post office's special flat-rate envelope convenient to use. Any amount of material that fits into the envelope may be mailed at the regular two-pound rate regardless of the weight of the material in the flat-rate envelope.

Priority Mail can be insured, registered, certified, or sent Collect on Delivery (COD) for an additional charge. Priority Mail is also the only way that the USPS sends heavier pieces of international mail.

First-Class Mail

Use first-class mail for sending letters, postcards, stamped cards, greeting cards, personal notes, checks, and money orders. All mail weighing more than thirteen ounces sent as first-class mail will be handled as Priority Mail.

Mail Services

Additional services such as certificates of mailing and certified, registered, COD, and restricted delivery can be purchased for first-class mail. Insurance can also be purchased. However, insured articles mailed at the first-class mail rate must contain only merchandise or material not required to be sent as first-class mail.

All first-class mail receives prompt handling and transportation. If your first-class mail is not letter size, make sure to mark it "First Class." First-class mail is generally delivered overnight to locally designated cities and within two days to locally designated states. Delivery by the third day can be expected for remaining outlying areas.

First-class mail in mailings of five hundred pieces or more qualifies for a postage rate discount if the mailer presorts and prepares the mail according to specific requirements. There is also a discount rate for properly presorted postcards. Pieces that cannot be presorted and prepared as required are residual mail and are paid at the full first-class letter or postcard rate.

Forwarding First-Class and Other Mail

First-class mail is forwarded at no charge for one year. Second-class mail, including magazines and newspapers, is forwarded at no charge for sixty days from the effective date of a change-of-address order. All post offices have information about holding mail, temporary changes of address, and forwarding and return of other classes of mail.

Other Special Mail Services

In addition to the services already outlined, the USPS offers a wide variety of other options to provide customers maximum convenience and to give individual pieces of mail special handling or protection.

Any piece of mail traveling by one of these special services must be so labeled. The appropriate marking (registered, insured, certified, delivery tracking, etc.) should be placed above the delivery address and to the right of the return address.

Post Office Box and Caller Services

Post office box and caller services are available at many post offices for an annual fee. Post office box delivery is a secure and private means of getting your mail any time the post office lobby is open. With post offices conveniently located near most businesses, you can get a jump on your day by picking up your company's mail at a post office box in the morning.

Caller (pickup) service, available when post office retail windows are open, is for customers who receive a large volume of mail or those who need a box number address when no boxes are available. Call your post office for more information.

Collect on Delivery (COD) Service

Use COD service when your company wants to collect for merchandise and postage when the merchandise is delivered. COD service may be used for merchandise sent by first-class mail, Express Mail, Priority Mail, third- or fourth-class mail, or registered mail. The merchandise must have been ordered by the addressee. The fee charged for this service includes insurance protection against loss or damage, although the service

Mail Services

is limited to items valued at a maximum of $1,000. COD service is not available for international mail.

Merchandise Return Service

Merchandise return service is available to authorized parties through a special permit. The service enables one of your company's customers to return a parcel and have the postage paid by you. Under this arrangement, the company provides the customer with instructions and a special label to attach to the parcel if it must be returned. The customer applies the label to the parcel and deposits it at a post office or in a mailbox. Unless the label is provided, the customer must pay the required postage charges.

Certified Mail

Certified mail service provides the mailer with a receipt and a record of the delivery of the item mailed from the post office from which it is delivered. No record is kept at the post office at which the item is mailed. Certified mail is handled in the ordinary mail and is not covered by insurance. The matter mailed usually has no intrinsic value, with the sender wishing only to be sure that it has been sent to the correct point of receipt. If the item mailed does have intrinsic value, it should be sent via registered mail, *not* certified mail.

Certified mail may be sent special delivery if additional postage is paid. An additional fee is also charged if delivery is restricted (only to the person named in the address) or if a return receipt is requested by the mailer.

Certificate of Mailing

At a fee somewhat lower than that for certified mail, a certificate of mailing will furnish evidence of mailing only. No receipt is obtained upon delivery of mail to the addressee. The fee does not insure the article against loss or damage to the item mailed.

Return Receipt

When the sender wants evidence that the mail was delivered, he or she should request a return receipt at the time the article is mailed. A return receipt can be purchased for mail that is sent COD or by Express Mail, is insured for more than $50, or is registered or certified. It identifies the article by number, the signer, and date of delivery. For an additional fee, the sender can get the addressee's correct address of delivery or can request restricted delivery service (see below).

Return receipt for merchandise service—another form of return receipt service, which provides a mailing receipt, return receipt, and record of delivery—is available for merchandise sent at first-class, Priority Mail, and third- and fourth-class rates of postage.

Restricted Delivery

Restricted delivery means that the sender's mail is delivered only to the addressee or to someone authorized in writing to receive mail for the addressee. Restricted delivery is offered in connection with return receipt service and is available only for registered mail, certified mail, COD mail, and mail insured for more than $50.

Restricted delivery mail addressed to officials of government agencies, members of the legislative and judicial branches of the federal government and state govern-

Mail Services

ments, members of the diplomatic corps, minors, and individuals under guardianship can be delivered to an agent without written authorization from the addressee.

Insurance

Protection against loss or damage to packages with contents valued in any amount up to $5,000 is available. The fee is based on the amount of insurance desired. Insurance can be purchased for third- and fourth-class mail, as well as for third- and fourth-class matter that is mailed at the Priority Mail or first-class mail rate. Insurance coverage up to $25,000 can be purchased on registered mail, the most secure service offered by the USPS. For articles insured for more than $50, a receipt of delivery is signed by the recipient and filed at the delivery post office.

Do not over-insure your packages since the amount of insurance coverage for loss will be the actual value, less depreciation. No payments are made for sentimental losses or for any expenses incurred as a result of the loss. For example, if you send a package containing a three-year-old computer that was originally purchased for $2,500, its actual value (due to depreciation) might be only $800. Even if you insured the computer for $2,500, if it were damaged or lost, the insurance would pay only the current value of $800.

Registered Mail

The most secure option offered by the USPS is registered mail. Registered articles are placed under tight security from the point of mailing to the delivery office, providing added protection for valuable and important mail. Return receipt and restricted delivery services are available for additional fees. Registered mail to Canada is subject to a $1,000 indemnity limit. For all other foreign countries, the indemnity is currently $40.45. First-class or Priority Mail postage is required on domestic registered mail.

There are special packaging requirements for registered mail. For example, you can't send a soft-sided package, put tape over the edges, or reinforce an old box with tape. The box must be able to accept a postage ink stamp, and slick tape surfaces will not.

Special Handling

Special handling service is required for parcels whose unusual contents require additional care in transit and handling. Special handling is not required for parcels sent by first-class mail, Express Mail, or Priority Mail. Examples of contents requiring additional care—and thus, special handling—include live poultry or bees. Special handling is available for standard mail only, including insured and COD mail. This service provides preferential handling to the extent practical in dispatch and transportation.

Special handling service is not necessary for sending ordinary parcels even when they contain fragile items. Breakable items will receive adequate protection if they are packed with sufficient cushioning and clearly marked "Fragile." Use registered mail for valuable or irreplaceable items.

Information on the Internet

A wealth of information is available at your fingertips when you visit the USPS's website at www.usps.com. You can look up ZIP + 4 codes, track your mail, get information on the latest postal rates, and find answers to frequently asked questions.

Mail Services

If you keep exploring, you can find postal news releases and learn about the history of the USPS. The Inspection Service has information on consumer fraud and other crimes and information about the service's history. The website is continually changing, so you should visit often for new postal information. You also have an opportunity via the website to make inquiries and request additional information.

Alternatives to the U.S. Postal Service

Although documents, letters, and advertisements are usually shipped through the USPS, it is likely that your company will also use an alternative form of service—for example, United Parcel Service or FedEx.

United Parcel Service

When it comes to shipping parcels, many businesses turn to the United Parcel Service (UPS), which specializes in overnight shipping in addition to its regular package shipping service. Its freight charges are comparable to other carriers; prices vary depending on how far your package is being shipped and how much it weighs.

United Parcel Service distance charges are based on zones—both ground transportation zones and air freight zones. The ground transportation zones can also tell you approximately how many working days it will take for your package to arrive at its destination. You can determine the zone by looking up the zip code of the package's destination on a UPS zone chart. Use the UPS website (www.ups.com) to find this information and order shipping supplies. You can also print labels for your packages at the website.

There are several ways to ship via UPS:

- Take your packages directly to the nearest UPS office or UPS store. You can find the location by calling UPS at 800-PICK-UPS (800-742-5877) or by checking the website.

- Bring your package to one of the local UPS pickup stations, found at hardware stores, print shops, and office supply stores, in addition to chains of mailbox and packaging stores. Because each of these locations has a specific time when the UPS truck arrives to pick up packages, be sure you know when it is before you make the drop-off. You also may want to note that some of these local pickup stations as well as mailbox and packaging stores charge a surcharge on top of the regular shipping costs.

- Call UPS and ask to have your package picked up at your location. Normally, UPS will schedule the package pickup for the next day. When calling, you will need the weight and dimensions of each package, along with the delivery address. The operator will give you a price for the shipment, which you will have to pay by cash or check when the package is picked up. There is a small additional charge for the pickup service.

- Set up a UPS account, so that you can schedule shipments by phone or using the UPS website. You do not have to provide any detailed information on the size or weight of your package or the delivery address. You can schedule a pickup from a UPS driver at your location. The fees for the shipment are charged to your account, which is billed to your business by UPS.

- Register with UPS for regular weekday pickups. This is the ideal choice for a company that does a lot of shipping. To make the arrangement, meet with a UPS representative, register your company, and pay a small deposit, usually based on the company's normal expected monthly shipping bill. UPS will then provide a shipping kit that contains various supplies. With these materials you can prepare your own shipments for a pickup each day. In addition to the shipping charges, there is a small weekly pickup fee, paid whether you have any outgoing packages or not.

UPS Services   The following is a list of UPS services:

- UPS Next-Day Air Early A.M.—Guaranteed delivery to major U.S. cities by 8 a.m., and most others by 8:30 a.m. on weekdays and 9 a.m. on Saturdays. In addition, 8:30 a.m. delivery is available for most major international cities.

- UPS Next-Day Air—Overnight money-back guarantee on delivery of letters, documents, and packages to all major U.S. metropolitan areas.

- UPS Next-Day Air Saver—3 p.m. delivery for commercial destinations and end-of-day for residential locations for packages shipped within the continental United States and from Alaska.

- UPS 2nd-Day Air A.M.—Guaranteed delivery by noon on the second business day for commercial deliveries in the continental United States. The service is also available from Alaska and Hawaii to the contiguous forty-eight states.

- UPS 2nd-Day Air—Economical, guaranteed second business day delivery of letters and packages.

- UPS 3-Day Select—Guaranteed three-day delivery. Developed primarily for longer-distance shippers who need time-definite delivery and higher levels of information, it is priced between traditional ground and air express services. The service is available to any shipper for delivery throughout the contiguous forty-eight states.

- UPS Ground—Guaranteed time-definite delivery that applies to commercial ground service throughout the contiguous forty-eight states.

- UPS Worldwide Express Plus—Guaranteed delivery of documents and packages to more than 150 cities in Europe by 8:30 a.m. on the second business day. In addition, there is guaranteed overnight delivery by as early as 8 a.m. to thousands of U.S. cities from Europe, Asia, Canada, Mexico, and Puerto Rico.

- UPS Worldwide Express—For urgent international shipments, a door-to-door, customs-cleared delivery to more than two hundred countries and territories. There is guaranteed overnight delivery of documents from major U.S. cities to the world's most important business centers. Document and nondocument shipments to other destinations worldwide are typically delivered in two business days.

- UPS Worldwide Saver—For delivery by the end of the day in more than two hundred countries. There is next-day delivery to Canada and Mexico, and second-day delivery to Europe and Latin America.

- UPS Worldwide Expedited—For routine shipments that don't require express delivery, a time-definite alternative that is faster than traditional air freight. This is a door-to-door, customs-cleared service available to major trading countries.

Mail Services

Shipments to most major destinations in Canada and Mexico are delivered in three business days and to Europe and Asia in four business days.

- UPS Standard Service—For routine shipments to and from Canada, this is a prompt, dependable service with low-cost, fully tracked ground delivery. Service is available to every address in all of Canada's provinces.

FedEx

FedEx Express and FedEx Ground offer a wide variety of package shipping services ranging from overnight letters to ground freight. You can set up an account for FedEx by calling 800-GoFedEx (800-463-3339) or by visiting the website at www.fedex.com. FedEx services include:

- FedEx Express: U.S.—For fast, reliable, time-definite delivery.
- FedEx Express: International—for shipping to more than 220 countries door to door by specific delivery times.
- FedEx Freight—For time-definite delivery of packages that weigh between 151 and 2,200 pounds.
- FedEx Freight International—For time-definite delivery of high-volume international shipments in twenty-four to seventy-two hours to major global markets.
- FedEx Ground–U.S.—For cost-effective, day-definite delivery for business-to-business packages.
- FedEx International Ground—For door-to-door delivery in three to seven days from the United States to Canada and Puerto Rico.
- FedEx Home Delivery—For deliveries to residences at extended hours, competitive ground rates, and backed by a money-back guarantee.

To ship a package with FedEx, follow these steps:

1. Pack your shipment in FedEx packaging or your own packaging. Shipping supplies, such as overnight letter envelopes, boxes, and shipping forms, can be ordered or picked up from one of many conveniently located FedEx locations. They can also be ordered from the FedEx website.

2. Log on to the www.fedex.com website and select a service. Then create a shipping label by filling out the same, address, and phone number of the recipient. You can print a shipping label on your laser or ink-jet printer.

3. Drop off your package at the nearest self-service FedEx drop box, staffed service center, FedEx authorized shipping center, or select post office locations around the country. You can locate one of the more than 48,000 drop-off locations using the www.fedex.com website. In addition to dropping off your package, you can schedule a pickup. No prequalification is needed for a FedEx pickup; however, there is a small surcharge added to the shipping cost.

Other Shipping Services

Air Freight

For special situations, such as large packages or packages that must be delivered to another city the same day, air freight services are available from many airlines and

Mail Services

specialty air freight companies. Some have special offices at the airport for same-day shipments. These shipments must usually be dropped off at the freight office and picked up at the destination freight office. The fees are much higher than other next-day air and two-day air shipments.

Trucking Freight

For large shipments and heavy or bulky packages, there are many trucking companies that specialize in hauling freight. These companies will load the shipment at your place of business, transport it to the destination, and unload it for a fee that is usually competitive. Depending on what you are shipping and where it is going, coast-to-coast shipping can take anywhere from seven to twenty-one days.

Courier Services

If you need to ship a package across town within a few hours, your best bet is a courier service. These companies operate in most large towns and cities and provide pickup and delivery within a few hours. The prices for these services vary depending on the distance traveled and the weight and size of the package. Most of the time, the charge is paid in advance by the sender. Courier services are bonded against theft or damage.

For documents and other small items, many taxi companies also provide a courier-type service. Check your telephone book for courier services or taxi services.

Mail Services

5

Travel Arrangements

Today's Business Traveler

In today's competitive market, companies routinely buy and sell products and services both across the country and around the world. Because of this situation, business-related travel is common to every type and every size of company.

A small business just getting under way may have interest only in local markets; however, as the business grows and expands, a larger domestic market and possibly international markets will be of greater interest. Thus, as a business grows and an owner's needs increase, your administrative duties will include keeping abreast of how to handle your employer's travel needs quickly and efficiently, no matter how far he or she goes.

Even if you work for a larger company that has an in-house travel department, it's useful to know the following procedures to troubleshoot for your boss when needed.

Getting the Trip Under Way

Your main purpose in making travel arrangements is to get your boss to his or her destination and back home again as smoothly as possible. Speed and cost may be other considerations. If you are a new administrative assistant or new to a particular office, see what the policies and precedents are for making travel arrangements. You may find helpful information in the files. There may even be a step-by-step procedures manual to consult, or you may find a special intranet Web page that contains travel information.

As you collect information for the trip, be sure to determine the following basics:

■ What is the purpose of the trip?

■ What are the desired departure and return times and dates?

■ What is the point-by-point itinerary?

■ Will the boss be traveling alone, or will other staff members or family members be traveling along?

■ What type of transportation does your boss desire? What is the best means of transportation available at that particular destination? If you're not sure, a travel agent can help you with some of this information even if arrangements are ultimately not made through the agency.

■ What is the lodging facility closest to the activities of the trip? If your boss's appointments are scattered throughout the city, perhaps a downtown hotel or an airport hotel or motel would be preferred.

Booking Travel Online

It is simple to make travel arrangements online. You can go directly to the website for an airline, hotel, or car rental company and make reservations or purchase tickets. You can also visit a travel website and make all the plans from one site. Some of the most popular travel websites include the following:

- Priceline: www.priceline.com
- Expedia: www.expedia.com
- Kayak: www.kayak.com
- Orbitz: www.orbitz.com

Hotel Reservations

If the meeting is in a major city, make the lodging reservations without delay because city hotels are often fully booked weeks in advance. Always get printed confirmation from either the website or from a confirmation email, which your boss should carry when traveling in case he or she arrives only to be told that no such reservation exists.

Some hotels also make airport shuttle or limousine reservations. If your boss needs either of these, make a reservation now. Have the date and the exact time of day the shuttle or limousine is needed, and add that to the reservation. Again, get a printed confirmation and provide a copy to your boss.

Hotels hold room reservations only until a specific deadline, typically 6 p.m. You can extend the reservation beyond that time limit by guaranteeing payment whether or not the boss arrives. To do this, you must give the hotel reservations person a credit card number. Remember that if the boss changes his or her mind about making the trip or staying at that hotel, the room charge will have to be paid anyway, since you've guaranteed arrival. However, most hotels and motels will allow you to cancel a guaranteed reservation without charge if you cancel before 6 p.m. on the day of arrival.

All of this presumes you know which hotel to choose. If your boss is traveling to a city he or she has never visited before or is going to a convention that does not recommend a particular hotel, investigate your choices using the Internet. If your boss has a favorite hotel chain, you can call the national reservations center for the chain or go to its website and find out if they have a hotel in the city your boss will be visiting. You can then make reservations using the national reservations center or website.

Transportation Reservations

Airline
You can purchase airline tickets by either calling the airline's reservation office or by visiting its website. Some airlines offer a discount for booking the travel online because it saves them the cost of ticketing agents.

As soon as you're in touch with the airline, you can instantly make a flight reservation and usually secure a preferred seat and rental car reservation as well. You'll need your employer's credit card number in order to confirm the tickets.

Check with your boss to determine when he or she wishes to travel, which airport to fly in and out of (if the destination has multiple airports), whether nonstop is required, and his or her seating preferences. Most airlines offer first-class and business-class seating in addition to coach; however, some budget airlines only offer one class of seating. Some airlines offer coach seating with extended leg room or exit rows for an additional charge.

Electronic Tickets   Electronic tickets, or e-tickets, allow you to print a ticket and boarding pass from your office computer printer. Some airlines also offer electronic tickets that can be downloaded to a smartphone. This requires the passenger to register with the airline as a frequent flyer and download the airline's mobile app. Most airlines also allow you to check in for a flight 24 hours in advance and then print a copy of the boarding pass.

Airport security and airline check-in locations require you to provide a government-issued photo ID, such as a driver's license. (The name on the ticket must match the name on the ID.) For international travel, a passport may be needed as identification. In addition, when flying on an e-ticket, you must have a printed copy indicating a flight departure for the current date.

This information is required in order to enter the secured area beyond the security screening checkpoint. Passengers who do not need to check baggage and already have an approved document (outlined above) may proceed through the security checkpoint directly to the departure gate.

Some employers require paper receipts for business travel expense reports. Some companies accept printouts of confirmation emails, but check your company's policy to find out what is acceptable documentation.

Train

In days gone by, rail travel was the way to go, with comfortable sleeping compartments and dining cars with fine food graciously served. But today, with time being money, most executives prefer air travel. Still, there are executives who either prefer not to fly or genuinely enjoy leisurely travel such as that provided by Amtrak. Railway travel is usually done when there is adequate time and easy access to rail terminals.

If your employer prefers rail travel, obtain a schedule for Amtrak trains as well as for commuter lines and connecting lines from the nearest rail station or at the Amtrak website at www.amtrak.com. A call to Amtrak at 800-USA-RAIL (800-872-7245) will also answer your questions.

Car Rental

Call the preferred car rental company's reservation office by consulting your telephone directory for a toll-free 800 number or make the reservation online by visiting the car rental company's website. Many car rental companies have frequent-renter programs that speed up the rental process both when making reservations and when picking up a car. Check with your employer to find out which car rental company is preferred and whether or not he or she has a frequent-renter membership. Also ask about the type of car your boss prefers.

Car rentals are handled much the same way as hotel reservations. You'll need to provide a credit card number in order to guarantee the reservation. You will also need to know the following in order to make a car rental reservation:

- City
- Specific rental location in the city
- Car pick-up time

- Car drop-off time
- Car class

The Itinerary

An itinerary—that is, a written travel agenda—is useful to both the executive and the administrative assistant who remains in the office. Quick reference to it can be made when questions arise. Perhaps the executive has forgotten the address or time for an appointment, or perhaps the administrative assistant, faced with a sudden emergency, needs to know exactly where the employer can be contacted.

Before preparing the written itinerary, confer with your boss, making notes of all activities on the trip. Show your employer a draft of the written schedule so that changes can be made or forgotten items added. Once the itinerary has been completed, it can be typed on small pocket-size cards or on plain paper or emailed to the traveler's smartphone. Figure 5-1 contains a sample itinerary.

FIGURE 5-1 Sample itinerary.

PAUL GROME
ITINERARY

Monday, June 1 (Dallas to New York)

8:00 AM	Leave Dallas residence by limousine for airport. (Limousine reservation attached.)
9:00 AM	Leave DFW Airport on American Airlines Flight 122, Seat 1B. (Ticket attached.)
12:40 AM	Arrive New York, JFK Airport. Limousine to Americana Hotel. (Limousine reservation attached.)
2:30 PM	Don Daley, president of Bryant Industries, will provide car for trip to his office, Chase Manhattan Plaza, Suite 1000. (Bryant Industries file in briefcase.)

Tuesday, June 2

9:00 AM	Appointment with Henderson, Smith & Jackson, Empire State Building, Suite 8000.
10:30 AM	Appointment with Mary Louise Henderson. (Henderson, Smith & Jackson file in briefcase.)
2:00 PM	Appointment with August Terrell, your hotel; meet in lobby. (Terrell Corporation file in briefcase.)
7:00 PM	Dinner, Don Daley's home (5203 Legendary Lane, New York; Telephone 212-555-6120).

Wednesday, June 3

7:45 AM	Leave hotel by limousine for airport. (Limousine reservation attached.)
9:45 AM	Leave JFK Airport on American Airlines Flight 292, Seat 12A. (Ticket attached.)
11:05 AM	Arrive Dallas. Limousine to office. (Limousine reservation attached.)

Before-the-Trip Checklist

Before your employer leaves on a trip, you should confirm the following:

- Airline tickets and frequent flyer number
- Lodging information and confirmation number
- Car rental information and confirmation number
- Money, travelers' checks, or credit card (alert the credit card company of your employer's intended travel, so that the company won't freeze your employer's account for suspected fraud)
- Passport, visa, driver's license, or international driving permit
- Itinerary
- Destination contact names, addresses, and phone numbers
- Meeting agendas
- Speeches, reports, and presentations
- Computer or iPad
- Cell phone

International Travel

If the boss's trip involves international travel, make plans well in advance because of the many details involved. He or she should be aware of both U.S. requirements regarding foreign travel and the requirements of the country or countries to be visited. There are many conditions imposed on business travelers that are different from those imposed on tourists.

For assistance in arranging an international business trip, you can contact the U.S. Department of State at www.travel.state.gov. You can also visit the U.S. Department of Commerce website at www.commerce.gov.

Visas and Passports

Most U.S. citizens need a passport to leave the United States and to reenter it. A passport is required by U.S. law for travel to North America, South America, Central America, the Caribbean, or Bermuda (under previous law, a passport was not required for such travel). Passports are not required for travel to U.S. territories (such as Puerto Rico). All travelers should always carry personal identification, such as a driver's license or a government-issued photo ID, which is at the least necessary to board planes.

In addition to a passport, many countries require a visa to enter. Usually, the visa must be obtained in advance and can't be purchased at the border or point of entry. Visas are issued by the individual embassies and consulates of various countries. Some countries charge a small fee, while others issue visas for free. Since the requirements can and do change often, even if your employer has obtained a visa in advance of a trip, double-check before your employer leaves to make sure the visa is still valid.

To find out more about passports and visas, contact the U.S. Department of State at www.travel.state.gov or call 877-487-2778.

Western Hemisphere Travel Initiative Enhanced Driver's Licenses

The Western Hemisphere Travel Initiative (WHTI) is an international agreement among the United States, Canada, and Mexico that allows for travel between countries using a WHTI Enhanced Driver's License in lieu of a passport. As of the publication of this book, the following states and provinces are issuing WHTI enhanced driver's licenses:

- Washington
- Michigan
- New York
- Vermont
- Manitoba
- British Columbia
- Ontario
- Quebec

Required Immunizations and Vaccinations

Anyone traveling internationally must have up-to-date information concerning required immunizations. The U.S. Department of Health and Human Services (DHHS) has information on required immunizations for travelers available by calling 877-FYI-TRIP (877-394-8747). You can also visit DHHS's Centers for Disease Control and Prevention on the Web at www.cdc.gov/travel.

Customs

When returning from foreign countries, the traveler must declare certain items acquired abroad to determine whether a tax is owed. Travelers returning home to the United States are allowed certain exemptions, which help cover the inevitable souvenirs. Articles totaling $800 (fair retail value in the country where purchased) are duty free, except for cigarettes, cigars, and liquor.

Beware: Travelers should not try to understate the value of an article or misrepresent the nature of any article. To do so could result in the seizure and forfeiture of the item, and the tax will still be assessed. If a traveler has doubt as to whether to declare an item, he or she should declare it and then ask the customs inspector about it. Complete and detailed information concerning customs regulations are available by visiting www.cbp.gov.

Time Zones

A variety of useful time zone–related information is available on the Web at www.timeanddate.com. The following is a list of abbreviations for time zones:

Standard

- *UTC.* Coordinated Universal Time, civil time, the one most often used by "ordinary" people. It also is known as Greenwich Mean Time.
- *UT.* Universal Time, based on the earth's rotation, often used in astronomy
- *TAI.* International Atomic Time, based on atomic clocks

European

- *GMT.* Greenwich Mean Time, as UTC
- *BST.* British Summer Time, as UTC + 1 hour

- *IST.* Irish Summer Time, as UTC + 1 hour
- *WET.* Western Europe Time, as UTC
- *WEST.* Western Europe Summer Time, as UTC + 1 hour
- *CET.* Central Europe Time, as UTC + 1 hour
- *CEST.* Central Europe Summer Time, as UTC + 2 hours
- *EET.* Eastern Europe Time, as UTC + 2 hours
- *EEST.* Eastern Europe Summer Time, as UTC + 3 hours
- *MSK.* Moscow Time, as UTC + 3 hours
- *MSD.* Moscow Summer Time, as UTC + 4 hours

United States and Canada

- *AST.* Atlantic Standard Time, as UTC – 4 hours
- *ADT.* Atlantic Daylight Time, as UTC – 3 hours
- *EST.* Eastern Standard Time, as UTC – 5 hours
- *EDT.* Eastern Daylight Saving Time, as UTC – 4 hours
- *ET.* Eastern Time, either as EST or EDT, depending on place and time of year
- *CST.* Central Standard Time, as UTC – 6 hours
- *CDT.* Central Daylight Saving Time, as UTC – 5 hours
- *CT.* Central Time, either as CST or CDT, depending on place and time of year
- *MST.* Mountain Standard Time, as UTC – 7 hours
- *MDT.* Mountain Daylight Saving Time, as UTC – 6 hours
- *MT.* Mountain Time, either as MST or MDT, depending on place and time of year
- *PST.* Pacific Standard Time, as UTC – 8 hours
- *PDT.* Pacific Daylight Saving Time, as UTC – 7 hours
- *PT.* Pacific Time, either as PST or PDT, depending on place and time of year
- *HST.* Hawaiian Standard Time, as UTC – 10 hours
- *AKST.* Alaska Standard Time, as UTC – 9 hours
- *AKDT.* Alaska Standard Daylight Saving Time, as UTC – 8 hours

Australia

- *AEST.* Australian Eastern Standard Time, as UTC + 10 hours
- *AEDT.* Australian Eastern Daylight Time, as UTC + 11 hours
- *ACST.* Australian Central Standard Time, as UTC + 9.5 hours
- *ACDT.* Australian Central Daylight Time, as UTC + 10.5 hours
- *AWST.* Australian Western Standard Time, as UTC + 8 hours

Time Zone Time Differences

Table 5-1 shows the time differences between countries and various time zones in the United States.

TABLE 5-1 Time Zone Time Differences

Country	GMT	USA Eastern	USA Central	USA Mountain	USA Pacific
A					
Afghanistan	+ 4.5 H	+ 9.5 H	+ 10.5 H	+ 11.5 H	+ 12.5 H
Albania	+ 1.0 H	+ 6.0 H	+ 7.0 H	+ 8.0 H	+ 9.0 H
Algeria	+ 1.0 H	+ 6.0 H	+ 7.0 H	+ 8.0 H	+ 9.0 H
American Samoa	− 11.0 H	− 6.0 H	− 5.0 H	− 4.0 H	− 3.0 H
Andorra	+ 1.0 H	+ 6.0 H	+ 7.0 H	+ 8.0 H	+ 9.0 H
Angola	+ 1.0 H	+ 6.0 H	+ 7.0 H	+ 8.0 H	+ 9.0 H
Antarctica	− 2.0 H	+ 3.0 H	+ 4.0 H	+ 5.0 H	+ 6.0 H
Antigua and Barbuda	− 4.0 H	+ 1.0 H	+ 2.0 H	+ 3.0 H	+ 4.0 H
Argentina	− 3.0 H	+ 2.0 H	+ 3.0 H	+ 4.0 H	+ 5.0 H
Armenia	+ 4.0 H	+ 9.0 H	+ 10.0 H	+ 11.0 H	+ 12.0 H
Aruba	− 4.0 H	+ 1.0 H	+ 2.0 H	+ 3.0 H	+ 4.0 H
Ascension	+ 0.0 H	+ 5.0 H	+ 6.0 H	+ 7.0 H	+ 8.0 H
Australia East	+ 10.0 H	+ 15.0 H	+ 16.0 H	+ 17.0 H	+ 18.0 H
Australia North	+ 9.5 H	+ 14.5 H	+ 15.5 H	+ 16.5 H	+ 17.5 H
Australia South	+ 10.0 H	+ 15.0 H	+ 16.0 H	+ 17.0 H	+ 18.0 H
Australia West	+ 8.0 H	+ 13.0 H	+ 14.0 H	+ 15.0 H	+ 16.0 H
Austria	+ 1.0 H	+ 6.0 H	+ 7.0 H	+ 8.0 H	+ 9.0 H
Azerbaijan	+ 3.0 H	+ 8.0 H	+ 9.0 H	+ 10.0 H	+ 11.0 H
B					
Bahamas	− 5.0 H	+ 0.0 H	+ 1.0 H	+ 2.0 H	+ 3.0 H
Bahrain	+ 3.0 H	+ 8.0 H	+ 9.0 H	+ 10.0 H	+ 11.0 H
Bangladesh	+ 6.0 H	+ 11.0 H	+ 12.0 H	+ 13.0 H	+ 14.0 H
Barbados	− 4.0 H	+ 1.0 H	+ 2.0 H	+ 3.0 H	+ 4.0 H
Belarus	+ 2.0 H	+ 7.0 H	+ 8.0 H	+ 9.0 H	+ 10.0 H
Belgium	+ 1.0 H	+ 6.0 H	+ 7.0 H	+ 8.0 H	+ 9.0 H
Belize	− 6.0 H	− 1.0 H	+ 0.0 H	+ 1.0 H	+ 2.0 H
Benin	+ 1.0 H	+ 6.0 H	+ 7.0 H	+ 8.0 H	+ 9.0 H
Bermuda	− 4.0 H	+ 1.0 H	+ 2.0 H	+ 3.0 H	+ 4.0 H
Bhutan	+ 6.0 H	+ 11.0 H	+ 12.0 H	+ 13.0 H	+ 14.0 H
Bolivia	− 4.0 H	+ 1.0 H	+ 2.0 H	+ 3.0 H	+ 4.0 H
Bosnia/Herzegovina	+ 1.0 H	+ 6.0 H	+ 7.0 H	+ 8.0 H	+ 9.0 H
Botswana	+ 2.0 H	+ 7.0 H	+ 8.0 H	+ 9.0 H	+ 10.0 H

(continued)

TABLE 5-1   (*continued*)

Country	GMT	USA Eastern	USA Central	USA Mountain	USA Pacific
Brazil East	− 3.0 H	+ 2.0 H	+ 3.0 H	+ 4.0 H	+ 5.0 H
Brazil West	− 4.0 H	+ 1.0 H	+ 2.0 H	+ 3.0 H	+ 4.0 H
British Virgin Islands	− 4.0 H	+ 1.0 H	+ 2.0 H	+ 3.0 H	+ 4.0 H
Brunei	+ 8.0 H	+ 13.0 H	+ 14.0 H	+ 15.0 H	+ 16.0 H
Bulgaria	+ 2.0 H	+ 7.0 H	+ 8.0 H	+ 9.0 H	+ 10.0 H
Burkina Faso	+ 0.0 H	+ 5.0 H	+ 6.0 H	+ 7.0 H	+ 8.0 H
Burundi	+ 2.0 H	+ 7.0 H	+ 8.0 H	+ 9.0 H	+ 10.0 H
C					
Cambodia	+ 7.0 H	+ 12.0 H	+ 13.0 H	+ 14.0 H	+ 15.0 H
Cameroon	+ 1.0 H	+ 6.0 H	+ 7.0 H	+ 8.0 H	+ 9.0 H
Canada Central	− 6.0 H	− 1.0 H	+ 0.0 H	+ 1.0 H	+ 2.0 H
Canada Eastern	− 5.0 H	+ 0.0 H	+ 1.0 H	+ 2.0 H	+ 3.0 H
Canada Mountain	− 7.0 H	− 2.0 H	− 1.0 H	+ 0.0 H	+ 1.0 H
Canada Newfoundland	− 3.5 H	+ 1.5 H	+ 2.5 H	+ 3.5 H	+ 4.5 H
Canada Pacific	− 8.0 H	− 3.0 H	− 2.0 H	− 1.0 H	+ 0.0 H
Cape Verde	− 1.0 H	+ 4.0 H	+ 5.0 H	+ 6.0 H	+ 7.0 H
Cayman Islands	− 5.0 H	+ 0.0 H	+ 1.0 H	+ 2.0 H	+ 3.0 H
Central African Rep	+ 1.0 H	+ 6.0 H	+ 7.0 H	+ 8.0 H	+ 9.0 H
Chad Rep	+ 1.0 H	+ 6.0 H	+ 7.0 H	+ 8.0 H	+ 9.0 H
Chile	− 4.0 H	+ 1.0 H	+ 2.0 H	+ 3.0 H	+ 4.0 H
China	+ 8.0 H	+ 13.0 H	+ 14.0 H	+ 15.0 H	+ 16.0 H
Christmas Islands	− 10.0 H	− 5.0 H	− 4.0 H	− 3.0 H	− 2.0 H
Colombia	− 5.0 H	+ 0.0 H	+ 1.0 H	+ 2.0 H	+ 3.0 H
Congo	+ 1.0 H	+ 6.0 H	+ 7.0 H	+ 8.0 H	+ 9.0 H
Cook Islands	− 10.0 H	− 5.0 H	− 4.0 H	− 3.0 H	− 2.0 H
Costa Rica	− 6.0 H	− 1.0 H	+ 0.0 H	+ 1.0 H	+ 2.0 H
Croatia	+ 1.0 H	+ 6.0 H	+ 7.0 H	+ 8.0 H	+ 9.0 H
Cuba	− 5.0 H	+ 0.0 H	+ 1.0 H	+ 2.0 H	+ 3.0 H
Cyprus	+ 2.0 H	+ 7.0 H	+ 8.0 H	+ 9.0 H	+ 10.0 H
Czech Republic	+ 1.0 H	+ 6.0 H	+ 7.0 H	+ 8.0 H	+ 9.0 H
D					
Denmark	+ 1.0 H	+ 6.0 H	+ 7.0 H	+ 8.0 H	+ 9.0 H
Djibouti	+ 3.0 H	+ 8.0 H	+ 9.0 H	+ 10.0 H	+ 11.0 H

Travel Arrangements

Country	GMT	USA Eastern	USA Central	USA Mountain	USA Pacific
Dominica	− 4.0 H	+ 1.0 H	+ 2.0 H	+ 3.0 H	+ 4.0 H
Dominican Republic	− 4.0 H	+ 1.0 H	+ 2.0 H	+ 3.0 H	+ 4.0 H
E					
Ecuador	− 5.0 H	+ 0.0 H	+ 1.0 H	+ 2.0 H	+ 3.0 H
Egypt	+ 2.0 H	+ 7.0 H	+ 8.0 H	+ 9.0 H	+ 10.0 H
El Salvador	− 6.0 H	− 1.0 H	+ 0.0 H	+ 1.0 H	+ 2.0 H
Equatorial Guinea	+ 1.0 H	+ 6.0 H	+ 7.0 H	+ 8.0 H	+ 9.0 H
Eritrea	+ 3.0 H	+ 8.0 H	+ 9.0 H	+ 10.0 H	+ 11.0 H
Estonia	+ 2.0 H	+ 7.0 H	+ 8.0 H	+ 9.0 H	+ 10.0 H
Ethiopia	+ 3.0 H	+ 8.0 H	+ 9.0 H	+ 10.0 H	+ 11.0 H
F					
Faeroe Islands	+ 0.0 H	+ 5.0 H	+ 6.0 H	+ 7.0 H	+ 8.0 H
Falkland Islands	− 4.0 H	+ 1.0 H	+ 2.0 H	+ 3.0 H	+ 4.0 H
Fiji Islands	+ 12.0 H	+ 17.0 H	+ 18.0 H	+ 19.0 H	+ 20.0 H
Finland	+ 2.0 H	+ 7.0 H	+ 8.0 H	+ 9.0 H	+ 10.0 H
France	+ 1.0 H	+ 6.0 H	+ 7.0 H	+ 8.0 H	+ 9.0 H
French Antilles (Martinique)	− 3.0 H	+ 2.0 H	+ 3.0 H	+ 4.0 H	+ 5.0 H
French Guinea	− 3.0 H	+ 2.0 H	+ 3.0 H	+ 4.0 H	+ 5.0 H
French Polynesia	− 10.0 H	− 5.0 H	− 4.0 H	− 3.0 H	− 2.0 H
G					
Gabon Republic	+ 1.0 H	+ 6.0 H	+ 7.0 H	+ 8.0 H	+ 9.0 H
Gambia	+ 0.0 H	+ 5.0 H	+ 6.0 H	+ 7.0 H	+ 8.0 H
Georgia	+ 4.0 H	+ 9.0 H	+ 10.0 H	+ 11.0 H	+ 12.0 H
Germany	+ 1.0 H	+ 6.0 H	+ 7.0 H	+ 8.0 H	+ 9.0 H
Ghana	+ 0.0 H	+ 5.0 H	+ 6.0 H	+ 7.0 H	+ 8.0 H
Gibraltar	+ 1.0 H	+ 6.0 H	+ 7.0 H	+ 8.0 H	+ 9.0 H
Greece	+ 2.0 H	+ 7.0 H	+ 8.0 H	+ 9.0 H	+ 10.0 H
Greenland	− 3.0 H	+ 2.0 H	+ 3.0 H	+ 4.0 H	+ 5.0 H
Grenada	− 4.0 H	+ 1.0 H	+ 2.0 H	+ 3.0 H	+ 4.0 H
Guadeloupe	− 4.0 H	+ 1.0 H	+ 2.0 H	+ 3.0 H	+ 4.0 H
Guam	+ 10.0 H	+ 15.0 H	+ 16.0 H	+ 17.0 H	+ 18.0 H
Guatemala	− 6.0 H	− 1.0 H	+ 0.0 H	+ 1.0 H	+ 2.0 H
Guinea	+ 0.0 H	+ 5.0 H	+ 6.0 H	+ 7.0 H	+ 8.0 H

(continued)

TABLE 5-1   (*continued*)

Country	GMT	USA Eastern	USA Central	USA Mountain	USA Pacific
Guinea-Bissau	+ 0.0 H	+ 5.0 H	+ 6.0 H	+ 7.0 H	+ 8.0 H
Guyana	− 3.0 H	+ 2.0 H	+ 3.0 H	+ 4.0 H	+ 5.0 H
H					
Haiti	− 5.0 H	+ 0.0 H	+ 1.0 H	+ 2.0 H	+ 3.0 H
Honduras	− 6.0 H	− 1.0 H	+ 0.0 H	+ 1.0 H	+ 2.0 H
Hong Kong	+ 8.0 H	+ 13.0 H	+ 14.0 H	+ 15.0 H	+ 16.0 H
Hungary	+ 1.0 H	+ 6.0 H	+ 7.0 H	+ 8.0 H	+ 9.0 H
I					
Iceland	+ 0.0 H	+ 5.0 H	+ 6.0 H	+ 7.0 H	+ 8.0 H
India	+ 5.5 H	+ 10.5 H	+ 11.5 H	+ 12.5 H	+ 13.5 H
Indonesia Central	+ 8.0 H	+ 13.0 H	+ 14.0 H	+ 15.0 H	+ 16.0 H
Indonesia East	+ 9.0 H	+ 14.0 H	+ 15.0 H	+ 16.0 H	+ 17.0 H
Indonesia West	+ 7.0 H	+ 12.0 H	+ 13.0 H	+ 14.0 H	+ 15.0 H
Iran	+ 3.5 H	+ 8.5 H	+ 9.5 H	+ 10.5 H	+ 11.5 H
Iraq	+ 3.0 H	+ 8.0 H	+ 9.0 H	+ 10.0 H	+ 11.0 H
Ireland	+ 0.0 H	+ 5.0 H	+ 6.0 H	+ 7.0 H	+ 8.0 H
Israel	+ 2.0 H	+ 7.0 H	+ 8.0 H	+ 9.0 H	+ 10.0 H
Italy	+ 1.0 H	+ 6.0 H	+ 7.0 H	+ 8.0 H	+ 9.0 H
J					
Jamaica	− 5.0 H	+ 0.0 H	+ 1.0 H	+ 2.0 H	+ 3.0 H
Japan	+ 9.0 H	+ 14.0 H	+ 15.0 H	+ 16.0 H	+ 17.0 H
Jordan	+ 2.0 H	+ 7.0 H	+ 8.0 H	+ 9.0 H	+ 10.0 H
K					
Kazakhstan	+ 6.0 H	+ 11.0 H	+ 12.0 H	+ 13.0 H	+ 14.0 H
Kenya	+ 3.0 H	+ 8.0 H	+ 9.0 H	+ 10.0 H	+ 11.0 H
Kiribati	+ 12.0 H	+ 17.0 H	+ 18.0 H	+ 19.0 H	+ 20.0 H
Korea, North	+ 9.0 H	+ 14.0 H	+ 15.0 H	+ 16.0 H	+ 17.0 H
Korea, South	+ 9.0 H	+ 14.0 H	+ 15.0 H	+ 16.0 H	+ 17.0 H
Kuwait	+ 3.0 H	+ 8.0 H	+ 9.0 H	+ 10.0 H	+ 11.0 H
Kyrgyzstan	+ 5.0 H	+ 10.0 H	+ 11.0 H	+ 12.0 H	+ 13.0 H
L					
Laos	+ 7.0 H	+ 12.0 H	+ 13.0 H	+ 14.0 H	+ 15.0 H
Latvia	+ 2.0 H	+ 7.0 H	+ 8.0 H	+ 9.0 H	+ 10.0 H

Travel Arrangements

Country	GMT	USA Eastern	USA Central	USA Mountain	USA Pacific
Lebanon	+ 2.0 H	+ 7.0 H	+ 8.0 H	+ 9.0 H	+ 10.0 H
Lesotho	+ 2.0 H	+ 7.0 H	+ 8.0 H	+ 9.0 H	+ 10.0 H
Liberia	+ 0.0 H	+ 5.0 H	+ 6.0 H	+ 7.0 H	+ 8.0 H
Libya	+ 2.0 H	+ 7.0 H	+ 8.0 H	+ 9.0 H	+ 10.0 H
Liechtenstein	+ 1.0 H	+ 6.0 H	+ 7.0 H	+ 8.0 H	+ 9.0 H
Lithuania	+ 2.0 H	+ 7.0 H	+ 8.0 H	+ 9.0 H	+ 10.0 H
Luxembourg	+ 1.0 H	+ 6.0 H	+ 7.0 H	+ 8.0 H	+ 9.0 H
M					
Macedonia	+ 1.0 H	+ 6.0 H	+ 7.0 H	+ 8.0 H	+ 9.0 H
Madagascar	+ 3.0 H	+ 8.0 H	+ 9.0 H	+ 10.0 H	+ 11.0 H
Malawi	+ 2.0 H	+ 7.0 H	+ 8.0 H	+ 9.0 H	+ 10.0 H
Malaysia	+ 8.0 H	+ 13.0 H	+ 14.0 H	+ 15.0 H	+ 16.0 H
Maldives	+ 5.0 H	+ 10.0 H	+ 11.0 H	+ 12.0 H	+ 13.0 H
Mali Republic	+ 0.0 H	+ 5.0 H	+ 6.0 H	+ 7.0 H	+ 8.0 H
Malta	+ 1.0 H	+ 6.0 H	+ 7.0 H	+ 8.0 H	+ 9.0 H
Marshall Islands	+ 12.0 H	+ 17.0 H	+ 18.0 H	+ 19.0 H	+ 20.0 H
Mauritania	+ 0.0 H	+ 5.0 H	+ 6.0 H	+ 7.0 H	+ 8.0 H
Mauritius	+ 4.0 H	+ 9.0 H	+ 10.0 H	+ 11.0 H	+ 12.0 H
Mayotte	+ 3.0 H	+ 8.0 H	+ 9.0 H	+ 10.0 H	+ 11.0 H
Mexico Central	− 6.0 H	− 1.0 H	+ 0.0 H	+ 1.0 H	+ 2.0 H
Mexico East	− 5.0 H	+ 0.0 H	+ 1.0 H	+ 2.0 H	+ 3.0 H
Mexico West	− 7.0 H	− 2.0 H	− 1.0 H	+ 0.0 H	+ 1.0 H
Moldova	+ 2.0 H	+ 7.0 H	+ 8.0 H	+ 9.0 H	+ 10.0 H
Monaco	+ 1.0 H	+ 6.0 H	+ 7.0 H	+ 8.0 H	+ 9.0 H
Mongolia	+ 8.0 H	+ 13.0 H	+ 14.0 H	+ 15.0 H	+ 16.0 H
Morocco	+ 0.0 H	+ 5.0 H	+ 6.0 H	+ 7.0 H	+ 8.0 H
Mozambique	+ 2.0 H	+ 7.0 H	+ 8.0 H	+ 9.0 H	+ 10.0 H
Myanmar	+ 6.5 H	+ 11.5 H	+ 12.5 H	+ 13.5 H	+ 14.5 H
N					
Namibia	+ 1.0 H	+ 6.0 H	+ 7.0 H	+ 8.0 H	+ 9.0 H
Nauru	+ 12.0 H	+ 17.0 H	+ 18.0 H	+ 19.0 H	+ 20.0 H
Nepal	+ 5.5 H	+ 10.5 H	+ 11.5 H	+ 12.5 H	+ 13.5 H
Netherlands	+ 1.0 H	+ 6.0 H	+ 7.0 H	+ 8.0 H	+ 9.0 H

(continued)

TABLE 5-1   (*continued*)

Country	GMT	USA Eastern	USA Central	USA Mountain	USA Pacific
Netherlands Antilles	− 4.0 H	+ 1.0 H	+ 2.0 H	+ 3.0 H	+ 4.0 H
New Caledonia	+ 11.0 H	+ 16.0 H	+ 17.0 H	+ 18.0 H	+ 19.0 H
New Zealand	+ 12.0 H	+ 17.0 H	+ 18.0 H	+ 19.0 H	+ 20.0 H
Nicaragua	− 6.0 H	− 1.0 H	+ 0.0 H	+ 1.0 H	+ 2.0 H
Niger Republic	+ 1.0 H	+ 6.0 H	+ 7.0 H	+ 8.0 H	+ 9.0 H
Nigeria	+ 1.0 H	+ 6.0 H	+ 7.0 H	+ 8.0 H	+ 9.0 H
Norfolk Island	+ 11.5 H	+ 16.5 H	+ 17.5 H	+ 18.5 H	+ 19.5 H
Norway	+ 1.0 H	+ 6.0 H	+ 7.0 H	+ 8.0 H	+ 9.0 H
O					
Oman	+ 4.0 H	+ 9.0 H	+ 10.0 H	+ 11.0 H	+ 12.0 H
P					
Pakistan	+ 5.0 H	+ 10.0 H	+ 11.0 H	+ 12.0 H	+ 13.0 H
Palau	+ 9.0 H	+ 14.0 H	+ 15.0 H	+ 16.0 H	+ 17.0 H
Panama	− 5.0 H	+ 0.0 H	+ 1.0 H	+ 2.0 H	+ 3.0 H
Papua New Guinea	+ 10.0 H	+ 15.0 H	+ 16.0 H	+ 17.0 H	+ 18.0 H
Paraguay	− 4.0 H	+ 1.0 H	+ 2.0 H	+ 3.0 H	+ 4.0 H
Peru	− 5.0 H	+ 0.0 H	+ 1.0 H	+ 2.0 H	+ 3.0 H
Philippines	+ 8.0 H	+ 13.0 H	+ 14.0 H	+ 15.0 H	+ 16.0 H
Poland	+ 1.0 H	+ 6.0 H	+ 7.0 H	+ 8.0 H	+ 9.0 H
Portugal	+ 1.0 H	+ 6.0 H	+ 7.0 H	+ 8.0 H	+ 9.0 H
Puerto Rico	− 4.0 H	+ 1.0 H	+ 2.0 H	+ 3.0 H	+ 4.0 H
Q					
Qatar	+ 3.0 H	+ 8.0 H	+ 9.0 H	+ 10.0 H	+ 11.0 H
R					
Reunion Island	+ 4.0 H	+ 9.0 H	+ 10.0 H	+ 11.0 H	+ 12.0 H
Romania	+ 2.0 H	+ 7.0 H	+ 8.0 H	+ 9.0 H	+ 10.0 H
Russia Central 1	+ 4.0 H	+ 9.0 H	+ 10.0 H	+ 11.0 H	+ 12.0 H
Russia Central 2	+ 7.0 H	+ 12.0 H	+ 13.0 H	+ 14.0 H	+ 15.0 H
Russia East	+ 11.0 H	+ 16.0 H	+ 17.0 H	+ 18.0 H	+ 19.0 H
Russia West	+ 2.0 H	+ 7.0 H	+ 8.0 H	+ 9.0 H	+ 10.0 H
Rwanda	+ 2.0 H	+ 7.0 H	+ 8.0 H	+ 9.0 H	+ 10.0 H
S					
Saba	− 4.0 H	+ 1.0 H	+ 2.0 H	+ 3.0 H	+ 4.0 H
Samoa	− 11.0 H	− 6.0 H	− 5.0 H	− 4.0 H	− 3.0 H

Country	GMT	USA Eastern	USA Central	USA Mountain	USA Pacific
San Marino	+ 1.0 H	+ 6.0 H	+ 7.0 H	+ 8.0 H	+ 9.0 H
Sao Tome	+ 0.0 H	+ 5.0 H	+ 6.0 H	+ 7.0 H	+ 8.0 H
Saudi Arabia	+ 3.0 H	+ 8.0 H	+ 9.0 H	+ 10.0 H	+ 11.0 H
Senegal	+ 0.0 H	+ 5.0 H	+ 6.0 H	+ 7.0 H	+ 8.0 H
Seychelles Islands	+ 4.0 H	+ 9.0 H	+ 10.0 H	+ 11.0 H	+ 12.0 H
Sierra Leone	+ 0.0 H	+ 5.0 H	+ 6.0 H	+ 7.0 H	+ 8.0 H
Singapore	+ 8.0 H	+ 13.0 H	+ 14.0 H	+ 15.0 H	+ 16.0 H
Slovakia	+ 1.0 H	+ 6.0 H	+ 7.0 H	+ 8.0 H	+ 9.0 H
Slovenia	+ 1.0 H	+ 6.0 H	+ 7.0 H	+ 8.0 H	+ 9.0 H
Solomon Islands	+ 11.0 H	+ 16.0 H	+ 17.0 H	+ 18.0 H	+ 19.0 H
Somalia	+ 3.0 H	+ 8.0 H	+ 9.0 H	+ 10.0 H	+ 11.0 H
South Africa	+ 2.0 H	+ 7.0 H	+ 8.0 H	+ 9.0 H	+ 10.0 H
Spain	+ 1.0 H	+ 6.0 H	+ 7.0 H	+ 8.0 H	+ 9.0 H
Sri Lanka	+ 5.5 H	+ 10.5 H	+ 11.5 H	+ 12.5 H	+ 13.5 H
St. Lucia	− 4.0 H	+ 1.0 H	+ 2.0 H	+ 3.0 H	+ 4.0 H
St. Maarten	− 4.0 H	+ 1.0 H	+ 2.0 H	+ 3.0 H	+ 4.0 H
St. Pierre and Miquelon	− 3.0 H	+ 2.0 H	+ 3.0 H	+ 4.0 H	+ 5.0 H
St. Thomas	− 4.0 H	+ 1.0 H	+ 2.0 H	+ 3.0 H	+ 4.0 H
St. Vincent	− 4.0 H	+ 1.0 H	+ 2.0 H	+ 3.0 H	+ 4.0 H
Sudan	+ 2.0 H	+ 7.0 H	+ 8.0 H	+ 9.0 H	+ 10.0 H
Suriname	− 3.0 H	+ 2.0 H	+ 3.0 H	+ 4.0 H	+ 5.0 H
Swaziland	+ 2.0 H	+ 7.0 H	+ 8.0 H	+ 9.0 H	+ 10.0 H
Sweden	+ 1.0 H	+ 6.0 H	+ 7.0 H	+ 8.0 H	+ 9.0 H
Switzerland	+ 1.0 H	+ 6.0 H	+ 7.0 H	+ 8.0 H	+ 9.0 H
Syria	+ 2.0 H	+ 7.0 H	+ 8.0 H	+ 9.0 H	+ 10.0 H
T					
Taiwan	+ 8.0 H	+ 13.0 H	+ 14.0 H	+ 15.0 H	+ 16.0 H
Tajikistan	+ 6.0 H	+ 11.0 H	+ 12.0 H	+ 13.0 H	+ 14.0 H
Tanzania	+ 3.0 H	+ 8.0 H	+ 9.0 H	+ 10.0 H	+ 11.0 H
Thailand	+ 7.0 H	+ 12.0 H	+ 13.0 H	+ 14.0 H	+ 15.0 H
Togo	+ 0.0 H	+ 5.0 H	+ 6.0 H	+ 7.0 H	+ 8.0 H
Tonga Islands	+ 13.0 H	+ 18.0 H	+ 19.0 H	+ 20.0 H	+ 21.0 H

(*continued*)

Travel Arrangements

TABLE 5-1   *(continued)*

Country	GMT	USA Eastern	USA Central	USA Mountain	USA Pacific
Trinidad and Tobago	– 4.0 H	+ 1.0 H	+ 2.0 H	+ 3.0 H	+ 4.0 H
Tunisia	+ 1.0 H	+ 6.0 H	+ 7.0 H	+ 8.0 H	+ 9.0 H
Turkey	+ 2.0 H	+ 7.0 H	+ 8.0 H	+ 9.0 H	+ 10.0 H
Turkmenistan	+ 5.0 H	+ 10.0 H	+ 11.0 H	+ 12.0 H	+ 13.0 H
Turks and Caicos	– 5.0 H	+ 0.0 H	+ 1.0 H	+ 2.0 H	+ 3.0 H
Tuvalu	+ 12.0 H	+ 17.0 H	+ 18.0 H	+ 19.0 H	+ 20.0 H
U					
Uganda	+ 3.0 H	+ 8.0 H	+ 9.0 H	+ 10.0 H	+ 11.0 H
Ukraine	+ 2.0 H	+ 7.0 H	+ 8.0 H	+ 9.0 H	+ 10.0 H
United Arab Emirates	+ 4.0 H	+ 9.0 H	+ 10.0 H	+ 11.0 H	+ 12.0 H
United Kingdom	+ 0.0 H	+ 5.0 H	+ 6.0 H	+ 7.0 H	+ 8.0 H
Uruguay	– 3.0 H	+ 2.0 H	+ 3.0 H	+ 4.0 H	+ 5.0 H
USA Alaska	– 9.0 H	– 4.0 H	– 3.0 H	– 2.0 H	– 1.0 H
USA Central	– 6.0 H	– 1.0 H	+ 0.0 H	+ 1.0 H	+ 2.0 H
USA Eastern	– 5.0 H	+ 0.0 H	+ 1.0 H	+ 2.0 H	+ 3.0 H
USA Hawaii	– 10.0 H	– 5.0 H	– 4.0 H	– 3.0 H	– 2.0 H
USA Mountain	– 7.0 H	– 2.0 H	– 1.0 H	+ 0.0 H	+ 1.0 H
USA Pacific	– 8.0 H	– 3.0 H	– 2.0 H	– 1.0 H	+ 0.0 H
Uzbekistan	+ 5.0 H	+ 10.0 H	+ 11.0 H	+ 12.0 H	+ 13.0 H
V					
Vanuatu	+ 11.0 H	+ 16.0 H	+ 17.0 H	+ 18.0 H	+ 19.0 H
Vatican City	+ 1.0 H	+ 6.0 H	+ 7.0 H	+ 8.0 H	+ 9.0 H
Venezuela	– 4.0 H	+ 1.0 H	+ 2.0 H	+ 3.0 H	+ 4.0 H
Vietnam	+ 7.0 H	+ 12.0 H	+ 13.0 H	+ 14.0 H	+ 15.0 H
W					
Wallis and Futuna Islands	+ 12.0 H	+ 17.0 H	+ 18.0 H	+ 19.0 H	+ 20.0 H
Y					
Yemen	+ 3.0 H	+ 8.0 H	+ 9.0 H	+ 10.0 H	+ 11.0 H
Yugoslavia	+ 1.0 H	+ 6.0 H	+ 7.0 H	+ 8.0 H	+ 9.0 H
Z					
Zaire	+ 2.0 H	+ 7.0 H	+ 8.0 H	+ 9.0 H	+ 10.0 H
Zambia	+ 2.0 H	+ 7.0 H	+ 8.0 H	+ 9.0 H	+ 10.0 H
Zimbabwe	+ 2.0 H	+ 7.0 H	+ 8.0 H	+ 9.0 H	+ 10.0 H

International Currencies

The following is a list of countries and their currencies. (Note that the euro is the currency of thirteen European Union countries: Austria, Belgium, Finland, France, Germany, Greece, Ireland, Italy, Luxembourg, Netherlands, Portugal, Slovenia, and Spain. It is also the official currency of seventeen states of the European Union, which includes Cyprus, Estonia, Latvia, Malta, and Slovakia.)

- Afghanistan: Afghani
- Albania: Lek
- Algeria: Algerian Dollar
- American Samoa: U.S. Dollar
- Andorra: Euro
- Angola: Angolan Lwanza
- Anguilla: East Carribbean dollar
- Antigua and Barbuda: East Carribbean dollar
- Argentina: Argentine Peso
- Armenia: Dram
- Aruba: Aruban Guilder
- Australia: Australian Dollar
- Austria: Euro
- Azerbaijan: Manat
- Bahamas: Bahamian Dollar
- Bahrain: Dinar
- Bangladesh: Taka
- Barbados: Barbados Dollar
- Belarus: Ruble
- Belgium: Euro
- Belize: Belize Dollar
- Bermuda: Bermudian Dollar
- Bhutan: Ngultrum
- Bolivia: Boliviano and Mvdol
- Bosnia and Herzegovina: Convertible Marks
- Botswana: Pula
- Brazil: Brazilian Real
- Bulgaria: Lev
- Cambodia: Riel
- Cameroon: CFA Franc
- Canada: Canadian Dollar
- Cape Verde Islands: Cape Verde Escudo
- Cayman Islands: Cayman Islands Dollar
- Central African Republic: CFA Franc
- Chad: CFA Franc
- Chile: Chilean Peso
- China: Yuan Renminbi
- Columbia: Columbian Peso
- Congo: CFA Franc
- Costa Rica: Colon
- Cote D'Ivoire: CFA Frac
- Croatia: Kuna
- Cuba: Cuban Peso
- Czech Republic: Koruna
- Denmark: Krone
- Djibouti: Djibouti Franc
- Dominica: East Carribbean Dollar
- Dominican Republic: Dominican Peso
- Ecuador: U.S. Dollar
- Egypt: Egyptian Pound
- El Salvador: Colon
- Ethiopia: Birr
- Europe: Euro
- Finland: Euro
- French Guiana: Euro
- Gabon: CFA Franc
- Gambia: Dalasi
- Georgia: Lari
- Germany: Euro

- Ghana: Cedi
- Greece: Euro
- Grenada: East Caribbean Dollar
- Guadeloupe: Euro
- Guatemala: Quetzal
- Guinea: Guinea Franc
- Guyana: Guyana Dollar
- Haiti: Gourde and U.S. Dollar
- Honduras: Lempira
- Hong Kong: Hong Kong Dollar
- Hungary: Forint
- Iceland: Krona
- India: Rupee
- Indonesia: Rupaih
- Iran: Rial
- Iraq: Dinar
- Ireland: Euro
- Israel: New Shekel
- Jamaica: Jamaican Dollar
- Japan: Yen
- Jordan: Dinar
- Kazakhstan: Tenge
- Kenya: Shilling
- Korea, North: North Korean Won
- Korea, South: Won
- Kuwait: Dinar
- Kyrgyzstan: Som
- Laos: Kip
- Latvia: Latvian Lats
- Lebanon: Lebanese Pound
- Lesotho: Loti
- Liberia: Liberian Dollar
- Libya: Dinar
- Liechtenstein: Swiss Franc
- Lithuania: Litas
- Luxembourg: Euro
- Macedonia: Denar

- Madagascar: Madagasy Franc
- Malaysia: Ringgit
- Maldives: Rufiyaa
- Mexico: Peso
- Mongolia: Tugrik
- Morocco: Dirham
- Mozambique: Metical
- Myanmar: Kyat
- Namibia: Rand
- Nepal: Rupee
- New Zealand: New Zealand Dollar
- Nicaragua: Cordoba Oro
- Niger: CFA Franc
- Nigeria: Naira
- Norway: Kroner
- Oman: Rial
- Pakistan: Rupee
- Panama: Balboa and U.S. Dollar
- Paraguay: Guarani
- Peru: Sol
- Philippines: Philippine Peso
- Poland: Zloty
- Qatar: Rial
- Romania: Leu
- Russia: Ruble
- Rwanda: Rwanda Franc
- Saudi Arabia: Riyal
- Senegal: CFA Franc
- Sierra Leone: Leone
- Singapore: Singamore Dollar
- Slovenia: Euro
- Somalia: Shilling
- South Africa: Rand
- Sri Lanka: Rupee
- Sudan: Dinar
- Suriname: Guilder
- Swaziland: Lilangeni

Travel Arrangements

- Sweden: Krona
- Switzerland: Swiss Franc
- Syria: Syrian Pound
- Taiwan: New Taiwan Dollar
- Tajikistan: Somoni
- Tanzania: Shilling
- Thailand: Baht
- Togo: CFA Franc
- Tonga: Pa'anga
- Trinidad and Tobago: Trinidad and Tobago Dollar
- Tunisia: Dinar
- Turkey: Lira

- Turkmenistan: Manat
- Uganda: Shilling
- Ukraine: Hryvnia
- United Arab Emirates: Dirham
- United Kingdom: Pound Sterling
- Uruguay: Peso Uruguayo
- Uzbekistan: Sum
- Venezuela: Bolivar
- Vietnam: Dong
- Yemen: Rial
- Zambia: Kwacha
- Zimbabwe: Zimbabwe Dollar

6

Meetings

Anatomy of a Meeting

Whether we like it or not, meetings are a regular and time-consuming part of business life. Because meetings require planning, coordination, and documentation, they are a major job responsibility for most administrative assistants.

The assistant's job includes sending invitations to in-house meetings, finding time in the schedules of meeting attendees, and selecting meeting times and locations. A thoughtful administrative assistant is careful to avoid scheduling meetings for early Monday morning or late Friday afternoon.

Some executive meetings are scheduled weekly. Despite their being routine, the administrative assistant must still schedule the meetings, send invitations, and send reminders. Work on routine meetings also involves creating meeting agendas that include the names of everyone attending the meeting; the date, time, and meeting location; and any advanced preparation required of the attendees.

Sometimes a meeting is called with only a moment's notice. When this happens, the assistant needs to coordinate the meeting by calling the attendees on the phone, seeing them in person, or using an email scheduling program such as Microsoft Outlook.

Types of Corporate Meetings

Every corporation holds an annual meeting of stockholders for the election of directors. During the year, it may also hold other meetings when the stockholders' consent is required for a proposed action, such as an increase or decrease in capital stock, an amendment of the corporate charter, or a merger.

Annual stockholder meetings have special legal requirements for when meeting notices must be sent. Printed notices are sent along with proxy voting forms and a return-address, postage-paid envelope.

As an administrative assistant, your duties include preparing notices of the meeting as well as a proxy form to be used in case a stockholder cannot attend. This proxy gives another person the right to vote for the stockholder. Notices and proxy forms must be sent to everyone concerned in accordance with the bylaws of the group. In most cases, these notices must be sent out three to four weeks in advance.

You must arrange for a meeting place and confirm that it will be ready for use at the time specified. You'll also type and distribute the agenda. On the day of the meeting, you should place all pertinent papers in a folder with the corporate seal on the conference table at the chairperson's seat.

If you act as the recorder of the meeting, sit beside the chairperson in order to hear every word distinctly. If you have difficulty hearing something, signal the chairperson, who will then ask for a repetition of what has been said. Before the meeting, read all resolutions and reports to be presented so you are familiar with them. In addition, obtain the list of the persons attending (which you should have from distributing the agenda), and check the absentees ahead of time rather than writing down names while the roll is being called. The greater your knowledge is of the meeting's purpose and the attendees, the easier it will be to record the meeting.

Corporate director meetings are specified by the corporate bylaws. Most companies have quarterly or yearly director meetings. A written notice of these meetings is not required by law. An administrative assistant may be asked to contact directors via phone, letter, or email to inform them of an upcoming meeting. The assistant will also be asked to track who is coming to the meeting and who has declined. A list of those attending the meeting should be created and made available at the meeting.

Other corporate meetings that are not regular events should be scheduled two weeks in advance. You should send out an invitation, agenda, and a follow-up reminder. The date, time, location, and subject should be clear in the invitation.

Outside meetings and conferences usually require printed invitations sent out as a mass mailing. Double-check all the information on a proof of the invitation before it is printed. Confirm the date, week, day, time, room, location, and names of all the speakers. No one should have to telephone the sponsor to get information that was inadvertently omitted from the invitation.

Scheduling Meetings

Scheduling meetings is one of the most common tasks for administrative assistants. In the past, scheduling a meeting was a time-consuming task that involved hardcopy invitations sent as interoffice memos. The telephone was usually the preferred method of confirming invitations. Today, with computer technology and groupware software such as Microsoft Outlook or IBM Notes, the task of scheduling a meeting requires only a few mouse clicks.

Despite the advances in technology, scheduling a meeting is not as simple as it looks. There is a lot of judgment involved. Anytime you bring together a group of people, there are many factors to consider. For example, you have to consider pecking order. Some members of the group are more important, so others must change their schedules to accommodate them. Decisions about where a meeting is held can be important as well. Is the meeting room large enough and supplied with the right equipment? Can it be reserved for the entire meeting?

Common Problems When Scheduling Meetings
The following are common problems that occur when scheduling a meeting:

- The meeting is scheduled and after everyone has been invited, you discover that some important participants can't attend. Another date has to be found. This can lead to a cycle of invitations and revisions.

- You ask the participants about their availability for a meeting, but the available dates and times are so limited that no common date and time can be found.

Meetings

- A meeting location is specified, and then it is later changed in a subsequent meeting notice. Some of the attendees follow the original meeting notice and end up in the wrong room.

- Repeated meeting notices and revisions are sent out, so that everyone is confused about where and when the meeting will be held or for what purpose.

- You use an Internet-based meeting scheduling tool, but outside participants don't have the same software.

- A work team uses an Internet system to schedule meetings, but eventually the team members get lazy about updating their schedules and begin to miss meetings.

- A meeting is scheduled and confirmed, but the location is already booked.

- No one sends a meeting reminder, and several attendees forget about the meeting.

- People are invited to a meeting but the meeting organizer didn't say what it is about, so they show up unprepared.

Meeting Agendas

The meeting agenda is like a roadmap for the meeting. It tells the participants what the plan is for the meeting, providing a sense of direction and purpose. A meeting agenda should include:

- Meeting start time
- Meeting end time
- Meeting location
- Topic headings
- Topic detail for each heading
- How much time each topic discussion is expected to last
- Which meeting participants will facilitate the discussion of a particular topic

Figure 6-1 shows a sample meeting agenda.

If you use word-processing software such as Microsoft Word, you can use agenda templates to create an agenda. To access the agenda templates, click the File Menu, then click New. In the search box type "Agenda" and then press ENTER. Figure 6-2 shows the agenda templates available in Microsoft Word 2013.

The Agenda Wizard will ask you specific questions about the meeting, and when you are finished it will create an agenda document. You can send the agenda as an attachment to a meeting invitation or print copies and bring them to the meeting.

Meeting Minutes

Meeting minutes are a record of what took place during a meeting. The minutes allow the meeting attendees to review the meeting later to look for outstanding issues and action items. In some cases, such as stockholder and board of directors meetings, the minutes are required by law and are included in the corporate minute book.

FIGURE 6-1   Sample meeting agenda.

OUTSOURCING PROJECT
Meeting Agenda

Meeting Called By:	Session No.:	Date:	Starting Time:
Mark Rivers		1/27/2015	9:00 a.m.

Location:	Dress Code (optional):	Ending Time:
Central Park Conference Room 11a		12:00 noon

Meeting Objective and Scope:

JAD Session—The Big Picture

Time:	Topic:	Discussion Leader:
9:30–9:35	Welcome and review agenda	Mark Rivers
9:35–9:55	Basic data flow for enrollments	Darlene Price
9:55–10:15	Ongoing data requirements including conversion needs	Darlene Price
10:15–10:35	Basic data flow for pay processing including negatives	Darlene Price
10:35–10:40	Break	
10:40–11:00	Basic data flow for 401(k) billing	Darlene Price
11:00–11:20	Basic data flow for termination processing	Darlene Price
11:20–11:40	Basic data flow for loans	Darlene Price
11:40–11:55	Basic data flow for discrimination	Darlene Price
11:55–12:00	Wrap-up	Mark Rivers

Facilitator:	Time Keeper:	Scribe:
Darlene Price		Debra Miller

Attendees:

Anne Fried	Mark Rivers	Donna Morgan	Tonya Smith
Debra Miller	Sally Roberts	Susan Mullins	Ebony Hollings
Tanya Sanchez	Mary McKnight	Daphne Johnson	Mike Harper
Kevin Wilson	Kendall Williams	Rita Zezula	Darlene Price

   While attending a meeting, you can make handwritten notes, type on a computer if the sound of the typing does not distract the meeting attendees, or use a recording device and transcribe the meeting later. Regardless of which method you use, make sure that all of the essential elements of the meeting are noted: type of meeting, company name, date and time, facilitator, main topics, and time of adjournment.

   Make a list of the expected attendees, or review the meeting agenda. As each person enters the room, you can check him or her off the list. Optionally, you can pass around an attendance sheet for everyone to sign as the meeting begins. If necessary, map out a seating arrangement for the meeting and be prepared to introduce any unfamiliar people.

FIGURE 6-2   The Agenda Wizard in Microsoft Word 2013.

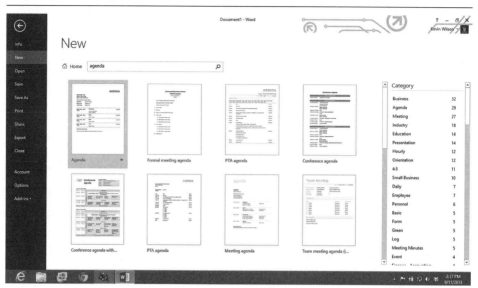

Screen shot used with permission from Microsoft.

If you prepare an outline in advance based on the agenda, you will already have the main topics written down and you can keep your notes organized.

When you transcribe the minutes, you should write them up in formal language according to the following outline:

- Name of organization
- Name of body conducting meeting
- Date, hour, and location of meeting
- List of those present and those absent
- Reading of previous minutes and their approval or amendment
- Unfinished business
- New business
- Date of next meeting
- Time of adjournment
- Signature of recorder

Avoid the mistake of recording every single comment. Instead, concentrate on getting the essence of the discussion by taking enough notes to summarize it later. Remember, minutes are a record of what happened at a meeting, not a record of everything that was said.

Always prepare ahead for meetings where you will take minutes. It's important that you understand the discussion without asking a lot of questions. Following the meeting, don't wait too long to write up the minutes. Always have a draft of the minutes approved by the meeting organizer or facilitator before distributing them to the attendees.

Figure 6-3 is an example of minutes for an organization.

FIGURE 6-3   Minutes of a typical meeting.

**Minutes of Meeting of
the Historical Society of the University of Texas
Hotel Driscoll, Austin, Texas
May 1, 2015**

At the meeting of the Historical Society of the University of Texas at Austin, some 100 charter members being present, the Society was called to order at 1:05 p.m. by Mr. John R. Combs, Chairperson, who requested Mr. Warren T. Scaggs to serve as Temporary Secretary.

Mr. Combs dispensed with the reading of the minutes of the last meeting because a copy had been previously distributed to all members.

A communication from the National Historical Society, read and accepted by the Society, dealt with the planting of redbud trees throughout America.

A communication from Miss Harriet Allen of New York City asked that the Society refrain from its normal pattern of conducting spring tours throughout the State of Texas. Several members, after the reading, expressed disagreement with the views given by Miss Allen.

There was no unfinished business.

New business was the election of officers for the remaining current year. The following nominations were announced by Mr. Warren T. Scaggs, Chairperson of the Nominating Committee:

President	Mrs. Rutherford Tinsdale
Secretary	Mr. Joseph Mapes
Treasurer	Mrs. Theodore R. Tollivar
Members of the Council	Ms. Louise Allen
	Mrs. Philip W. Crossman
	Mr. John Stobaugh
	Mrs. John C. McCann

After an unanswered call for nominations from the floor, it was moved by Mrs. William R. Metcalfe that the Secretary cast one ballot for officers nominated. The motion was seconded and carried, and the officers were declared elected.

The next meeting of the Historical Society of the University of Texas at Austin will be held on June 11 at the Hotel Driscoll in Austin, Texas, at 1:00 P.M.

After congratulations to the newly elected officers by the Chairperson, the Society adjourned at 3:25 p.m.

Warren T. Scaggs
Temporary Secretary

Corporate Minutes

All corporations must document the minutes of shareholder and board of directors meetings. In fact, in many states, the absence of proper meeting minutes may be a liability for the corporation, especially in situations where the shareholders are also on the board of directors or where there are close relationships among board members. All corporations in the United States are required to hold annual shareholders' meetings to elect directors. In addition, the bylaws of most corporations require the board of directors to have annual meetings. At these corporate meetings, the following actions will normally be approved by the board of directors:

- Election of officers of the corporation
- New business policies and plans
- Creation of committees and assignments
- Issuing and selling stock
- Approval of the sale, transfer, lease, or exchange of any corporate property or assets
- Approval of mergers and reorganizations
- Adoption of a pension, profit-sharing, or other employee benefit plans and stock-option plans
- Approval of corporate borrowing and loans
- Entering into joint ventures
- Designating corporate bank accounts and authorized signatures
- Changing an officer's compensation
- Entering into major contractual agreements

Small corporations have informal meetings where these matters are discussed. Large corporations have formal meetings. In both cases, the board of directors must pass a resolution to approve the action. Therefore, the meeting minutes are a record of the board's consent and the discussion surrounding the decision.

Resolutions

Formal resolutions may be made in one of these forms:

- WHEREAS it is necessary to . . . ; and
- WHEREAS conditions are such that . . . ; and
- Therefore be it
- RESOLVED, That . . . ; and be it
- RESOLVED further, That . . .

Note that the word *whereas* is in caps with no comma following it; the first word after it is not capitalized unless it is a proper name. The word *resolved* is also set in caps but is followed by a comma and a capital letter, or by the word *further,* then a comma, and then a capital letter.

In formal resolutions, the facts are stated simply:

. . . and the following resolution was unanimously adopted: RESOLVED, That . . . .

Office Meetings

Your boss may ask you to record in written form a meeting of various office personnel or perhaps department heads. Elaborate minutes are not required as long as the group is not a governing body within the company, such as the board of directors. Figure 6-4 is a sample report of an office meeting.

Meetings

FIGURE 6-4   Sample report of an office meeting.

Meeting of the United Way Committee
January 12, 2015

Attendance:

   A meeting of the department managers was held in the office of John Smith, Executive Vice President, at 9 a.m. on January 12, 2015. Mr. Smith presided. Present were Martha Johnson, Philip Smith, Martin Allen, Raymond Martinez, Eloise Randolph, Anthony Guerrero, and Patricia Reese. James Augustine was absent.

Items Covered:
1. How the company can participate fully in the United Way campaign. Raymond Martinez reviewed last year's company goals and how these goals were reached. Anthony Guerrero suggested our goal for the present year be increased by 10 percent. Recommendations were made by each person present.
2. These suggestions and recommendations will be discussed and voted upon at the February 2 meeting of the committee.

Adjournment:
The meeting was adjourned at 10 a.m.

                                    Martha Johnson, Recorder

Conferences

Sometimes an administrative assistant will be asked to assist in the planning and coordinating of conferences for the company. This involves preparing for the event, carrying out your responsibilities during the conference, and follow-up activities after it's over.

Planning for the Conference

The planning for a conference involves consideration of the following tasks related to the conference facilities and the speakers:

- Booking the conference site
- Making reservations for hotel rooms, selection of room sizes, and price range
- Confirming auditorium sizes and breakout rooms
- Scheduling catering and beverage service
- Confirming smoking locations
- Inspecting facilities you haven't seen before
- Sending letters of invitations to speakers
- Following up with confirmation letters to the speakers and conference site
- Obtaining background information, photos, and résumés of the speakers

Preparing Conference Materials

As the conference time approaches, you will need to confirm all necessary supporting materials: table and chair rentals, reports, financial statements, advertisements, meeting agendas, itineraries, and executive travel folders.

If it is your responsibility, you will need to make arrangements for printing packets, maps, tickets, and awards. You may also need to make arrangements for local tours and special outside events to entertain the speakers, attendees, and their spouses. Many times, additional family members accompany the spouses when attending a conference, and any thoughtful conference organizer has made arrangements for shopping trips, outside restaurant gatherings, tickets to sporting events, museum tours, and other local attractions.

You will need to coordinate with the conference site to plan meals, refreshments, coffee breaks, and banquets. This should involve evaluating menus in advance and planning what will be served.

You may also be involved in preregistration and registration. This requires organizing a filing system for those attendees who preregister and having badges made. During the registration on the first day of the conference, you may be involved in staffing the registration desk. You should organize registration materials alphabetically. All conference materials should be assembled in packets with programs, brochures, reports, name tags, meal tickets, and so forth.

Confirm with the conference site any audiovisual equipment or meeting supplies you may need. Breakout rooms will need chalkboards or whiteboards, easels with large pads of paper, and marker pens or chalk. Conference rooms may need lecterns, microphones, overhead projectors, video players, video projectors, projections screens, television monitors, and a public address system. Usually this involves filling out a reservation request form with the conference facility. Also make sure you order extra projector bulbs and extension cords.

If your conference involves international guests, you may need to make arrangements for a translation service.

Two weeks before the conference, you should mail all pre-work to attendees and you should ship any supplies and conference materials to the conference site.

If it is appropriate, you may need to arrange for press coverage by contacting media outlets, arranging for a photographer to take photos during the conference, and sending out press releases.

Finally, you'll need to coordinate any security concerns with the conference location's security service. You may also need to coordinate parking with the conference location's parking attendants. You will need to provide the security service and the parking attendants with a formal agenda with event times, additional security protection needed, and parking requirements.

During the Conference

While the conference is under way, your duties may include checking meeting rooms and making sure all necessary materials are available. Confirm that the lighting and heating are functioning, refreshments are available, audiovisual equipment is available and functioning, and that the room is clean.

As conference guests arrive, you should greet and welcome them to the conference. Be a host and introduce people, escort people who need directions, and be helpful where you can.

If you are asked to work the registration desk, you may need to provide statistics on who will attend the various events. Prepare lists of participants with names and addresses.

You may be asked to attend some meetings and take minutes, handle correspondence requests, or route incoming express shipments. You may write and distribute a conference newsletter, coordinate messages among participants, or meet with media representatives and photographers.

After the Conference

Each day after the conference, remove any surplus literature and conference packets from the meeting rooms. Inform the conference site staff regarding any catering items left in the meeting rooms. Make sure any audiovisual equipment is properly secured. Also move and secure any other rental equipment. Any lost and found items should be taken to the conference site receptionist.

When you return to the office, you may need to complete follow-up reports or other conference-related mailings. You may need to send thank you letters to speakers or distribute meeting minutes.

Finally, you will need to calculate expenses and fill out expense reports. As a last step, update the meeting file with your notes. With everything fresh in your mind, write down what went well and what challenges you faced. If you have ideas on how to make improvements, put them down on paper in the file.

Conference Notes

If your employer asks you to report on all that is said in a conference, make place cards for the members of the group who are expected to meet. As they enter the room, direct them to sit where they have been assigned. In front of your own seat, arrange tabs showing the names of the members in the same order as they are seated around the table so that you will know who is speaking at each given moment. This will enable you to take your notes in the form of a dramatic dialogue. Preface one remark with "Hansen" if the man whose name is Hansen has spoken; preface the next remark with "Rosen" if the next voice has come from the seat you assigned to Mrs. Rosen; and so forth.

When you transcribe your notes, you can show the discussion in this dialogue form, if that's acceptable to your employer. Alternatively, you can insert a full stage direction such as "Mr. Hansen replied:" or "The next speaker was Mrs. Rosen, who said . . . " In either case, open your transcription with a list of those present, giving the full name or initials and office held, if any, for each.

A recording device is usually used, but you should be ready if it's not available. It may be wise to take notes even when a recording device is used because, unless the meeting is held under strict discipline, there may be a jumble of voices. Your notes will help you decipher the recording.

7

Time Management

Overview of Time Management

Time management is an essential skill for an effective administrative assistant. People who use time management techniques are usually the highest achievers in life and business. If you learn time management techniques, you'll be able to work effectively, even under pressure.

The key aspect of time management involves a change in focus. You must concentrate on the end result, not just on staying busy. Many people find themselves very busy throughout the day, but they don't achieve much because they are not focusing on the right things. The famous Pareto Principle, sometimes called the "80:20 Rule," sums it up nicely: 80 percent of the unfocused effort generates only 20 percent of the results. By using time management techniques, you can optimize your time and energy by focusing on results that have the greatest payoff. This will ensure that you'll get the greatest benefit from the time you have available.

Controlling Procrastination

If you've put off important tasks from time to time, you are like many people. We all sometimes procrastinate to some degree. One of the first keys to effective time management is not to let procrastination stop you from achieving in your career. The key to controlling your urge to procrastinate is to recognize when you are doing it and to take action to better manage your time and effort.

People procrastinate when they put off something they should be doing in order to do something else that is more enjoyable. People who procrastinate may work just as long and hard as everyone else, but they spend their time on the wrong tasks. Sometimes this comes from not being able to prioritize tasks effectively.

If you spend the day being bombarded with one thing after another, you might focus on the most recent task, considering it always to be the most urgent even though an earlier project might actually be more important. Similarly, you might decide to tackle the endless list in the order the tasks were assigned, even though that list might not be in priority order.

Feeling overwhelmed by an assignment is another cause of procrastination. You can't figure out how to get started, or doubt you have the skills to complete the job, so you put it off in favor of doing other things you feel capable of accomplishing. The problem is that the challenging assignment isn't going away.

Other causes of procrastination include waiting for the right mood to take on an important task, being afraid of failure, being too much of a perfectionist, or not having good decision-making skills.

Whatever the reason you find yourself procrastinating, you must be honest with yourself and take action. The first thing you should do is make sure you understand the priorities of your assignments. Communicate with your boss or the individual making the assignment and find out when it is due. When there is a conflict between two projects, ask which is more important. Many times your boss may make a request early in the day, only to have a more important assignment come up later. By asking your boss which task takes priority, it's easy to focus your effort where it is needed most.

Maintaining an Activity List

To get a better idea of how you are spending your time and what you are actually accomplishing, make a list of your daily activities. After you've recorded several days of activity, analyze the list to see how much time you've spent doing low-priority tasks.

As you examine the list, start by eliminating tasks that are not your responsibility. Are you doing things that someone else in the organization should be doing? Are you doing personal activities at work or sending non–work-related emails?

Try to reduce the number of times you switch between tasks. For example, rather than stopping every half hour to read and reply to email, you could schedule time twice each day to focus solely on email.

Use your activity list to help prioritize your to-do list. Schedule the most challenging tasks for the time of day when your energy is highest.

Creating Action Plans

Whenever you find yourself facing a large project that seems overwhelming, it's time to create an action plan. An action plan is a list of all the tasks you need to accomplish in order to complete an entire project. It's different from your to-do list because it focuses on a single goal.

To create an action plan, first list all the tasks that need to be accomplished to achieve the goal and put them in the order they need to be completed. As you put tasks on the list, try to break each task into smaller subtasks. Listing a few items may cause you to think of others.

Keep the action plan nearby as you begin working through the plan item by item. If additional tasks are needed that were not on the original plan, revise the plan and work from the new version.

After you've completed the project, go back and review the final version of your action plan. Could you have done anything differently? Were you missing some steps? Would a different order of tasks have been better? Use your action plan as a learning experience to make improvements in the action plans you create in the future.

Keeping a To-Do List

If you feel overwhelmed by looming deadlines or sometimes forget to do something important, you badly need to start keeping a to-do list. A to-do list is a prioritized list

Time Management

of all of the tasks you need to accomplish. The most important tasks are at the top of the list; the least important are at the bottom.

Many people who become effective at time management say that keeping a to-do list is one of the main reasons they are successful. By keeping a list in one place of everything you need to do, it's difficult to forget something. If you review the list each morning and reprioritize it, you can easily tell what needs immediate action. Without a to-do list, you have to juggle everything in your head. When you accidentally forget to do something, people will think you are unreliable. With a to-do list, you're organized and more responsible. Because of this, keeping a to-do list can be critical to the success of your career.

To create a to-do list, start by writing down all the tasks you need to accomplish. Larger projects should be divided into smaller tasks, similar to an action plan. Keep subdividing larger tasks until each item on your to-do list will take no more than one to two hours to complete. Once you've written everything down, you can prioritize your list by assigning letters or numbers. For example, all items that have a high priority should be assigned the letter A. All items that have extremely low priority should be assigned the letter F. Continue to prioritize your to-do list using letters B, C, D, and E. After your first pass, review the high-priority items and see if any of them can be demoted. When you are finished prioritizing, sort the list, putting the high-priority tasks at the top of the list. You may find it easier to use word-processing software to create your to-do list, since it is simple to revise and sort.

People use their to-do lists in different ways. Some create a smaller daily version with a list of all the items they plan on completing that day. They then review the master list each morning and create a new daily to-do list.

You may find that some of the low-priority tasks are carried around from one to-do list to the next for several weeks or even months. There's no need to worry about this, though you should not forget about such items entirely. If one of the low-priority tasks has an imminent deadline, you'll need to raise its priority level.

Scheduling

So far this chapter has focused on organizing your daily tasks. Scheduling is where your plans become reality. Scheduling is the process during which you examine the amount of time you have available each day, and you plan how you will use it to accomplish the tasks you've identified. By scheduling time to work on each task, you will understand what you can realistically accomplish. You'll be able to make the best use of the time you have available, designating time for those must-do items. You'll be able to schedule time for the unexpected, so you'll be prepared for the twists and turns business life may throw your way. As a result, you'll reduce your stress level by not overcommitting to others. A schedule allows you to take control of your time and your life.

Scheduling is best if you do it regularly, such as the beginning of each week or month. The first step is to determine the times each day when you will work on your tasks. This depends on the nature of your job and your personal situation. Next, block out the time in your schedule. If you use calendar software or Microsoft Outlook's calendar feature, you can schedule work time in your calendar to keep other people from scheduling meetings for you during these periods.

After scheduling your work time, the next step is to review your to-do list and schedule the high-priority tasks in your work periods. Make sure you leave time available for the unexpected and schedule contingency time.

The time that is left in your schedule is your discretionary time. This is the time you can use to learn new things, plan, organize yourself, and prioritize. If you find that you have little or no discretionary time, you need to revisit your list of tasks and determine if they are all absolutely necessary or whether they can be accomplished in some abbreviated way.

8

Keeping Accurate Records

A Critical Duty

Keeping accurate records and maintaining an up-to-date filing system are important responsibilities for most administrative assistants. Every filing system ever conceived requires the person maintaining it to approach the duty with a sense of pride. He or she must be confident that any file can be retrieved quickly, perhaps even as the employer is still requesting it on the telephone.

Most companies today, even small businesses, store their letters and documents in their computers and automatically maintain them there or on a network drive. (However, as administrative assistants know only too well, even with computers, the amount of paper correspondence and documents to be saved seems to grow daily.)

Large companies often have a central file department where all papers are kept by competent file clerks. Other companies maintain files by division, and small companies may have only a few file cabinets for their entire operation. In these cases, it's the administrative assistant who is usually responsible for record keeping and maintenance. But no matter what your usual duties, you should be familiar with the various filing systems used in both small and large offices.

Getting Ready

It's often tempting, especially at the end of the day, simply to throw a file in its own folder. Don't. Filing is an important duty, no matter how tedious it seems. Instead of trying to get rid of that file or piece of paper as quickly as possible, approach it with these questions always in mind: Where could I easily find this tomorrow (or next week, or next year)? What's in this letter or document that would cause me to recall where I'm placing it in the file now?

Follow this checklist before you start to file:

- Prepare the papers by separating personal correspondence from business correspondence and documents.

- Check all stapled papers to be sure that only papers belonging together have been stapled together.

- Remove all paper clips. They not only crowd the file but also can catch papers that should not have been clipped to them.

- Mend any torn papers with tape.

■   Underline in bright pencil or with a marking pen the name or subject under which the paper is to be filed.

On the file folders, use staggered tabs or one-position tabs. The straight-line tab, all in the center or in the far right position on the edge of the folder, is often preferred.

When various sets of files are used, it's wise to tab each set with a different color label. For example, use white for correspondence, blue for subject files, and green for case files. Each category then has its own color for quick recognition.

On labels, type the name of the folder on the first line beginning two or three spaces from the left edge. Use initial caps and lowercase letters, and abbreviate freely. Leave two spaces between name and any number.

Basic Filing Systems

Common or basic filing systems that might be used in a business office include the following: alphabetical, subject, geographical, numeric, and combination subject (though the office would probably be a very large one with many technical files to utilize the last). About 90 percent of offices use the alphabetical system.

Two less-used systems are the decimal filing system and the group name system (sometimes called the phonetic filing system). The decimal system, based on the Dewey decimal classification system, is used primarily in libraries. The material being filed must be organized under ten or fewer main headings numbered 000 to 900. In turn, each main heading is divided into ten or fewer subheadings numbered from 10 to 90 and preceded by the correct hundreds digit. Each subheading may then be subdivided into ten or fewer further headings numbered from 1 to 9, preceded by the correct hundreds and tens digits.

The group name or phonetic system is used when there are a great many names involved, as in census surveys. Names that sound alike but are spelled differently are grouped together according to pronunciation rather than spelling: Allan, Allen, Allyn; Nielsen, Neilson, Nealson; Schneider, Snider, Snyder.

Alphabetical System

The alphabetical system is the most widely used filing method because it's the most efficient and least complicated. Material is filed alphabetically according to name. No cross-indexing is necessary. A label should be typed for each name and applied to the tab on each folder.

Papers are placed in the folder in chronological order, with the most current date in front. The folders are filed behind alphabet guides (obtainable in any office supply store). When there is heavy correspondence with one client, several folders may be needed to hold all current material. In this case, it's a good practice to separate the material into time periods: one folder for the year 2015, another for the year 2016, and another for 2017. If several projects have been handled for that customer, one folder may be labeled FLORIDA, another NORTH DAKOTA, another MICHIGAN, and so on.

If only the current year's files are kept handy (with previous years' files stored elsewhere), it's useful, for at least the first few weeks of the new year, to have the old year's files and the new year's files placed back to back or side by side. Of course, a

Keeping Records

different year will be on each file tab, perhaps a different color as well: red for 2015, for example, and yellow for 2016.

Subject System

This classification is used when papers are called for by subject, rather than by a person's or a company's name. Subject classification may be needed when dealing with, say, advertising, brand name products, or materials of all kinds.

You should be thoroughly familiar with the papers flowing through the office and across your desk before attempting to set up this kind of system. The list of subjects must be comprehensive, as simple as possible, and in alphabetical order or by number code. The alphabetical list is usually preferred so that a cross-index is not necessary. Papers in the subject folder are arranged chronologically, always with the latest date in front.

Subject Index

While an index of files is not required for a small filing system, it's imperative for large companies. And since most small businesses hope to grow, it's a good practice to maintain a filing system from the start. The subject index will prevent the filing of material under a new heading when a folder has already been set up for that subject, perhaps under a different title. It also permits a person other than the administrative assistant to trace information in the file.

An index card is made for each subject heading or subheading. Each subheading shows the main heading under which it is filed. Cross-reference cards are made if the subject is complex. The employer may indicate on the paper where he or she wants it to be filed, while the administrative assistant may have formerly filed that subject under another heading. A cross-reference enables both to find the paper later. The index cards are filed alphabetically.

How to Alphabetize for Filing and Indexing

Individual or Personal Names   The names of people are alphabetized by their surname. When surnames are the same, the position is naturally determined by the letters that follow:

- Smith, Mary B.
- Smith, Ned
- Smithson, John

When two or more similar names are of unequal length, file the shorter name first:

- Smith, M.
- Smith, Mary
- Smith, Mary C.
- Smith, Mary Charlene

Individual surnames with prefixes are alphabetized as each is written and are considered to be one word, whether or not they are written as one word:

Keeping Records

- Mason, Tim
- McFarland, John
- Merrill, Jane
- Vane, K.
- Van Houton, Mae
- Vargas, Louise

A religious title or foreign title is alphabetized when it is followed by a first name only:

- Brother Thomas
- Burton, Francis (Rev.)
- Friar Tuck
- Queen Elizabeth
- Sister Mary Rose
- Tilton, Sarah (S.S.J.)

Company or Business Names   Words joined by a hyphen are treated as one word. However, if the hyphen is used instead of a comma in a business name, the individual parts of the name are treated as separate words, and therefore the name is indexed by the first word alone. The second name of the hyphenate is used only when needed, similar to a given name:

- Johnson, Samuel
- Johnson-Smith & Company
- Johnson, Steven
- Johnson, Victor

Whether a company name is composed of a compound word or is spelled as two words, it is alphabetized as if it were one word:

- New Deal Loan Company of America
- Newdeal Marine Works
- Suncity Shipbuilding Corporation
- Sun City Tannery

The exception is when a company name contains the name of a person. In this case, alphabetize by using the surname, followed by first name, then middle initial or middle name if any. The exception is the names of schools. These are alphabetized as written, as are other organizations, businesses, or institutions. See Table 8-1.

Single letters used as words are treated as words and arranged alphabetically preceding word names:

- BB Shop
- BBB Service Company
- Bakery Heaven
- Brighton Clothes Company

Keeping Records

TABLE 8-1   Filing When the Company Name Contains a Person's Name

Name	Filed As
American Petroleum Co.	American Petroleum Co.
Mary Brown Café	Brown, Mary Café
John Dillard Company	Dillard, John Company
Dillard Stores	Dillard Stores
Joyce Kilmer High School	Joyce Kilmer High School
May's Floral Center	May's Floral Center
John C. Wilson Realty	Wilson, John C. Realty
Wilson Realty Company	Wilson Realty Company

TABLE 8-2   Filing Abbreviations

Name	Filed As
St. Luke's Church	Saint Luke's Church
Jas. Smith	Smith, James
Chas. Williams	Williams, Charles

When two or more similar company or business names are of unequal length, file the shorter name first:

- National Bank
- National Bank of Commerce
- Bronson Club
- Bronson Club of New York City

Miscellaneous   Abbreviations are alphabetized as if spelled in full. See Table 8-2. Designations following names are alphabetized according to natural order of age:

- Smith, James III
- Smith, James, 2d
- Smith, James, Jr.
- Smith, James, Sr.

Articles, prepositions, conjunctions, and the ampersand are disregarded in alphabetizing:

- Thomas & Anderson, Inc.
- Thomas, Brown R.
- Washington Bank, The
- Workshop for the Blind

When words end in *s,* the *s* is considered part of the name:

- Leon Neon and Light
- Leon's Art Supplies

If a name contains a number, do not put it in "numerical order" with other numbered names. Alphabetize it as if the number were spelled out:

- 1020 Building Corporation (one thousand twenty)
- 13 Park Avenue Studio (thirteen)
- 21 Club (twenty-one)

Titles are disregarded:

- Jones, R. L. (Dr.)
- Simms, Carlotta (Countess)
- Smith, Nancy (Miss)

Exception: If a company name starts with a title, the title is considered to be the first word:

- Queen Mary Boat Company
- Sir John Thomas Cigar Company
- Viceroy of India Silk Company

File Cabinets

A standard file cabinet has four drawers that accommodate material written on 8½-inch by 11-inch typing or computer paper. An office with many legal-size papers (8½ inches by 13 or 14 inches) will need a wider cabinet made specifically for these sizes.

Your file cabinet should be near your desk, since you will go to it frequently throughout the workday. Label each drawer of the cabinet either horizontally (left to right) or vertically (top to bottom). If an alphabetical system is used, the top drawer might be labeled "A–G," the second drawer "H–M," and so forth.

Many secretarial desks have a built-in file drawer, handy for files used often so you can reach for them quickly without having to leave your desk to go to the larger cabinet.

Organizing Your Computer Files

As an administrative assistant, you will create and work with many different documents, presentations, and graphics each day. Most of these documents will be in electronic form and will be stored on your computer. After a while, you may be storing thousands of documents. To avoid losing documents and to save time finding the documents you need, a good electronic filing system is needed.

Just as you wouldn't store all of your paper files on your desk, to avoid file clutter you need to organize the files and folders on your computer. What follows are some tips to help you organize your computer files.

Keeping Records

FIGURE 8-1   Documents Library in Microsoft Windows 8.

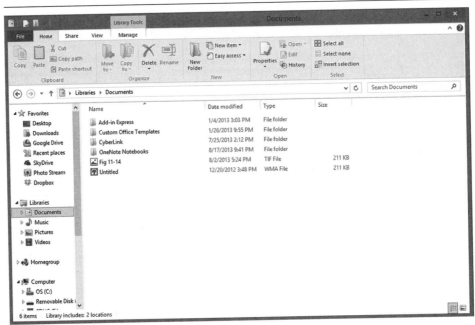

Screen shot used with permission from Microsoft.

Using Documents Library

Start your filing system by taking advantage of the default folder in Windows named "Documents." In Windows 7 (and older Windows versions), If you click START > DOCUMENTS, you can view the Documents Library. The folder already includes default folders for Documents, Music, Pictures, and Videos. You can customize the Documents Library to include other folders for different projects, customers, or tasks. You can create new folders by clicking FILE > NEW > FOLDER. A new folder will be created with the name highlighted. You can then type in a name.

In Windows 8, you can view the Documents folder by clicking DESKTOP from the Start screen, then clicking the FILE EXPLORER icon on the taskbar at the bottom of the screen. The File Explorer icon looks like a file folder. From the File Explorer window, you can double click the DOCUMENTS icon. The rest of the steps for creating your filing system are the same as in Windows 7.

Use an upside-down tree structure to organize your file folders, with fewer folders at the top and more folders nested within. This structure will make it easier to locate files and to back them up by dragging the highest level folder to a backup location.

To create new nested folders, open the top-level folder and then right-click and select NEW > FOLDER. You can then name the new folder. Figure 8-1 shows the Documents Library with its list of folders.

Naming Your Files

You should use a consistent method when naming files. Short names are best because long files names are more difficult to read. In general, avoid using punctuation or spaces in file names, as some programs are confused by special characters. You can use abbreviations for common topics such as MTG for "meeting" or PROJ for "project."

File names should include easy-to-remember names of projects, coworkers, customers, products, or model numbers.

It is a best practice to include the date in a numeric form (such as 100216 for October 2, 2016) along with your initials and a version number. Version numbers can be abbreviated as V1, V2, and so forth.

Storing and Grouping Files

It is a best practice to group files within folders by file type. For example, you should store all of your Word documents together for a particular project and keep them separated from any PowerPoint or Excel files.

For graphic files, use the Medium or Large Icon folder view in order to see a small version of the graphic.

If you use the Details folder view for viewing documents, you can view more information about your files by clicking the column headings to add or remove headings. For example, you can view the file name, size, date created, date modified, and author. You can also sort the files by any of the column headings. Click the heading for descending sort. Click the same heading again for an ascending sort.

It is a best practice to separate your ongoing work from your completed work. To keep your files better organized, search through your files once a month and copy old project folders and files to remote storage, such as a network drive, Windows SkyDrive, flash drive, CD, or DVD.

When a folder contains more than thirty documents, you should consider creating subcategory folders. For example, if you store meeting minutes in one folder, you should create subcategory folders for each month.

Using Shortcuts

You can store files temporarily on your desktop, but don't make it a habit. The best practice is to store the file in its appropriate folder within your filing system, and then create a shortcut and place the shortcut on the desktop. The shortcut is a pointer that points to the original file. To create a shortcut, right-click the file and from the pop-up menu, click CREATE SHORTCUT. You can then drag the shortcut to your desktop.

Backing Up Your Files

If you store all of your files within the Documents Library, you can easily back up your files by copying the contents of the library to another drive, a network drive, an Internet Cloud drive, a flash drive, or a CD or DVD. You can schedule automated backups of your computer files in Windows 7 by clicking START > CONTROL PANEL > SYSTEM AND SECURITY > BACK UP YOUR COMPUTER. In Windows 8, you can schedule automated backups by accessing the File History function. (See Chapter 11 for instructions.)

Viewing Files

As you create the file folders for your electronic filing system, you should create a folder view for each folder. After creating a folder, click the Change Your View icon and select a view. Icon view is best for graphic files, while List or Details is best for documents.

Keeping Records

Using Recent Items

To find files with which you've just worked, you can use the Recent Places folder. This folder is available from the Start Menu on earlier versions of Windows; however, in Windows 7 you must manually add it to the Start Menu. To do this, right-click on the Taskbar and select PROPERTIES. On the Taskbar and Start Menu Properties dialog box, click the START MENU tab. Then click the CUSTOMIZE button. On the Customize Start Menu dialog box, scroll down and put a check in the RECENT PLACES checkbox. Then click OK to close the Customize Start Menu. Click OK again to close the Taskbar and Start Menu Properties dialog box. In the future, you'll be able to access recently used items by clicking START > RECENT PLACES.

In Windows 8, RECENT PLACES is already listed as one of your Favorites by default.

Using More Than One Computer

If you work on more than one computer, the best way to keep track of your files is to create a special folder that can be copied back and forth using a flash drive. For example, you might create a folder called "briefcase" that contains copies of all your current work.

Another solution is to add dates and version numbers to your files, so that when you copy a file from one computer to another, you won't accidentally wipe out the latest version.

A third solution when working on more than one computer is to store your files on removal storage, such as a flash drive. You can then share the drive between the two computers. However, when using a flash drive, it is a best practice to keep a backup copy of all your files stored on a more permanent medium, such as a network drive, SkyDrive, or hard drive. That way, if you accidentally lose the flash drive, you will still have access to recent versions of your files.

Keeping Records

Office Equipment and Computers

9

Office Equipment

Telephones

Telephone service has come a long way since it was invented in the late 1800s. In the early days, telephone service was primitive and selective. Not everyone had a telephone, nor could you call everyone or everywhere. Only towns that put up the poles and ran the wires had service, and even then, many people had to share a telephone line.

Today, telephone service is taken for granted. Businesses use voice mail and computerized answering machines to take messages, to network computers across town or across the country, and to send fax transmissions to offices around the world. Let's start with the basic business services that allow you to call across the street.

Private Branch Exchange

You may have seen in old movies a switchboard operator struggling with a tangle of wires and plugs. Today's larger businesses have replaced the switchboard operator with a private branch exchange (PBX) system. A PBX is a computerized telephone management system that is ideal for a company with many employees and individual phone extensions. It allows a single telephone number for a business to be accessed at the same time by numerous outside callers. As each call is received, it is automatically routed to the appropriate extension via a touchtone phone or with the help of a receptionist or operator.

Multi-Line Telephones

A multi-line telephone system is often the preferred choice in a small business. It allows you to answer an incoming call from anywhere in the office and to route it to another telephone at the touch of a button. If one line is being used, you can access another line to make an outgoing call.

VoIP Telephones

Voice over Internet Protocol (VoIP) is a technology that is rapidly growing in popularity in many businesses today. This technology allows for sending telephone audio over the Internet rather than traditional telephone lines. The advantage is low-cost local and long-distance telephone service.

The IP phones look just like normal phones, but instead of the normal RJ-11 phone connectors, they use an RJ-45 Ethernet connector and are connected to your computer network. IP phones have all the software and hardware to handle IP calls.

79

Other Business Telephones

A wide variety of other available business telephones combine telephone service with computer operations. Many of these more sophisticated telephones are equipped with special features, such as buttons and lights to designate different lines. More modern telephones use computer-like LED (light-emitting diode) displays to designate and select lines as well as to indicate the number dialed. Others are programmable to store frequently called numbers in the telephone's memory. Some have speaker telephones built in to free up one's hands while talking. Still others have automatic redialing, intercom capabilities, and built-in answering machines.

Voice Mail

When you're away from your desk and no one else can cover your telephone, it's important that you use a voice-mail system. You don't want to miss critical calls for your boss or yourself. Customers now expect the use of such devices, no matter what size company you work for.

Computerized voice-mail systems accept incoming calls and route them to various voice mail boxes for each employee. All messages are stored in the company's phone system computers or by the telephone company.

Integrated Messaging

Integrated messaging is a service that allows voice-mail messages to be received as email attachments using email software such as Microsoft Outlook. The message normally includes caller-ID information such as the phone number or email address of the person calling you. You can listen to your messages by opening the email and clicking the attached audio file.

Special Telephone Services

Many telephone companies have a variety of special services that enhance the performance of your business telephone system, no matter which model you have. These services may vary from one part of the country to another. Here is a description of some of the more common services available:

- *Call waiting* is useful for individuals who and for small businesses that have only one incoming telephone line. When you're on one call, you are alerted by a tone that another incoming call is waiting. If you wish, you can put the current call on hold and switch to answer the new incoming call.

- *Select call waiting* permits only the calls the user has programmed into the telephone to beep you in the call-waiting mode.

- *Call forwarding* allows you to redirect calls intended for your telephone to another telephone of your choice—ideal when you or your boss must spend extended time at another location.

- *Select call forwarding* enables you to program your telephone with a list of only those people you want to be able to contact you at the forwarding number.

- *Three-way conferencing* allows you to call more than one person at a time so that three or more people can participate in the same conversation.

- *Caller ID* shows you on a visual display the name and number of the person calling. Caller ID lets you use your telephone like a pocket pager, enabling you to decide whether to take the call, return it later, or ignore it.

- *Busy number redial* continues to dial a busy number automatically until the line is free. The telephone then alerts you when the line is ringing.

- *Selective call acceptance* allows you to program your telephone with a list of only those people you want to contact you. When a person on that list calls, the call rings through to your telephone. No other calls are allowed to get through.

- *Voice message* enables callers to leave a message that you retrieve later, just like an answering machine. Voice message is similar to voice mail; however, no special equipment is required at a user's location.

Toll-Free Numbers

One long-distance service can benefit your company's customers: a toll-free number, sometimes called a "Watts" line. As the owner of an 800 number, your company pays for all incoming long-distance charges. A toll-free number is an expense, true, but it's more than just a convenience for your distant customers. It can be a selling point in whether your company makes the first sale at all.

Because of the demand for toll-free numbers, telephone companies have made a variety of other three-digit prefixes available in addition to 800, including 888, 878, 877, 866, and 855.

900 Numbers

The 900 prefix is often associated with information lines that require the caller to pay a per-minute fee for the time on the call. This fee is charged to the caller's telephone bill and paid to the owner of the 900 number. Some small businesses involved in mail order have tried using 900 numbers, but often it is reserved for technical help, not for customers who want to order a product.

Teleconferences

One way to reduce travel costs associated with meetings is to use teleconferencing. Teleconferences can be scheduled in advance with a long-distance carrier. With a reservation, you can link up different callers from around the country at the same time.

There are two basic ways to conduct a teleconference. In the first, each caller dials a special telephone number at a designated time and is connected to the group teleconference one by one. In the second, an operator calls and connects each individual to the teleconference. The cost of the teleconference includes a setup fee and an hourly fee for each caller along with the long-distance charges for each individual.

Teleconferences are often combined with Web conferences, where attendees are not only connected via the telephone but also view a presentation on the Web.

Fax Machines

While faxes are increasingly being replaced by email, there are still millions of fax machines in use, and millions more faxes are sent annually.

Today's fax machines are faster and more versatile than ever. There are even products available that tie your fax machine to your office telephone's voice messaging system. Those products make it as easy to check for fax messages when you're out of the office as it is to check for voice messages.

Computer Fax

In addition to dedicated fax machines, there are also fax modems available for personal computer systems. A fax modem will connect your computer to the phone lines to send and receive data and allow your computer to send and receive faxes.

To send a fax, you first compose the document on the computer electronically. Then, without having to print out the document and take it to a fax machine, you access the software that comes with the fax modem and transmit the document just as a regular fax machine does. Incoming faxes are stored in your computer's memory like a graphic. You can read the fax using the software or print it out with your printer.

Office Computers

Companies of all sizes routinely use personal or desktop computers in the office. Computers allow employees to be more productive by automating many repetitive tasks, such as word processing, billing, and filing. They come in a wide variety of configurations for both Microsoft Windows and Apple Macintosh operating systems.

When most people use a PC, what they are really using is a computer system. The computer itself may be no larger than a single integrated circuit chip soldered to a circuit board inside the computer's case. However, the user interfaces with a variety of other elements that together make up the computer system. These elements, called *peripheral devices*, include the keyboard, monitor, mouse, disk drives, and printer.

A true computer system usually consists of five elements:

1. An input device, such as a keyboard or mouse, that allows you to communicate with the computer.

2. An output device, such as a monitor or a printer, that allows the computer to communicate back to you.

3. A processor that allows for the manipulation of your data. The central processing unit (CPU) is the brains of the computer system.

4. A storage system, such as a hard disk drive, that allows you to save your work electronically.

5. Software that provides instructions for the computer in the form of programs.

Hardware

How you operate your computer and what type of work it can perform depend on how your system is equipped. From the outside, the computer is just a case to house the electronic components. There are a variety of different computer designs, such as the desktop system, laptop, or tablet computer.

All computers have a power switch on the system unit, located on the front of the case or on the back. Depending on which brand of computer you use, there will also probably be drives mounted inside the system unit and USB (universal serial bus) connectors for connecting various devices such as a keyboard and mouse. Looking at the back of a typical PC, you will normally see USB ports for the printer, keyboard, and mouse, a network port, and a video port for the monitor.

The computer's operating system and programs are stored on a *hard disk* drive that is mounted inside the system unit. In addition, most computers have a *DVD* drive. Each disk drive is given a letter, number, or name so that it's easy to load and save information to or from a particular drive location. On Microsoft Windows computers, the hard drive is called drive C. The DVD drive would be called drive D. On Apple Macintosh computers, the drives are given names or labels.

The PCs are usually designed to be expandable. For this reason, it's possible to remove the case should you need to get inside to install a new component. Many people are afraid to open the computer case, yet the more familiar you are with your computer, the better able you will be to troubleshoot little problems that arise from time to time. Computer repairs and upgrades are simple skills to acquire, yet they are invaluable, especially in terms of time saved.

Inside the system unit of a typical computer you will see a metal box, which is the computer's power supply. This *transformer* converts the power from the wall outlet into electricity that can be used by the computer. You'll see the hard disk drive that is mounted inside the case. And you'll see the *motherboard*, which occupies most of the inside of the computer. This large circuit board contains various chips and your processor. On the motherboard, you will see various slots for plug-in expansion boards. *Expansion boards* are available for a variety of purposes. They easily plug into the motherboard expansion slots so you can add a device such as a high-performance video card.

Other key components in your computer are the *memory* and the *processor*. The amount of memory your computer has determines the amount of workspace available for data. For example, if you are working with a large word-processing document or a large accounting program with a lot of data, you might eventually see messages on your monitor screen that the computer is running low or is out of memory. Most computers allow for upgrading the amount of memory. For most Windows and Macintosh computers, you can add to the computer's memory by plugging in memory chips, which are what provides your computer's memory. Memory chips can be plugged into slots on the motherboard of your computer to increase system memory. Your computer will likely have between two and four slots for memory and usually come with between 4 to 8 gigabytes (GB) of memory.

Computer performance and speed are determined mainly by the type of processor chip included with your computer. Also important in evaluating speed and performance is the *clock speed* of your processor. Clock speed is the speed at which messages from the computer processor travel to other parts of the computer, such as the disk drives, hard drive, monitor, and printer. Speeds ranging up to several gigahertz (GHz) are available today.

The key point to remember when you're choosing a company computer is that better speed and performance usually translate into greater productivity. Therefore, an investment in a good computer system can help you do more in less time.

Memory

Computer memory is often very confusing to new computer users, because it implies that the computer will remember your data automatically. However, this is not the case: If you create a document with a word processor but don't save it and then turn off your computer, the document will be lost. Unfortunately, most computer users learn this lesson the hard way. Long-term storage of data is handled by the hard disk drive, not by the computer's memory.

Your computer's memory is that area where programs and data are temporarily copied from a CD, DVD, or hard disk drive so that you can use them. Moving programs and data into memory is called *loading* or, on some systems, *opening*. It is just like taking a document out of a file cabinet and putting it on your desk. Unlike this analogy, however, when a computer loads a program or a document into memory, it only takes a copy—leaving the original intact on the disk. You can modify the original by saving your latest work with the same name as the original, or you can retain the original and keep a new version by saving the new version with a slightly different name.

Random access memory (RAM) is the area of memory where your programs and data are loaded. Memory is measured in terms of bits, bytes, kilobytes, megabytes, and gigabytes. Electronically, the RAM in your computer is made up of lots of little electric switches that are turned on or off. For programming purposes, "on" is given a numerical value of 1, and "off" is given the numerical value of 0. Therefore, programs and data are represented as lots of 1s and 0s. Each character in the alphabet is represented by a special code made up of 1s and 0s. Each group of eight 1s and 0s is called a *byte*; 1,024 bytes equal a kilobyte, 1,024 kilobytes equal a megabyte, and a gigabyte is 1,000 megabytes.

The same is true for numbers and graphics on your monitor. Some computers use a 32-bit system. That means that it takes a combination of 32 1s and 0s to form each character or graphic. Other more advanced computers use 64-bit systems.

Another way some computers access even greater amounts of memory is to use *virtual memory*. Computers can use part of the computer's hard drive as if it were extra RAM. Virtual memory is slower than RAM memory and is used primarily when multiple programs are loaded and running at the same time. The program not being accessed by a user can be temporarily swapped to virtual memory.

Read-only memory (ROM) is another type of memory that is built into the computer and cannot be changed by programs. ROM chips contain a permanent set of instructions that support the overall operation of the computer. Essentially, they function automatically and require little attention from most computer users.

Computer Input Devices

In order to use computers, you need some way to communicate with them. This process is known as *input*. There are many types of input devices. Probably the most common is a keyboard. By simply typing on a keyboard, you send information to the computer for processing. In order to see what it is you have typed, most computers use a *monitor*. As characters are typed on the keyboard, they appear on the monitor screen.

Among the most familiar devices for input are game controllers such as *joysticks*. These devices allow a game player to communicate information to a computer informing it of key decisions necessary to play a game. A similar device is a *mouse*, a hand controller that is used in some software applications and operating systems for a variety of different computers. A mouse is used to select menu choices and to move a *cursor*, or pointer, around on the monitor screen. Similar to a mouse is a *track ball*. Many small portable computers use *touchpads*, since the operator may be using the computer where there is no desktop available for a mouse.

Another useful form of input designed originally for disabled individuals is *voice recognition*. Voice recognition and natural language speech systems interpret the human voice into signals that a computer can understand as input. Voice recognition systems are now popular and can be used to select menu items in software and, in some cases, even to create text for a word-processing document or spreadsheet.

For graphic artists and designers and others who need to input precise drawings, a special drawing device called a *graphics tablet* is available. A graphics tablet consists of a plastic board containing a grid of fine electrical wires. A special drawing pen is used to draw. When the pen comes into contact with the grid of wires, information on the location of the pen is sent to the computer in order to create a graphics image on a monitor screen.

Another input tool used by graphic artists is the *scanner*. There are various models available. Some you hold in your hand; other desktop models operate much like a copy machine. With the desktop version, you place an original document into the scanner, and the scanner copies an image of the document or graphic into the computer's memory. When the document is text, special optical character recognition software is often used. This software takes the images input from a scanner and compares them against various text styles in memory. It then translates the scanner image into text for your word processor.

Finally, *digital cameras* can be used to acquire digital images that can be transferred into a computer and used in desktop publishing applications.

Computer Output Devices

When you work with a computer, most of your attention will be focused on output devices. This is where you see the results of your work. The most common output devices found on computer systems are the monitor and the printer. Both output devices are available in many different models.

The Monitor

Monitors display information by painting the screen with tiny dots of color called pixels. Today, there are several different types of monitors to fit various needs. Most are flat-screen liquid crystal display (LCD) monitors that come in different screen sizes.

The crispness of the monitor's picture is measured in dot pitch, refresh rate, and resolution. Dot pitch is the distance between pixels. The better the dot pitch, the better the monitor can display lines and curves. The refresh rate is the speed at which the monitor repaints the screen. Refresh rates are measured in Hertz (Hz). A low refresh rate will produce a noticeable flicker on the monitor. Resolution is the screen image size that can be displayed on the monitor as measured in horizontal and vertical pixels.

The Printer

Along with video display monitors, the other most popular form of output for a computer system is a *printer*. Printers produce a hardcopy paper version of what is on your display screen. There are several different types of printers available.

Ink Jet Printer   Ink jet printers produce letter-quality output by spraying ink through a series of tiny nozzles onto the paper to form each letter. Ink jet printers can print in black and white and in color. In fact, some ink jet printers can produce photographic-quality output that rivals traditional photographic film prints.

Laser Printer   Perhaps the most successful and popular method of producing letter-quality text is with a laser printer. Although laser printers are more expensive than ink jet printers, their quality and speed have made them popular among all types of computer users. Laser printers function similarly to copy machines. A graphics image of the computer output is sent to the laser printer, which also has a computer processor. The laser printer then uses a laser to display an image on an electrically charged drum surface. Once the charged surface comes into contact with a powdered or liquid toner, the toner sticks in the image areas and falls off the non-image areas. When paper comes into contact with the drum, the toner is transferred to the paper, producing an image.

Color Laser Printers   Recent advances in color printing have resulted in laser printers that use multicolored toners for producing color output.

Printer Performance

The performance of a printer is determined by its resolution, memory, and speed. Printer resolution is the sharpness of the image the printer can produce on paper. Resolution is measured in dots per inch (dpi). For draft-quality text printing, a dpi setting of 300 is sufficient. For letter-quality printing, a dpi setting of 600 is good. For photographic-quality printing, a resolution of 600 dpi or better is needed.

The dpi settings affect the speed of the printer. Most ink jet and laser printers can print three to six pages per minute, depending on the type of image. Photographic-quality images may take much longer. Laser printers tend to be the fastest printers available.

Printers have built-in memory that helps speed up the printing process. If you print large documents or documents with complex graphics, having additional printer memory will enhance printing speed.

Another device for reproducing computer output is a *plotter*, or large format printer, which draws the computer output in large format. This is often used in architectural and design offices.

Storage Devices

The ability to store, search for, and retrieve specific information from permanent data storage media is ideal for helping secretaries organize the department or company—and keep it organized. Using the computer's electronic filing system, you should see a great time savings for yourself as well as an increase in your productivity and efficiency in day-to-day business activities.

A computer stores your work in two areas, one temporary and one permanent. The temporary storage is your computer's memory, its RAM. We've already discussed computer memory, but it's important to remember that information stored in RAM is stored only as long as the computer is turned on.

The Hard Drive

The main permanent storage device is the computer's *hard drive* (sometimes called a *fixed disk*), which can be either internal (mounted inside the computer case) or external (in its own case connected to the computer via a cable). A hard drive is actually a stack of disks coated with a magnetic coating, similar to audiotape or videotape. Information is saved on a hard drive much the same way a song is recorded on audiotape. The computer's electronic signals are recorded on the magnetic hard drive disk, and when you want the information back, the hard drive "plays back" those signals. Saving information on a hard drive is called *writing* to the drive; playing information back is called *reading*. It is also possible to erase information on a drive, which is called *deleting*.

Disk storage capacity is measured in units called *bytes*. As previously discussed, a byte is made up of 8 bits of information. One thousand twenty-four bytes is a *kilobyte*, or K for short. A *megabyte* is 1,024 K. One thousand megabytes is a *gigabyte* (often called a "gig"). One thousand gigabytes is a *terabyte*. Hard drives can store billions of bytes.

Tape Backup

One specialized storage medium is available solely for the purpose of making backups. Tape backup drives use a cartridge tape to back up your hard drive and all your data. A tape backup drive is much slower than a hard drive, so it's not very useful for normal day-to-day use as a storage medium. However, special software combined with a tape backup drive can automatically back up your data periodically so you'll also be protected in the event of hard drive failure.

CD-ROM and DVD-ROM

Another data storage medium is a *CD-ROM*. This system uses a compact disk to store computer data. Approximately 600 megabytes can be stored on one CD-ROM. If you have a CD-ROM drive that can create—or "burn"—CDs, you can also use it for making backups of your data. These drives are often called CD Recordable (*CD-R*) or CD Read and Write (*CD-RW*) and can store approximately 600 megabytes of data.

Making the move from the entertainment center to the computer are *DVD-ROM* drives. These drives can store several gigabytes of data and are often also used for viewing DVD movies on your computer. DVD recordable (*DVD-R*) and DVD Read and Write (*DVD-RW*) drives are also available. They can record DVD data disks that can store 4 to 9 gigabytes of data.

Flash Drives

Flash drives are small portable devices that can connect to the USB port on your computer for storing and transferring data from one computer to another. Flash drives are about the size of your car keys and can store data for ten years or more without being plugged into a power source. These inexpensive devices come in a variety of sizes ranging from a few megabytes up to several gigabytes.

Laptop Computers

Many offices use small laptop computers in place of desktop computers to give employees mobility and flexibility when using their PCs. With a laptop, everything is combined into one unit: CPU, monitor, hard drive, DVD-ROM, modem, and network card, as well as other devices like speakers and microphones. Laptop computers can be upgraded with larger hard drives and additional RAM. You can connect them to printers, a phone line, and an office network, or to an external monitor, keyboard, and mouse. One nice feature of a laptop computer is the built-in battery. This battery will power the computer for several hours without needing to be connected to a power outlet.

While you can connect an external mouse to a laptop computer, a variety of built-in pointing devices are available. Most laptops use a touchpad with buttons or a pointing stick positioned next to the G and H keys that resembles the eraser of a pencil.

When you are in the office, some laptops can be connected to a port replicator or docking station. When connected to one of these expansion units, you can use an external monitor, keyboard, and mouse just like a desktop computer system.

Tablet Computers

Tablet computers are mobile computers that feature a touchscreen and Wi-Fi or cellular network connectivity. Tablet computers include models like the Apple iPad, Samsung Galaxy, or Microsoft Slate. These lightweight computers allow you to use your finger rather than a mouse to make selections. Some models do not include a keyboard, and instead an on-screen keyboard is used.

Maintaining Your Computer

For the most part, there is little you need to do to maintain your computer system. However, as for any machine, there are a few things you can do that will help your computer last longer and operate smoothly.

ScanDisk

This is a utility that comes with your computer that can detect and fix hard disk errors that cause performance problems. In the latest versions of Windows, this utility is called CHKDSK. These utilities run automatically if a computer loses power unexpectedly. You can also run these utilities periodically to check the condition of your hard disk drive. To run the utility in Windows 7 and earlier versions, double click MY COMPUTER, then right-click your hard disk drive. From the pop-up menu, click PROPERTIES. On the Properties window, click TOOLS, then in the Error-Checking section, click CHECK NOW.

In Windows 8, access the DESKTOP and click the FILE EXPLORER icon. Then right-click your hard disk drive. From the pop-up menu, click PROPERTIES. On the Properties window, click TOOLS, then in the Error-Checking section, click CHECK NOW.

Disk Defragmenter

As you use your computer, the files you save get divided and spread in different available spaces on your hard drive. The more spread out or fragmented they get, the more the performance of your computer is affected. A disk defragmenter recombines files and resaves them in one continuous location. This reorganizes your hard drive and improves disk efficiency.

Disk Cleanup

As you work with various documents, print, view Web pages, and so forth, temporary information gets stored on your computer. These temporary files can grow in size and eventually squeeze out room for other things. It's a good idea to delete these files from time to time.

Backing Up Your Data

If your hard drive fails, you could lose all your data. Since your hard drive is like a very large filing cabinet filled with important and often confidential data about the business you work for, protecting that information is very important. Therefore, you should back up your hard drive frequently by making copies of all data onto an external hard drive, a network drive, a backup tape, diskettes, a CD-R, a CD-RW, a DVD-R, or a DVD-RW.

There are also a variety of online backup services available where you can pay a monthly or annual fee and have a backup copy of your files stored offsite. These services allow you to make periodic automatic backups over the Internet. Popular online backup services include the following:

- My PC Backup: www.mypcbackup.com
- Just Cloud: www.justcloud.com
- Backup Genie: www.backupgenie.com
- iBackup: www.ibackup.com
- Zip Cloud:www.zipcloud.com
- Sugar Sync: www.sugarsync.com
- Mozy: www.mozy.com
- Crash Plan: www.crashplan.com
- Carbonite: www.carbonite.com
- SOS Online Backup: www.sosonlinebackup.com

Copy Machines

Another essential office tool is the copy machine. Although the advent of word-processing typewriters and personal computers has reduced reliance on copiers to some extent, because you can make additional paper copies by printing out duplicates, many documents that do not originate from your word processor or PC require copies.

Many small businesses use a local print shop for copies; however, considering the amount of time lost going back and forth to the shop and the convenience and relative cheapness of having your own copier, purchasing or leasing a copier for the business may be a good idea.

Copiers and laser printers function similarly. They are often referred to as "nonimpact printing." Rather than have a hammer strike a ribbon to produce type on the page like a typewriter, copiers use a photographic process involving static electricity.

When you place a document to be copied inside a copy machine, a very strong light is projected on the original. The image of the original is then projected to an electrically sensitive rotating drum. The dark and light areas of the original affect the electric charge on the print drum. After being exposed to the original, the copier drum turns through a powder called toner, which sticks to the electrically charged areas. The drum then comes into contact with a fresh piece of copier paper, transferring the toner to the paper, thus creating a copy.

More advanced copiers magnify the projection of the light from the original to the copier drum, thus enlarging or reducing the size of the reproduction. Many copiers use

Office Equipment

microprocessors to store images and to automate many of the functions such as sorting, collating, and making two-sided copies. With the use of multicolor toners, color copies can be produced. Other copiers have automatic document feeders, paper trays, sorters, and even built-in staplers. The choice of features makes for a wide range of prices.

Binding Systems

Binding systems are used to create professional-looking bound reports, presentations, and proposals. One of the most common systems is the plastic comb binding system. This is an ideal solution for binding standard letter-size documents in-house. The system includes a punch press that punches up to twenty sheets of 20-pound paper per punch and binds documents sheets with two-inch plastic binding combs. A paper guide and ruler are used to align sheets accurately.

Laminators

Laminators are often used to preserve photographs and to create quick reference cards, place mats, badges, and ID cards. A paper document is placed into a clear plastic lamination pouch and then run through the heated laminator, which seals the document in a protective hard plastic covering.

Overhead Projectors

Overhead projectors and video projectors are often used in meetings and presentations to large groups. With an overhead projector, presentation materials are copied or printed on clear plastic transparency pages called foils or transparencies. The transparencies are then placed on the light table of the overhead projector, and a powerful light passes through the transparency and projects an image on a screen. The transparencies can be written on during a presentation for everyone in the meeting to see.

Video projectors are often used to display videos, television images, or computer data. With a video projector, presentation slides can be created using a program such as Microsoft PowerPoint. The slides are then displayed on a screen by the video projector. When the presenter wants to change slides, the mouse button is clicked or the space bar on the keyboard is pressed.

Paper Shredders

As a security measure to protect sensitive documents, paper shredders are used to destroy draft copies and old documents as an alternative to throwing them in the trash. Paper shredders vary in size from small models that fit on top of a trash can to large free-standing models.

10

Mobile Computing

If you have access to a tablet or smartphone and are allowed to use it at work, you can check your email, check your schedule, and view your documents while you are away from your desk. Since many executives use these tools to stay in touch, some expect their administrative assistants to also use them. What this often means is that your boss may continue to send you requests even after you've gone home for the day. How you respond to off-hour requests when you are not "on the clock" is something you must discuss with your boss.

This chapter explores how to use the communications and file-sharing tools available with the Apple iPad and iPhone, as well as with the Android operating system for Android smartphones and tablets.

iPad and iPhone

The iPad and iPhone are powerful tools that give administrative assistants a mobile office where they can still answer phones, check email, and view their computer files while away from their desks. In this section, we will take a look at procedures for checking voice mail, setting up conference calls, conducting video calls, sending and receiving email, viewing contact information, audio recording, and file sharing.

Voice Mail

The first time you access voice mail, you'll be asked to create a voice mail password and record your greeting. Until you do this, a default greeting is played whenever someone calls and their call goes to voice mail. To change your voice mail greeting, follow these steps:

1. On the HOME screen, tap the PHONE icon.
2. At the bottom of the screen, tap the VOICE MAIL icon.
3. Tap GREETING.
4. Tap CUSTOM.
5. Tap RECORD.
6. Say your new greeting.
7. When you finish, tap STOP.
8. To review your message, tap PLAY.

Conference Calls

You can use your iPhone to easily create a conference call involving up to five people depending on your cellular provider. To conduct a conference call, follow these steps:

1. On the HOME screen, tap the PHONE application.

2. Tap the KEYPAD button to dial a number.

3. After the person you've called answers, you can add more people to the conference call by tapping ADD CALL.

4. The first person you called is placed on hold. You can then dial another number.

5. When the second person answers, tap MERGE CALLS.

6. Repeat these steps to add up to five people to the call.

FaceTime

If you and your boss both have iPhones, you can make video calls using FaceTime. No setup is required, but you do need a Wi-Fi network in order to make or receive a video call. To use FaceTime, follow these steps:

1. On the HOME screen, tap the PHONE application.

2. Tap the KEYPAD button to dial a number.

3. Tap the FACETIME button.

4. When the voice call is established, the other person's image appears on your screen. A smaller inset image shows what the other person sees.

Email

The Mail program on your iPhone and iPad works with most popular email systems including Yahoo, Google, Hotmail, AOL, and others. You can also configure your business email so that it goes to your phone or tablet.

Add a New Account   Follow these steps to add a new email account to your iPhone or iPad:

1. To add an email account to your phone, from the HOME screen, tap the SETTINGS icon.

2. Tap the bottom of the screen to simulate scrolling down.

3. Tap MAIL, CONTACTS, CALENDARS (Figure 10-1).

4. On the Mail, Contacts, Calendars screen, tap ADD ACCOUNT.

5. Tap one of the mail services from the list.

6. Tap in the NAME field.

7. Tap the keyboard to enter a name.

8. Tap the EMAIL field.

9. Tap the keyboard to enter an email address.

10. Tap the PASSWORD field.

11. Tap the keyboard to enter a password.

12. Tap the NEXT button.

13. The iPhone or iPad verifies the account and adds it to the Mail program.

FIGURE 10-1   The Mail, Contacts, and Calendars screen.

Screen shot used with permission of Apple Computer.

Read Email Messages   Follow these steps to check and read email messages on your iPhone or iPad:

1. On the HOME screen, tap the MAIL icon.

2. Your messages are displayed showing you who it is from, the subject line, and a short preview of the message.

3. Tap the message to view the complete message.

4. To delete a message, tap the TRASH CAN icon.

5. To return to the inbox, tap the INBOX button.

6. To see additional messages, you can scroll through the list by touching and dragging your finger up or down.

7. When you receive a message that has an attachment, you will see a paper clip icon. To view the attachment, first open the message.

8. The attachment appears as an icon within the message. To view the attachment, tap the attachment. The attachment is displayed.

9. To return to the message, tap the MESSAGE button.

Sending Email Messages   Follow these steps to create and send an email message from your iPhone or iPad:

1. From the Inbox, tap the PENCIL AND PAPER icon in the bottom left corner.
2. The New Message screen appears. The cursor will be blinking in the To field. You can enter an email address by typing it in.
3. You can add additional email address if you want by typing them. You can also select one of your contacts by clicking the + icon.
4. A list of all your contacts is displayed. Scroll through the list to find the correct contact.
5. The contact information is displayed. Tap to select the email address.
6. Back on the New Message screen, the next step is to enter a subject. Tap the SUBJECT field.
7. Tap the keyboard to enter a subject for the email.
8. Tap below the Subject field to begin typing your message.
9. Tap the SEND button to send the message.

Replying to an Email Message   Follow these steps to reply to an email message on your iPhone or iPad:

1. To reply to a message while you are reading it, tap the LEFT POINTING ARROW at the bottom.
2. From the menu, tap REPLY.
3. A new message is created and the To field and Subject are already filled in. All you need to do is enter your reply. Tap the keyboard to enter a reply.
4. Tap the SEND button to send the reply.

Forwarding an Email   Follow these steps to forward an email message on your iPhone or iPad:

1. To forward a message while you are reading it, tap the LEFT POINTING ARROW at the bottom.
2. From the menu, tap FORWARD.
3. A new message is created. Enter the person's email address or select one of your contacts using the + icon.
4. Tap below the Subject line.
5. Tap the keyboard to enter a message.
6. Tap the SEND button to forward the message.

Contacts

You can store information about the people with whom you communicate in your Contacts list. When you want to make a call or send a text message or email, rather than having to remember and manually enter a phone number or email address, you can select the person from your contacts.

You can take a picture of your contacts and include a picture. You can also import and use pictures you receive from email messages and text messages. You can store

Mobile Computing

several phone numbers for your contacts. To call the person, tap to select one of his or her phone numbers. You can store several email addresses for your contacts. To send an email to the person, touch to select his or her email address. You can store your contact's home or work address. To see a map and get directions, touch the address. To send a text message to your contact, tap the SEND MESSAGE button. To establish a video conference with your contact, touch the FACETIME button. Note: You must be connected to a Wi-Fi network in order to conduct a FaceTime video conference.

Adding Contacts   There are several ways you can add people to your Contacts list. You can enter the information manually, you can add people who call you or send you messages, and you can sync the contacts from your computer. Follow these steps to create a new contact:

1. To create a contact from someone who has called you, tap the PHONE app.
2. View the recently received calls by touching RECENTS at the bottom of the screen.
3. You'll see a list of recent calls. Tap the INFORMATION ICON to see the details of the call.
4. You'll see the Info screen with information about the call. Touch the CREATE NEW CONTACT button at the bottom of the screen.
5. Add information about your new contact, including a photo, first and last name, company, phone numbers, and email address.
6. If you scroll to the bottom of the screen, you can add the contact's website and address.

Creating a New Contact from Scratch   Follow these steps to create a new contact from scratch:

1. Tap the PHONE app.
2. Touch the CONTACTS button at the bottom of the screen.
3. You'll see a list of contacts. To add a new contact, touch the + button.
4. Add information about your new contact.

Syncing Contacts from Your Computer   To sync contacts from your computer, you need to maintain a contacts list in an email program, such as Outlook or Gmail. Follow these steps to sync the contacts from your computer:

1. You can use iTunes to sync your phone to your computer to import contacts into your phone.
2. Click to select your phone in the DEVICES list to the left.
3. Click the INFO button at the top.
4. You'll see a "Sync Contacts with" pane.
5. Click the button to select the source of your contacts.
6. Your contacts can be stored in Outlook, Google, Yahoo, or in your Windows or Apple Macintosh contacts.
7. Once you've selected a sync source, choose whether to sync all contacts or specific ones you select manually.
8. When you are ready, click the SYNC button.

Mobile Computing

Managing Contacts   After you have added contacts to your phone, the next step is managing them. You can edit information about your contacts, and if you no longer want a particular contact, you can delete it. Follow these steps to edit and delete contacts:

1. To access your contacts list, tap the PHONE application.
2. Tap the CONTACTS icon at the bottom of the screen.
3. A list of your contacts displays.
4. Select the contact you want to edit.
5. Tap the EDIT button.
6. Update any information you want about this contact.
7. Tap the field you want to edit.
8. You'll see a keyboard that allows you to enter the new information.
9. When you are finished entering the information, tap the DONE button.
10. If you want to delete a contact, once again, access the contact as you've just seen, and touch the EDIT button.
11. Scroll down to the bottom of the screen.
12. Tap the DELETE CONTACT button.
13. A second DELETE CONTACT button will display, allowing you to confirm your choice.

Searching for Contacts   The main reason for having contacts in your phone is to make it easy to find and use them when you want to call or send a text message. Follow these steps to search for a contact:

1. When sending a text or email message, on the New Message screen, when the cursor is in the To field, all you need to do is start typing the name of your contact.
2. A list will appear below. You can either select someone from the list, or keep typing to narrow the list.
3. When the list is narrowed down to one person, select the contact from the list.
4. An alternative is to click the + icon on the NEW MESSAGE screen.
5. A list of your contacts displays.
6. One option is to scroll through the list until you find your contact. Or, you can touch the alphabetical listing to the right to jump deeper within your list of contacts. In either case, when you find the right person, select him or her in order to send a message.

Audio Recording

There are a variety of free audio recording applications that can be installed on your iPhone or iPad that will allow you to record meetings and record dictation. This allows your phone or tablet to double as a digital audio recorder. The audio files that you record are saved in your phone or tablet's memory, and you can play them back for transcribing using the same application. You can also transfer the files to your computer using iTunes or iCloud (see Sharing Files Between Devices, below).

Password Security

To protect your security, it's a good idea to have your phone or tablet passcode protected. To add password protection to the iPhone or iPad, do the following:

1. On the HOME screen, tap the SETTINGS icon.
2. On the Settings screen, tap GENERAL.
3. Tap PASSCODE LOCK.
4. Tap TURN PASSCODE ON.
5. On the Set Passcode screen, enter a four digital passcode.
6. Reenter the passcode a second time to confirm it.
7. The next time you access your phone or tablet, you'll need to enter the passcode.
8. After entering the correct passcode, you'll see your Home screen.

Wi-Fi Access

Whenever you send emails or surf the web using your iPhone or iPad, if you are not connected to a Wi-Fi network, you will be using part of your data allowance from your cellular provider. Whenever a wireless network is available, you can quickly access it by going to Settings. Follow these steps to join a Wi-Fi network:

1. From the HOME screen, tap SETTINGS.
2. Tap WI-FI.
3. Tap the OFF button next to Wi-Fi.
4. The phone will search for available Wi-Fi networks.
5. To join a network, select it from the list.
6. You'll join the network automatically if it is not password protected. If the Wi-Fi network is password protected, you'll need to get the password and enter it here.
7. Tap the JOIN button.
8. You'll be connected to the Wi-Fi network. Since this network is now configured, if you return to this location, your phone or tablet will automatically connect to this network.

Calendar and Appointments

The iPhone and iPad Calendar app can make it easy for you to stay on schedule. The Calendar can subscribe to Google, Yahoo, Microsoft Outlook, or iCal calendars to sync your schedule on your computer to your phone or tablet and vice versa.

You can view the Calendar on your iPhone by tapping the Calendar icon on the Home screen.

Subscribe to a Calendar   To subscribe to a calendar or to sync your iPhone or iPad to your computer's calendar, follow these steps:

1. From the HOME screen, tap the SETTINGS icon.
2. Tap MAIL, CONTACTS, CALENDARS.
3. Tap ADD ACCOUNT.
4. Tap one of the mail services from the list.
5. Tap in the NAME field.

6. Tap the keyboard to enter a name.

7. Tap the EMAIL field.

8. Tap the keyboard to enter an email address.

9. Tap the PASSWORD field.

10. Tap the keyboard to enter a password.

11. Tap the NEXT button.

12. The iPhone or iPad verifies the account and adds the calendar.

Add Events to the Calendar   Follow these steps to add events to your iPhone or iPad calendar:

1. While viewing the calendar, tap the + icon in the top right corner of the screen.

2. On the ADD EVENT screen, enter the title of the event.

3. Tap the LOCATION field.

4. Tap on the keyboard to enter the location.

5. Tap the STARTS field.

6. On the STARTS & END screen, slide the rolling date and times to set start date and time.

7. Tap the ENDS field.

8. Slide the rolling date and times to set end date and time.

9. If necessary, you can make the event an All Day event and you can adjust the time zone.

10. Tap DONE to continue.

11. On the Add Event screen, tap the DONE button.

Viewing Calendar Events   Follow these steps to view your schedule on your iPhone or iPad's calendar app:

1. To view a particular event on the calendar, on the HOME screen tap the CALENDAR icon.

2. On the ALL CALENDARS screen, tap a particular date on the calendar.

3. The dot next to the date signals you that events are scheduled on this date. Events are listed below. Tap the event to view the details.

4. To return to the calendar, tap the DATE button in the top left corner.

Reminders

The Reminders app on the iPhone and iPad works in conjunction with the Calendar to remind you of items on a specific date and time. The Reminders app can function as a task list or to-do list. It can automatically sync with your calendar accounts, such as your Google or Yahoo calendar, or a Microsoft Outlook Calendar.

Add a Reminder   Follow these steps to add a reminder:

1. Tap the REMINDERS app on the HOME screen.

2. On the REMINDERS screen, today will be the default date. Tap the CALENDAR icon in the top left corner to select another date.

3. On the DATES screen, tap the date for the reminder.

4. Tap the + icon.

5. Tap on the keyboard to type the reminder.

6. Tap the DONE button.

7. To set a specific time for the reminder, tap the newly added reminder.

8. Tap the REMIND ME field date and time.

9. On the REMIND ME screen, Tap the DATE field.

10. Slide the rolling dates and times to select a new time.

11. Tap DONE.

12. Tap DONE again.

View a Reminder   Follow these steps to view a reminder:

1. Tap the REMINDERS app on the HOME screen.

2. A list is displayed. Tap a reminder to view it.

3. To delete a reminder, tap the DELETE button.

4. Tap the red DELETE button to confirm.

5. To mark a reminder as completed, tap the box next to the item.

6. A checkmark appears that marks the item as completed.

Sharing Files Between Devices

There are several ways to share files between your computer and your iPhone or iPad. You can sync files using iTunes or using iCloud, or you can use applications like Dropbox, SkyDrive, or Google Drive.

iTunes   When you connect your iPhone or iPad to a computer via the USB cable, and open iTunes on your computer, your phone or tablet will show up in the iTunes library pane under Devices. If you select your phone or tablet, information about your device will be displayed in the main window of iTunes (Figure 10-2). To back up the contents of your phone or tablet, you have the option to back it up to iCloud or to your computer.

In addition to syncing your phone and computer using a USB cable, if you have a Wi-Fi network, you can choose to sync using Wi-Fi.

If you click the Info menu, you have choices to sync contacts in your computer's email program with the contacts in your iPhone. You can also sync the calendar between your phone and computer. Further down the screen, you can sync your email accounts, and you can sync the bookmarks from your computer's web browser.

iCloud   Another way you can keep your iPhone, iPad, and computer in sync is to use Apple's iCloud service. iCloud stores your photos, apps, contacts, and calendars in a cloud storage system, and shares your files between your iPhone, your iPad, and your computer. With iCloud, if you schedule an appointment using your computer's calendar, the appointment also appears on your iPhone. You can also backup the contents of your iPhone to the cloud. With iCloud you get a free email account and five gigabytes of storage for your mail and documents.

FIGURE 10-2   iTunes Sync Menu.

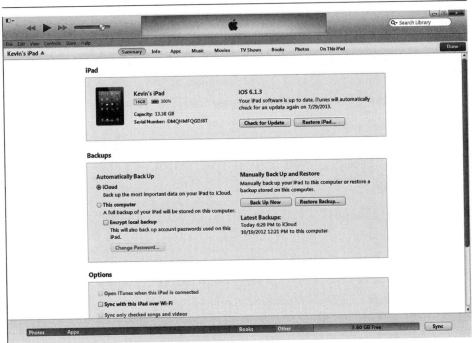

Screen shot used with permission of Apple Computer.

Follow these steps to set up iCloud on your iPhone or iPad:

1. To choose what information to store in iCloud, tap the Settings icon on the Home screen.
2. Tap iCloud (Figure 10-3).
3. Enter your Apple ID if it is not already there. If you don't have an Apple ID, tap Get a Free Apple ID.
4. Tap the Password field and enter your password.
5. Tap Sign In.
6. You can select which items you want to store in the cloud.
7. Tap Storage & Backup.
8. Tap the button for iCloud Backup.
9. Tap OK to confirm.
10. You have now successfully configured iCloud.

iCloud for the Mac and PC   If you want to share data between your computer and your iPhone or iPad using iCloud, you need to install iCloud software on your computer. There is a version for the Mac and the PC available at www.apple.com/icloud.

On the Macintosh, on the latest version of the OS X operating system, you can find iCloud in the System Preferences. Sign into your Apple account, and then select which things to store and share on iCloud.

FIGURE 10-3   iCloud settings.

Screen shot used with permission of Apple Computer.

On a Windows PC, you'll find iCloud in the Control Panel. Sign into your Apple account, and select the services you want to enable.

For both the Mac and the PC, you'll need to open iTunes and enable automatic downloads. You can do this by accessing STORE PREFERENCES.

Dropbox   To share other types of documents between your computer and your phone, such as word processing documents, PDF files, spreadsheets, and other business or personal documents, you might consider using an app such as Dropbox.

Dropbox offers a free account and software that installs on both your computer and your iPhone or iPad. You can find it at www.dropbox.com.

Dropbox acts like a storage drive on your computer. Just drag and drop files you want to share into the Dropbox drive. The files are automatically copied to the Dropbox cloud. When you install the Dropbox app on your iPhone or iPad, you can then access the files on your mobile device.

Google Drive   Another service that is similar to Dropbox is Google Drive. With Google Drive, you can create, view, and upload files from your Google Drive website. You can also install Google Drive on your Mac or PC and use it like a disk drive (Fig-

FIGURE 10-4   Google Drive on a PC.

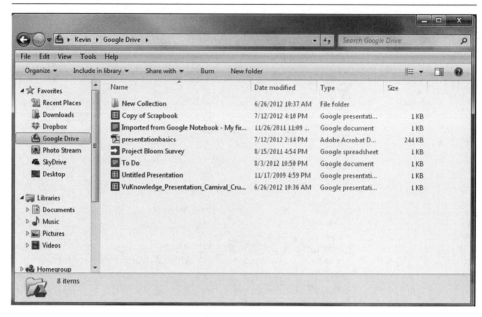

Screen shot used with permission of Google Inc. and Microsoft.

ure 10-4). Just drag and drop files you want to share into your Google Drive folder. When you install the Google Drive mobile app for the iPhone or iPad, you can then access the files. Google Drive is available at www.google.com.

SkyDrive   SkyDrive is a service from Microsoft similar to Dropbox and Google Drive. With SkyDrive, you can create Microsoft Office documents on your computer using a web-based application available at www.live.com. If you install the SkyDrive mobile application on your phone or tablet, you can access your SkyDrive files.

SkyDrive also has a PC application that makes SkyDrive appear as a disk drive on your computer. You can drag and drop files that you want to share into your SkyDrive folder and they'll be available for use on your phone or tablet.

Android

Most of the mobile computing applications we have discussed that are available with the iPhone and iPad are also available for Android phones and tablets. Android is a mobile operating system created by Google and licensed for use on various manufacturer's smartphones and tablets. There are many different versions of the Android operating system available depending on the device; however, most versions include email and calendars that allow administrative assistants the freedom to be mobile while still having access to their main office tools.

Google Account

The first time you open a Google application on your Android device, you will be required to sign into your existing Google account. If you don't already have a Google account, you can create one. The Google account gives you access to Gmail, Google's email application, as well as the calendar app. You can create a Google account by visiting www.google.com.

Conference Calls

You can establish a conference call by adding one caller at a time to a call. Follow these steps:

1. To make the first call, from the HOME screen, tap the PHONE KEY to open the keypad.
2. Enter the number using the keypad, and tap the CALL KEY to make the call.
3. After you've established a connection with the first party, to add more people to the call, tap the MENU KEY, then tap ADD CALL.
4. Dial the number of the second person or select him or her from your list of contacts by tapping CONTACTS.
5. Tap the CALL KEY to make the call. Both calls are displayed on the call screen; however, the initial call is locked and put on hold.
6. Tap MERGE CALL to merge the calls into a conference call.

Contacts

You can add contacts to your Android device and sync them with the contacts in your Google account or on your computer's email application.

Importing Contacts from Your Computer   Follow these steps to import your contacts from an email program such as Outlook:

1. Save your contacts to a file from your computer's email program. For example, in Outlook, click FILE > OPTIONS > ADVANCED > EXPORT.
2. On the IMPORT AND EXPORT WIZARD, click EXPORT TO A FILE, then click NEXT.
3. On the EXPORT TO A FILE dialog, click COMMA SEPARATED VALUES (WINDOWS), then click NEXT.
4. Select the CONTACTS folder, then click NEXT.
5. Click the BROWSE button.
6. Navigate to a place where you want to save your export file, then add a name to the FILE NAME field.
7. Click the OK button.
8. Back on the EXPORT TO A FILE dialog, click NEXT.
9. Click FINISH.
10. After the file has been saved, click OK on the OUTLOOK OPTIONS window.

    Follow these steps to import your contacts into your Google account:

1. Go to www.google.com and sign into your Google account.
2. Click GMAIL from the menu bar.
3. Click the down arrow next to GMAIL and select CONTACTS.
4. Click IMPORT CONTACTS.

Mobile Computing

5. On the IMPORT CONTACTS message screen, click the BROWSE button.

6. Navigate to where you saved your Outlook contacts export file, select the export file, and click OPEN.

7. Back on the IMPORT CONTACTS message screen, click IMPORT.

After importing your computer's contacts into your Google account, your Android device will automatically sync with your Google account and give you access to the contacts.

Adding a Contact Manually   You can add contacts manually to your Android device by following these steps:

1. From the HOME screen, tap the PHONE KEY and enter the new contact's phone number.

2. Tap the MENU KEY > ADD TO CONTACTS > CREATE NEW CONTACT.

3. Add details about the contact.

4. Tap SAVE when you are finished.

Searching for Contacts   To search for contacts on your Android device, follow these steps:

1. From the HOME screen, tap the APPS KEY.

2. Tap CONTACTS.

3. Tap in the SEARCH field and enter the contact name using the keypad. You can also tap the letters at the right side of the screen.

Email

Your Android device will typically include an Email app as well as a Gmail app. You can use the Email app to read email from other email providers.

The first time you open the Email app, a setup wizard guides you through the process of adding an email account. Normally, you'll just need to enter your email address and password.

You can add multiple email accounts by following these steps:

1. From the HOME screen, tap the EMAIL app.

2. Your default email account will open. Tap the MENU button.

3. Tap SETTINGS.

4. Tap the + ADD ACCOUNT button.

5. Enter the email address and password, then tap NEXT on the keyboard.

6. The new email account will be added.

Checking Email   After setting up your email account, you can check email by tapping the EMAIL app on the HOME screen. A list of email messages is displayed. Tap a message to read it. The message will be displayed, and the message list will display to the left. Figure 10-5 shows the Email app for Android.

Deleting a Message   To delete a message from the message list, tap the box to the left of the message and then tap the DELETE icon that looks like a trash can. To delete a message after reading it, just tap the DELETE icon.

FIGURE 10-5   Email for Android.

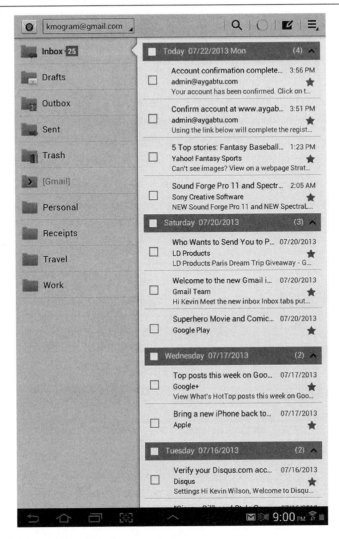

Creating and Sending an Email Message   To create a new email message, follow these steps:

1. From the HOME screen, tap the EMAIL app.

2. In the Email app, tap the COMPOSE button.

3. Enter an email address in the To field.

4. Enter the subject and text of the message.

5. Tap ATTACH to attach a file to your message. Select the type of File and browse or it.

6. Tap SEND to send the message.

7. Sent messages are stored in the OUTBOX folder.

Using the Calendar

You can view your calendar by tapping the Calendar app on the Home screen. To view an event, tap the date. The events for that date are displayed.

Adding an Event   Follow these steps to add a new event to your calendar:

1. Tap the + button in the Calendar app.
2. Enter a name or title for the event.
3. Check the date and enter the start and end date and time for the event.
4. Tap the Location field and enter the location.
5. Tap the Description field and add a description of the event.
6. To repeat the event, tap the Repeat field and select how often you want to the event to repeat.
7. To add a reminder, tap the + for the Reminder field and select how much in advance you want to be reminded about this event.
8. Tap Save to save the event in the calendar.

File Sharing

You can access Microsoft Office and Adobe Acrobat documents on your Android device using the same file-sharing tools mentioned earlier for the iPhone and iPad. These include Dropbox, Google Drive, and SkyDrive.

With the Polaris Office app that comes installed on the Android device, you can view, create, and edit Microsoft Office and Adobe Acrobat documents on your device. The documents can be email attachments that you have downloaded to your device; files that you've downloaded from Dropbox, Google Drive, or SkyDrive; or files that you copy to your device when it is connected to your computer.

Creating a Document   To create a document using Polaris Office, follow these steps:

1. From the Home screen, tap the Apps Key, then tap Polaris Office.
2. Tap the New icon to start a new document.
3. Tap to select a document type.
4. Enter contents using the keyboard at the bottom of the screen or by using the edit menu across the top of the screen.
5. When you are finished, tap the Save icon.
6. Tap the Back Key to exit.

Viewing a Document   To view a document you've downloaded from an email or one that you created using Polaris Office, follow these steps:

1. From the Home screen, tap the Apps Key, then tap Polaris Office.
2. Tap Browse to search folders and documents stored on your Android device.
3. To view a document stored in SkyDrive, Google Drive, or Dropbox, tap Clouds then select your cloud storage service.
4. Move to the folder that contains the file you want to open.
5. Tap the document that you want to view or edit.

FIGURE 10-6   Polaris Office toolbar.

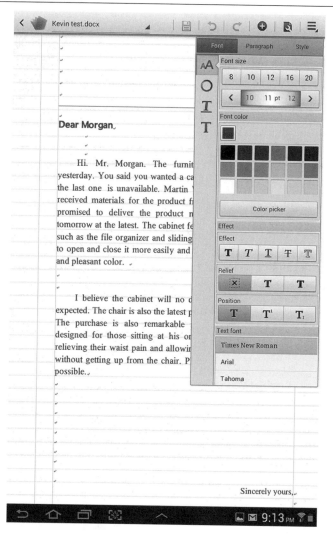

Polaris Office Document Tools   To create and edit documents, Polaris Office has a toolbar that offers access to many useful functions. You can access the toolbar by first selecting something in the document, such as text or a photo, then selecting the TOOL-BAR icon. There is a toolbar for editing text, one for editing photos, another for spreadsheet formulas, and another for formatting slides. Figure 10-6 displays the Polaris Office Toolbar.

Voice Recorder

There are a variety of audio recording apps available for Android devices and they all allow for easy recording of voice memos, dictation, and meetings. Just access the Voice Recorder app from the Home screen and tap the RECORD button to begin recording. Tap the record button again to stop recording. You can play the file back on your Android device, or you can email the file to yourself for listening on your computer.

Android to Computer Connections

You can connect your Android device to your computer using a USB cable. After making a successful connection, the Android device shows up as one of your computer's disk drives, allowing you to copy files back and forth. You may need to install special driver software for your Android device that is available from the manufacturer's support web page.

Wi-Fi Connection

To access a Wi-Fi connection for Internet access, follow these steps:

1. From the Home screen, tap the APPS Key.
2. Tap SETTINGS.
3. Tap the Wi-Fi switch to turn it on.
4. A list of Wi-Fi networks that are within range will be displayed.
5. Tap to select the desired network.
6. If the network is password protected, enter the password.
7. The Wi-Fi network will show a status of "Connected."

11

Using Microsoft Windows

Operating Systems

An operating system is the underlying software that allows other programs—such as word processors, databases, and spreadsheets—to operate with similar menu choices, processes, and functions. The operating system, sometimes called the OS, is a set of rules that other programs must follow. The operating system serves as an intermediary, handling communications between your software and the computer's hardware.

Microsoft Windows is the most widely used computer operating system. There are several alternative operating systems, including Apple OS for Macintosh, Unix, and Linux. Because Microsoft Windows is by far the most commonly used operating system in business today, this chapter discusses the features of Windows.

How Does Microsoft Windows Work?

As the operating system, Microsoft Windows provides instructions to the computer's "brain" for how to access disk drives, how to print, and even how to add 2 + 2. Think of the operating system as the interface between you and the computer components. Tell the operating system what you want to do, and it completes the task—if it is told in the proper way.

Microsoft Windows has a graphical user interface (GUI). In simple terms, everything can be done with a point and click from a mouse. Graphics are used to create an understandable interface with the user. With Microsoft Windows, you can graphically see what you need to do and can accomplish it through the graphic interface. The secret is to know what you want to accomplish.

There are a variety of versions of Microsoft Windows available, depending on the age of your computer and how often your business upgrades its computers. The most recent versions include Windows XP, Windows Vista, Windows 7, and the latest version Windows 8. While earlier versions are similar to operate, Windows 8 offers some dramatic differences in order to allow for touchscreen operation on tablets as well as computers. Because of these differences, we will focus part of this chapter on Windows 7 and another part on Windows 8.

The Windows 7 Desktop

The Windows 7 Desktop is the screen you see when you turn on your computer and Windows loads. As you use Windows 7, you will be rearranging, removing, and placing

109

FIGURE 11-1   The Windows 7 desktop.

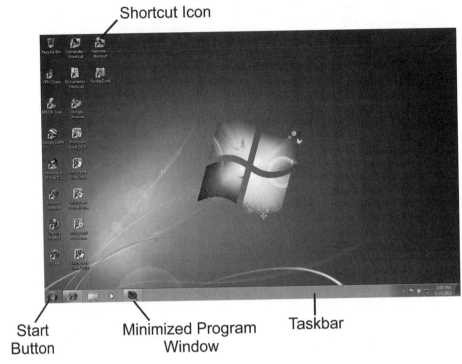

Screen shot used with permission from Microsoft.

items on the Desktop, just like a real desktop. The Desktop includes a variety of features such as:

■ Desktop icons like My Computer

■ The Taskbar

■ The Start button

The Taskbar occupies the bottom edge of the Desktop by default. It can be moved to the top or either side, or it can be made to disappear and reappear when you need it.

Figure 11-1 shows a typical Desktop after newly installing Windows 7. The Taskbar along the bottom contains the START button on the left and the time on the right. Open applications and folders are represented by buttons on the Taskbar at the bottom of the screen. These buttons come and go depending on which programs or folders you have open at any given time.

The Start Menu
The Start Menu (Figure 11-2) is opened by clicking on the START button at the left-hand end of the Taskbar. As an operating system, Windows 7 presents an interface to you, the user. The job of the interface is to give you the means of commanding the computer to perform actions like launching programs, copying files, and activating a printer. Normally, once the operating system is started, you're supposed to know what to do next. Of course, new users often do not know what to do next, so Windows 7 provides a clearly marked starting place, the START button.

FIGURE 11-2   The Start Menu.

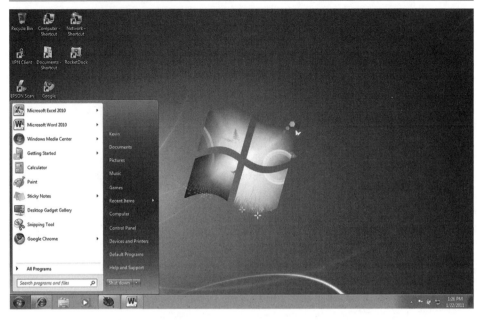

Screen shot used with permission from Microsoft.

As a beginner, you will use the Start Menu as home base for most operations you perform in Windows 7. Later, as you gain experience, you'll be creating folders and icons and will have the option of not using the Start Menu as much. Be aware that like most things in Windows 7, the Start Menu may vary depending on certain programs and options that may be installed on your system. In addition, the Start Menu contains several options that have nothing to do with starting things. In fact, one command is Shut Down, the opposite of starting. Before we go any further, we'll need to mention two possibilities that may occur at any time, even though they may seem out of sequence at this point: (1) the computer may be shut down; and (2) individual programs, said to be "frozen," may be shut down.

Shutting Down Windows 7

One option on the Start Menu is Shut Down. Although there is nothing to stop you from just switching off the computer, doing so without choosing the Shut Down procedure may result in lost data and corrupted files.

When you choose Shut Down, the screen dims and a new menu appears that gives you several options. Here you can click the YES button to shut down, or you can make another selection first and then click YES. If you choose to shut down, Windows 7 will spend a few moments closing files, and then will display a screen informing you that it is okay to turn off the power.

Closing a Frozen Program

If you have had any experience with personal computers, you will be familiar with the circumstance where the computer stops responding and becomes "frozen." Should your computer become frozen, you can press the CTRL + ALT + DEL keys simultaneously.

Then navigate to the Task Manager or Task List depending on which version of Windows you are using. When you do this, a list of tasks that are currently running will appear in a dialog box called Close Program. From this task list, you can do one of four things: (1) You can end the task (stop the program) that is causing the problem, perform a normal shutdown, reboot (i.e., restart) the computer immediately without a normal shutdown, or cancel and return to where you left off. (2) To end the task, you would make a guess at which program is causing the problem, select it from the list, and then click END TASK. (3) If this does not unfreeze the computer, you can try a normal shutdown by recalling the task list (by pressing CTRL + ALT + DEL again), then choosing SHUT DOWN. (4) If that doesn't work, you can press CTRL + ALT + DEL while the task list is displayed to force a system reset. If nothing else works, press and hold the on/off button on the front of the computer for a few seconds to force a system shutdown.

Starting a Program

The next option on the Start Menu that we'll look at is Programs. When the pointer is on Programs, a new menu appears to the right of the Start Menu.

As we'll discuss in more detail later, the little arrowheads to the right of some of the options mean that another menu will appear when you point to that option. To start a program, you select it from the Programs Menu with your mouse and then click. The program will then load and appear on your screen.

Resizing a Window

If the program window occupies your entire screen with no part of the desktop background visible, it may be maximized. If your window is maximized, you'll see three buttons in the upper right corner of the window.

If the center button looks like two small overlapping windows, your window is maximized. Each time you run a program, you'll notice that a new button appears on the Taskbar at the bottom of the screen. The button is labeled with the program name. When the Taskbar becomes crowded, the buttons are automatically made smaller to accommodate more of them. When the buttons are too small to show the program name, you can point to a button and wait a second or two, and the complete caption will appear in a little pop-up box.

To resize a window, you drag its border. You can do this by moving the mouse pointer to the border. When you are in the correct spot, the pointer will change to a two-headed arrow pointing left and right. You can then click and drag the window to a new size.

You can reshape both dimensions of a window by dragging the lower right corner. Position the mouse pointer over the corner until you see a diagonal sizing pointer. Then click and drag the mouse to change the dimensions. Some windows cannot be sized beyond certain limits. While using Windows 7, you'll frequently need to resize and move windows to arrange your desktop for efficiency.

Minimizing, Maximizing, Restoring, and Closing Windows

When you wish to get a window off the screen temporarily but have its program continue to run or its window instantly available, you can minimize it. To do this, you click the MINIMIZE button in the top right corner of the screen. When you do this, you'll notice that the window appears to zip down to the Taskbar. Technically, the window is still "open," so it appears on the Taskbar. To restore it, just click its button on the Taskbar.

If you need more space to work in an application window, you can maximize it to cover the entire screen. Just click the MAXIMIZE button in the top right corner of the window. If you maximize a window, the three buttons in the upper right corner of the window change. The MAXIMIZE button is replaced by a new button, called the RESTORE button. If you click the RESTORE button, the window returns it its original size.

When you wish to close a program or folder, you click the CLOSE button in the upper right corner of the window. It is the button that is marked with an X.

Using Scroll Bars

When the material inside a window won't fit the current window size, scroll bars will automatically appear to allow you to move the view and reveal the rest of the space.

Within each scroll bar there is a scroll slider. At the ends of each scroll bar there are small arrow buttons. The length of the slider gives you some indication of the proportion of the whole that you are viewing. You use the scroll bars to move within the viewing space. To move a small increment at a time, you click on the arrow buttons at the ends of the scroll bars. You can also click and drag the slider up or down (or left or right on the horizontal scroll bar).

Using scroll bars is one of the basic techniques for using Windows 7. Scroll bars appear in windows, dialog boxes, and anywhere a screen display needs additional space for items.

Using Explorer to View Files and Folders

The program you use to manipulate files is called Explorer. You can start Explorer by clicking the START button, then point to the Programs, and then click ACCESSORIES. Windows Explorer is in the Accessories folder.

The window is divided into two panes (Figure 11-3). On the left is a tree diagram of disk drives and folders. On the right is a list of the files and folders contained within the selected folder in the tree.

Files and Folders

People talk about having information stored on their computers. The most common questions are: Where is the information stored, and how do you find it? Here are two definitions that you need to understand first.

1. *File:* A file is a document that has been created or an application that has been installed on the computer. Files are similar to piles of projects on your desk. They are the actual pieces with which you work.

2. *Folder or Directory:* A folder is a directory or the organizer for the files. Folders can be used to store all the pieces of a software package that are needed to run the software or to organize documents that are created. Folders organize files into logical groups. Folders can hold other folders. The first folder you come to is called the Directory, and the folders inside the first folder are the Subdirectories. The ultimate decision of how to organize a folder is up to you, since you will have to find and access files and folders for later use.

FIGURE 11-3   Windows Explorer.

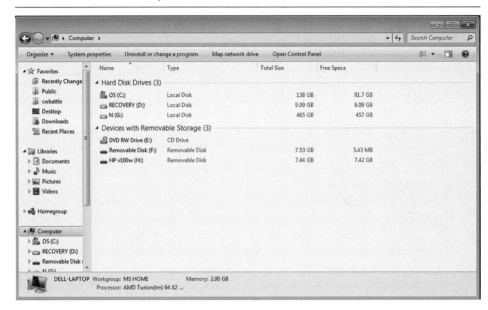

Screen shot used with permission from Microsoft.

Placing a File in a Folder   To place a file in a folder, you only need to drag and drop it. When you drag the file, be sure to point to the icon, not the name of the file. Dragging by the name will work, but sometimes you'll try to drag a file that is already selected when you click it to drag it. If the file is already selected, clicking on the name switches to edit mode (so you can type a new name), and you can't drag it then. If you always drag the icon, you will avoid this potential pitfall. When you drag to the target folder, that folder will become highlighted when you are pointing at the correct spot.

Deleting a File or Folder   You use the same procedure to delete files and folders. When you delete a folder, all the files and other folders within it are also deleted. You can use one of three techniques to delete files or folders:

1. You can drag it to the Recycle Bin icon on your desktop.

2. You can open its context menu and click DELETE.

3. You can select it and press the DELETE key on your keyboard.

Windows Help

There are two types of help: the online help for Windows 7 itself, and the online help for the various applications running in Windows 7. Software manufacturers use the built-in facilities of Windows Help, so most applications have similar help features.

Table 11-1 lists ways you can call for help. Because applications differ, not all these methods are always available.

When you access Windows Help, you'll see three tabs along the top, labeled Contents, Index, and Find. Table 11-2 lists what they do. The most useful of these is the Index, since most often you know the topic you want help with.

TABLE 11-1   Windows Help

Help about Windows 7	Open Start Menu, click HELP.
General help in an application	Open application's Help Menu.
Specific help about a current procedure	Press F1.
Help about a screen object	In some applications, click the Toolbar HELP button, then click the object.
	In some applications, press SHIFT + F1, then click the object.
	In some applications (and Windows 7 itself), dialog boxes have a question mark button. Click it, then click the object in the box.
General help about a dialog box	Some dialog boxes have HELP buttons. Also try F1.

TABLE 11-2   Windows Help Features

Contents	Presents help like a book or outline with chapters, topics, and subtopics.
Index	Searches for key words in topics, like a book's index.
Find	Full text search for words within the entire help system, including the body text of the help screens.

Help from Applications   Applications have their own help systems. Usually, they use the same model as Windows 7, so they should look and behave in a familiar manner.

In many applications, pressing the F1 key while something is selected or while you are performing some function will give you help about the object or procedure. Since you often need help to start a procedure, you may find that selecting help from the menu and using the search feature will be the most often-used technique.

Pop-Up Help   Some applications have automatic pop-up reminders to help you remember the functions of the various on-screen buttons. If you hold your mouse pointer over any of the buttons on a program's toolbar, a pop-up label appears, and a more detailed explanation is shown at the bottom of the window. Making the pointer remain still while pointing at an object is called hovering in some manuals. Many of the more recent Windows 7 applications from different publishers use the pop-up help technique when you hover over a button.

Menus

Most applications and folder windows have menu bars. A menu bar is a list of menus. When you click the name of a menu, it drops down. This is called opening a menu or pulling down a menu. The most common menu choices include File, Edit, View, Tools, Window, and Help. In some menus, an arrowhead appears to the right of some of the listed options. This means that when you point to it, another menu will appear. Options that are followed by an ellipsis (three periods) will display a dialog box. Options with nothing after them will execute immediately.

Once a menu is opened, you can move to another menu with the mouse or with the left and right arrow keys. The same actions work vertically within each menu, so that you can point to an option with the mouse or use the up and down arrow keys to point to one.

You can close a menu without making a selection by clicking on the menu name again, clicking anywhere except on a menu option, or by pressing the ESCAPE key (on the keyboard) twice.

Sometimes menus can be used to make settings, and the settings can be indicated on the menu. If you decide not to display, say, the Toolbar, you can click that item. The menu will close, and the Toolbar will disappear. The next time you open the View Menu, the Toolbar item will not be checked off.

Using Pop-Up Context Menus   The right-hand mouse button is used often in Windows 7. Usually, it produces a pop-up menu that is sometimes called a context menu because it contains options appropriate for the specific object you are pointing to. Most applications also use context menus.

Sometimes when a context menu appears, several of the options are grayed out. Grayed-out items do not work, because they are not appropriate for your current situation.

Objects on the Windows Desktop have their own context menus. If you point to any of the icons on the desktop and right-click, a context menu appears.

Dialog Boxes

Often when you select an item from a menu, such as Print, a new small window will appear on the screen (Figure 11-4). These windows are called *dialog boxes*. Dialog boxes are used to adjust various settings. For example, with the Print dialog box, you can select the quality of the printing, the size of the paper, the number of copies, and so forth.

Within a dialog box you'll often use what are called *radio buttons*. Radio buttons are round, and the selected one has a dot in it. Radio buttons are always in groups of two or more, and one of them is always selected. When you select another one, the previously selected one is deselected, just like when you punch a station button on a car radio.

Dialog boxes may also contain text entry boxes. When you click in one of these blanks, an insertion point (also called a cursor) will appear, indicating where the next character you type will appear. You can use this technique to edit the default value. (Be aware that, typically in a numeric entry space, you will not be allowed to enter non-numbers.)

To close a dialog box, you can choose one of the command buttons. Usually, you have a choice of OK and CANCEL. Choosing OK closes the dialog box and accepts your entries; CANCEL closes the dialog box but ignores any changes you made. If the dialog box also has a CLOSE button in the upper right corner, it has the same effect as the CANCEL button.

Saving Files

While working on a document, you'll want to save it frequently to prevent loss of any of your work. The first time you save a new document, you'll be prompted to give it a file name, and you'll need to select a folder in which to save it.

FIGURE 11-4   The Print dialog box in Microsoft Word.

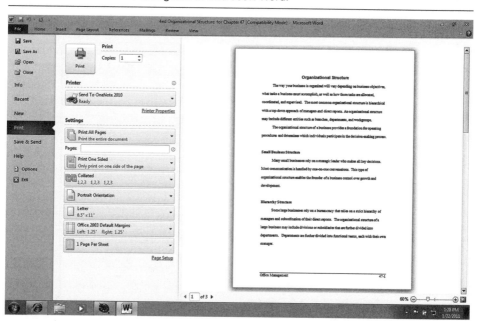

Screen shot used with permission from Microsoft.

You can save by opening the File Menu and choosing SAVE or SAVE AS (Figure 11-5). In an application such as Microsoft Word, you can click the SAVE button on the Toolbar. The first time you save an unnamed document, the Save As dialog box appears. Thereafter, each time you click the SAVE button, the document is saved immediately (no dialog box appears) under the same name. Should you wish to save it with a new name, you can open the File Menu and choose SAVE AS.

The Save As dialog box is called a *common dialog box* because Microsoft provides it as a tool that can be utilized by anyone writing programs for the Windows 7 operating system. Most Microsoft programs and many applications from other companies use the common dialog boxes rather than design their own. This is a great advantage to users, since once they have learned the standard common dialog boxes, they will know how to perform the same function in many different programs.

The Save As and Open dialog boxes are very similar. They contain many of the features of the Explorer, including the ability to point to a drive and folder. In addition, the Save As and Open dialog boxes can be used for some file management tasks, such as deleting or renaming files and folders and creating new folders. While the basic function of the Open dialog box is to allow you to select or enter the name of the file you wish to open, the main function of the Save As dialog box is to allow you to choose where you wish to save a file and to give it a name of your choice.

The file is created on the disk. Once the file is saved the first time, you can continue to work on the document and save at intervals. When you click the SAVE button, the current version of the file will be saved immediately in the same folder and with the same file name, overwriting the previous version. This will happen without asking you for a file name.

FIGURE 11-5   The Save As dialog box in Microsoft Word.

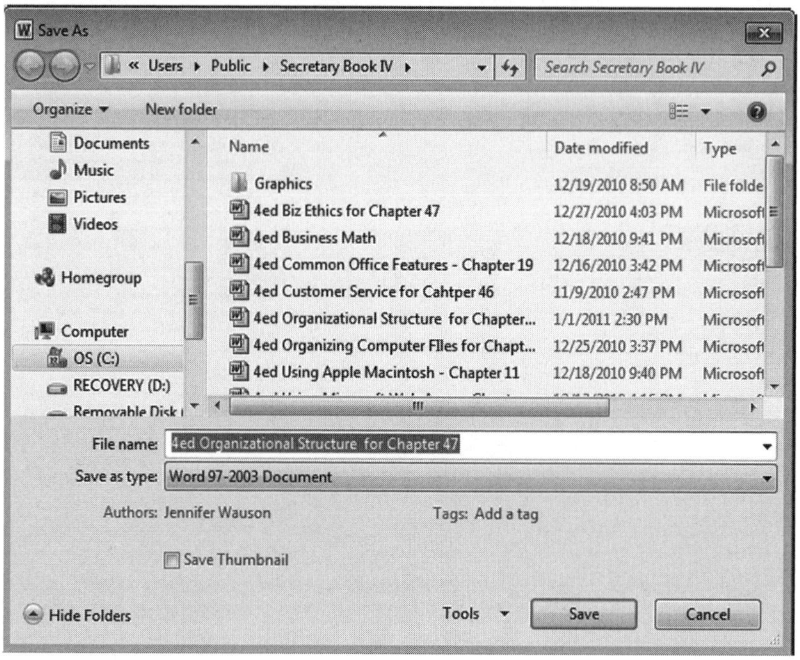

Screen shot used with permission from Microsoft.

Printing Files

You can print a document by clicking the File Menu and then clicking PRINT. Many programs also have a print button on a toolbar. Sometimes this button will cause the Print dialog box to open, but many times the toolbar button will make the document print one copy immediately to the currently selected printer without displaying the dialog box.

On the Print dialog box, you can choose which printer you wish to use, in case you have more than one (such as you might on a network). You can also choose what portion of the document you want to print and the number of copies. Though this is the common dialog box for printing in Windows 7, other applications will often use different, though similar, boxes. Usually, they will offer additional options.

Windows 7 will also allow you to print by dragging and dropping a file icon onto a printer icon.

Finding a File

The Find program is a very useful tool, so we are going to cover it in some detail here. You can start it several ways, but the most convenient way is the F3 key. When you press F3 on the keyboard, the Find dialog box appears. When you command Find to locate a file, it will begin searching from the folder or drive shown in the Look In blank. If you specify a folder as the starting point for the search, Windows 7 will find it faster.

If you open a folder—either in Explorer or in its own window—then start Find with F3, that folder will be the Look In folder.

Here is an important note. The F3 key does not start Find unless the Desktop, Taskbar, a folder, or Explorer has the focus. In other words, if you are working in an application, that application's window will have the focus, and the F3 key will perform whatever function is assigned to it by the application. If the application does not use the F3 key, nothing will happen when you press it. If you want to start Find while working in an application, be sure to click the Desktop or the Taskbar first. Some applications, such as the Microsoft Office Suite, have their own built-in Find-like features, so in actual practice, you will probably seldom use the Windows Find program while running an application.

Wildcard Searches   You can search for files by entering only part of the file name, or you can limit your search by using special symbols called wildcards (Table 11-3). For example, you can find all files on drive C with "win" in the file name. A fairly long list of files should appear. The files can appear in several formats. The window containing the list of files acts exactly like a folder containing files or Windows Explorer. You can move and copy files, delete them, or work with them in the appropriate application. You can sort and reverse-sort the listed files by clicking on the column headers.

You can also use wildcards similar to those used in old DOS to search for files. Although your system may be set so that it does not show all the three-character extensions for the file names, they are still used, even with long file names. For instance, if you wish to display all the executable program files, you can use the wildcard *.exe. That tells Windows 7 to find all files, regardless of name, with the extension "exe".

Date Searches   Each time you create a file, the date and time are saved with the name. When the file is modified, the date and time are updated. Sometimes you might need to find a file whose name you do not remember, but you know you modified it in the last two or three days. The first place to look would be the Documents option on the Start Menu, since it remembers the last fifteen files you modified. Failing that, you can have Find show you files in a certain date period.

TABLE 11-3   Wildcards That Can Be Used with Find

Name	What will be searched for
*	All files and folders
.	All files and folders
*.	All files (not folders)
Xyz	All files and folders with xyz in the name or extension
xyz	All files and folders with xyz in the name or extension
*.xyz	All files with the extension xyz
xyz.*	All files with the name xyz and any (or no) extension
?xyz	All files and folders where xyz is preceded by one or more characters
??xyz	All files and folders where xyz is preceded by at least two characters
x?yz	All files and folders where x is followed by one unknown character, then the letters y and z

Advanced Searches   You can find files and folders based on type, size, or even text contained in the file. When searching for text, you should be aware that such searches may take a while, so you should narrow the search as much as possible by specifying a specific folder, if possible, or other criteria such as date.

Shortcuts

Shortcuts are small files that "point" to other files, folders, and programs. When you open a shortcut, the object to which it points opens. This allows you to store objects in an appropriate place in the hierarchy of folders, but access them from another location, usually the Desktop or the Start Menu. So, for example, the Calculator program is stored in the Windows folder. It might just as easily be stored in some folder several layers deep. That might be the best place to keep it so that your computer is properly organized, but it makes it difficult to find when you want to use it. One solution to this problem is to place a shortcut to the Calculator program on the Desktop. You can place a shortcut in any folder.

The Desktop itself is actually a folder. The rule is that when you drag a program (application) object to a folder, such as the Desktop, the default action is to create a shortcut. However, when you drag a file or folder to a folder, the default action is to move (if the folder is on the same drive) or copy (if the folder is on a different drive). Since this can get confusing for many people, it is suggested that you always right-click objects, then pick the action you want from the Menu.

How to Use Shortcuts   You should use shortcuts almost all the time. You can rename them all you want without affecting the original, and you can place copies in as many folders as you want. Almost all objects on the Desktop are shortcuts. You rarely place an original program, file, or folder on the Desktop.

Deleting Files, Folders, and Shortcuts

You can delete files, folders, and shortcuts by selecting them, and then doing one of the following: (1) dragging them to the Recycle Bin icon, (2) pressing the DELETE key on your keyboard, or (3) opening the right-click Context Menu and choosing DELETE.

Recovering Deletions   If you wish to recover a file that you deleted, you can do so by just dragging it out of the Recycle Bin window (Table 11-4). The Recycle Bin can be set so that once the files in the Recycle folder occupy a certain percentage of space on the drive, the oldest files will be automatically deleted permanently. You can also manually permanently delete files from the Recycle folder by selecting them in the Recycle Bin window and deleting them again, using either the DELETE key or the Delete

TABLE 11-4   What Happens When You Delete an Object

Object	What Happens When Deleted
File	The file is moved to a special folder called Recycle Bin.
Folder	All files in the folder, as well as files in subfolders, if any, are moved to the Recycle Bin. The folders are erased when you select Empty Trash.
Shortcut	The shortcut is moved to the Recycle Bin, but not the object to which it points. It remains untouched.

Using Microsoft Windows

command from the Context Menu. You can also right-click the mouse on the Recycle Bin and click EMPTY RECYCLE MENU from the Context Menu.

Control Panel

The Control Panel contains a group of utility programs that allows you to make adjustments to your computer, the Windows operating system, and the drivers for hardware devices. Certain icons are added to the Control Panel when you install programs and features in Windows 7. The key functions for which you will use the Control Panel include:

- Changing your desktop background, color scheme, or screen resolution
- Setting the clock
- Installing a new printer
- Adding users to your computer
- Setting up security features
- Adding the computer to a network
- Backing up your computer's data

Depending on which version of Windows your computer is running, there may be different icons and views for the Control Panel. Figure 11-6 shows the Windows 7 Control Panel.

FIGURE 11-6 The Control Panel in Microsoft Windows 7.

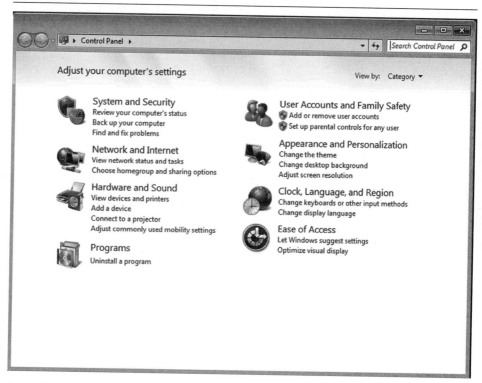

Screen shot used with permission from Microsoft.

Date/Time   Your computer contains an internal clock and calendar. (You can make this same dialog box appear by right-clicking the clock on the Taskbar.) Date/Time allows the user to set the date and time on the computer's clock. The computer clock is used to label files with the date and time they are created and modified.

Display or Personalization   Your screen can be customized through the Display icon. (In Windows 7, this is the Appearance and Personalization icon.) This dialog box can also be accessed by right-clicking on the Desktop and choosing Properties or Personalize.

The desktop background can be set to a color and pattern, or you can make it display a graphic file. A graphic file displayed on the background is called *Wallpaper*. The Background tab allows you to set a pattern or choose a graphic file for wallpaper. Wallpaper graphics can be small or can fill the entire screen. If they are small, Windows 7 gives you the option of repeating them to fill the entire screen. This is called *Tiling*. If you like, you can make your own wallpaper files in Windows Paint. Once you make the file, you just use the BROWSE button to tell Windows 7 the name and location of the file.

Besides setting the colors of the standard parts of the Windows 7 screen, you can set a number of other things, such as spacing of icons and the fonts used in title bars and menus. Once you have set your screen to the way you like it, you can just begin using Windows 7, and your settings will become the default. If you would like to change to other arrangements from time to time, you can save your settings as a *Theme* by giving it a name. Windows 7 has a group of preset themes, too.

Screen Saver   Another popular feature is the Screen Saver. This is a screen that appears after a preset time period of no activity. The original purpose of screen savers was to prevent static images from burning in and damaging the monitor's screen. Modern monitors are rarely damaged by static images, but screen savers are a very popular way of personalizing computers, and most monitor manufacturers still recommend them.

Display Settings   The Display Settings is where you can change the resolution of your monitor and the number of colors displayed. Typical resolutions are 800 × 600 and 1,024 × 768. Higher resolution allows you to fit more on your screen; however, text and icons are smaller and harder to read.

Mouse Pointers   You can modify the settings of your mouse to make it comfortable for yourself. When you run the Mouse Utility, you will see four tabs on the dialog box. The first tab, Buttons, allows you to reverse the buttons. Left-handed users may prefer to have the buttons reversed. The left button takes on the actions of the right button, and vice versa. You can also set the double-click speed, and there is a little test area to check the different double-click settings.

You can choose different mouse pointers, including animated ones. You can also save your choices in a scheme, just as you can for the appearance options.

Printers   You may have one or more printer icons, each one representing a printer that is available to you, either connected to your computer or through a network. Though you will usually print while using an application, you can also drag a document file from the Explorer or a folder window and drop it on a printer icon. This will cause the document's associated application to start and print the document.

Using Microsoft Windows

In most cases, a print job is *spooled* first, which means the output from the application is sent to a temporary disk file, then to the printer. This allows large print jobs to be transferred to the spool file quickly, allowing you to go on working while the document is printed from the spooler. If you print several jobs in rapid succession, they will form a queue, waiting for the printer to become available. Or, if you are attached to a network, several other people may be printing on the same printer, and all the documents will form a queue.

The printer icon in the Control Panel allows you to view the queue. The window that appears is where the print queue would be shown. On networks, unless you are the system administrator, you cannot rearrange or cancel print jobs except your own.

Keyboard Shortcuts
There are a variety of keyboard shortcuts that allow you to perform common Windows 7 functions without using the mouse to click through the menus. Some shortcuts involve pressing more than one keyboard key at the same time. Table 11-5 shows a list of Windows 7 keyboard shortcuts.

Windows 8

Windows 8 offers two user interfaces and is a radical redesign compared to earlier versions of Windows. One interface, the Desktop, functions very similar to Windows 7 and earlier versions, while the new Modern User Interface, Modern UI, is designed for touch-enabled tablets, laptops, and PCs. You can easily switch back and forth between both interfaces depending on which environment you like and whether you are using a touchscreen device.

Microsoft Account
With Windows 8, you have the option of signing on as a local user or using your Microsoft account. With a Microsoft account, you can download and use apps from the Microsoft Store, sync your PC settings across different devices, and access Microsoft SkyDrive's cloud storage service.

Microsoft accounts include a free email account, such as @hotmail.com, @live.com, or @outlook.com. If you already have one of these email accounts, you can use it to sign into Windows 8. Obtaining a Microsoft account is free, and you can sign up at www.live.com.

Start Screen
The Start Screen is the first place you arrive when you sign into Windows 8. It is a wide scrolling screen filled with colorful tiles for various built-in applications such as web browsing, news, sports, shopping, travel, and stocks. If you have Microsoft Office installed on your Windows 8 device, there will be tiles for your individual Office applications, such as Word, Excel, and PowerPoint.

The Start Screen is designed to be wider than your display, and therefore you must scroll sideways to see additional application tiles. You can click and drag the horizontal scrollbar at the bottom of the screen, or you can use a mouse wheel to scroll.

You can move the tiles around on the Start Screen and group certain ones together. To move a tile, just click and drag it to a new location on the Start Screen. You can

Using Microsoft Windows

TABLE 11-5   Windows 7 Keyboard Shortcuts

Function	Keyboard Shortcut
Help	F1
Open the Start Menu	CTRL + ESC
Switch between open programs	ATL + TAB
Quit a program	ALT + F4
Delete item permanently	SHIFT + DELETE
Lock the computer	Windows Logo key + L
Copy	CTRL + C
Cut	CTRL + X
Paste	CTRL + V
Undo	CTRL + Z
Bold	CTRL + B
Underline	CTRL + U
Italics	CTRL + I
Activate menu bar options	F10
Open a shortcut menu for a selected item	SHIFT + F10
Open Windows Task Manager	CTRL + SHIFT + ESC
Open a drop-down list box	ATL + DOWN ARROW
Bypass the auto-run feature in a CD or DVD	Hold SHIFT while inserting CD or DVD
Display the System Menu	ATL + SPACEBAR
Close the current window	ATL + F4
Switch between multiple windows in the same program	ATL + F6
Rename an object	F2
Find all files	F3
Turn on or off Sticky Keys	Press SHIFT five times
Select the currently selected button	ENTER
Select the Cancel button on a dialog box.	ESC

remove a tile by right-mouse clicking on the tile, and then clicking UNPIN FROM START from the App Bar at the bottom of the screen (Figure 11-7).

Apps
The applications that are visible on the Start Screen are called apps. You can get additional apps (both free and paid) by clicking the Store tile. To launch an application from the Start Screen, just click once on the app tile.

FIGURE 11-7 Start Screen with App Bar Visible.

Screen shot used with permission from Microsoft.

Every software application installed on your computer does not necessarily show up on the Start Screen as a tile. In order to see all the apps installed, right-mouse click the Start Screen, and click ALL APPS on the App Bar at the bottom of the screen. You'll see icons for all installed apps.

If an app you often use is not already showing up as a tile on the Start Screen, you can add it. When viewing All Apps, if you right-mouse click the icon for an application, you can then click PIN TO START to add a tile to the Start Screen.

Desktop

The Desktop is a tile on the Start Screen that gives you access to the second Windows 8 interface. While this interface is similar to Windows 7 and earlier versions, there is no Start button or Start Menu. Instead, you use the File Explorer, which is available as an icon on the taskbar, to find and launch applications and access data files. You add shortcuts to the desktop just as you can with earlier versions of Windows.

Some applications do not install as tiles on the Start Screen, and instead will give you the option to install a shortcut on the Desktop. Some applications also come in two flavors, one for the Desktop and one for the Start Screen. For example, there are two versions of the web browser Internet Explorer installed with Windows 8: one version that runs from the Start Screen and another version that runs from the Desktop. Each version has slightly different features.

Charms Menu

There are several ways to navigate back to the Start Screen from the Desktop, and one of the easiest ways is to access and use the Charms Menu. The Charms Menu is a set of commonly used system commands that can be accessed from the right side of the screen. Swipe inward from the right edge of the screen when using a touchscreen device

FIGURE 11-8   Charms Menu in Windows 8.

Screen shot used with permission from Microsoft.

and the Charms Menu will appear. If you are using a mouse, move the mouse pointer to the upper or lower right corners of the screen (Figure 11-8).

The Charms Menu includes options for Search, Share, Start, Devices, and Settings. To access the Start Screen from the Desktop, just access the Charms Menu and click START.

Searching

Since there is no Start button or Start menu with Windows 8, the recommended way to find applications and data files is to use the search function. Just access the Charms Menu and then click SEARCH. You can filter your results by clicking Apps, Settings, or Files.

You can also search from the Start Screen by just typing your search criteria. The Search function will automatically appear and start showing you results as you type.

App Bars

The apps that run from the Start Screen typically do not have traditional menus or ribbon bars across the top of the application. Instead, these apps use App Bars that appear at the bottom or top of the screen to display functions and commands.

To access the App Bar, right-mouse click in an open space on the app or use the keyboard combination Windows Key + Z.

Recent Apps

To see recently used apps, swipe in from the left edge of the screen when using a touch-screen device, or when using a mouse, click the mouse in the upper or lower left corners of the screen. Images of each recently used app will appear along the left side of the screen. To access one of these apps, just click it.

There is also an image of the Start Screen in the list of recently used apps. This is another way to return to the Start Screen from the Desktop.

Closing an App
Applications that you run from the Desktop operate like traditional Windows applications. You can close them by clicking the red X in the top right corner of the screen. Start Screen apps do not have the same interface and do not have an Exit button. To close an open Start Screen app, just click and drag the apps toward the bottom of the screen.

Working with Two Apps on the Same Screen
If you need to work with more than one app at a time on the same monitor, Windows 8 has a feature that positions both apps side by side. Start by opening the first app, and then click the top of the app and drag it down. The app window will shrink, a vertical dividing bar appears, and you can drag the app to one side of the screen and release it there. You can then open a second app, and it will snap into the spare space on the screen. You can click and drag the vertical dividing line to show more of one app or the other.

Shutdown Windows 8
Windows 8 offers "Connected Standby" that allows your computer to go into sleep mode instead of being shut down. If you prefer to go ahead and power off your computer at the end of the workday, first bring up the CHARMS menu, select SETTINGS, click the POWER button, and then select SHUT DOWN. You can also press CTRL + ALT + DEL on your keyboard and then click the POWER button followed by SHUT DOWN.

Working with Contacts
The Start Screen has a built-in People app that keeps track of all your contacts. The People app can be set up to integrate with your email program as well as your Microsoft account, Facebook, Twitter, and LinkedIn. All of your email contacts from these sources will be automatically added to the People app.

To import your contacts from a particular account, while viewing the People app, access the CHARMS menu, click SETTINGS, click ACCOUNTS, and then click ADD AN ACCOUNT. Click the icon for the type of account, then enter the user ID and password. The People app will sync with the account and import your contacts.

You can scroll through your list of contacts by clicking the horizontal scrollbar, or you can search for a particular person by accessing the CHARMS menu, clicking SEARCH, and then typing the person's name. You can use the asterisk as a wildcard when searching.

To view the details about a contact, just click the name. You can view his or her email account, and other information such as the address and details from his or her profile, if the contact was imported from a social media site such as LinkedIn.

To add a new contact, right-mouse click on the blank area of the People app, and from the App bar, click NEW CONTACT. You can then fill in the fields with information about the new contact. Click SAVE when you are finished.

Depending on your preference, you can sort your contacts by first or last name. To change the way your contacts are sorted, access the CHARMS menu, click SETTINGS,

FIGURE 11-9   Mail App in Windows 8.

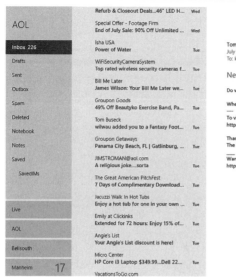

Screen shot used with permission from Microsoft.

and then click OPTIONS. Click SORT MY CONTACTS BY LAST NAME to switch the sorting on or off.

Mail App

Windows 8 has a built-in email app on the Start Screen that can consolidate all of your email accounts into one place (Figure 11-9).

To add an email account, while viewing the Mail app, access the CHARMS menu, click SETTINGS, click ACCOUNTS, and then click ADD AN ACCOUNT. Click the icon for the type of account, then enter the user ID and password.

When you open the email account, you'll see tiles on the bottom left of the screen for each of your email accounts. Click a tile to view mail for that account. You'll see a list of messages to the right. Click a message to see the message displayed.

To create a new email message, click the + button. To delete a message, after selecting it, click the TRASH CAN button. To reply to a message, click the REPLY button.

Email Signature   To add an email signature to your account, when the Mail app is open, access the CHARMS MENU, click SETTINGS, and then ACCOUNTS. Select the account, then click the USE AN EMAIL SIGNATURE switch. Enter your email signature just below.

Email Formatting   The Mail app allows you to format your email messages with different font styles, sizes, and colors, as well as bold, italics, and underlined. Just right-click to show the App bar, then select the appropriate formatting button.

Email Priority   You can designate your email messages with low, normal, or high priority so the recipients will know how important your message is. After creating and writing a message, click the SHOW MORE link under the address fields, then select the priority from the drop-down list.

FIGURE 11-10 Screen Resolution in Windows 8.

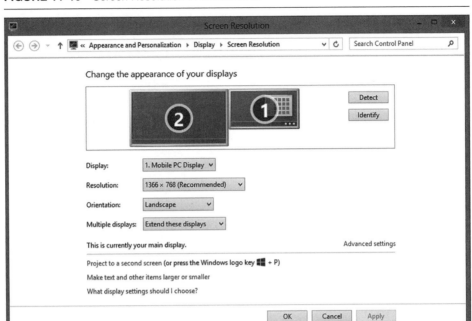

Screen shot used with permission from Microsoft.

Calendar App

Windows 8 includes a Calendar app on the Start Screen that allows you to keep track of your schedule. When you click a date on the calendar, you can create a new event. You can enter the date, time, duration, and location. You can also add a message.

To add reminders, set up repeat events, and to invite other people, click SHOW MORE on the New Event screen.

Connecting to a Projector or Second Monitor

If you need to connect your computer to a projector for a presentation or meeting, it is much easier with Windows 8 than it has been in the past. After connecting the projector to your computer, from the Start Screen, click DESKTOP. Then, right-click the desktop, and select SCREEN RESOLUTION. From the Screen Resolution window, click PROJECT TO A SECOND SCREEN (Figure 11-10).

File Explorer

File Explorer, the file management application that can be accessed from the taskbar on the Desktop, replaces the Windows Explorer available in earlier versions of Windows. Windows Explorer used a menu system, while File Explorer uses Ribbon bars similar to Microsoft Office. The Ribbon is minimized when you first open File Explorer. To show the Ribbon, click the down arrow next to the Help button in the top right-hand corner of the window (Figure 11-11).

FIGURE 11-11   File Explorer in Windows 8.

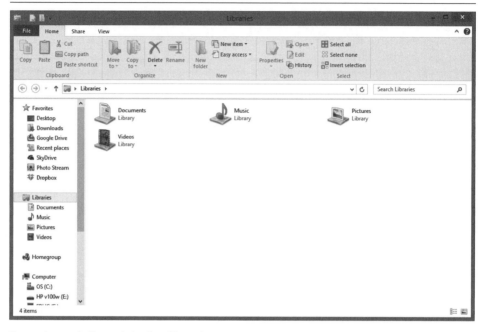

Screen shot used with permission from Microsoft.

Quick Access Toolbar   Just above the Ribbon in File Explorer is the Quick Access Toolbar. This small toolbar includes shortcuts for undo, redo, delete, and rename. You can select which shortcuts you want to display on the Quick Access Toolbar by clicking the down-arrow button and then selecting your choices from the Customize Quick Access Toolbar menu.

Windows Defender

In previous versions of Windows, it was important to install a third-party antivirus program. Windows 8 comes with a basic level of protection with Windows Defender. It defends against viruses and spyware.

You may need to update Windows Defender from time to time. You can do this by accessing the Action Center. To do this, access the CHARMS menu, then click SEARCH, followed by SETTINGS. Then, type "Action Center." When the icon for Action Center is displayed, click it to open it.

On the Action Center window, you'll see an area for Security. Click the down-arrow next to Security to see if Windows Defender is on (Figure 11-12). If you need to update Windows Defender, you'll see a notice that says "Windows defender is out of date." Just click the UPDATE NOW button to download an update.

Windows Update

To keep your computer up to date, make sure Windows Update is set to automatically download and install updates. You can access Windows Update by bringing up the CHARMS menu, then click SEARCH, SETTINGS, and then start typing "Windows Up-

FIGURE 11-12   Action Center in Windows 8.

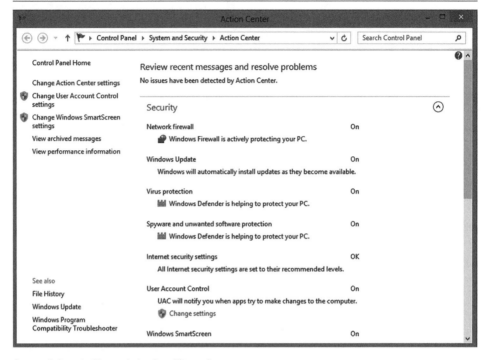

Screen shot used with permission from Microsoft.

date." Click the icon for Windows Update. Click on any important updates and then click INSTALL.

Installing App Updates

You can install apps from the Windows Store that will appear as tiles on the Start Screen. The individual apps may need to be updated occasionally, and they do not update automatically with Windows Update. When updates are available, you will see a number in the bottom right corner of the Windows Store tile. To install updates, click the WINDOWS STORE tile, and then click the UPDATES link in the upper right corner of the screen. Finally, click the INSTALL button.

File History Backup

It is important to back up your files on a regular basis, and Windows 8 has a backup system called File History. You can configure File History to automatically back up your files to an external drive or network drive. If you need to retrieve a file that you backed up, you can restore an older version using File History.

To configure File History, access the CHARMS menu, click SEARCH, and SETTINGS. Then, start typing "File History." Click the FILE HISTORY icon when it appears.

On the File History window, click SELECT DRIVE, and then choose an external or network drive, then click OK. Click TURN ON to begin the backup process (Figure 11-13). If you click ADVANCED SETTINGS, you can select how often the backup occurs.

FIGURE 11-13   File History in Windows 8.

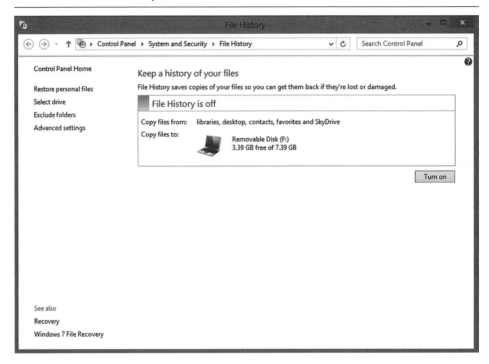

Screen shot used with permission from Microsoft.

If you need to restore a file, you can return to File History and click RESTORE PER-
SONAL FILES.

Task Master

If you are in the middle of something with Windows 8 and the computer locks, Windows 8 will try to automatically fix the problem. If that doesn't work, you can manually close problem applications by using the Task Manager.

The easiest way to access the Task Manager is to press CTRL + SHIFT + ESC on
your keyboard. Task Manager will load. You can then click the PROCESSES tab, find the
problem app in the list, and click END TASK (Figure 11-14).

Recover, Refresh, and Resetting Windows 8

Windows 8 has several built-in tools to help you handle problems with your computer.
You can create a system recovery drive in case your system crashes or your hard drive
fails, you can refresh your Windows 8 installation, or you can reset your Windows 8
installation back to its factory-default settings.

Recovery   You can create a recovery DVD or a recovery flash drive that you can use
if your Windows 8 system fails to startup. To create the recovery drive, first close all of
your applications, then access the CHARMS menu, click SEARCH, click SETTINGS, and
then start typing "recovery." Click the CREATE A RECOVER DRIVE icon. Click YES and

Using Microsoft Windows

FIGURE 11-14   Task Master in Windows 8.

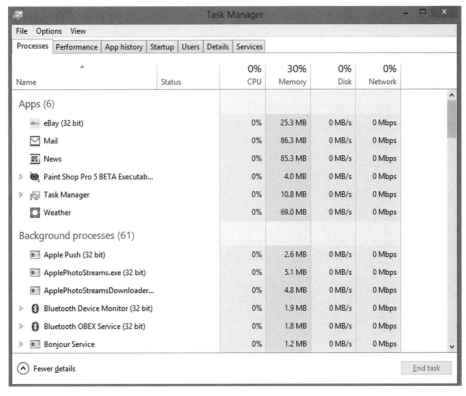

NEXT, and then connect a USB drive. You also have the option of creating a recovery DVD. When you are ready, click the CREATE button. When the recovery drive has been prepared, click FINISH. Label your recovery drive or disc and put it in a safe place.

Refresh   You can refresh your Windows 8 installation without losing your data. Apps that you've installed from the Windows Store on the Start Screen will be preserved, but any other applications installed from the web or discs will be deleted and will have to be reinstalled.

To refresh your Windows 8 installation, access the CHARMS menu, click SEARCH, Click SETTINGS, and then start typing "refresh." Then click the REFRESH YOUR PC icon and follow the on-screen instructions.

Reset   When you switch computers or want to completely reinstall everything on your PC, you can reset it back to the factory-default settings. This process completely removes all your data and applications, so make sure you have backed everything up before you begin.

To reset your Windows 8 installation, access the CHARMS menu, click SEARCH, click SETTINGS, and then start typing "reset." Click the icon for REMOVE EVERYTHING AND INSTALL WINDOWS and follow the on-screen instructions.

TABLE 11-6   Windows 8 Keyboard Shortcuts

Keyboard Combination	Function
Windows Logo Key + Start Typing	Search
Ctrl + plus(+) or Ctrl + minus(–)	Zoom in or out on a large number of items such as apps pinned to the Start Screen.
Ctrl + scroll wheel on the mouse	Zoom in or out on a large number of items such as apps pinned to the Start Screen.
Windows Logo Key + C	Open the Charms Menu.
Windows Logo Key + F	Open the Search charm to search files.
Windows Logo Key + H	Open the Share charm.
Windows Logo Key + I	Open the Settings charm.
Windows Logo Key + J	Switch the main app and snapped app.
Windows Logo Key + K	Open the Devices charm.
Windows Logo Key + O	Lock the screen orientation (portrait or landscape).
Windows Logo Key + Q	Open the Search charm to search apps.
Windows Logo Key + W	Open the Search charm to search settings.
Windows Logo Key + Z	Show the commands available in the app.
Windows Logo Key + spacebar	Switch input language and keyboard layout.
Windows Logo Key + Ctrl + spacebar	Change to a previously selected input.
Windows Logo Key + Tab	Cycle through open apps (except desktop apps).
Windows Logo Key + Ctrl + Tab	Cycle through open apps (except desktop apps) and snap them as they are cycled.
Windows Logo Key + Shift + Tab	Cycle through open apps (except desktop apps) in reverse order.
Windows Logo Key + PgUp	Move the Start Screen and apps to the monitor on the left.
Windows Logo Key + PgDown	Move the Start Screen and apps to the monitor on the right.
Windows Logo Key + Shift + Period (.)	Snaps an app to the left
Windows Logo Key + Period (.)	Snaps an app to the right

Windows 8 Keyboard Shortcuts

Windows 8 allows you to use shortcut keys on your keyboard in order to perform many tasks. Table 11-6 shows a list of Windows 8 keyboard shortcuts.

12

Using Apple Macintosh

Overview of the Apple Macintosh

While many Apple Macintosh computers can run Microsoft Windows in a dual operating system mode, they also feature Apple's own operating system, OS X. Regardless of which operating system is used, Apple Macintosh computers can run the most common business applications including Microsoft Windows.

Navigating with Mac OS X

There are multiple options for finding files and programs in OS X, including the Dock, the Finder, and the Apple Menu.

The Dock is a bar across the bottom of the screen that stores icons for frequently used programs. You can open a program by clicking its icon on the Dock, and when you are working with several open programs at the same time, you can easily switch between them by clicking their Dock icons. You can add a program to the Dock simply by dragging its icon to the Dock.

The Finder is a navigational tool that allows you to locate files and programs stored on the Macintosh. You can access the Finder on either the Dock or the Apple menu.

The Apple Menu can be accessed by clicking the small apple icon in the top left corner of the screen. This menu includes access to the system preferences as well as shutting down the Mac; however, it also includes a list of recently accessed items that makes it easy to open the programs or files that you use the most often.

A shortcut to a program or file called an *alias* can be created and moved to the desktop for easy access. Many Macintosh computers have an alias that represents the computer's hard drive that is positioned in the top right corner of the screen. You can double-click the hard drive icon to find files and programs (Figure 12-1).

Opening and Closing Programs

Mac OS X programs can be found on the Dock, in folders on the hard drive, or on the desktop. Programs are represented as icons.

To open a program from the Dock, single-click the icon. To open a program from its icon on the desktop, double-click the icon.

FIGURE 12-1   Apple Mac OS X.

Screen shot reprinted by permission from Apple Computer.

The normal location for installed programs is the Applications folder on the hard drive. You can access the programs by double-clicking the hard drive icon on the desktop, and then click APPLICATIONS. A window will open displaying icons for all the installed programs. Double-clicking any of the program icons will open the program.

After working with a program, it is best to close the program before you shut down the computer. First, make sure you save your work before closing a program. Each program will have a menu item with the program's name, in addition to typical menus like File, Edit, View, and so forth. To close a program, click the program menu, and then click QUIT. You can also close a program using the keyboard combination command + Q.

Working with Files

It is a good practice to make a backup copy of your work files and then store the backup copy on some type of external storage, such as a network drive, a CD or DVD, or a flash drive. If something should happen to the original file, you can access your work on the backup copy.

To copy a file, first select the file. Then, select the File Menu and click DUPLICATE. The copy will appear in the same location as the original with the word "copy" added to the name.

You can also copy a file by dragging and dropping it onto a different drive. Just open the target drive's window on your desktop, and drag the file you want to copy to the drive window and release the mouse. If the new location where you want to store the copy is on the same drive as the original, you must hold down the option key while you drag and drop.

Dragging and dropping a file from one folder to another without holding the option key is how you move files in order to organize your work. It is a good idea to follow the procedures for organizing your computer files as described in Chapter 8, Keeping Accurate Records.

You can name your files almost anything you want; however, there is a 32-character limit including spacing and punctuation. If your files will eventually be used by you or someone else on a Windows-based machine, it is a good idea to keep the file names short.

To rename a file, select the file, and then click the name a second time. A shaded box will appear around the file name. You can then type the new name. When you are finished, click anywhere else on the screen.

From time to time you should delete old, unnecessary files in order to free up space on your drives. To delete a file, you can drag and drop it on the trash can icon on the Dock. An alternative is to select the file, and then click the File Menu followed by MOVE TO TRASH.

Files that are moved to the trash can stay in the trash until it is emptied. That way if you delete something by mistake, you can click the trash can icon to see a window with icons of all the deleted files. To undelete a file, just drag it back out of the trash can.

When you are certain that the files in the trash should indeed be deleted, in the Finder Menu, click EMPTY TRASH. A dialog box will inform you that the files will be deleted permanently if you proceed. To empty the trash, click OK.

In your role as an administrative assistant, you should organize the files you create in folders. You can create a new folder by clicking the File Menu and then selecting NEW FOLDER. Name your folders the way you would name the file folders in your filing cabinet. You can rename a folder the same way you rename a file. Click the name and a highlight box will appear around the file name. Then type the new name. You can organize your files by dragging and dropping them into the appropriate folders.

There are several options for viewing the files stored within a folder. The View options allow you to select whether you want to view the files as icons, in lists, or in columns. The toolbar on any folder window provides three icons for changing the view of the files. When you view your files as a list, you will see the file name and size, the date it was last modified, and what kind of file it is. When you view your files in columns, the columns will show the hierarchical structure of files and folders, which makes it easy to navigate. You can also arrange you files so they sort according to name, date modified, date created, size, or kind. Clicking the column header will cause the files to sort by the particular header you pick.

Rather than having to click and drag a group of files one by one, you can select multiple files by pressing and holding the command key as you click. After you've made all your selections, release the command key and then drag and drop the group of files.

If you share your files with coworkers but need to prevent their being changed, you should change the permissions on the file. To do this, select the file, and then click the

File Menu. From the File Menu, click GET INFO. Click the arrow next to OWNERSHIP & PERMISSIONS. On the Ownership & Permissions dialog box, click the Access drop-down list and select either READ ONLY access, NO ACCESS, or READ & WRITE ACCESS.

Creating an Alias

An alias is a shortcut that can be used to open files, folders, or programs. Rather than having to navigate using the Finder, you can create an alias and put it on the desktop.

To create an alias of a file, folder, or program, click the item, and then from the File Menu click MAKE ALIAS. The alias will appear next to the original. You can then rename the alias just like any other file and then drag and drop it on your desktop.

If you decide you don't need the alias any longer, you can delete it from your desktop without harming the original file, folder, or program.

Saving Files

Saving files that you create using an Apple Macintosh OS X is almost the same as saving files created in Microsoft Windows. Click the File Menu for the application, and then click SAVE. The Save dialog box is used to add the file name and to select the location where the file will be saved.

To save an existing file with a new name, select the File Menu and click SAVE AS. You can then give the file a new name on the Save As dialog box.

Copy, Cut, and Paste

With an Apple Macintosh, you can easily copy, cut, and paste text or graphics from one place within a document to another or from one document to another. You can perform these tasks using either mouse commands or keyboard commands.

To copy with the mouse, select the text or graphic to be copied, then from the Edit Menu, click COPY. To do the same thing with your keyboard, after selecting the item, press command + C.

To cut something out with your mouse, select the text or graphic to be cut, then from the Edit Menu, click CUT. You can do the same thing on your keyboard by pressing command + X.

To paste something that you have copied to the clipboard, place your cursor where you want the item pasted, and from the Edit Menu, click PASTE. The keyboard equivalent is command + V.

The same process works whether you are copying and pasting within a document or between documents. In fact, you can usually copy and paste items between different Mac applications. Just follow the previous steps to copy the item, then switch to the new document or application, and follow the steps outlined above to paste.

Printing

You can print documents in Mac OS X by clicking the File Menu and then selecting PRINT. The Print dialog box will allow you to select the printer, the number of copies desired, and which page numbers to print. After adjusting the settings, click the PRINT button.

To add a printer to the list, from the Print dialog box, click the printer drop-down list and select EDIT PRINTER LIST. The Printer List dialog box will display. On the toolbar, click Add. From the Printers Menu, select ADD PRINTER. Using the lists, select the printer you want to use, then click ADD. You have the option at this point to make this your default printer by clicking MAKE DEFAULT.

Mouse and Keyboard Commands

One difference between an Apple Macintosh OS X and a Microsoft Windows computer is that the Mac mouse has only one button. In order to perform some of the features typically performed in Windows using a right-mouse click, the Mac uses a combination of mouse and keyboard commands.

The Open Apple or Command key is used in combination with other keys or the mouse to perform shortcuts that you would normally do by accessing a series of menu options. For example, to print a document you can follow the steps described in the previous topic, or you can press Command + P. Most Mac applications use the same keyboard combinations for common shortcuts.

In order to access the right-mouse click menus, holding down the CTRL key while clicking an item, will cause the Quick Menu to appear for that item. You can use the mouse to scroll through the menu a select a Quick Menu option.

Spotlight Functions

One of the most useful features available in Mac OS X is the spotlight feature. Spotlight is an indexing search that catalogs every program and every word of every document on your computer. You can use Spotlight to quickly locate anything on your computer in just a matter of seconds, rather than navigating through folders and trying to find a particular document. To access Spotlight, click the blue magnifying glass in the top right corner of the screen, then start typing the first few letters of the program or file you're looking for, and the results start coming up instantaneously. You can also access Spotlight using the keyboard combination Command + Space.

Print to PDF

It is easy to create Adobe Acrobat PDF files with Mac OS X. Within any program, once you select the Print function, a Print dialog box will display. In the bottom left corner of the dialog box is a PDF button, which allows you to save your file as a PDF file.

Keyboard Shortcuts

Keyboard shortcuts typically use the Command key along with another key to perform actions that could be accomplished with a series of mouse clicks. The following table shows a list of common Mac keyboard shortcuts.

TABLE 12-1   Apple Macintosh Keyboard Shortcuts

Action	Keyboard Command
Open a file	Command + O
Close a file	Command + W
Save a file	Command + S
Print a file	Command + P
Open a new document	Command + N
Cut	Command + X
Copy	Command + C
Paste	Command + V
Check spelling	F7
Bold text	Command + B
Italicize text	Command + I
Select all	Command + A
Undo a previous action	Command + Z
Redo a previous action	Command + Y

Using Apple Macintosh

13

Email

Email is short for *electronic mail*. It involves the exchange of written messages sent over computer networks such as the Internet. In many offices, email has replaced written memos, drop-by office visits, and even phone calls. Email provides a written record of office communications. You can send messages to groups of people simultaneously, attach files, and include hyperlinks to websites. Email is one of the most popular and effective tools for communicating with others over the Internet. With email, you can send a message to anyone in the world who has email access—and, barring technical difficulties, the message will be received in a matter of minutes.

Email Accounts

An email account allows you to connect to a network and the Internet. This is done through an Internet Service Provider, or ISP. The ISP helps you get connected to the network using a dial-up telephone connection, DSL, cable modem, WiFi, or cellular connection. When you establish an account with an ISP, the ISP will provide you with the following:

- *Email address.* In most cases, this will be your name or nickname, followed by the @ sign and an ISP identifier that will most commonly end with the extension .com or .net.

- *POP server.* This is the name of your incoming mail server. POP stands for Post Office Protocol. This is the ISP's computer that receives incoming email messages addressed to you.

- *SMTP server.* This is the name of the outgoing mail server. SMTP stands for Simple Mail Transfer Protocol. This is the ISP's computer that processes the email messages you send.

- *User name.* This is usually the part of your name that appears in your email address before the @ sign. Some ISPs use your entire email address. The user name is used to access the ISP's system along with your password.

- *Password.* This is the secret code you'll use to keep your email private.

In many offices, an administrative assistant will obtain an email account from the company's system administrator. This person will assist you in setting up your computer to send and receive email and will provide you with your user ID, password, and email address.

141

Passwords

Passwords can sometimes be case-sensitive. If your email password is all uppercase letters, you will need to press the SHIFT key while entering your password.

You should never store your password around your computer. Your password should be something that is easy to remember. If you are assigned a password that is hard to remember, change it yourself. Most email systems encourage you to change your password often. The best passwords combine letters and numbers and are at least six characters in length. Never use your name, your user name, your telephone number, your birth date, your Social Security number, or family names as passwords. Also, never use any real word that can be found in the dictionary without combining it with numbers.

Email Programs

Email can be accessed from a website. This is often called Web mail. You can also use email software provided by your ISP. However, in most businesses, the most commonly used email programs include:

- Microsoft Outlook
- Windows Live Mail
- Windows 8 Mail
- Macintosh Mail
- Google Mail (Gmail)

All email programs have similar features such as file folders for organizing mail, toolbars, a menu bar, a message list, and a message view window. The most commonly used toolbar or menu bar commands include:

- New Message—to create a new message
- Print—to print a paper copy of a message
- Read—to view a message in a separate window
- Reply—to reply to a particular message
- Reply to All—to reply to everyone copied on a previous message
- Send and Receive—to send out mail you've written and receive new messages
- Forward—to send an email you've received to someone else
- Attachment—to send a computer file along with your email message

Microsoft Outlook

Microsoft Outlook is a more advanced email management program that is included with the Microsoft Office suite of programs. Microsoft Outlook is one of the most common email programs used by businesses today. In addition to sending and receiving email, users can also manage their personal calendar, schedule meetings with coworkers, and manage contacts. Microsoft Outlook can also be integrated with voice-mail systems so that voice messages can be retrieved and played on your computer. Microsoft Outlook is discussed in more detail in Chapter 25, Using Microsoft Outlook. Figure 13-1 shows a screen image of Microsoft Outlook.

FIGURE 13-1   Microsoft Outlook.

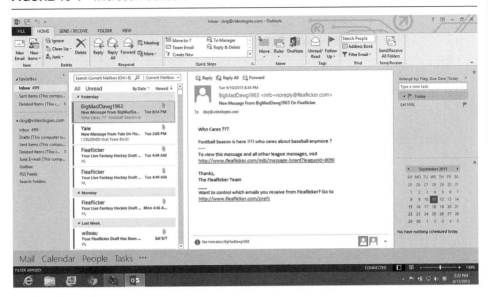

Screen shot used with permission from Microsoft.

FIGURE 13-2   Windows Live Mail.

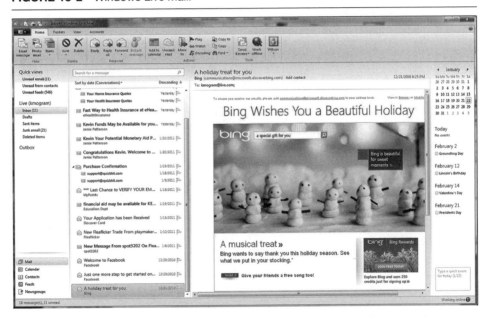

Screen shot used with permission from Microsoft.

Windows Live Mail

Windows Live Mail comes with Windows 7 and functions similarly to Outlook. Windows Live Mail includes a built-in search box that lets you search for specific content in all your email messages. There is also a junk mail filter that helps reduce the amount of spam. Figure 13-2 shows a screen image of Windows Live Mail.

FIGURE 13-3   Apple Macintosh Mail.

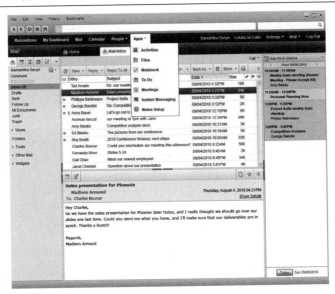

Screen shot reprinted by permission from Apple Computer.

Windows 8 Mail

Windows 8 Mail comes with Windows 8 and is an app that is included as a tile on the Start Screen. Windows 8 Mail is discussed in Chapter 11, Using Microsoft Windows.

Apple Macintosh Mail

Apple Macintosh Mail is a program that comes with the Apple OS X operating system used on Macintosh computers. Mail is a multifaceted program that allows for customizing mail messages with personalized stationary. It can be used as a memo pad and for keeping a to-do list. Incoming email messages can be easily added to a to-do list in order for you to stay organized.

Mail is a full-featured email application that includes most of the same functionality as Microsoft Outlook. Figure 13-3 shows a screen image of Macintosh Mail.

Managing Email

When you receive mail, the email program stores it in your Inbox. When you click the Inbox, you will see a list of messages you have received. When you select a message from the list, the body of the message is displayed in a window. You may read other messages by clicking on the listings in the Inbox window.

The icon to the left of a message indicates whether or not the message has been read. In Microsoft Outlook and Windows Mail, unread mail has a sealed envelope to the left of the message. When you read a message, its icon automatically changes to an open envelope.

After you have read a message, it remains in your Inbox. You can reduce the clutter in your Inbox by moving the messages to other folders. You can also use menu items

FIGURE 13-4 New Mail window in Microsoft Outlook.

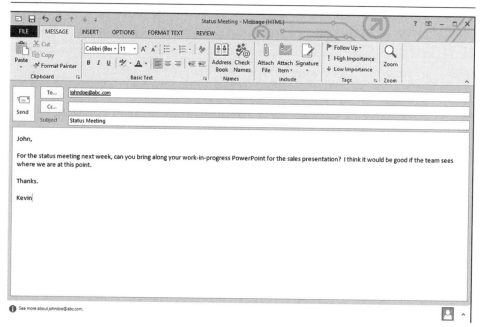

Screen shot used with permission from Microsoft.

to move a message to the Deleted Items folder or, once the message is highlighted, you can simply press the DELETE key.

You can print a message by opening it and clicking the PRINT icon on the toolbar. To compose a new message, you click the NEW MAIL icon on the toolbar. A New Message window then appears. Figure 13-4 shows the New Mail window in Microsoft Outlook.

To send a message, click the SEND button on the toolbar. The message will be stored in the Outbox folder until you click SEND AND RECEIVE. In Lotus Notes, you have to click REPLICATE to send and receive mail.

Sending Attachments

Whenever you email a message to someone, you have the ability to send additional files along with your message as an attachment. In Microsoft Outlook, you click the ATTACH icon on the toolbar. The Insert Attachment dialog box will appear. You can navigate to the appropriate file and attach it to the email message. You'll then see the attachment listed or shown as an icon, along with your message.

When you receive an attachment, the email program lets you know by showing you a small icon next to the message in your Inbox. In some email programs an attachment shows up as a paper clip icon. When you open the message, you will see a listing for the attachment or an icon embedded within the document. Double-clicking the icon will open the attachment file.

Reasons for Sending Attachments

There are a number of reasons one chooses to send someone an attachment. Here is a partial list of reasons:

- The recipient can use the attached file to add, edit, or make revisions.
- You need a document to arrive ready to print and distribute.
- The recipient needs the document immediately.
- You need to send a single document to many different recipients.
- The recipient is going to distribute the document to others.

Alternatives to Sending Attachments

You should avoid sending attachments when they are unnecessary. You can avoid sending attachments by:

- Cutting and pasting word-processing data into your email message.
- Placing the files on a website or File Transfer Protocol (FTP) site for downloading.
- Sending the files on a CD or DVD.
- Faxing the document.
- Printing the document and sending it via regular mail or overnight express.

Problems with Attachments

Email attachments can be big and take a long time to download if the recipient has a slow connection. There can also be translation problems when the recipient doesn't have the right program or the correct program version for opening and using the attachment. In addition, many viruses spread across the Internet through infected attachments.

Email Protocol for Sending Attachments

Unless you send attachments to someone on a regular basis, you should always check with the recipient before sending an attachment. Make sure the person has the right software and can handle downloading the file.

When you send an attachment, use the email message as a cover letter. Explain what the attachment is and why you are sending it. You can use compression software if you are sure the recipient also has the same software. Compression software reduces the file size and download times for users with slower dial-up Internet connections.

Always keep in mind that the formatting of a document may change on the recipient's computer. Many files, such as Microsoft Word documents, are printer-dependent. That means that their layout on the screen and on paper is dependent on what model printer is installed.

If you want to make sure a document will look the same on the screen and when printed on a recipient's computer, use Adobe Acrobat. Adobe Acrobat uses a file format called Portable Document Format (PDF). Adobe Reader, which lets you open and read PDF files, can be downloaded for no charge from the Adobe website at www.adobe.com. To create an Acrobat document, you need to purchase Adobe Acrobat creation software. After the software is installed on your computer, you will be able to create Acrobat documents by printing your document to the PDF printer, which acts as a software-only printer connected to your system. Instead of printing your document on paper, your document is printed as a PDF file and stored on your hard drive.

Attachment Protocol for Recipients

Don't get upset when you can't open an attachment. When this happens, send a reply and explain the problem. If necessary, ask for word-processing documents to be saved as text or have the document printed and mailed.

You should know what kind of attachments you can open. Each program has a file extension—a dot and three characters—added to the file name. The file extension is used by a program to identify its own data files. When you examine an attached file extension, it will tell you what program is needed. The following is a list of common file extensions and the program needed to open them:

- doc and docx—Microsoft Word
- txt—Microsoft Word, WordPad, or Notepad
- rtf—Microsoft Word
- pdf—Adobe Acrobat Reader
- xls and xlsx—Microsoft Excel
- ppt and pptx—Microsoft PowerPoint
- pps—Microsoft PowerPoint
- jpg—Windows Paint
- bmp—Windows Paint
- gif—Windows Paint
- mp3—Windows Media Player
- mov—Quicktime Player
- avi—Windows Media Player
- zip—WinZip or other compressed file

Be careful with executable file attachments. These files are actually programs that could install a virus. Executable file extensions like exe, vbs, com, drv, dll, bin, and sys can easily contain viruses. You should always use anti-virus software and keep it up-to-date. Don't open file attachments from people you don't know. Some viruses come embedded within legitimate files, such as Microsoft Word macro viruses. Because of this, you should always download file attachments to your hard drive and scan them with your anti-virus software before opening them.

Hyperlinks in Email Messages

There is a limit on how large of an attachment you can send with an email message. The maximum size varies depending on the recipient's Internet service provider. One alternative to sending a file attachment is to post the file somewhere on the Internet and to send a link to the file within an email message. In most email programs, when a Web address appears in the body of a message, it shows up as a hyperlink that the recipient can click to view or download.

Organizing Your Email

When you receive messages in your email program, they automatically go to the Inbox. In time, the number of messages you receive may crowd the Inbox and make it difficult to keep track of information. You can create new folders to organize your messages. You can then drag and drop messages from the Inbox to the various folders to store and save them.

It is important for an administrative assistant to keep a good filing system for email messages. You may want to create separate file folders for projects, personnel, clients, or subjects. You can create folders within folders to further organize your messages.

Email Address Book

All email programs have an address book to help you manage your email contacts. There are two ways to generate listings for the address book: you can enter the information manually, or you can add to a list through a menu command. Once you've added names to your address book, you'll want to start using it to address messages.

Signature Files

A signature file is a small text file that can be added automatically at the end of your email messages. Signature files are created in ASCII text format, which is a format that can be read by any program on any computer.

The content of this file should include your name, title, company name, address, phone, company website, and you email address.

Returned Mail

Sometimes a message you send cannot be delivered. When this happens, you will receive a message notifying you that your mail has been returned. There are a number of reasons this could happen. Often, the cause may be temporary problems with your ISP, or the host server of the intended recipient may not have been online when your message arrived. In addition, you may have made an error in the intended recipient's address. Should a message be returned to you, read the routing information that appears at the top of the message. Verify that you sent the message to the proper address. If the problem persists, notify your ISP or the person you're trying to send mail to.

Instant Messaging

Instant messaging is a form of rapid response email that allows a user to send multiple email messages back and forth to another person when both parties are online at the same time. Rather than sending a series of email messages that must be read and replied to individually, instant messaging allows the two users to chat with each by typing short messages to each other.

Instant messaging allows you to store a list of people whom you want to contact with instant messages. You can send a message to anyone on the list who is online.

FIGURE 13-5   Skype Instant Messaging.

Screen shot used with permission from Microsoft.

When you send an instant message to someone, a message window opens where you and the other person can type messages that both of you can see. Figure 13-5 shows a screen capture of Skype.

There are a variety of instant messaging programs available, including:

■ America Online Instant Messenger (AIM)

■ Skype

■ Yahoo Messenger

In addition to being able to type text messages back and forth, the most popular instant-messaging software allows for sending files, images, video, and sounds.

Email Protocol for Administrative Assistants

Since email is a written form of communication, you should follow proper email protocols in order to look professional. You can do this by using proper language and accepted rules.

Addressing Your Email

To send a message to someone, enter his or her email address in the To field. Always verify the correct email address of a recipient. Sending just one email to the wrong person could be a disaster. If a person is already in your address book, many programs fill in the address automatically when you click on the name.

The CC field is for "carbon" copies. You should add recipients to this field when you want them to have a copy of a message but do not need a response from them. You should use this field sparingly, unless you are certain the recipient knows why he or she is receiving a copy of the message. Using this field can be confusing, since many people consider CC messages as FYI (for your information).

The BCC field is for blind "carbon" copies. When you add a recipient to this field, any recipients in the To or CC field will not know the person in the BCC field was copied. In most cases, you should not use the BCC field to send secret messages behind someone's back. This can be an email etiquette disaster. Instead, use the BCC field to send messages to a list of people in order to keep their email addresses private.

Subject Line

Most email recipients decide when and whether to read a message based on the subject line. Always add a subject to the subject line. Some computer novices and ultra-busy executives forget to add a subject line. Even if you have to reply to a message you receive that does not have a subject line, always add one yourself.

Keep your subject short. Many email programs limit the subject line message to forty characters or fewer. Avoid starting your subject out with "RE." Many programs automatically insert "RE:" in the subject line when you reply to a message. You may want to capitalize the subject like a book title; that is, capitalize the first letter of each word except for articles and infinitives.

Always be very specific with your subject lines. A subject like "ISS Meeting on Tuesday" is better than "Meeting." Make the subject meaningful. If the message generates a back-and-forth conversation, you'll know what the message is about after you received it for the third time.

Message Greetings

Email should always have a personal greeting and include customized information. With email, there's no need for the inside address, date, and all the normal things that go into a business letter. However, standard business letter protocol still applies with email.

If this is the first time you have sent an email to a recipient, introduce yourself and explain why you are writing. Be respectful of people you don't know.

Body of the Message

Be respectful of the recipient's time. Keep your messages short. If one sentence will do the job, use one sentence. If you have to switch subjects, it's best to send a separate email so it can be filed separately.

Use the active rather than passive voice in your message. In the active voice, the speaker (or subject of the sentence) is the "doer" of the action being described. In the passive voice, the speaker (or subject) is the recipient of the action. For example, an expression in active voice is: "The committee drafted documents." Alternatively, this idea expressed in the passive voice would be: "Documents were drafted by the committee." Active voice is more direct and more easily understood.

Keep your language gender-neutral. Avoid using sexist language such as, "The salesman should configure his email program." Instead, you could say: "The sales person should configure the email program."

If you make a request in an email message, don't forget to add "please" to your request. If someone does something for you, a polite "thank you" is always nice.

Always spell-check your messages. Most email programs have a built-in spell-check feature. Always proofread your messages before you send them. Many people don't bother to read their messages before they send them, and it shows. Most spelling and grammar errors can be eliminated if you read your messages before clicking SEND.

You can use common abbreviations and acronyms in your business emails if you are certain the recipient understands them.

Avoid using all capital letters in the body of your message. In Internet tradition, this means yelling. However, if you need to emphasize a word—such as DANGER or WARNING—that's okay.

HTML Format Versus Plain Text

You can choose whether to send your messages in HTML format or plain text. The HTML format allows you to format your message just like word processing; however, the recipient must be using an email program that recognizes HTML format. Within an office where everyone is using the same email program, such as Microsoft Outlook, it's okay to send formatted messages using HTML format. With plain text messages, all formatting information is disregarded.

For external emails, you should assume that the recipient is using a plain text email system. Therefore, when you send external emails, you should not use:

- Italics
- Bold
- Underlining
- Multiple colored or sized fonts
- Bullets
- Any special symbols or fonts
- Tabs
- Spacing to indent paragraphs

Even for internal emails, you should refrain from formatting your email to look like a desktop publishing job. Your message format should be basic and easy to read. Use paragraphs, and double-space between them. Don't double-space after periods. Most people now use a publishing style that requires only one space after a period.

Emoticons

Emoticons are little sideways faces created using punctuation marks. For example, the emoticon :-) means smile. Emoticons are often used to signal to your reader that you are being sarcastic or making a statement with a tongue-in-cheek attitude. They can also be used to soften a message.

Use emoticons sparingly. They should be avoided at work.

Sign-Offs

For business email, you should always end your message with a formal sign-off. *Sincerely, regards*, or *best wishes*, followed by your name, are the best salutations for formal messages. For informal communications, you can sign off with just your name. For external emails, always include your contact information: name, title, company name, address, email address, and phone and fax numbers. Alternatively, include your contact information in your signature file.

When to Respond to Emails

In deciding how often to read and respond to email, you must balance your workload between productive work and spending all day doing email. Of course, your manager or a customer should get a quicker response than someone else if you are busy.

With most emails personally addressed to you, you should respond by the end of the business day. Even if the email requires that you perform a task or do some research, you should let the sender know you got the message and when he or she can expect you to complete the task.

You can use templates for frequently asked questions, such as directions to your office. You can create a template message in your word processor and cut and paste it into your email message.

When you send email to external recipients, you should not expect a reply as quickly as you would with an internal email. Unless a message is urgent, you should wait a few days, even up to a week, before resending the message. Remember, if a message is urgent, you can always call on the phone.

Messages Sent to the Wrong Address

If you ever receive an email message by mistake, send a reply to the sender along with a copy of the message, and let the sender know that he or she used the wrong email address. Of course, this does not apply to any junk emails you may receive.

Quoting from a Previous Email

When you reply to a previous email, send a copy of the previous message or a few lines as a quote. This will help the recipient know to which message you are replying. Most email programs automatically copy the previous message if you click REPLY on the toolbar. You have the option of including the entire message or deleting everything except the section you want to reference. You should quote when you are answering a question, when you are commenting on a point made in a previous email, or when you think it will be helpful. If you use selective quoting, you can mark the previous message by using two "less than" symbols (<<) and two "greater than" symbols (>>) on each side of the quote.

When you include a copy of a previous message or a quote, always type your message above the quote or copy. This will prevent the recipient from having to scroll down to find your message.

Handling Email Overload

When you find your Inbox swamped with messages, answer the most recent messages first. This will help you avoid answering questions or dealing with issues that may have already been resolved. In addition, by answering the most recent messages first, you maximize your appearance of promptness.

Don't spend all day reading and replying to email. You should read and respond to all non-urgent messages at one time—perhaps after lunch or at the end of the business day. File or delete messages you have already read and responded to. This will reduce the clutter in your Inbox.

Filtering Messages

There are filters built in to email programs like Microsoft Outlook. Filters allow you to sort messages directly to specific file folders, bypassing your Inbox. Filters do take some time to set up, but they are well worth the time. Some ideas for filters include separating the following:

- Mail from particular people
- Internal email from external email
- Messages that do not include your company's domain name
- Messages where your email address is in the CC or BCC field
- Messages from mailing lists or newsgroups
- Personal email from family and friends

Urgent Messages

You should mark a message as "urgent" or "high priority" only when it really is. Never cry wolf with your email by getting in the habit of marking all your messages "urgent." In fact, when you have an urgent message to send, you should consider whether email is the best medium for the message. Perhaps a telephone call would be more effective.

Return Receipt

On an internal email system, you can choose whether to be notified via email when a recipient receives your message. When the message is read, you get a read receipt.

Return receipts are usually not supported for external emails sent over the Internet. In many cases, the receipt tells you only that the message made it to the recipient's email server. There are delivery receipt options in Microsoft Outlook that give the recipient the option of acknowledging the delivery of the message.

Some email programs allow you to read a message in a preview window without actually opening the message. If the recipient never actually opens and reads your message, you won't get a return receipt.

If you send a message with a return receipt and do not get a receipt, or if you request something and do not get a response, send out a reminder message. For internal messages, give the recipient until the end of the day to respond. For external messages, give the recipient several days to a week to respond.

Rules for Forwarding Messages

Forwarding a message can be both good and bad. It's good because it allows you to easily share information with others. It's bad because any message you forward may end up becoming public.

When is it okay to forward messages? Not as often as most people think. Unless a person gives you permission to forward a message, you should not forward it. There may be many reasons someone would not want his or her message forwarded. The message may be for you only, the tone might not be appropriate for others, or the sender may not want to share his or her email address.

If you don't want a message you send to be forwarded to someone else, how should you let the recipient know? Make it clear that the message is just for him or her.

Before forwarding a message that contains a history of replies, check to make sure that everything in the message is appropriate before you forward. Remove any unnecessary or sensitive content.

Always keep in mind that email is not private. Anything you write might be forwarded. Not everyone follows the correct protocols. One of the best rules to follow for email communication is to not write anything in an email that you would not want someone else to read.

You should never forward jokes and chain letters to anyone at work. You never know when someone might find them offensive. However, if you receive a lot of forwarded messages, you can set up a filter that looks for messages with FW on the subject line.

Is it necessary to reply to forwarded messages? The answer is usually no, unless you find that there is something in the message that specifically applies to you or one of your responsibilities.

Mass Mailings

Any time you need to send a single message to a group of people, you can always just add all of the addresses to the To and CC fields. However, this means you are sharing everyone's email address with everyone on the list. To avoid this, you can either create a group or use the BCC field. When you use the BCC field, none of the email addresses are revealed. You do need to put at least one email address in the To field; however, that can always be your own email address.

You should never use the BCC field to send a message behind someone's back. This is considered impolite.

Creating a Group

Many email programs like Microsoft Outlook will allow you to create a group of email addresses from your address book and save the list with a unique name. When you send a message to the group, everyone in the list receives the message.

Some company email systems have preconfigured groups. Be careful when sending emails to these groups. Know who these individuals are before you include them in a mass mailing.

Reply to All

If you receive a mass mailing and click REPLY TO ALL, everyone on the list will get a copy of your reply. This can be dangerous if done by mistake. When replying to a message, always make sure you click REPLY rather than REPLY TO ALL unless you really do intend to send a reply to everyone on the list.

Some email programs will allow you to set a preference that will prompt you when you click REPLY TO ALL. This feature helps prevent clicking REPLY TO ALL by mistake.

General Email Guidelines for Business

Email is not always the best medium for a message. Sometimes it is best to use the telephone or speak with a coworker in person rather than sending an email message.

Email is appropriate in business communications for things like directions, requests, information to be saved, information to be copied, and company-wide announcements.

What Messages Are Inappropriate for Business Email?

The following are examples of situations where email is an inappropriate medium for communication:

- Thank you notes
- Long memos

- Yes or no answers
- Job praise
- Telling your boss you are sick
- Requests for raises, promotions, or resignations
- Jokes
- Flirting
- Gossip
- Anything illegal or unethical

The Tone of Your Email at Work

When you email your boss, do not use a casual tone, even if you are friends. Keep your emails businesslike. You never know when your boss may need to forward one of your messages to a superior.

Never write an email when you are angry. Take time to calm down before you fire off a message you'll later regret.

International Email

There are special rules that apply to international business emails. Start by addressing the recipient as Mr. or Ms. and his or her surname. Do not use the recipient's first name. Keep the tone of your email formal, and avoid humor that might be misunderstood. Convert all your measurements to metric, and be careful about calendar dates. The date 2/06/17 means June 2, 2017 in Europe, not February 6, 2017. To be clear, always write out the month, day, and year.

If your message concerns money, be specific about what currency you are talking about. If you ask the international recipient to call you, provide him or her with the appropriate telephone country code. Also watch out for time-zone confusion. If you say you'll call the recipient at 5 p.m., make sure you are clear about whose 5 p.m. you mean.

Auto Respond Messages

When you are out of the office for longer than one business day and will not be able to respond to your emails, you should use an out-of-office notice that auto responds to your emails. An auto-respond message can be set up in your email program. It will automatically send a message to anyone who sends you a message while you are away. Your auto-respond message can inform the senders that you are away and will respond to their emails at a specific time when you return.

Email Hoaxes

From time to time you may receive forwarded hoaxes. You should be suspicious of any message that says, "Forward this to all your friends." Many times, these chain letters are simply ways to harvest email addresses for junk emailers.

If you are suspicious that a message may be a hoax, you can check the following websites dedicated to exposing Web-related hoaxes:

- urbanlegends.about.com
- hoaxbusters.ciac.org

You can also do a search of the particular message content in Yahoo.com or Google.com.

Spam

Spam is another word for junk email. These are the unsolicited sales offers and scams that try to trick the unsuspecting email user. Many Internet Service Providers have filters that attempt to eliminate spam; however, many spam messages still slip through. You can reduce the amount of spam you receive by setting up filters that look for subject line phrases like *free, hot, money, hi, hello*, and *info*. You should also report any spam messages to your Internet Service Provider. You can also report spammers to the U.S. government's Federal Trade Commission by sending an email to uce@ftc.gov or fill out a complaint form at www.ftc.gov.

Never reply to spam. This will cause you to receive even more, because now the junk emailer will know your email address is real. Also, never click on any Web links in a spam message or call any telephone numbers listed.

Email Viruses

There are many different types of computer viruses that spread via email. These viruses can clog up your hard drive and slow down your computer, destroy files, compromise access to your computer, and automatically spread viruses to other computers.

One of the most common ways to get a computer virus is from an email attachment. The attached file is either infected or is itself a virus. You should always use anti-virus software and keep it updated. Anytime you receive a file attachment, download it and scan it with your anti-virus software.

Email Privacy

Email is not private. Not only may your messages be forwarded to others, but your company has the right to read anything you write or receive via email. Because your employer pays for the computer, Internet connection, and your time, your business email account belongs to the company. Even if you delete email, it is still available for a company to view. The same rules apply for Web surfing and telephone usage.

14

Using the Internet

The Internet represents a vast global resource for collecting, disseminating, and distributing information. The Internet's underlying technologies enable instantaneous communication and collaboration across the entire globe. Individuals, businesses, educational institutions, communities, libraries, government bodies, and other organizations are able to share information like never before. The popular media have come to call this vast new digital world "cyberspace."

With the Internet, the possibilities are infinite. Businesspeople can check in with the home office from anywhere, or they can email proposals to sales prospects instantaneously. In short, the Internet has changed our perception of time and space.

Simply put, the Internet is composed of millions of computers linked into tens of thousands of computer networks. These networks, which span the globe, are then connected to one another.

The World Wide Web

Today, the World Wide Web (www), generally referred to as "the Web," makes up a very large percentage of total Internet traffic. Just about every for-profit and nonprofit company, university, library, school, and government, as well as millions of individuals, now have a presence on the Web. The Web uses the same underlying protocols as the Internet but has supplemented them with several additional technologies that have made the Internet far more accessible to computer users around the world. These include browser software, search engines, and HTML (HyperText Markup Language).

The Web was introduced to the Internet as a text-only system. With the release of the Mosaic browser—the first graphical browser—in 1993, the popularity of the Web grew. Soon after, Netscape appeared on the scene with its first Web browser, Netscape Navigator. Microsoft also developed its Web browser, Internet Explorer. Both Netscape and Explorer were quickly accepted and surpassed Mosaic in use. Both browsers were faster, contained more features, and were easily acquired by downloading them from websites.

Today, Web documents can include text, graphics, video, and sound. The World Wide Web gives you access to true multimedia documents from all over the globe.

157

Connecting to the Internet

In order to connect to the Internet, you need a modem, network, or Wi-Fi connection; browser software; and an ISP (Internet Service Provider).

Modems, Networks, and Wi-Fi Connections

A modem is a device that translates and transmits signals sent over phone lines, cable, or radio signals. In many personal homes, a cable or DSL modem is used to connect to the Internet. In many businesses, computers connect to a network (commonly an Ethernet network) using cables that connect to each computer.

A wireless network router can be connected to the Internet for broadcasting a radio signal that allows connections without a cable. These wireless networks are called Wi-Fi networks. Laptop computers have built-in Wi-Fi network adapters that can connect to a wireless office network.

Browser Software

Browser software is used to read the documents available on the World Wide Web. Browser programs read, interpret, and present documents. Microsoft's Internet Explorer, FireFox, Google Chrome, and Safari are some of the most widely used Web browsers.

ISPs

ISPs, or Internet Service Providers, are companies or organizations that provide access to the Internet. ISPs maintain several *servers*, which are computers dedicated to providing high-speed access to the Internet.

The speed at which data can travel to and from your computer is determined by a number of factors, including the processor in your computer, the speed of the ISP's servers, and the type of data line connecting computers along the way. Data can be carried on a standard phone line. Improved technology has resulted in the creation of the ISDN line, which can carry data about four times faster than a standard phone line, and the T1 line, which can carry data about one hundred times faster than an ISDN line. Even faster is a T3 line. A T3 line represents twenty-eight T1 lines and has the "backbone" speed of major Internet connections in the United States.

Fast Internet connections are sometimes referred to as "broadband." Broadband connections include the following:

- DSL—a digital subscriber line service that connects at high speed over a telephone line
- Cable modem—a high-speed connection provided by a cable television company
- Satellite modem—a high-speed connection provided by a satellite subscription service
- Wireless modem—a high-speed connection that uses radio and cellular telephone signals

Besides providing direct access to the Internet, some ISPs also contain several options to make your online activity user-friendly and more interesting. These options may include chat rooms, entertainment ideas, travel services, online catalogs for home shopping, and so forth.

Using the Internet

HyperText Markup Language

The Web is based on the principle of *hypertext*. Hypertext is a method of navigating through documents using *links*. Hypertext is a "nonlinear" medium. That is, aside from a site's home page, there is no beginning, middle, or end to hypertext documents. You can link from a home page to a page that discusses the latest news, and then link from that page to a different site altogether for related information.

Links are embedded into a Web page through a coding system called the Hyper-Text Markup Language (HTML). When you activate one of these links by clicking on it, the Web makes the connection to the host computer that houses the document you requested, and it retrieves the documents without involving the user in the underlying file-transfer process.

Web Pages and Websites

A *Web page* is a document, almost like a word-processing document, that can be displayed by your Web browser. Web pages contain text, graphics, sounds, animation, downloadable files, and hyperlinks.

A *website* is an organized group of Web pages. For example, this book could be put on the Web and would be considered a website. Each of the chapters could be considered a web page.

When you visit a website, the first page that appears is called the *home page*. The home page contains links to other pages on the website. If this book were a website, the home page would likely contain a table of contents, with each listing being a hyperlink that would take you to the chapter or page you select.

Internet Addresses

How does the browser find a particular document? It employs an addressing method known as the Universal Resource Locator (URL). Each page on the Web has its own URL. A look at how a URL is put together might make it easier to visualize how documents are found.

Here is an example of a URL: http://www.videologies.com/assistant.htm. The first section (http) is the *protocol*. This indicates the type of Internet service the URL uses; in this case, it is hypertext transfer protocol—http. When typing a URL using a modern browser, you usually do not have to include the http:// prefix. It is automatically added when you access the site. The two slash marks (//) indicate that the next section of the URL will be a domain name. In our example, the *domain name* consists of videologies.com. This is enough information to direct the browser to the host computer. When it reaches the site, it will pull up the default home page, unless a particular file is specified.

Each type of organization has its own domain. A few of the more common domains are listed in Table 14-1.

The last section of the URL—after the slash (/)—specifies a file located within that domain. If you do not enter a specific file name, the URL will generally take you to the home page of the site you are requesting. In this case, we want to reach a particular file named assistant.htm. It will pull up the default home page, unless a particular page is specified—in this example, assistant.htm is the page specified.

TABLE 14-1   Common Domains

Domain	Organization
.com	Business/commercial
.org	Organization
.gov	Government
.edu *or* .k12	Educational institution
.net	Network provider
.mil	Military agency
.co	Country-level domains
.info	Commercial and personal sites
.biz	Commercial
.name	Personal

Using a Web Browser

Many of the features and functions of the Microsoft Explorer browser are the same or very close to those of Google Chrome, Firefox, or Safari. The features you will use the most often include:

- Menu bar
- Toolbar
- History list
- Favorites
- Help
- Address box
- Status bar

Figure 14-1 shows a Web page in Microsoft's Internet Explorer.

The Menu Bar

Menu bars are common to most Windows and Macintosh applications. They include categories of functions you'll use the most often when working. Choices include File, Edit, View, Go, Bookmarks, Tools, Windows, and Help.

The Toolbar

The toolbar includes buttons for the most common functions you'll use when browsing the Web. Toolbars can be customizable with features you use the most often; however, the default versions of the programs include the following:

- Back—to view the last Web page you viewed
- Forward—to return to the original Web page after you have clicked the BACK button to view a previous Web page

FIGURE 14-1   Web page on Microsoft Internet Explorer.

Screen shot used with permission from Microsoft.

- Stop—to stop loading a Web page
- Refresh—to reload a Web page to check for an update
- Home—to load the starting Web page that opens whenever you start your browser
- Search—to access the browser's Web search function
- Favorites—to access a website you have added to your list of favorite websites
- History—to access any of the Web pages you have viewed in the past

Bookmarks and Favorites

All browsers feature a bookmark function that keeps an electronic record of favorite pages. (In Internet Explorer, the bookmark feature is called Favorites.) No matter what it is called, the feature maintains a list of URLs that can be accessed whenever you want to return to your favorite websites.

Printing a Web Page

There are two ways to print a Web page. You can click the PRINTER icon on the browser's toolbar. If you are using Internet Explorer, you can also click the File Menu and then click PRINT. Depending on the type of Web page, the Print window may ask which frame you wish to print. Frames are a way of dividing up the information on a Web page so that it almost looks like a magazine page layout. You can choose to print one particular frame or all of the frames on the page.

Saving a Web Page

You can download and save a Web page to your computer's hard drive. By doing this, you can view the page again without having to be online.

To save a Web page in Internet Explorer, click the File Menu, then click SAVE AS. The Save Web Page window will appear and allow you to browse to a location where you want to save the page.

Downloading and Uploading Files

When you are viewing Web pages with your Web browser, your browser is *downloading* files to your computer. These files are stored temporarily in your computer's memory as you view them. As just described, you can choose to save a Web page to your hard drive in order to access it when you are offline.

Downloading involves the transmission of a file from the Internet to your computer. Sometimes you will find links to files on Web pages that are available for downloading. These files may be data files, new programs, drivers for particular devices, graphics, music, and so forth.

Uploading is the opposite process. You transmit a file from your computer to another computer on the Internet. For example, if you apply for a job online, you might want to upload your résumé. In most cases, this is done by clicking the appropriate link to upload a file, then browsing your computer's hard drive to locate the file you want to send.

If you are involved in publishing documents and other information for websites, you will need to use a File Transfer Protocol (FTP) program. An FTP program works similarly to Windows Explorer. After logging onto a website with a user name and password, you will see two windows on your screen. One window shows the files on your computer's hard drive. The other window shows the files on the website. You can then drag and drop files using your mouse from your computer to the website in order to start the FTP process.

Cookies

Whenever you visit a website, your browser stores information about your visit on your computer. This information is called a *cookie*. A cookie stores information, such as your user ID and user preferences, so you don't have to retype them the next time you visit the site. Cookies are often used by Web marketers to learn your likes and dislikes so they can try to sell products. Unfortunately, this means your privacy is at risk.

You can set your browser to disable cookies if you wish. You can do this by viewing your browser's Preferences or Options Menu.

Search Tools

There are millions of pages on the World Wide Web. How do you begin to find the information you're interested in? Various companies have developed programs that search the Web for the information you're looking for. A number of sites on the Internet provide this service and are commonly called *search engines.*

Search engines serve as a sort of automated reference librarian. Search engines find pages on the Web based on key words you provide. There are a variety of engines and tools to help you find what you're looking for. For example, Google.com, Bing.com, and Yahoo.com can help you find sites on the Web.

Yahoo! is a Web guide that organizes listings into categories and subcategories. It is among the most popular search tools because it allows users to register their own websites. You'll be able to find the latest additions to the Web using Yahoo!

The list of categories in a Web guide is most useful when you have a broad subject in mind. The guide's hierarchical structure can help you narrow your topic as you go along. For instance, you could search an extremely broad topic, such as "weather," using the categories provided by a Web guide.

The following is a list of popular search sites:

- Google: www.google.com
- Bing: www.bing.com
- Yahoo: www.yahoo.com
- Ask: www.ask.com
- AOL: www.search.aol.com
- My Web Search: www.mywebsearch.com
- Blekko: www.blekko.com
- Lycos: www.lycos.com
- Dogpile: www.dogpile.com
- WebCrawler: www.webcrawler.com
- Info: www.info.com
- Infospace: www.infospace.com
- Search: www.search.com
- Excite: www.excite.com
- Good Search: www.goodsearch.com
- Duck Duck Go: www.duckduckgo.com

Conducting a Search

Because of the sheer volume of information on the Web, broad searches generate a great number of results.

Some search engines don't return results based on categories and concepts. Instead, they look for the occurrence of the key words you put in your search request within all the documents in their registries. This approach has both advantages and disadvantages.

The main advantage is breadth. A search for the key word "hurricane" may turn up interesting documents that refer to hurricanes but are not entirely devoted to hurricanes. For instance, a general science magazine may have a good article on hurricanes. While you may not find it in a directory search, because it wouldn't be listed under the category "hurricanes," you would likely find it in a key word search. A disadvantage is that, in addition to useful references, you'll also pull up every page with the word "hurricane," whether it's relevant or not.

The simplest way to get good results from a search engine is to determine in advance precisely what you are looking for and then enter as many words as you can think of to describe it. Thus, while searching for "hurricanes," you should use the engine AltaVista. AltaVista ranks the search findings by matching them to the search text. If your search text involves a number of words or phrases, AltaVista will rank Web pages that have all the search text requirements above those that contain only a single element of the search text. For example, Web pages containing all the words of the search text "hurricane, radar, image, Atlantic, ocean," will be ranked above those that contain only one or two of those words.

Effective Search Strategies

Two key terms used in comparing search engine performance are *recall* and *precision*. Having a high recall rating indicates that a search engine returns a great number of documents from a search. High precision refers to the percentage of returns that actually match your search criteria. The goal on which to focus is to increase the precision of your searches.

You can achieve more efficient search results through the use of *search syntax*. There are a few simple syntax elements that can greatly help you to refine your search. Incorporating search syntax into your queries makes each search far more effective in finding the information you want. In other words, it will increase the precision of your search.

Advanced searching alerts the search engine to the relationship between your key terms. You can specify that *all* your terms must appear, *any* of your terms must appear, or that the terms must appear in a specific order. Moreover, you can specify that certain words do not appear. This feature would be helpful if you were searching for information on pythons and wanted to exclude documents dealing with the British comedy group Monty Python.

You indicate the relationships between your key terms by placing *operators* between them. For example, adding a plus sign (+) between words in your search will produce results that include all of the words in your search. *Note: Be sure to refer to a search engine's Help page before doing an advanced syntax search. The Help page will indicate which operators are recognized in that search engine.*

Boolean Searches

HotBot also lets you perform Boolean searches. This is the search syntax that professional research librarians use. While Boolean searches can get complicated, knowing a few of the operators involved will help you refine your searches. The following are some useful operators. (Note that they are typed in all capitals.)

AND	Placed between two words to indicate that the document must contain both words
OR	Placed between two words to indicate that the document can contain one or both words
NOT	Placed before a word to indicate that this word must not appear in the document
NEAR	Placed before a word to indicate that these words must occur within ten words of each other

Using the Internet

Searching Within a Site

You've seen that there are many ways to search. However, just because you have found a good site, it doesn't mean that the search is over. You'll find that even good sites contain a lot of filler. The goal is to cut through the filler and find the material that is useful and helpful to you. It is easy to get lost in a large website. Here are some standard rules for searching a very large website:

- Clearly identify the desired information. In other words, clarify the search.

- Think through the possible search terms that could be used.

- Remain focused in your search. Don't be pulled into surfing if you are trying to find something specific.

Error Messages

When using a browser, an error message can come up for a number of reasons. Different problems will generate different error messages.

The Web is a dynamic and ever-changing environment; while pages are constantly created, others are removed. If you encounter a page, or a site, that does not exist, you will receive an error message. Here are some of the error messages you may encounter:

- *Unable to Locate Server*—If the browser is unable to locate a particular host computer (also called a server), you receive a message indicating the situation.

- *Page Does Not Exist*—If you try connecting to a specific Web page that does not exist, you receive another type of error message. Rather than a dialog box, an actual Web page appears, advising you that the site you requested is not a valid URL.

- *Server Busy or Unavailable*—When there is too much traffic on the Internet, or if you try to access an overwhelmingly popular site, you may receive an error message.

Plug-Ins

Your Web browser has various features that allow it to display graphics, play sounds, and run animations. Some specialized tools are required to access content on certain websites. For example, some sites provide streaming audio or video content. These sites usually require a special plug-in be installed in order to access the content.

Some of the most common plug-ins include Apple Computer's QuickTime Player, Adobe's Flash, and Acrobat Reader.

Websites of Interest to Administrative Assistants

The following websites may be of special interest to administrative assistants:

- 1-800-Flowers—www.1800flowers.com—an online florist

- All One Search—www.allonesearch.com—a search engine for finding reference sources, quotes, and other language usage resources

- Amazon.com—www.amazon.com—an online bookstore that is searchable by title, author, or topic; also sells CDs, DVDs, and other products

- American Management Association—www.amanet.org—Resources and training information for administrative assistants and their managers

- Bankrate.com—www.bankrate.com—a listing of mortgage rates across the country

- Better Business Bureau—www.bbb.org—a list of Better Business Bureau services

- BusinessTown.com—www.businesstown.com—a site dedicated to business resources that includes sample letters and forms, travel information, accounting and finance, and office procedures

- Career Builder.com—www.careerbuilder.com—a listing of thousands of job postings, resume listings, and employer information

- CitySearch—www.citysearch.com—a listing of entertainment, restaurants, hotels, and shopping for various U.S. cities

- CNN—www.cnn.com—an online news resource

- Dice-www.dice.com—a listing of job postings

- Dictionary—www.dictionary.com—an online dictionary and thesaurus

- EDGAR Online—www.edgar-online.com—a repository of corporate filings by public companies to the Securities and Exchange Commission

- E-Trade Financial—www.etrade.com—an online stock trading resource

- Expedia Travel—www.expedia.com—an online travel agency for booking airline flights, hotels, and car rentals

- Federal Express—www.fedex.com—an express shipping service for overnight letters, packages, and freight

- FindLaw—www.findlaw.com—a directory of legal resources, law firm listings, and legal news

- Fodor's Online Travel Guides—www.fodors.com—a listing of restaurant and hotel reviews for various cities around the world

- Idea Café—www.ideacafe.com—a collection of resources available for small businesses

- InfoSpace—www.infospace.com—a search engine that finds telephone numbers, addresses, and email address of people nationwide

- Insure.com—www.quotesmith.com—a website with information on various types of insurance products

- Internal Revenue Service—www.irs.gov—The website of the IRS, with downloadable tax forms and tax information

- LinkedIn—www.linkedin.com—a social networking site for professionals

- MapQuest.com—www.mapquest.com—an online map that can provide driving directions between any two streets in the United States

- Monster.com—www.monster.com—a listing of job postings

- National Fraud Information Center—www.fraud.org—information on common scams
- New York Times—www.nytimes.com—an online version of the newspaper
- Office Depot—www.officedepot.com—an online office supply store
- Office Max—www.officemax.com—an online office supply store
- Priceline.com—www.priceline.com—a resource for purchasing air travel, hotels, and car rentals at reduced prices
- Small Business Administration—www.sba.gov—a listing of resources available for starting, financing, and running a small business
- Staples—www.staples.com—an online office supply store
- Travelocity—www.travelocity.com—an extensive travel guide for booking air travel, hotels, and car rentals anywhere in the world
- True Careers—www.truecareers.com—a listing of job postings
- United Parcel Service—www.ups.com—a shipping service for packages
- U.S. Census Bureau—www.census.gov—a website with statistical listings for individuals and businesses
- U.S. Federal Government—www.fedworld.ntis.gov—a resource listing U.S. federal government websites, publications, agencies, tax information, and jobs
- USA Today—www.usatoday.com—an online version of the newspaper
- Wall Street Journal—www.wsj.com—an online version of the newspaper
- Weather Channel—www.weather.com—an online weather report for anywhere in the world
- WebMD—www.webmd.com—a website with an extensive library of health-related information
- Zip Codes—zip4.usps.com/zip4—a site that lets you locate zip codes by typing in an address and a city

Using the Internet

15

Web Conferencing

Overview of Web Conferencing

Web conferencing is growing in popularity as a way to hold meetings with people from different locations without having to leave the office. A Web conference (sometimes called a webinar) allows the meeting to take place at a central online location so participants can share PowerPoint slides, view software demonstrations, or brainstorm ideas using a shared whiteboard. By combining a Web conference with an audio teleconference—where participants interact over the telephone—there's almost no need for in-person meetings.

Typically, an administrative assistant will handle all aspects of setting up and running a Web conference at which his or her manager will be a speaker or presenter. By having someone who focuses solely on the technology aspects of the Web conference, it frees the presenter to focus on the content and interactions with the participants.

Businesses often use Web conferencing for marketing meetings, sales presentations, training sessions, human resources announcements, employee orientations, and shareholder meetings. Web conferencing can help slash travel budgets, save travel time, and encourage more interaction between distant groups of people. The lack of face-to-face interaction can be solved by adding interactive polling, question and answer sessions, software application sharing, and video cameras.

Web conferencing vendors provide the software necessary for hosting a Web conference and the support necessary for teleconferencing. By signing up with a vendor, you can get an account, install the software, and begin hosting your first Web conference in a matter of minutes. Some of the most popular Web conference vendors are the following:

- InterCall—www.intercall.com
- WebEx—www.webex.com
- GoToMeeting—www.gotomeeting.com
- Citrix—www.citrix.com
- Lync Online—office.microsoft.com/en-us/lync/

Web Conferencing Software

Many Web conferencing vendors offer feature-rich software applications that allow for a dynamic interactive experience. Some of these features include:

- *Application Sharing*—Allows for sharing a software application on the presenter's desktop with the participants of the Web conference. Control of the application can be passed to conference attendees to demonstrate features, make changes, or collaborate. Application sharing is often used in training sessions, where the presenter acts as an instructor demonstrating how to use new software.

- *Screen Sharing*—Allows for sharing anything on the presenter's screen with the participants of the Web conference. This is often used when the presenter wants to demonstrate features of the computer's operating system or show two or more software applications simultaneously.

- *Presentation Sharing*—Allows the presenter to upload a PowerPoint slide presentation to share with the conference participants.

- *Whiteboard*—Allows the presenter and participants to draw diagrams and write notes on the screen.

- *Monitoring*—Allows the presenter to see a roster of attendees, to control access to shared documents and shared applications, and to grant co-moderator status.

- *Audio Controls*—Allows the presenter to mute or un-mute the participants' phone lines.

- *Web Tours*—Allows the presenter to display Web pages and share them with the conference participants.

- *Annotation Tools*—Allows the presenter and attendees to control an on-screen pointer, highlight parts of the screen, draw objects and diagrams, and type text on the screen.

- *File Transfer*—Allows the presenter to share files with the participants.

- *Chat*—Allows the attendees to type messages to the presenter or to each other. This feature is often used by the presenter to take participants' questions throughout the Web conference.

- *Polling*—Allows the presenter to provide a set of questions with multiple-choice answers to quiz the participants or to get feedback.

- *Recording*—Allows the presenter or individual participants to record a presentation in order to watch and listen to it later.

- *Web Camera*—Allows the presenter and participants to add webcams to the Web conference in order to see each other.

- *Reporting*—Allows the presenter to see a report following the Web conference showing the roster, participant activity, chat, and polling results.

- *Virtual Computer Lab*—Allows the presenter to send participants to specially configured computers for hands-on training.

Organizing a Web Conference

To hold a Web conference, you need a computer with an Internet connection, Web conferencing software, and a telephone line. The conference participants can access from a dial-up Internet connection if that's all they have available; however, it's recommended that the presenter have a high-speed Internet connection such as a DSL, a cable modem, or a T1.

To start a meeting, you use the Web conferencing software to schedule a specific date and time. The software then lets you send out invitations to attendees, with information on how to join the Web conference. The attendees can then join the conference by following the instructions in their invitation to sign on to a particular website or by clicking a hyperlink that automatically connects them to the conference. The attendees may need to install the Web conferencing software, which is a process that takes only a few minutes the first time they use the service.

Securing Your Meeting

One way to make sure that only invited participants attend your Web conference is to require a conference password. You can specify a password for each meeting and include it in your invitation. Since you may use the same account for many Web conferences, it is possible that someone who attended a previous session could attend a current session if you fail to password-protect the conference.

Another way to secure your meeting is to schedule an unlisted meeting. Unlisted meetings do not show up on the meeting calendar for your account.

You can also require your attendees to register for the meeting. You can then accept or reject each registration request.

Teleconference Information

Most Web conferencing vendors also offer teleconference services that provide you with a toll-free call-in number along with an access code and personal identification number. The call-in number and access code are included in the conference invitation. The presenter calls in first and uses the personal identification number to start the call.

One low-cost option is to use an Internet phone conference, using Voice over Internet Protocol (VOIP) technology. With this technology, the audio portion of the Web conference is transmitted over the Internet. The presenter and participants must use microphones and speakers connected to their computers in order to talk and listen. Usually, a VOIP teleconference is best if only one person, usually the presenter, is talking.

Microsoft Outlook Integration

Many Web conferencing vendors have software that will integrate with Microsoft Outlook's meeting scheduler. By installing the Outlook integration software, a presenter can schedule a meeting in Microsoft Outlook and include Web conference information in the meeting request. The meeting request serves as a conference invitation to the participants. The request also schedules the meeting automatically on the presenter's Web conference account calendar.

Participant Systems Check

A systems check is a quick process that participants need to go through in advance of the Web conference. This process usually involves having the participant do a pre-meeting installation of the Web conferencing software. Most Web conferencing vendors have a link on their websites that allow new users to install the necessary software before the Web conference.

To reduce the number of technical issues at the beginning of your Web conference, you should provide step-by-step instructions in your invitation that encourage participants to perform a systems check and to install any necessary Web conferencing software. Even if participants have attended Web conferences using the same system in the past, it is still a good idea to have them test their system. Changes to the vendor's software, upgrades to a user's computer, or even operating system and browser security updates could cause the Web conferencing software to suddenly stop working.

Some participants may have trouble installing the Web conferencing software during the systems check because of restrictions on software downloads put in place by the information technology (IT) department. These restrictions are usually put in place for security purposes and to help prevent the spread of computer viruses. If this happens, the user may try to install the Web conferencing software and nothing will happen. If possible, the presenter should contact the IT department and find out if any of the participants will have this issue. If so, make sure you consult with the IT department to authorize the download and to provide instructions for participants on how to work around this issue.

Sample Meeting Invitation
Figure 15-1 is a sample invitation for a Web conference using WebEx.

Planning Your Web Conference

As you plan your Web conference presentation, use the following checklist:

- Determine your discussion topics first. Remember, less is more, so try not to cover too much information in one session.

- Decide how much time should be spent on each discussion topic. It's best if your Web conference lasts no more than sixty to ninety minutes. It is difficult to keep participants' attention beyond this length.

- Think about what the participants will see on the screen for each of your discussion points. Try to spice up the presentation visually, rather than just using text bullets for every discussion point. Use pictures or charts when possible to illustrate your points.

- Identify ways you can add interactivity to your meeting so you can test your participants' understanding. You can use polling and chat questions, breakout sessions, or a shared whiteboard, or you can turn over control of a software application to the participants.

- If more than one person will be facilitating the Web conference, decide who will present each portion of the presentation. Decide how you will transition from one person to another. Will you all be in the same room, or will each of you be connected to the conference separately?

- Identify in advance who will field questions from the participants. You may want to line up several subject matter experts and have them join the conference in order to answer questions.

Sample Web Conference Agenda
Because a Web conference can get fairly complicated to produce, it's a good idea to create an agenda for the facilitators in advance of the conference. This is especially important if you plan to utilize tools such as a shared presentation, application sharing, polling questions, and so forth. Table 15-1 is a sample agenda for a new product rollout.

FIGURE 15-1 Sample Web conference invitation.

Hello,
You are invited to attend a Web conference using WebEx.

Session Details
Topic: Isha Foundation
Date: September 23, 2015
Time: 10:00 a.m. EST
Session Number: 46297
Session Password: Sadhguru
Teleconference Number: 1-800-555-2973
Teleconference Pass Code: SJV101

To access the conference, you will need to conduct a systems check well in advance of the meeting to ensure you are able to view the Web content. Even if you have attended a Web conference using WebEx before, it's important to conduct a systems check. Site configuration changes, such as an upgrade, can affect your computer's ability to access the Web conference.

To Perform the Systems Check:
1. Go to http://www.webex.com
2. Click the **Training Center** tab.
3. Click **Set Up** on the left-hand side of the screen.
4. Click **Training Manager.**
You will be prompted through a short software setup to determine if your computer is compatible. If your computer fails the system check, contact WebEx technical support at _____.

To Join the Session on the Internet:
1. Log on to http://www.webex.com
2. In the box under the words "if you know your meeting number, join here," type the session number and then click **Join**.
3. Follow the prompts for a short software download to access the Web conference.
4. Dial into the audio portion of the call.

Thank you

Presenting at a Web Conference

Keep the following tips in mind in preparing for the Web conference, running it, and handling post-conference tasks.

Preparing for the Web Conference

Always test your access to the conference software, your presentation, and other features that you intend to use before the actual conference. Hosting a conference in a conference room away from your regular computer may result in technical issues that should be resolved in advance.

TABLE 15-1   Sample Web Conference Agenda

Time	Discussion Topic	Presenter	What Participant Sees	Test for Understanding
10 min	Welcome/introduction • Welcome • Conference guidelines • Agenda • 4 Ps of marketing	Jennifer	PowerPoint Slide 1 PowerPoint Slide 2 PowerPoint Slide 3 PowerPoint Slide 4	Sign in using Chat Polling questions
15 min	Product • Definition • Features • Future enhancements • What's in it for me?	Kevin	PowerPoint Slide 5 Shared Browser Shared Browser PowerPoint Slide 6	Allow participants to direct
5 min	Pricing • Packages • Marketplace fit	Jim	PowerPoint Slide 7 PowerPoint Slide 8	Polling questions
15 min	Promotion • Marketing efforts • Advertising • Talking points • Ask for the sale	Jennifer	Shared Browser Shared Browser PowerPoint Slide 9 Sale Document	Allow participants to direct Download document
5 min	What happens next • Launch date • Your role • Our role	Kevin	PowerPoint Slide 10 *Your Role* Document *Our Role* Document	Polling questions Download document
10 min	Open forum/questions • Feedback • Questions • How to log out	All	Whiteboard Chat	Polling questions

Make sure all the files and documents you want to share are organized in a single folder so you can easily locate them during the meeting. Always clear your Web browser's cache before beginning a meeting. It's also a good idea to restart your computer before launching the Web conferencing software. This ensures that there aren't any conflicts from other applications you may have been running earlier.

If you plan to use polling, create all the questions before the meeting start time. Some Web conferencing software allows you to create and save your polling questions. Other systems may require that you enter them manually during the conference. If you have to enter them manually, you should type them into a word-processing document and then be ready to copy and paste them into the Web conferencing software.

Always join the Web conference and teleconference at least ten to fifteen minutes before the scheduled time. Be prepared to help participants join the Web conference. You should be familiar with the steps for installing the Web conferencing software for first-time attendees and assisting users whose computer skills may be lacking.

The administrative assistant should assist the presenter in driving the presentation and interacting with the Web conferencing software. This allows the presenter to focus on the message rather than the technology involved. The assistant can also monitor the chat window to see questions and respond to them without bothering the main presenter.

Include a welcome slide for your presentation that includes the title and teleconference access number. This gives the participants something to see when they first join the Web conference. Include meeting guidelines and technical assistance information on the second slide in your presentation.

Running the Web Conference

During the presentation, minimize background noise by telling participants to turn off their cell phones. Remind the participants to avoid sidebar conversations, or use the audio controls to put the participants on mute. If you will be un-muting their phones at the end of the conference to take questions, remind the participants not to put the conference call on hold. If their telephone system plays background music, everyone will hear the music.

Remind everyone how to use the Web conferencing software's features to ask questions, raise their hand, or to send chat messages.

During your presentation, use the annotation tools to point to areas on the slide, highlight text, and write notes. When you move from one slide to the next, wait a few moments for your participants' screens to catch up.

When sharing a presentation or document, open the application with which it was created and share the application. For example, if you have a PowerPoint presentation, rather than uploading the slides, you can open the presentation in PowerPoint on your desktop and then share the open PowerPoint application. This allows you to make edits if necessary.

Use Web browser sharing to take participants on a Web tour, rather than giving them a Web address and asking them to review the site later on their own. By taking them on a tour, you can ensure that they see the features you want. Use the full-screen mode when showing slides, sharing applications, or conducting Web tours.

If a brainstorming discussion occurs, use the whiteboard feature to take notes. This keeps everyone focused on the Web conference and allows everyone to follow along. In addition, most Web conferencing software allows you to save the whiteboard text at the end of the conference.

Provide handouts to your participants at the beginning of the meeting. If you are conducting a PowerPoint slide presentation, you can share the presentation and allow participants to print a copy. You can improve the performance of your presentations by limiting the number of animations, slide transitions, and screen captures. Try to limit the number of slides in your presentation to no more than thirty slides. If you must have more slides to cover your content, create a separate presentation and switch presentations in the middle of the conference.

Keep a watchful eye on the time. If discussions get too lengthy, ask participants to hold their questions until the end.

Give your participants a break if your Web conference is going past ninety minutes. Everyone needs a chance to stretch and use the restroom after ninety minutes, so add an "intermission" to your longer conferences. Just tell everyone to leave the Web conference running and return to the conference at a specified time.

It's always considerate to record the presentation for invited participants who are unable to attend. Most Web conferencing vendors allow you to record the on-screen activities and combine them with the telephone audio for access at a later time. Some vendors require special equipment in order to capture the telephone audio, so make sure you check with your vendor before you attempt to record a session. If you decide to make a recording, make sure everyone knows the call is being recorded.

If by accident you are kicked out of your own conference because of some technical glitch, don't panic. Just communicate what happened over the audio part of the call and then log back in. This is also good advice to share with your participants who may have the same thing happen to them. If they lose the audio or Web portion of the conference, they should simply log back on or call back in.

Handling Post-Conference Tasks

When your conference ends, thank everyone for participating. If you made a recording of the presentation, let everyone know when the recording will be available. You can send out a post-meeting email to the participants that includes a hyperlink to the recorded version.

Be sure to hang up the phone and close the Web conferencing software when you are finished. Be careful about making any comments about what happened during the conference, in case you are still connected and some of the participants are still listening.

When you close the Web conferencing software, save the chats, polling questions, and whiteboard text that was created during the conference. Some systems will save these items for you automatically.

Web Conferencing

16

Data Security

Information = Profit

Information about your company is valuable, not only to your company but also to unscrupulous people outside your company. Such information includes confidential records such as bank transactions or corporate credit card numbers. It also includes paper or computer files about customers, new products, sales strategies, and so on. Consider how damaging it would be to your company if such records were lost or destroyed or if they were stolen by a competitor. That's why data security is critical to protect computer information from theft, misuse, and disaster.

The misuse of computer information ranges from unauthorized use of computer time to criminal acts like sabotage. It all falls under one general category that many people call "computer crime." Surveys show that over half of the government departments and industrial organizations in the United States have experienced some form of computer crime. Because of this growing epidemic, it's important that you understand the different types of computer crime in order to protect yourself and your company's information.

Determining What Is a Crime

There are different degrees of computer crime, from breaking into other people's computers in order to steal or sabotage data, to making illegal copies of software to give to a friend. All of it is wrong.

Probably the most often committed offense is theft of computer time. It ranges from the innocent borrowing of someone's computer without permission to the theft of computer time from a business for personal use and gain. Theft of computer time—especially involving large computers, such as one running an office network—can easily translate into a theft of money. Besides the theft of time, unauthorized use of a computer also involves unnecessary wear and tear on the equipment and software.

The best way to judge whether a personal activity might be considered a criminal act is to compare it with the use of a company vehicle. Would it be wrong to borrow a company car or truck without asking? Would it be wrong to use the company car on the weekend for personal use? Would it be wrong to fill up one's personal car with gas and charge it to the corporate account? We know your answer is "Yes, it would be wrong," so keep this comparison in mind when using business computer equipment and software yourself and when overseeing others' use of it.

Threats from Outside

Today's companies are using computer communications in ever-increasing ways, and these same applications are in the hands of criminals. Working from the privacy of their own homes, would-be criminals often gain access to an organization's computers for the purpose of stealing or altering information. This electronic trespassing or vandalism has several variations, which are referred to by their own slang terms:

- *Hacking*—breaking into computer systems to gain access to restricted or private information
- *Crashing*—breaking into a computer system in order to shut it down or turn it off
- *Trashing*—altering or erasing a computer's data files
- *Viruses*—malicious computer programs that destroy data or open unauthorized access to a computer

Threats from Inside

One of the most serious threats to the security of business data comes from insiders: those working within a company who decide to misuse computer or data files as a form of vengeance or for financial gain. This type of computer crime is extremely harmful, since it may involve information worth thousands and thousands of dollars. If a computer crime happens in your company, any insider could be a suspect. However, there are certain individuals who are likely to be investigated first:

- Disgruntled employees often take their vengeance out on the computer system in the form of sabotage.
- A competitor or an employee who has recently quit or been terminated may be responsible for theft of computer data or software.
- Outside users of a computer system via a communications system may attempt authorized sale of information, such as customer lists.
- Computer programmers may attempt to take their programs with them or to create hidden embezzlement schemes.
- Computer operators may alter or erase data on purpose.
- Computer system engineers may attempt to alter security information or passwords.

Software Piracy

Software piracy is another major computer crime problem. Individuals are sometimes allowed to make copies of their programs for protection purposes, but the sale and/or the distribution of those copies to friends and other computer users is a violation of federal copyright laws.

With the growing concern over the copying problem, many software publishers have been forced to devise elaborate copy protection schemes. Piracy may not affect your company directly, but the cost of combating piracy is eventually passed along to you as the consumer.

Data Security

Apprehending Criminals

Computer criminals have often been hard to apprehend as a result of a lack of understanding on the part of law enforcement agencies and the judicial system. However, things are beginning to change. Many states are leading the way with special legislation aimed at stopping software piracy. Other new laws make it a crime to trespass electronically on a computer system even if there is no damage or theft. Many cities are establishing special police units to combat computer crime.

Protecting Your Company's Data

Audit Logs

There are steps you can take to protect your company's data from these human threats. Audit logs are a record of who has been using a computer system. As a user logs onto a computer, it records the time, the name of the user, the files that person accesses, and when the person logs off. The computer then keeps the data in a special security file.

In some cases, an audit log can tell whether files have been altered. The use of audit logs is usually provided as part of security password software that can be installed on individual computers. If a computer crime occurs, the log can furnish the authorities with evidence they might need to prosecute.

Codes

Special data encryption techniques code your data files and your communications automatically. Someone who is attempting to intercept and manipulate the information would receive a file that looks like random symbols, thus preventing use of the data.

Computer Viruses

One type of computer crime that is a big concern to even the smallest business is the computer virus. A virus is a program developed by a computer vandal who finds pleasure in creating havoc. This program "infects" other programs, causing them to malfunction or to fail completely. Viruses are passed from computer to computer via email and by copying files from one computer to another. Some viruses will only display messages; others can damage your hard drive and the files stored there. Some virus programs even try to extort money from victims in order to receive a software antidote.

To combat the rapidly growing virus problem, there are a variety of virus protection software programs available on the market (Table 16-1). The key to selecting and using one of these programs is to purchase the most current edition and then update it on a regular basis.

Most virus protection programs are designed to look for and destroy viruses that are known at the time the program was written. As new viruses appear, an older virus protection program may fail to detect them.

Symptoms of Viruses

When a virus attacks your computer, you may see the following effects:

Data Security

TABLE 16-1   Anti-Virus Software

Company	Internet Address	Anti-Virus Software
Microsoft	www.windows.microsoft.com/en-us/ windows/security-essentials-download	Windows Security Essentials
Norton	www.norton.com	Norton Internet Security
ZoneAlarm	www.zonealarm.com	ZoneAlarm Extreme Security
F-Secure	www.f-secure.com	F-Secure Internet Security Suite
Kaspersky	www.kaspersky.com	Kaspersky Internet Security Suite
Trend Micro	www.trendmicro.com	Titanium
Panda	www.cloudantivirus.com	Panda Cloud Antivirus
G Data	www.gdatasoftware.com	G Data Antivirus
AVG	www.avg.com	AVG Internet Security
Frisk Software	www.f-prot.com	F-PROT Antivirus
Eset	www.eset.com	NOD32 Antivirus

- The virus continuously makes a copy of itself and uses up all the free space on your hard drive.
- A copy of the virus may be sent to all of the addresses in your email address list.
- The virus may reformat your hard drive and wipe out all your files.
- The virus may install hidden programs that allow people to access your computer without your knowledge or permission.
- You experience a sudden degradation in system performance.
- Your anti-virus software stops working for no reason.
- Strange messages appear on your screen.
- Strange music or sounds play from your speakers.
- A program installed on your computer suddenly disappears.
- Your computer will not start.
- There is a lot of communications activity.
- The computer takes a long time to start.
- You get "out of memory" error messages.
- You cannot install new programs.
- A disk utility such as ScanDisk reports serious errors.
- A disk storage partition suddenly disappears.
- Anti-virus software indicates a virus has been found.

Data Security

Firewalls

The only way to make a computer completely secure is to not use other people's data files and to completely disconnect from the Internet. Obviously, this is not practical. A firewall is a security system that protects a computer from attacks. It blocks access to a computer's communications ports, monitors the installation of new software, and controls which programs have access to the Internet.

There are both hardware and software firewalls available. Hardware firewalls are usually available within network routers and broadband modems. Software firewalls are available within Microsoft Windows and as add-on software products.

Firewalls block both incoming and outgoing threats. Incoming threats come in the form of communication port scans that look for an entrance into a computer in order to affect it with a virus. An outgoing threat occurs when a computer becomes infected with a virus or spyware. These malicious programs attempt to communicate with other computers on the Internet to spread themselves and steal information. A firewall limits access to only the programs the user authorizes.

Windows Defender is a firewall that is available with Windows. Internet security programs, such as Norton Internet Security and ZoneAlarm, are also available.

Maintaining Your Computer's Security

To prevent virus infections, hacker attacks, and other types of computer crime, do the following:

- Always use anti-virus software and keep it updated with the latest virus signature files.
- Install operating system security updates and software updates.
- Install and use firewall software.

Acts of Nature

Mother Nature can be an enormous threat, even causing a computer system to fail and lose data permanently. Floods, lightning, tornadoes, hurricanes, and fires could completely destroy your office computer and all your data files, resulting in the failure of the business and loss of everyone's job, since business records, client lists, accounting records, and much more would all be lost.

Electrical surges or voltage spikes can damage the computer's important electronic components. These surges can also disrupt and scramble data storage media like the hard drive. A complete power outage can shut down a computer system, causing loss of all data in the memory. (Steps you can take to prevent such problems can be found below.)

Mechanical Problems

Mechanical problems can cause storage media such as the hard drive to fail, resulting in the loss of all data stored there. Sudden changes in temperature or humidity, or bumping or dropping a computer system when the hard drive is operating, can result in what's called a head crash—or hard drive failure. (Again, steps to prevent such problems appear below.)

Data Security

A Security Checklist

There are a variety of ways to protect your company's data and make it more secure from both human and natural threats. You may wish to use some of these methods for your own computer. If you have office management responsibilities, you may also want to make changes for your entire department or company. To protect your data:

- Investigate theft prevention devices, which can lock a computer to a desktop.

- Prevent electrical noise and power surges from damaging your computer system through the use of surge suppressors. A surge suppressor plugs into the wall, and the computer system plugs into it for power.

- Get even more security with a device known as an *uninterruptible power supply*. It will power your computer system for a limited period of time in the event of a power outage. Then, if an outage does occur, you'd have ample warning to save your data.

- Make a backup copy of all data stored. The methods to back up your data range from printing out your files on paper to making regularly scheduled backups of your files on CD-ROM or DVD-ROM, backups on network drives, or backups on Internet or "cloud" drives.

Coping with Disaster

It is a good idea to insure your company's computer system and software. If you work in a small company, you may want to check with your boss to see if he or she has this insurance. But in the case of a disaster, getting reimbursed for the cost of the equipment can't ever replace the valuable data that the business relies on.

Most large organizations have disaster plans that shift data-processing jobs from one location to another and protect data by storing them in two or more locations. A small business should also have a disaster plan just in case. As secretary, you can get the ball rolling.

A good disaster plan should address the following questions:

- Is backup computer equipment available?
- Are backup software and data files available?
- What should employees do in the event of a disaster?
- What projects and tasks have priority?
- Are essential business supplies available?

Taking the time to create a disaster plan and to inform all employees in the company that it is essential. If the company is very small, even having an extra computer system, software, and supplies at someone's house may be a good start. It's like an extra insurance policy, and it may help all of you keep your jobs should disaster strike.

Data Security

17

Troubleshooting Computer Problems

There is nothing more upsetting than being in the middle of an important project and having trouble with your computer. Almost every computer user has experienced times when his or her computer didn't operate properly. Perhaps the computer crashed and lost your work before you saved. Perhaps the computer started running very slowly or wouldn't turn on at all. In many cases, just turning a computer off and back on does the trick. This process, called rebooting, resets the computer's memory, processes, and programs.

Sometimes, though, you need to do more than reboot, but you must determine what you should do. Many people are afraid to troubleshoot computer problems; the solutions, however, to some of the most common problems can be quite simple. With some help, you can diagnose and correct most problems.

In most large offices, a computer Help Desk is available. If you experience a problem, you can call the Help Desk and someone will come to take a look at your computer. In smaller businesses, you may have to call an outside vendor, who may first attempt to troubleshoot the problem over the telephone. Whether you work for a large or small business, though, the result is the same: lost time.

This chapter will help you troubleshoot some of the most common problems yourself so you can get back to work without waiting for a service technician. There are separate sections for Windows PC troubleshooting and Macintosh troubleshooting. Make sure you consult your owner's manual before you open your computer and attempt any repairs yourself.

Microsoft Windows PC Troubleshooting

Computer Won't Turn On

If your computer won't turn on, you first need to check the simple stuff. Look to make sure the power cord has not come loose from the wall or the back of the computer. Check the switch on the surge protector. Make sure the surge protector is turned on and plugged in. Has the surge protector blown a fuse? If so, you may be able to push the reset button to reset the surge protector. Make sure there is power to the wall outlet where the computer or surge protector is plugged in. Will anything else work in this outlet?

Computer Freezes or Crashes

Freezing occurs when the computer become completely inactive. There are no error messages, the mouse doesn't move, and the computer does not respond to keyboard commands. Crashing is similar to freezing, but the computer usually displays some type of error message. A program may close unexpectedly, but the rest of Microsoft Windows continues to function.

If your computer freezes or crashes frequently, it could be the sign of a hardware problem. Sometimes this is the result of a device that is not installed properly, such as a new video card, memory, or a hard drive. Sometimes a component will fail after the machine has warmed up.

Usually, it's a good idea to have a computer technician examine your computer when you experience frequent freezing and system crashes.

Computer Comes on with a Blue Screen

If you turn on the computer and a blue screen appears that says the computer was not properly shut down, it will normally begin doing a scan for errors. This occurs when the computer was improperly shut down the last time you used it. The system scans for errors on the hard drive that can occur when you turn off the hardware without shutting Microsoft Windows down properly. To properly shut down the system in Windows 7, always go to the Start Menu on the taskbar and click SHUT DOWN from the pop-up menu. In Windows 8, access the CHARMS menu, click SETTINGS > POWER > SHUT DOWN.

Computer Runs Very Slowly

There are several reasons your computer might start running very slowly, ranging from viruses to the system's not having enough memory or hard drive space. Use anti-virus software to help combat viruses. To check your system memory in Windows 7 or earlier, click START, CONTROL PANEL, SYSTEM AND SECURITY, SYSTEM. To check your system memory in Windows 8, access the CHARMS menu, click SEARCH, SETTINGS, and start typing "System". Then, click the SYSTEM icon. The System window will tell you how much memory your system has. It is recommended that your system have at least 4 GB of RAM. If your system has less, see about getting more memory. Figure 17-1 shows the System window in Windows 8.

While viewing the System window, you can adjust the performance of your Windows system by clicking ADVANCED SYSTEM SETTINGS. There you will find a setting for performance. Click the SETTINGS button for Performance. You can then adjust the visual effects for better performance. On the Advanced tab of the Performance Options box, you can adjust the processor settings, memory usage, and virtual memory. Virtual memory is necessary, but the use of it by your computer slows your system. With virtual memory, when your computer system runs low on RAM, it offloads some of its memory to your hard drive. Since your hard drive is much slower than RAM, your computer is forced to slow down.

Another thing to check when your computer appears to be running very slowly is the space available on your hard drive. In Windows 7 or earlier, click the Start Menu, click COMPUTER, then right-click on the c: drive icon, and then click PROPERTIES. In Windows 8, from the Start screen, click DESKTOP, then click the FILE EXPLORER icon on the taskbar. You can then right-click on the C: drive icon. The Properties box shows the capacity of the C: drive as well as how much space is used and how much space is still available. Figure 17-2 shows the C: drive Properties box.

FIGURE 17-1   System window in Windows 8.

Screen shot used with permission from Microsoft.

If most of your C: drive is being used, this can cause your system to run slowly. If this is the case, try using the Windows Disk Cleanup program, which will suggest files you can delete. To access Disk Cleanup in Windows 7 or earlier versions, click the START button on the taskbar, and then click ALL PROGRAMS, ACCESSORIES, SYSTEM TOOLS, and DISK CLEANUP. In Windows 8, access the CHARMS menu, click SEARCH, click SETTINGS, and type "Disk Clean". Then, click FREE UP DISK SPACE BY DELETING UNNECESSARY FILES. Windows then checks the drive and the Disk Cleanup program begins to run. The Disk Cleanup program tells you how much space can be freed and displays a list of files that should be deleted. You should run Disk Cleanup once a month to manage the space on your hard drive.

Another thing you can do to improve your computer's performance is to defragment your C: drive. Over time, the files on your computer begin to get fragmented and stored on various open spaces on the drive, rather than being stored as one contiguous file. Because the files are broken up over multiple locations, this process is called fragmentation. When the computer goes to access one of these fragmented files, it takes longer to load. The Disk Defragmentation tool optimizes the performance of your computer by reorganizing the files on your hard drive into contiguous blocks. You should defragment the files on your hard drive once month.

To run Disk Defragmentation in Windows 7 and earlier versions, exit all the programs and turn off your screen saver. Then, click the Start Menu, click COMPUTER, then right-click on the C: drive icon. Then click PROPERTIES. Click the DEFRAGMENT NOW button to begin the process.

FIGURE 17-2   C: drive Properties box.

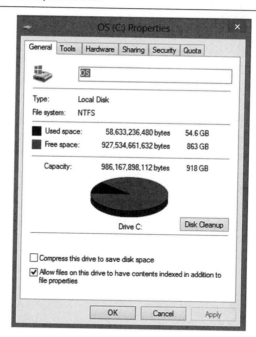

In Windows 8, access the CHARMS menu, click SEARCH, click SETTINGS, and type "Disk Defrag." Then click DEFRAGMENT AND OPTIMIZE YOUR DRIVES.

The Monitor Is Blank

Many computers have a built-in energy saver that will put the system to sleep after a period of time. The monitor appears to be off, while the power light goes from green or blue to amber or black. To wake up your system, just move your mouse around or type a key on the keyboard. After a few moments, the system will power back on.

If the system is not in sleep mode, check to make sure the power switch is turned on. When the power is turned on for a monitor, the power light will usually show green or amber. Green tells you that the monitor has power and is receiving a video signal from the computer.

If you can't see the power light, check to see if the power cord is tight in the back of the monitor and to the power strip or wall socket. Also make sure the monitor video cable is tightly connected to both the back of the monitor and to the back of your computer.

If the power is on and all the cables are okay, check to make sure the monitor's brightness and contrast controls are not turned down. These controls are on the monitor; however, the location varies depending on the manufacturer.

Before assuming the monitor is broken, you might want to try another monitor connected to your computer. If that monitor works, then you can probably isolate the problem to your original monitor. If the replacement monitor also doesn't work, then the problem is likely with your computer's video card or the integrated video on the system board. In either case, you should have the computer serviced.

No Signal Input Sign on Monitor

Sometimes the monitor comes on and you see a box on the screen with red, green, and blue stripes, along with the message "No signal input." This means that the monitor is on but it's not receiving a signal from your computer. Just turn on the computer first, before turning on your monitor.

Mouse Won't Work

If your computer's mouse won't work or stops working while you are in the middle of a project, try the following troubleshooting steps. Check to make sure the mouse is connected to the computer. If the mouse cable is disconnected, reconnect it and, if necessary, restart your computer.

Sometimes just turning your computer off and then back on will cause a nonfunctioning mouse to start functioning again. You can also try using a different mouse. If there is an unused computer around the office, try borrowing its mouse to conduct a test. It is best to turn off the computer, connect the replacement mouse, and then turn the computer back on. If the replacement mouse works, then you've isolated the problem to your old mouse. It's probably time to buy a new one.

If you just installed a new mouse and it doesn't work, you must also install the new mouse software.

If you are in the middle of working when your mouse stops working, you can press the CTRL + s keys on the keyboard to save your work. Table 17-1 shows the keyboard shortcuts if your mouse stops working.

Keyboard Won't Work

If your keyboard stops working, check to make sure the keyboard is connected to the computer. If the keyboard cable is disconnected, reconnect it and restart your computer.

Another thing you can do is press the CRTL + ALT + DEL keys on the keyboard at the same time to bring up the Task Manager. Use the mouse to select a program that says "not responding" and click the END TASK button. Repeat this process until all the tasks are ended. Check to see if the keyboard starts working again.

Sometimes just turning the computer off and back on will cause the keyboard to start working again. If your mouse is still working, click START on the taskbar, and then click SHUT DOWN. Unplug the keyboard connection from the back of the computer and reinsert it tightly. Wait a few moments and then restart the computer.

Number Keypad Doesn't Work

The NUM LOCK must be on for the number keypad to work. If you press the NUM LOCK key on the key pad, the NUM LOCK button will light on the keyboard. The NUM LOCK key is located in the upper left corner of the number keypad.

Keyboard Error or No Keyboard Found

If you start your computer and see a message that says "Keyboard Error" or "No Keyboard Found," then the computer is not seeing the keyboard. Check to make sure the keyboard cable is connected to the computer.

Check to see if any lights display on the keyboard. Press the NUM LOCK button on the number keypad of your keyboard and see if the NUM LOCK light appears.

TABLE 17-1   Keyboard Shortcuts If the Mouse Stops Working

Keys to Press	Action It Causes
Windows logo keys or CTRL + ESC	Opens the Start Menu located on the taskbar
CTRL + ALT + DELETE (DEL)	Opens the Close Program dialog box, which contains a list of applications to be closed and command buttons for Ending Task, Shutting Down, and Cancel
ALT + F4	Closes all open programs and shuts down
Windows logo key + R	Opens the Run dialog box
Windows logo key + M	Minimizes all open windows
SHIFT + Windows logo key + M	Undoes minimizing of all windows, tiles horizontally, tiles vertically, or cascades windows
Windows logo key + E	Opens Windows Explorer, My Computer
Windows logo key + D	Minimizes all windows and undoes minimizing of all windows
tab	Moves focus to next option in open window
enter	Chooses the OK button, opens a window selected using Window key + TAB
esc	Closes a dialog box, cancels
Windows logo key + BREAK	Opens the System Properties box
Windows logo key + TAB	Selects the taskbar buttons
CTRL + N	Opens a new document
CTRL + O	Opens the Open File dialog box
CTRL + S	Opens the Save dialog box
CTRL + P	Opens the Print dialog box
UP arrow or DOWN arrow	Selects the previous or next item
PAGE UP or PAGE DOWN	Selects the item up or down one screen
HOME or END	Selects the first or last item in the list box

Try switching keyboards with another computer. If the replacement keyboard works, then it's probably time to toss your old keyboard and get a new one.

Printer Won't Work

If the printer isn't working, you need to determine if the problem is with the printer, the cable, or your computer. Check the printer's owner's manual for information on how to use the printer's built-in self-test mode. When the printer is in self-test mode, it will print a test page. If the self-test is successful, you can assume the printer is OK.

Test the connection between your computer and the printer in Windows 7 by clicking START, DEVICES and PRINTERS, and then right-click the icon of the printer that is not responding. Click PROPERTIES and then click the PRINT TEST PAGE button. If Windows can't print a test page, then click the printer cable and make sure it is connected. In

Windows 8, you can access your printer by accessing the CHARMS menu, and clicking DEVICES.

If multiple printers are available, try printing to another printer. If you can print to another printer, then your computer is okay and there's a problem with the connection to the other printer or with the failing printer itself.

Check to make sure the printer isn't having paper feed problems. Check to make sure the printer doesn't need a new ink jet or toner cartridge.

Is the printer shared on the network? If so, then usually a shared printer is connected to another computer on the network. That computer must be turned on before the shared printer is accessible.

Non-System Disk or Disk Error

If the computer makes a funny sound, your hard drive may have failed. Try turning off the computer and turning it back on. If that doesn't work, contact your Help Desk or call a computer repair company.

Operating System Not Found

If you receive a message that the "operating system was not found," this usually means there is a problem with the hard drive or with your installation of Microsoft Windows. Try running the Windows Install disk to repair your Windows installation.

Numeric Error Code Displayed on Screen

When the computer displays a numeric error code, there could be a problem with the hardware settings stored in the computer's BIOS (basic input-output system). Turn the computer off and restart it. If that doesn't help, call your Help Desk or contact a computer repair company.

HDD Controller Failure Message

When the computer displays a message indicating that there is an error with the FDD or HDD controller, there is a problem with the hard drive or the cables that connect them. Turn the computer off and restart it. If that doesn't help, call your Help Desk or contact a computer repair company.

Hard Drive Won't Save or Load Files

One of the first symptoms that your hard drive is having a problem is that it will have trouble saving or loading files. One way to check the health of your system is to run the ScanDisk utility. If your computer was not shut down properly, when the system restarts, ScanDisk will automatically run to check for errors. You can also run ScanDisk yourself, performing either a Standard scan, which checks files and folders for errors, or a Thorough scan, which will test files, folders, and the disk surface for errors.

To start the ScanDisk tool, exit all programs and turn off the screen saver by right-clicking the WINDOWS DESKTOP and selecting PERSONALIZE from the pop-up box. Click the SCREEN SAVER icon, and then select NONE from the drop-down box. Click the APPLY button and click OK. Then in Windows 7 or earlier versions, click the START button, ALL PROGRAMS, ACCESSORIES, SYSTEMS TOOLS, and then SCANDISK. In Windows 8, access the CHARMS menu, click SEARCH, click SETTINGS, and type "Scandisk". Then, click DEFRAGMENT AND OPTIMIZE YOUR DRIVES.

Beeping Noises During Startup

Beeping sounds usually mean there is a problem with the computer's hardware, such as the video card or memory. Turn the computer off and restart it. If that doesn't help, call your Help Desk or contact a computer repair company.

Windows PC Software Troubleshooting

Program Locks Up

When a program locks up while you were in the middle of work, test to see if the keyboard is still responding by pressing the CAPS LOCK key. Try typing CTRL + Z to undo whatever you just did or press the ESC key.

If necessary, restart the computer by typing CRTL + ALT + DEL. This will bring up the Windows Task Manager. You can then check the status of the running applications. If any of the programs have a status of Not Responding, click that program, and then click the END TASK button. The bad news is that whatever you were doing on the program since the last time you saved will be lost. If necessary, restart the computer by typing CTRL + ALT + DEL to bring up Windows Task Manager. Then click SHUT DOWN from the menu, and then click RESTART.

If nothing else works, press the START button on your computer and hold it for ten seconds to restart the system.

Computer Starts in Windows Safe Mode

Windows Safe Mode is a limited version of Windows that loads when your computer is having trouble. Windows is smart enough to know when there's a problem and will automatically run Safe Mode, or give you the option to load Safe Mode, when your start the system.

In some cases, you may want to force the computer to load into Safe Mode. You can do this by holding down the F8 key on the keyboard just before Windows would normally start loading. You'll see the Windows Startup Menu and you can select Safe Mode from the list of options. You can tell you are in Safe Mode because the screen resolution will be a standard 640 × 480 resolution with 16 colors and you'll see the words "Safe Mode" on the screen.

In Windows Safe Mode, the system loads with a minimum set of device drivers so the PC can function at a basic level. You won't be able to print or use the Internet, but you can still do some troubleshooting. For example, if you installed new software that caused a problem, you could load Windows in Safe Mode in order to uninstall the program.

Not Enough Virtual Memory Message

If your computer has been on for a while and you have used several different programs, you may need to restart your system. If you repeatedly get a message that there is not enough virtual memory, you may need to have additional memory installed in your computer.

As stated earlier in this chapter, virtual memory is actually hard drive space that is used as system memory when your computer runs out of RAM. In Windows 7, you can adjust the amount of hard drive space that is used for virtual memory by clicking the

START button, CONTROL PANEL, SYSTEM AND SECURITY, SYSTEM, and ADVANCED SYSTEM SETTINGS. Click the SETTINGS button. On the Performance Options box, click the ADVANCED tab. In the Virtual Memory section, click the CHANGE button. You can click the drive you want to use for virtual memory and the amount of space you want to use for this purpose. When you are finished, click the SET button, then click OK. Click OK again on the Performance Options box, followed by OK on the System Properties box.

In Windows 8, access the CHARMS menu, click SEARCH, SETTINGS, and start typing "System". Then, click the SYSTEM icon, and ADVANCED SYSTEM SETTINGS.

Fatal Exception Error

If you are running a program and suddenly a blue screen appears with the message "Fatal Exception Error," the only way to respond is to restart your computer. Any changes made since your last save will be lost. Fatal exception errors can occur when you are working on a file from a removable storage device such as a flash disk, and you remove it before the system has finished reading from it. Sometimes a particular program will cause fatal exception errors on a regular basis. You might also get fatal exception errors after installing a new program or a new device. If this happens, use Windows Safe Mode to uninstall the program. Check the software or hardware vendor's website for the correct software or drivers for your operating system. If you install incompatible software or hardware drivers, it could be the cause of fatal exception errors.

Missing Program Error Message

If you normally start a program from a shortcut icon on the desktop and suddenly one day get a Missing Program error message, this usually means that the program has been deleted or moved or become corrupted.

If you moved the program, delete the old shortcut on your desktop and create a new one. The program may have been accidentally deleted. Search your computer for the missing program by clicking the START button, then clicking SEARCH. (In Windows 8, access the CHARMS menu and click SEARCH.) If you find the program, try running the program from its new location. If the program appears to be missing, you may have to reinstall the program.

Using System Restore (Windows 7)

System Restore allows you to take your computer back in time to a point where you know it was working okay. To use this feature, you must first enable it by scheduling restore points. To access System Restore, click START, ALL PROGRAMS, ACCESSORIES, SYSTEM TOOLS, and SYSTEM RESTORE. Choose CREATE A RESTORE POINT, and then click NEXT. Name the Restore Point, then click the CREATE button. When the process is finished, click CLOSE.

To restore the system back to your restore point, start System Restore, and then choose RESTORE MY COMPUTER TO AN EARLIER TIME. Click the NEXT button, and then pick the date of your restore point. Click NEXT, and then click NEXT again. Click the OK button. You can set System Restore to automatically create Restore points at various times each week.

For information about Windows 8 file history, refreshing, and recovering, see Chapter 11.

Apple Macintosh Troubleshooting

Apple Macintosh systems can also experience problems ranging from system startup issues to software issues. Make sure you consult your owner's manual before you open your computer and attempt any repairs yourself.

System Does Not Start

If your Macintosh won't start when you turn on the power, first check the power cord at both ends. Make sure it is securely connected to the back of the Mac and to the wall outlet or power strip. If the computer is connected to a power strip, make sure the power strip is connected to the wall outlet and turned on. Check to make sure the power strip hasn't blown a fuse. You can check this by bypassing the power strip and plugging your Mac's power cord directly into a wall outlet.

Check the other cables and connections, such as the keyboard and mouse cables, and any network cables. Check all the cables carefully for bent pins. Sometimes a bent pin will cause the system to short electrically and the system won't power on to protect itself.

Also check the screen brightness and make sure the brightness and contrast are not turned down low.

System Starts and Freezes

If your Mac starts up and then freezes, try restarting the system. Unplug all peripheral devices except for the mouse and keyboard. For example, unplug any printer, network cables, scanners, or other USB devices. Then try restarting the system again. If it starts, you can troubleshoot which peripheral device is having problems by reconnecting them one by one and restarting each time.

Sometimes programs add plug-ins to the system. These plug-ins are called *extensions* in the Macintosh world. To see if a software extension is causing the problem, restart the computer while holding the SHIFT key down. This turns the extensions off. If the computer restarts, then remove all the extensions and add them back one by one. Restart the Mac after each addition. You can manage your extensions using Extensions Manager.

System Starts with Sad Mac

If the system starts with a sad Mac icon, restart the system using the Mac OS operating system disk and reinstall the system. Then run a hard disk drive checking tool such as Disk First Aid, MacCheck, or Norton's Disk Doctor.

Applications Unexpectedly Quit

If you have an application that quits functioning, close all your applications and restart the computer. If the program continues to quit periodically, try reinstalling the program. Check online and make sure the program is compatible with the system software you are using. Check the stats for the amount of memory needed to run the application.

Application Busy or Missing

If you try to open a data file and get the message "Application Busy" or "Application Missing," you should locate the application and start it first, then try opening the file.

Computer Troubleshooting

If the application won't open, try reinstalling it. If there are two copies of the application, delete one.

System Locks Up

If you are in the middle of doing something and the system locks up, type COMMAND – OPTION + CONTROL + ESCAPE and then select YES to force quit. Save all documents, quit all applications, and then restart the Mac.

To prevent system crashes, add more memory to the system, check for duplicate system folders, or duplicate applications.

You should also use Extension Manager to look for any extension conflicts. If necessary, use the installing disks to install a clean version of the operating system and any applications.

Time and Date Incorrect

If the time and date are incorrect, and you make changes but the changes won't stick, you may need to reset the PRAM (Parameter Random Access Memory) or rebuild the desktop. Control Panel settings that won't stick can also be a signal that the system board is going bad.

Control Panel settings are stored in PRAM. To reset the PRAM, turn off the system completely and then turn it back on. As the system is powered on, hold the COMMAND + OPTION + P + R keys until the system makes two chimes.

To rebuild the desktop, restart the system while holding the COMMAND + OPTION + SHIFT keys until a message appears. Then click OK.

Hard Drive Problems

If your hard drive makes a funny sound or if you have trouble reading or saving files from your hard drive, restart your Macintosh and run the Disk Utilities program. If you can't access the hard drive, try to reinstall the Macintosh operating system from the installation disk.

Also try resetting the PRAM and rebuilding the desktop. To reset the PRAM, as the system is powered on, hold the COMMAND + OPTION + P + R keys until the system makes two chimes. To rebuild the desktop, restart the system while holding the COMMAND + OPTION + SHIFT keys until a message appears. Then click OK.

Monitor, Printer, Keyboard, and Mouse Problems

To troubleshoot monitor, printer, keyboard, or mouse problems on the Macintosh, follow the same procedures outlined earlier for troubleshooting problems with a Windows PC.

CD Won't Eject

If you have a CD or DVD that is stuck inside the Macintosh, press the SHIFT + COMMAND + I key. Then restart the computer. While restarting, press the mouse button. If this doesn't work, try inserting a paper clip in the small hole in the front of the CD/DVD-ROM drive.

18

Office Ergonomics

You can think of ergonomics as a way of designing tools and equipment to suit individual needs. For a number of years, there have been efforts to improve ergonomics, primarily in manufacturing and product design. But improvements can also be made for office workers.

Ergonomics addresses three aspects of your workplace: the physical, the environmental, and the personal. An example of a physical aspect is creating a good fit between you and your computer workstation. An example of an environmental aspect is eliminating glare on your monitor screen by improving the lighting in your work area. An example of a personal aspect is the need to take periodic breaks throughout the day to restore your energy and improve comfort.

Recognizing Signs of Discomfort

Early recognition of physical symptoms allows you to make adjustments, seek help, and eliminate further discomfort. So how can you recognize the early signs and symptoms? Well, only you can listen to what your body is telling you. If you feel any fatigue, tension, or discomfort in any part of your body, take immediate action to relieve it. It's important to pay attention to the early signs and symptoms to avoid conditions that may lead to further discomfort.

Other symptoms include limbs that feel heavy or in which you feel a dull ache. You might also have joint or muscle discomfort. Be aware of problems with your eyes, including dry or itchy eyes, redness, aches, or blurred vision. You can also get headaches from eyestrain.

How can you recognize the advanced signs and symptoms of work-related problems? Consider the following:

■ Do you notice tingling, numbness, or coldness in joints and extremities?

■ Is there a loss of strength or dexterity in your hands?

■ Do you have difficulty turning door knobs, grasping things, or holding onto things?

What should you do if you experience these symptoms? Remember first that these symptoms are likely temporary and might have nothing to do with your work. For example, these symptoms might result from recreational activities, such as sports, hobbies, and home projects, or from medical conditions, such as arthritis, diabetes, pregnancy, or obesity.

193

Whatever their source, it's important to address these symptoms early and seek appropriate medical attention. Early intervention is the key to avoiding prolonged discomfort.

Whether at work or play, examine the risk factors in your activities.

- Are you involved in prolonged, intensive activities without breaks?
- Is your desk arranged so that you must extend yourself to reach the phone or reference materials?
- Do you sit in one position and rarely move about? Rarely take rest breaks? Rarely if ever stretch? You should take a break at least once each hour.
- Do you use too much force when gripping a pen or pencil?
- Do you lean or rub against hard surfaces such as the edge of a desk?
- Do you perform visually intensive tasks without breaks?
- Do you work in an area where there are wide temperature shifts, drafts, breezes, poor or irregular lighting, or excessive noise?

Your Desk and Chair

There are three preferred ways to sit at your desk. First, sitting upright is perhaps the most familiar posture when working at a computer. When seated, the angle between your upper and lower body should be approximately 90 degrees. Your back should be supported and erect. Your feet should be supported by the floor or a footrest. This is a good all-around posture for working at the computer.

A second popular sitting position is called reclining. In this position, you lean back in your chair. Make sure your back is fully supported and your buttocks are not shifted forward, which causes your lower back to not be supported. Your feet should be supported by the floor or a footrest. This is a good posture for viewing information on your monitor or for reading documents.

The third way to sit is called declining. In this posture, your upper body is upright while your thighs are declining slightly and your feet are firmly on the floor or a footrest. The seat back is adjusted almost vertically to provide back support. This is also a good posture for keyboarding work.

Adjustments to Your Chair

To enhance your comfort, you can make four main adjustments to most office chairs. These are adjusting the seat pan height, the backrest height, the backrest tilt, and the armrests. Let's look at each of these adjustments in more detail.

You should adjust the seat pan height so that your elbows are approximately at keyboard height when your elbows are next to your body. Your thighs should be approximately parallel to the floor with your feet resting firmly on the floor. If your feet are not resting firmly on the floor, you need a footrest. This seat pan height adjustment prevents your thighs from being compressed so blood flow is not restricted. This reduces fatigue in your legs. This adjustment also encourages you to sit more erectly and to use the backrest of your chair, which reduces stress on the lower back.

The backrest height adjustment makes sure that your lower back is supported. For most people, their lower back is at the same height as their elbows when the elbows are next to their body. When adjusted correctly, the lumbar support of the backrest should fit the curvature of your lower spine. This adjustment helps your lower back to maintain its natural curvature and thereby provides even compression on spinal disks and less fatigue of your back muscles.

The backrest tilt adjustment involves the angle between the backrest and the seat pan. It should be no less than 90 degrees. You should avoid adjusting the backrest too far back to where your arms are stretched out to reach the keyboard. You should also avoid adjusting the backrest too far forward where you are too close to the keyboard and cause too much bend in your elbow.

The armrest adjustment involves adjusting the height of the armrests so that the elbows rest naturally on the armrests without slouching or shrugging your shoulders. If possible, you should adjust the width between armrests so that the armrests are directly underneath your elbows. The correct adjustment of the armrests reduces the loading of the arm on the shoulder.

Other Ways to Adjust Your Seating

What if you must use a nonadjustable chair? Just because the chair is "nonadjustable" doesn't mean you can't still make adjustments. You can make an existing chair more ergonomically sound by physically adjusting the height and adding lumbar support. You can adjust the height by adding a cushion on top of the seat pan. Finally, you can add a back support cushion, pillow, or even a rolled up towel to give yourself lumbar support.

You can lower the height of your work surface by obtaining a lower-height work surface, or, as a last resort, have the Facilities staff cut down the height of the legs. You might also consider adding an adjustable-height or lower fixed-height keyboard tray to your work surface.

You can raise the height of a work surface by obtaining a higher-height work surface or by adding blocks under the workstation's legs.

Positioning Your Computer Keyboard and Mouse

The keyboard and mouse are typically the main interface between a user and a computer system. Therefore, if you work with a computer system, you probably use your keyboard and mouse extensively.

How can you set up your keyboard and pointing device to maximize comfort? There are several things you can do. You can place them properly and, if necessary, you can acquire keyboard and mouse accessories.

To set up your keyboard properly, start by placing it directly in front of the monitor with the home position keys, G and H, centered to the screen. Sit so that your elbow angle is approximately 90 degrees. Maintain a straight line across the hand and forearm. This might require you to lower the keyboard off the rear legs. Placing your keyboard properly helps you maintain a neutral posture, thereby improving comfort (Figure 18-1).

Pointing devices such as a mouse, trackball, or glidepoint should be positioned to maximize comfort. You should place the device at the same height as the keyboard and as close to the keyboard as possible. For right-handed people who don't use the ten-key numeric keypad, you might want to consider using a keyboard without this keypad.

FIGURE 18-1 Positioning your keyboard.

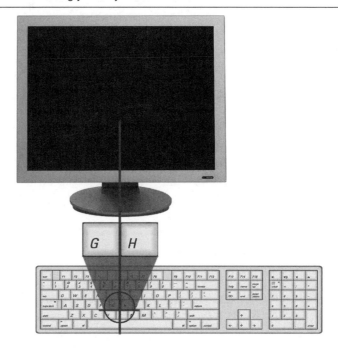

Positioning your pointing device correctly helps you maintain a neutral posture, thereby improving comfort.

Several keyboard and mouse accessories are available that can assist you with your comfort. Adjustable keyboard trays and platforms are designed to position the keyboard at various heights to help keep your wrists and arms in a neutral, relaxed position. Adjustable keyboard trays can slide in and out from underneath a work surface. Some models have a separate height and tilt adjustment.

Palm rests can be helpful in the use of both the keyboard and the mouse. These soft foam or gel strips are designed to raise your palms and keep your wrists straight. If you use a palm rest, it should not be used while keying but only to rest your palms between periods of keying.

Positioning Your Computer Display

The location and orientation of your display depends on the lighting characteristics in your work area, the viewing distance and angle, and glare control.

Glare control is key to avoiding eyestrain and the accompanying discomfort it can cause. You should keep in mind that the best way to correct screen reflections is to remove their source. The need for antiglare screens suggests that the workplace is not arranged or lit properly.

Many sources that can cause glare reflections on a properly positioned display will likely cause distracting glare in a person's normal field of vision. Screen glare can result from too much light falling on the screen (for example, light from windows or lamps), or bright areas of the environment that reflect onto the screen (such as a white shirt or blouse).

Office Ergonomics

Proper lighting is really a relative term. Lighting that is good for one task may be inappropriate for another. The general attitude in most offices is that more is better, but this is not necessarily true for working at your computer. If you are reading paper documents, you need bright light, but if you are viewing a display, you need less light. The best solution for most offices is to reduce the overhead lighting so that the computer screen is more easily read, then supplement with task lamps.

If possible, choose a workplace setup location where the screen is perpendicular to any windows and away from any bright light sources such as task lamps. You should consider using an antiglare screen if it is impossible to control the source of the glare. You should also adjust the monitor's contrast, brightness, and color controls to suit your individual comfort level. This may require changing these controls during the day as room light varies.

Special screen cleaners are available to clean dust, dirt, and fingerprints from the display or antiglare screen. You can also try a damp cloth.

After you've located your display properly in your work area to avoid glare, you need to fine-tune the position in relationship to your body. Your display should be centered behind your keyboard. The height of your display depends on your eye height while seated. The top of the display, not the top of the screen, should be even with or a little lower than your horizontal line of sight.

For people of shorter stature, you should avoid placing the display on top of your desktop computer system. This makes it nearly impossible to position the keyboard and display properly. Either the monitor will be too high or the keyboard will be too low. If, in your work, you look primarily at source documents, place the source documents directly in front of you and the display slightly off to the side.

If you need to raise the display, stands are available that can provide a comfortable viewing height in order to reduce eye and neck discomfort. If you wear glasses with bifocals, trifocals, or progressive lenses, and you find yourself looking through the bottom or top of your glasses to view the screen, you should adjust the display until you don't have to tilt your head up or down to see the screen.

What if you have a laptop instead of a monitor? In a fixed office setting, you might consider getting a "Y" connector and using an external keyboard and mouse. You can then set the laptop on a raised platform behind the keyboard to raise the screen to the proper height. Another option is to obtain a separate display for office use.

The distance between your eye and the display should be whatever is comfortable for you. You should be able to easily read the characters on the screen. You should not have to lean forward or back to read the screen. One good rule of thumb is to sit at an arm's length from the display with your hand in a fist position.

You can tilt the display up or down as necessary. Try to maintain a 90-degree angle with your line of site. Also be careful not to pick up glare from overhead lighting. By following these simple placement guidelines for displays, you can avoid possible eyestrain, awkward neck positions, and neck and back discomfort.

Arranging Your Workstation

The way you organize the elements of your workplace to fit your individual needs is an important consideration in working comfortably. Make sure you have sufficient desk area to allow you to position your keyboard, pointing device, display, and other items in a way that works best for you.

Organize your desk to reflect the way you use work materials and equipment. Place the equipment you use most often, such as your telephone, within the easiest reach. Avoid placing objects where they reduce your freedom of movement. For example, don't place a computer tower or boxes under your desk too close to your legs. The key here is to maintain an orderly desktop to reduce unnecessary movements or awkward postures. This will help to improve your comfort.

Task lamps can be used to provide lighting for reading documentation or to illuminate specific work areas. You should be careful when placing task-specific lighting to avoid glare on your computer screen and to avoid getting direct light in your eyes. Having the proper lighting will help you reduce eyestrain and its accompanying discomforts.

If your job involves working with documents, you should place the source documents properly to avoid eyestrain and awkward neck positions. One useful accessory is a document holder. When positioned properly, a document holder reduces the amount of movement required when looking back and forth between the screen and the document. Some document holders sit on your desk and are adjustable. Other models attach to the side of the display. You should position the source document at the same distance as your display and next to your display. The main thing is for the document to be on the same plane and angle as the display. If you spend most of your time transcribing, you should position your source documents directly in front of you and place your display off to the side.

How many times a day do you pick up a telephone? It's probably a lot, right? The main thing here is to avoid cradling the handset between your ear and shoulder, which can lead to neck discomfort. If you use a telephone for the majority of your day, you should consider obtaining a telephone headset. A variety of sizes and types of telephone headsets are available. You should find one that fits you comfortably and is compatible with your telephone. If you are unsure of compatibility, consult the telephone manufacturer's literature.

Sustained Work

No matter how well your workstation is set up, you should take frequent breaks. These breaks in your work are important as they help you to avoid fatigue. Frequent ergo-b reaks are important when you perform sustained, intensive, or highly repetitive work. Even if you just change positions or stand up and stretch at your workstation, it will help.

When working at your computer, it is recommended that you take a short break at least once each hour. These breaks can be from thirty seconds to five minutes long and can go a long way toward reducing fatigue. If you do take a short break from your workstation, don't just go somewhere else to sit. It is more beneficial to get up and move around. For example, stand while taking a phone call. Stand while having a face-to-face conversation with a colleague. Go make copies at the copy machine. Or just take a break from the keyboard and change your position in your chair and read mail or other documentation.

It is also a good idea to rest your eyes occasionally throughout the day. Your eyes can become fatigued; however, this is a temporary condition and is not harmful to your eyes. The muscles in your eyes that work to focus on near and far objects become fatigued when they focus for extended periods of time on near objects. Your eyes experience the least stress when they are focused on objects twenty feet away or farther.

Computer display users tend not to blink as frequently as people performing other reading tasks. Eye dryness from this staring effect is increased by low humidity in the office.

If you have difficulty reading your screen, consider increasing the default font size or improving the screen resolution.

If you wear glasses, keep the lenses clean and keep your prescription current. In fact, even if you don't wear glasses, you should have periodic eye exams. Most people's vision changes over time.

Keyboarding Techniques

The ergonomic principles behind proper keyboarding technique start with your body position relative to the keyboard. Maintain a relaxed and neutral hand and arm posture to improve comfort. Your shoulders should not be hunched up. Your arms should be comfortably at your side with your elbows bent at approximately 90 degrees. The keyboard should be approximately at elbow height, which allows the forearm and hand to be in a straight line and parallel to the floor.

The proper keyboarding technique involves a few guidelines you should keep in mind while you are working. If you notice that you are doing something incorrectly, you should stop and make adjustments.

Keep a soft touch on the keyboard. Use as little pressure as possible. Your hands should glide over the keys. If your hands remain in a fixed position, your fingers tend to overreach for the keys. Keep your fingers in a relaxed posture similar to when you rest your hand gently and naturally on a table. Try not to extend your pinky fingers and thumbs while typing. Avoid resting your hands on the palm rest while typing. Use the palm rest only when you are not typing. To reach the keys that are farthest away, such as the function keys, move your entire hand instead of reaching with your fingers.

Office Ergonomics

Office Productivity Software

19

Common Microsoft Office Features

Microsoft Office is a suite of programs that includes Word, Excel, PowerPoint, Access, Publisher, and OneNote. All of these programs share common features, such as the ribbon bar, command tabs, smart tags, screen tips, and help.

The Ribbon Bar and Command Tabs

The ribbon is a bar across the top of Microsoft Office programs that displays most of the functions you'll need as icons (Figure 19-1). There are several customizable ribbon bars available. Across the top of the ribbon bar are command tabs that allow you access different ribbon bars. For example in Microsoft Word, there are command tabs for File, Home, Insert, Page Layout, References, Mailings, Review, and View.

The tools on each ribbon bar are divided into groups. For example, in Microsoft Word on the Home tab, the ribbon bar has groups for Clipboard, Font, Paragraph, Styles, and Editing. In the lower left corner of each ribbon bar group is an icon for accessing a dialog box with additional functions.

Smart Tags

Smart tags are small icons for a function that appears within your document after you perform a certain action. For example, after pasting text into a document, a smart tag icon will display with options for formatting the newly pasted text. If you continue typing, the smart tag icon disappears.

Screen Tips

If you are unsure what a particular icon on a ribbon bar does, hover your mouse over the icon without clicking and a screen tip will display. The screen tip gives you a brief description of the function.

FIGURE 19-1   Ribbon bar in Microsoft Word.

Screen shot used with permission from Microsoft.

Help

Help is available in all Microsoft Office programs by clicking the question mark icon in the top right corner of the ribbon.

Customizing the Ribbon Bar

You can customize any of the ribbon bars with additional functions that you commonly use. To customize a ribbon bar, right-click on the ribbon bar and select CUSTOMIZE THE RIBBON. The Word Options dialog box will display (Figure 19-2). You can then select a particular ribbon bar from the list on the right, and then select functions from the list on the left. The ADD button will add a function to the ribbon bar that is selected. You can remove functions from a particular ribbon bar by selecting the function from the list on the right, and then clicking the REMOVE button.

Quick Access Toolbar

A small toolbar called the Quick Access Toolbar is available in Word, Excel, Access, and PowerPoint. It is visible on every ribbon bar regardless of which command tab you've selected. You can view the Quick Access Toolbar by right-clicking on the ribbon bar and then select SHOW QUICK ACCESS TOOLBAR.

The Quick Access Toolbar can be customized by right-clicking the toolbar, and from the Word Options dialog, selecting the functions you would like to display on the toolbar.

Cut, Copy, and Paste

The cut, copy, and paste functions are the same within all Microsoft Office applications. In fact, you can copy text from one program and paste it into another program.

To cut text from a document, select the text with your mouse and then on the Home tab, click CUT. You can also press the keyboard command CTRL + X to cut text.

To copy text, select the text with your mouse. Then on the Home tab, click COPY. You can also press the keyboard command CTRL + C. To paste copied text, click your mouse where you want the text to appear, and then on the Home tab, click PASTE. You can also press CTRL + V on your keyboard as an alternative.

All of the Microsoft Office applications have a clipboard that will temporarily store the last 24 selections that you have copied. You can access the clipboard by click-

FIGURE 19-2   Word Options for customizing the ribbon bar.

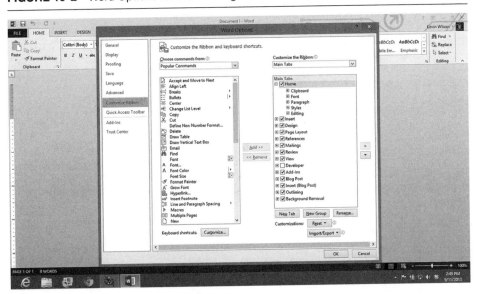

Screen shot used with permission from Microsoft.

ing the icon in the bottom right corner of the Clipboard group on the Home tab. The clipboard will be displayed with a list of files that have been copied.

Spelling and Grammar Checking

Spell checking is turned on by default in Microsoft Office applications. The software will check for misspelled words as you type and highlight them for you with a squiggly red underline.

If you find it distracting for the software to check spelling and grammar while you type and would rather check your documents when you are finished, you can turn off the automatic checking by accessing the FILE tab, click the OPTIONS button, the Word Options dialog box displays and you can change the setting for CHECK SPELLING AS YOU TYPE.

To manually check the spelling of your finished document, click the Review tab, and then click SPELLING AND GRAMMAR. The Spelling and Grammar dialog box will display words or sentences that it questions. Alternatives are suggested that you can select, or you can ignore the questioned text if you are sure it is correct. Some technical terms and phrases may be picked up by the software as being incorrect even though they are correct and commonplace in your particular business.

Using Clip Art

You can use clip art in most of the Microsoft Office applications to add images to your documents to make them more attractive. Microsoft Office includes some clip art when the program is installed on your computer; however, additional clip art is

FIGURE 19-3   Smart Art in PowerPoint.

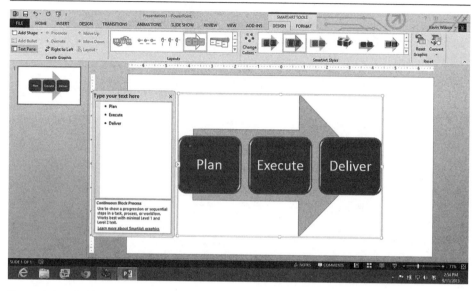

Screen shot used with permission from Microsoft.

available online and can be easily downloaded from within your Microsoft Office application.

To insert clip art in Office 2010 and earlier versions, click the Insert tab and then select CLIP ART. In Office 2013, on the Insert tab click ONLINE PICTURES and then click OFFICE.COM CLIP ART. In the Search box, enter a keyword or two that describes the kind of clip art you want. A list of images displays.

Using Smart Art

Smart Art is a function in Microsoft Office applications that allows you to create diagrams and charts. To insert Smart Art into your document, click the Insert tab, and then click SMART ART. You can then select a diagram or chart from the list.

After inserting Smart Art into your document, you can format it using the Smartart Tools tab. Here you will find a variety of functions for enhancing the look and feel of the chart. If you click the inserted Smart Art itself, you can add text and change the size (Figure 19-3).

Using WordArt

Word Art is a function that allows you to display text in a more creative way in Microsoft Word, Excel, and PowerPoint.

To access Word Art, select the Insert Menu and then select WORD ART. A list of styles is displayed from which you can select. The Edit WordArt Text dialog box displays and allows you to enter your text, select a font, font size, font color, and style. When you click the OK button, the WordArt is inserted like a piece of clip art into your document.

Drawing

You can draw shapes to create diagrams or flowcharts using the Shapes function, which is available on the Insert menu within Microsoft Office applications.

To create a frame in a Microsoft Word document that contains several drawing objects, click the Shapes function and select NEW DRAWING CANVAS.

To draw a particular shape, click the Shapes function and then select the desired shape. Then, click and hold the mouse on the document where you want the shape to start. Drag the mouse to create the desired shape. When you release the mouse button, the shape appears in your document.

You can also use the Shapes function to create text boxes. Text boxes can be useful to highlight headlines and key points in reports and newsletters. Just select the Text Box shape from the list of Shapes. After clicking your mouse and dragging to create the text box, clicking within the textbox will allow you to enter the desired text.

Converting Documents

Files from older versions of Microsoft Office programs will open automatically in Office 2013 in "compatibility view." When viewing an older file in compatibility view, you'll find that there is some limited functionality, especially when using drawing tools like SmartArt. You can quickly convert an older file to a newer file format by clicking the File Tab, and then clicking SAVE AS. On the Save dialog box, click the SAVE AS TYPE box and select the native format for the particular Office application. As an example, the native format for Word 2007 or 2010 is "Word Document."

Microsoft Office 2007 and 2010 files must be converted in order to be used in older versions of Microsoft Office. You can install updates in some earlier versions of Microsoft Office that allow them to automatically convert the newer file formats for viewing and editing in older versions. To convert a newer format file for use in older versions, just follow the same save-as procedure as above, and, on the Save dialog box, click the SAVE AS TYPE box and select WORD 97-2003 DOCUMENT.

Adobe Acrobat PDF Files

When you want to send a file to someone but don't want any changes made to the document, the best file format is Adobe Acrobat PDF. Adobe Acrobat PDF files are files that can be viewed by anyone using a free version of Adobe Acrobat Reader, available at http://www.adobe.com. Adobe Acrobat files are also known as PDF files, which stands for "Portable Document Format." PDF files cannot be easily edited without a professional version of Adobe Acrobat.

To create a PDF version of one of your documents, all you have to do is use the Save As function and select PDF from the Save As Type box.

Keyboard Shortcuts

Keyboard shortcuts are available for accessing most Microsoft Office functions instead of having to use a mouse to navigate to the various tabs and ribbon bars. Table 19-1 is a list of keyboard shortcuts.

TABLE 19-1   Microsoft Office Keyboard Shortcuts

Function	Keyboard Shortcut
Open a file	CTRL + O
Close a file	CTRL + W
Save a file	CTRL + S
Print a file	CTRL + P
Create a new document	CTRL + N
Cut	CTRL + X
Copy	CTRL + C
Paste	CTRL + V
Check spelling	F7
Bold text	CTRL + B
Italicize text	CTRL + I
Remove text formatting	CTRL + Spacebar
Select all	CTRL + A
Undo	CTRL + Z
Redo	CTRL + Y
Cancel action	Esc
Move up one line	Up Arrow
Move down one line	Down Arrow
Move one screen up	Page Up
Move one screen down	Page Down
Move to the end of a document	CTRL + End
Move to the beginning of a document	CTRL + Home

Microsoft Office (side tab)

Office 365 On Demand

An Office 365 subscription includes the ability to use several applications over the Internet without having to install them on your computer. These apps are streamed over the Internet. Unlike the Office Web Apps, which are free scaled-down browser-based versions of the Office applications, the Office On Demand applications are the full versions. Office On Demand includes streaming versions of Word, Excel, PowerPoint, Access, and Publisher.

When you have an Office 365 subscription and you sign into Microsoft account, you'll see My Office. Here, you can access files stored in your SkyDrive, and you can launch Office On Demand applications. When you click to launch an application, the application streams to your computer and opens. This is the full featured version of the Microsoft Office application and can be accessed from any computer.

20

Using Microsoft Word

Word processing can greatly improve your overall productivity. And although there are great differences among word processing software programs, almost all allow you to create documents, edit and format these documents, and print them. Other features include spelling checkers, style and grammar checkers, mail merge, and the ability to store documents electronically.

The most common word processing software found in businesses is Microsoft Word. The latest version available when this book went to press was Word 2013. This chapter provides useful tips for administrative assistants on how to use Microsoft Word 2010 and 2013.

Microsoft Word's screen features individual tabs, each with its own function-filled ribbon bar. Figure 20-1 shows an image of Microsoft Word with the various parts of the screen labeled.

The Home tab is used the most often, since it contains groups for making font choices, paragraph formatting, styles, clipboard functions, and find and replace.

Creating Documents

The first time you open Word, it will automatically create a blank document for you. If you need to create a new blank document while Word is already running, follow these steps:

1. Click the File tab.
2. Click NEW.
3. Click the Blank Document template.
4. (Word 2010) Click CREATE.

Typing
When a new document has been created, you can begin typing and entering data.

Moving Around an Existing Document
An on-screen pointer called a *cursor* shows where text will appear when typed. You can use your mouse to move the cursor from one character to another, up or down, or left and right, in order to make corrections, edit, or format the text. You can also move the cursor by using the arrow keys on the computer keyboard.

209

FIGURE 20-1   Microsoft Word functions.

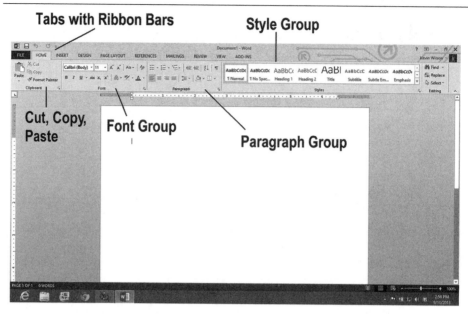

Screen shot used with permission from Microsoft.

Editing Documents

For administrative assistants, one of the best time-saving features of Word is the ability to make changes very easily, without retyping the entire document. Many administrative assistants start a document by typing without regard to format or the look of the finished document. They then come back, make revisions, and change the format. By coming back to spell-check, proof, and make corrections, they can remove most typos and sentence structure problems prior to printing out a copy of the document.

Deleting

To delete text from a document, several choices are available. Some keyboards have a BACKSPACE key, and others have a key marked DELETE.

When you type the BACKSPACE key, the cursor moves to the left one space and erases the character that was displayed there. When you type the DELETE key, the character that occupies the same space as the cursor is erased. You can also use your mouse to highlight the specific character or word to be deleted and then press the DELETE key.

Undo

When you delete text, it's stored in a temporary memory buffer. The buffer stores the last thing you deleted, such as a word, sentence, paragraph, or even whole pages. In case you inadvertently delete something, Word has an Undo function.

You can access the Undo function by clicking the Undo Typing icon in the top left corner of the Word window. You can also access the Undo function by pressing CTLR + Z on your keyboard at the same time.

Cut and Paste

Moving text from one location to another is one more useful feature of Microsoft Word. Just click and drag the mouse to highlight a block of text such as a sentence, paragraph, or group of paragraphs. Once the text is highlighted, select CUT or COPY from the Home tab to put the text (or a copy of it) into the temporary memory buffer. Next, use the mouse to navigate through the document to the location where the text should be inserted. By clicking the mouse on this location and selecting PASTE from the Home tab, you remove the text from the memory buffer and insert it into the new location.

Search

Microsoft Word provides the ability to search for and find a particular string of characters or words anywhere in a document. This feature comes in handy for finding names in a mailing list or other specific information from a document.

In order to search an entire document, position the cursor at the beginning of the document. The Find function is on the far right end of the Home tab. Once Find has been selected, you'll be asked to type the characters or words you want to find.

Search and Replace

A related function is Search and Replace. It is useful whenever a word that is scattered throughout a document must be changed. You can access the Replace function on the far right end of the Home tab. Once Replace has been selected, you enter the word or phrase you want to find and the replacement word or phrase. You have the option of replacing all of the instances of the search word or phrase at one time, or you can review each instance individually and make the replacement decision one at a time.

Many users save time by using Search and Replace as a time-saving shortcut. If these users frequently have to type a long, complicated word or phrase in a document, they will type substitute characters instead, such as "xxx." Since "xxx" would normally not appear in a document, the user can later access the Search and Replace function. This function then finds "xxx" and allows the user to type in a replacement string—the long, complicated word or phrase.

Formatting Documents

Many administrative assistants start by typing text and later going back to make adjustments to the way the document will look when printed on paper. This is a process known as *formatting*. There are many different ways to format a document—for example, by changing the margins, the line spacing, or the type style and size of the characters.

Margins and Tabs

Microsoft Word allows you to set the left and right margins. A ruler that runs just below the tabs is used for setting margins and tabs. Tabs can be added by clicking in the desired spot on the ruler. Tabs allow you to indent your text at the beginning of a paragraph or to line up columns of data.

If the ruler is not visible, you can turn it on by clicking RULER on the View tab.

Using Microsoft Word

Line Spacing

Line spacing is changed by selecting the Line and Paragraph Spacing icon on the Home tab. The menu provides options for changing the amount of spacing between each line. There are options for adding a specific amount of space before and after each paragraph. You can change the spacing of an existing paragraph by selecting it with your mouse and then making a selection from the Line and Paragraph Spacing function.

Justification

Justification is the way a block of text lines up on the page with the margins. Word offers four options for justification. Any block of text can be aligned flush with the left margin or the right margin. Another choice is full justification, which aligns the text flush with both the left and the right margin—like typesetting in a book. This is done by adding spaces between the words of each line. A fourth option is centered justification, used to center titles and other text in the middle of a line.

The justification settings in Microsoft Word are available as icons on the Home tab.

Character Formatting

Another major document-formatting tool is the character format. Text can be printed in a variety of different styles, such as underlined, bold, and italics. In addition, the characters themselves can be printed in many different sizes and typefaces called *fonts*.

Microsoft Word comes with a number of fonts and font sizes already installed. Additional fonts can be purchased as software to increase your number of choices. Some fonts are used to display text on the screen, and others are used by the printer. Some printers include fonts that are installed when the printer drivers are installed on your computer.

You can select the character formatting using the icons on the Home tab. You can change the formatting of existing text by first highlighting the text with your mouse, and then selecting the appropriate formatting icon on the Home tab.

Page Formatting

Additional formatting options are available for entire documents or sections of a document. For example, the page layout determines the top, bottom, left, and right margins for all text on a page. In addition, headers and footers can be inserted on each page for page numbers, the date, or the name of a document.

You can adjust the page formatting on the Page Layout tab. Headers and footers can be adjusted on the Insert tab.

Styles

If you create a specialized format for a document, rather than manually format each section, you can create what are called *styles*. Styles allow you to define individual formatting characteristics such as margins, justification, font size, and font style and give them a name that can be accessed from a menu on the ruler.

Built-in styles are available in the Styles section of the Home tab. You can create a new style based on existing text that you have formatted by selecting the text, then right-click and select STYLES > CREATE A STYLE. (In Word 2010 select STYLES > SAVE THE SELECTION AS A NEW QUICK STYLE.)

Printing Documents

When a document has been created and formatted, getting that document printed on paper is the ultimate goal for most Microsoft Word users. The Print function allows you to specify additional information about the way the document should appear on paper: for example, which pages of the document are to be printed, whether the printing itself should be draft mode or letter quality, how many copies should be made, page orientation (portrait versus landscape), paper size, and whether the printing will be one-sided or two-sided.

Microsoft Word has a print-preview feature that displays on the monitor the overall layout of how the printed document will appear on paper. In this way, you can see the formatting options before time and paper are wasted printing an incorrect document. Before printing any document, it's important that you first save the document to your computer's hard drive. Since printing involves a hardware connection between two different devices, occasionally there are problems that cause a computer to "hang up" when trying to print. If you have not saved your document, you could lose it if this happens.

Some of the biggest problems for many word processing users are printer related. The printer might print something you didn't intend, or perhaps it might not print at all. In order for the computer to communicate with a printer, print driver software is required. This software is usually supplied with the printer but can also be included with some word processing software. It's important that you specify the type of printer you are using and how it's connected to the computer.

The Print function in Microsoft Word is available on the File menu. You can also access the Print function by typing CTRL + P on the keyboard.

Saving and Loading Documents

One of the main benefits of using Microsoft Word is the ability to save your documents electronically and to retrieve them to use again. In this way, common business documents such as letters, invoices, and contracts can be created once, saved, and then customized as needed. This feature eliminates having to re-create a letter or document every time it is needed.

Saving a document is an electronic way of recording the data on the computer's hard drive or some other storage medium. Before you can save a document, you'll be asked to name the document and to designate where you want to save it. Give your document a unique name that will make it easy to find later. Some administrative assistants include the date and draft number in the document name.

If your computer is equipped with multiple hard drives, you must specify on which drive you want to save the document. It is also a good idea to create folders and filing system on each drive (see Chapter 8, Keeping Accurate Records).

Loading or opening a document that has been previously saved involves specifying the name of the document you want to open and telling the computer on which drive it is saved. When a document is loaded from the hard drive into the computer's memory, only a copy of the document is loaded. The original saved version is still stored on the disk. If you make changes to the document and save it again using the same name, only the most recent version will be saved on the disk. The original version is wiped out, and the new version is saved in its place. To save both versions of a document, you need to alter the name of the new version. Even if you change just one letter or char-

FIGURE 20-2   Review tab in Microsoft Word.

Screen shot used with permission from Microsoft.

acter in the name, the new version will be saved in a different space, and the original version will still be intact on the disk.

Fortunately, Microsoft Word has built-in protection that warns you when an original version of a document is about to be overwritten. Microsoft Word tells you that a previous version of the same document already exists and asks you to confirm that you really want to wipe out the old version.

Advanced Word Processing Features

Microsoft Word has some advanced features that may be of use to you in your work. For example, if you create long manuscripts or reports, features such as indexing, sorting, footnote tracking, automatic hyphenation, and tables may be of help. Check the online help for Microsoft Word if you wish to employ these powerful tools.

Spelling and Grammar Checker

Microsoft Word's spelling checker automatically looks for spelling errors. There is also a grammar and style checker that can analyze the mechanics of your writing. A built-in thesaurus can provide synonyms for words used in your document.

You can access the spelling and grammar checker and thesaurus on the Review tab. Figure 20-2 shows the Review tab.

Macros

Microsoft Word can utilize macros to help customize and shorten repetitive processes. A macro is a way of recording a series of keystrokes or commands and recalling them by using a single keystroke or key combination. For example, you might have to type a long medical term repeatedly throughout a document. Rather than type it over and over, you might create a macro that with just a two-key combination automatically types the longer word.

You can create a Macro by selecting MACROS on the View tab, and then select RE-CORD MACRO. You will be asked to name the macro and assign a keyboard combination that will call the macro. You then record the keystrokes you want to save in the macro.

Creating an Address List

You may need to keep a list of contacts, such as employees or customers, for use in correspondence and telephone calls. In addition to being able to use the list as a reference source, you can use your address list with the mail-merge feature in Microsoft

Using Microsoft Word

FIGURE 20-3   Page Layout tab in Microsoft Word.

Screen shot used with permission from Microsoft.

FIGURE 20-4   Insert tab in Microsoft Word.

Screen shot used with permission from Microsoft.

word to create customized form letters and emails. For information on creating mail-merge letters, see Printing and Emailing Mail-Merge Letters, later in the chapter.

To create your address list, gather information about your contacts and decide the types of information you want to include. A simple address list includes names, addresses, phone numbers, and email addresses. Other information may be added as needed by you and your manager, such as department, hire date, spouse's name, children's names, and so forth. These categories of information will be the headings for your address list table.

Figures 20-3 and 20-4 show the Page Layout and Insert tabs that you will need to access when creating an address list table.

Follow these steps to create an address list table in Microsoft Word:

1. Open a blank Word document by clicking FILE > NEW, then click BLANK DOCUMENT.

2. Click the Page Layout tab.

3. In the Page Setup group, click ORIENTATION. From the submenu, click LANDSCAPE. Your page layout should change to landscape view.

4. Click the Insert tab.

5. In the Tables group, click TABLE. From the submenu, click INSERT TABLE. The Insert Table dialog box will display.

6. Select the number of columns based on the categories of information you want in your address list. For example, first name, last name, address, city, state, zip, phone, and email would require eight columns.

7. Select the number of rows based on an initial estimate of the number of people you need to add to the list. (You can always add more rows later.)

8. Click the OK button. The table will be inserted into the document.

Using Microsoft Word

9. Add the categories of information as the headings in the top row of the table. Put each one in a different table cell.

10. To format the heading, select the first row in the table to highlight it, click the Home tab, and click the Bold icon in the Font group.

11. To add shading to the heading, if it is not still selected, select the first row in the table, then click the Shading icon in the Paragraph group on the Home tab. From the submenu, select one of the light gray colors.

12. To repeat the same heading on additional pages of the table, select the heading row, then right-click. From the right-click pop-up menu, select TABLE PROPERTIES. The Table Properties dialog box will display.

13. Click the Row tab on the Table Properties dialog box, then click the checkbox for REPEAT AS HEADER ROW AT THE TOP OF EACH PAGE.

14. Click the OK button.

15. To add a title to your address list, click the Insert tab, and in the Header and Footer group, click HEADER.

16. From the submenu, click EDIT HEADER. The Header and Footer tools will display, allowing you a space to type the header.

17. Right-click in the header and from the pop-up menu, click the CENTER JUSTIFICA- TION icon to center your text on the page.

18. Type the title of your address list. When you are finished, click the CLOSE HEADER AND FOOTER icon in the Close group.

19. Save your address list and give it a name.

20. You are now ready to enter the personal information about your contacts in the list. Remember to save your work often.

Creating and Printing Address Labels

Labels can be printed using Microsoft Word for use in addressing correspondence, organizing paper files, and creating items such as name badges.

The best place to start is with the label or paper stock that you want to use for the desired type of label. Avery makes a variety of label stock ranging from sticky labels for addresses to labels for DVDs. Each type of label is identified with a product code number.

While Avery is the dominant brand of label available at most office supply stores, you can find less expensive alternatives. Just make sure the Avery equivalent code is located on the packaging somewhere.

Microsoft Word allows you to customize your labels using templates that match the Avery label coding. You can customize the font, font size, font style, color, and layout. You can also add graphics or pictures to your labels.

When you use Microsoft Word to create labels, you'll have several choices:

■ You can create an entire page of the same label.

■ You can create a page of unique labels.

■ You can create and print one single label.

■ You can print mail-merge labels using an existing address list.

Using Microsoft Word

FIGURE 20-5   Mailings tab in Microsoft Word.

Screen shot used with permission from Microsoft.

When creating labels and mail merges, you will use the Mailings tab. Figure 20-5 shows the Mailings tab.

Entire Page of the Same Label

When you need to organize numerous items with the same information, such as the materials for a meeting or workshop, you can use Microsoft Word to print an entire page of the same label. Before you get started, make sure you have your label stock product code number.

Follow these steps to create an entire page of the same label:

1. Open a blank Word document by clicking FILE > NEW, then double-click BLANK DOCUMENT.

2. Click the Mailings tab.

3. In the Create group on the Mailing tab, click LABELS. The Envelopes and Labels dialog box will display with the Labels tab active.

4. Click the OPTIONS button. The Label Options dialog box will display.

5. Select the label brand from the Label Vendors drop-down list, then select the label stock product code from the Product Number list. Click OK to continue.

6. In the Address text box, type the text for your labels.
   a. To pick the font, right-click and select FONT.
   b. On the Font dialog box, select the FONT tab.
   c. Select the font, font size, font style, color, and layout.
   d. Click OK to continue.

7. On the Envelopes and Labels dialog box in the Print pane, make sure the radio button for FULL PAGE OF SAME LABEL is selected.

8. Load the labels into the printer.

9. Select the paper source in Microsoft Word by clicking the OPTIONS button, then select the correct tray on your printer, then click OK.

10. To print just one sheet of labels, click the PRINT button.

11. To print several pages of labels or to save your labels as a Word document, click the NEW DOCUMENT button. A new document will display.
   a. Save the labels by clicking the FILE tab, and then clicking SAVE. Name the file, select the location to save it, then click SAVE.
   b. To print several pages of labels, click the Microsoft Office button, and then click PRINT > PRINT. Make any adjustments necessary on the Print dialog box and then click OK.

Page of Unique Labels

When you need to print many different labels, such as address labels, you can create a new document label page and manually type your labels. Before you get started, make sure you have your label stock product code number.

Follow these steps to create a page of unique labels:

1. Open a blank Word document by clicking FILE > NEW, then double-click BLANK DOCUMENT.

2. Click the Mailings tab.

3. In the Create group on the Mailing tab, click LABELS. The Envelopes and Labels dialog box will display with the Labels tab active.

4. Click the OPTIONS button. The Label Options dialog box will display.

5. Select the label brand from the Label Vendors drop-down list, then select the label stock product code from the Product Number list. Click OK to continue.

6. Load the labels into the printer.

7. Select the paper source in Microsoft Word by clicking the OPTIONS button, then select the correct tray on your printer, then click OK.

8. Click the NEW DOCUMENT button. A new document will display with a table. Each table cell represents one label.

9. Enter the contents for each label. To move from one label to the next, press the TAB key on your keyboard.

10. Save the labels by clicking the FILE tab, and then clicking SAVE. Name the file, select the location to save it, then click SAVE.

11. To print the labels, click the Microsoft Office button, and then click PRINT > PRINT. Make any adjustments necessary on the Print dialog box and then click OK.

Single Label

When you need just one label, such as a single address label, you can specify the row and column where you want your label printed on your label stock. Before you get started, make sure you have your label stock product code number.

Follow these steps to create and print a single label:

1. Open a blank Word document by clicking FILE > NEW, then double-click BLANK DOCUMENT.

2. Click the Mailings tab.

3. In the Create group on the Mailing tab, click LABELS. The Envelopes and Labels dialog box will display with the Labels tab active.

4. Click the OPTIONS button. The Label Options dialog box will display.

5. Select the label brand from the Label Vendors drop-down list, then select the label stock product code from the Product Number list. Click OK to continue.

6. In the Address text box, type the text for your labels.

7. To pick the font, right-click and select FONT.

8. On the Font dialog box, select the Font tab.

9. Select the font, font size, font style, color, and layout.

10. Click OK to continue.

11. On the Envelopes and Labels dialog box in the Print pane, make sure the radio button for SINGLE LABEL is selected. Then, select the row and column on the label sheet where you want your label to be printed.

12. Load the labels into the printer.

13. Select the paper source in Microsoft Word by clicking the OPTIONS button, then select the correct tray on your printer, then click OK.

14. Click the PRINT button. The label will be printed without accessing the Print dialog box.

Mail-Merge Labels

Whenever you have a list of addresses as a file in Word or Excel, you can use the mail-merge feature in Word to set up a label and print one for each address in the file. You can also use this same feature to print mail-merge envelopes (see Printing and Emailing Mail-Merge Letters, later in the chapter). Before you begin this procedure, you must first create your address list.

Follow these steps to print mail-merge labels:

1. Open a blank Word document by clicking FILE > NEW, then double-click BLANK DOCUMENT.

2. Click the Mailings tab.

3. In the Start Mail Merge group on the Mailing tab, click START MAIL MERGE. The Start Mail Merge submenu will display.

4. Select LABELS from the submenu. The Labels Options dialog box will display.

5. Specify the paper tray to use on your printer by clicking the Tray drop-down arrow and making a selection from the list of trays.

6. Select the label manufacturer by clicking the Label Products drop-down list.

7. Select the type of label you are using by clicking the Product Number scroll box. The most common address labels are Avery 5160 Address.

8. Click the OK button to continue.

9. In the Start Mail Merge group on the Mailing tab, click SELECT RECIPIENTS. From the submenu, click USE EXISTING LIST. The Select Data Source dialog box will display.

10. Click the Look In down arrow to locate and find the address list file on your computer. Select the file, and then click the OPEN button.

11. To select the names and addresses to use for the mail merge, in the Start Mail Merge group on the Mailings tab, click EDIT RECIPIENT LIST. The Mail Merge Recipients dialog box will display.

12. Select the recipients you want to print by making sure the check box next to the name and address is selected. Click the OK button to continue.

13. To insert the merge fields, click your cursor in the top left label on your document.

14. In the Write and Insert Fields group on the Mailings tab, click INSERT MERGE FIELD, then select the correct field from the submenu. For example, select FIRST NAME. Add a space on your document to separate fields such as first name and last name. Add any additional fields. Press ENTER on your keyboard to move to the next line in your document to add other fields, such as the company name or address. Press ENTER again and repeat the process to add fields for the city, state, and zip. You will need to add the comma in your document between the city and state fields.

15. To use the same fields for all the labels on the page, in the Write and Insert Fields group, click UPDATE LABELS.

16. When you are finished adding all the necessary fields to the address, click PREVIEW RESULTS. You will see a preview of the first recipient's label.

17. When you are ready to print, in the Finish group, click FINISH & MERGE. From the submenu, click PRINT DOCUMENTS. The small Merge to Printer dialog box displays.

18. To print labels for all the recipients, click ALL. To print an envelope only for the record currently selected, click CURRENT RECORD. To print the labels in batches, enter a range in the text boxes. Click the OK button when you are finished. The Print dialog box will display.

19. Make any necessary adjustments on the Print dialog box.

20. Load the label stock into your printer.

21. Click the OK button on the Print dialog box.

Printing Envelopes

Printing address information directly on an envelope gives your correspondence a professional look.

Before you begin this procedure, you should familiarize yourself with how to load an envelope into your printer. Generally this is accomplished by manually feeding an envelope in one of the paper trays. Sometimes this requires removing the normal paper stock. Check the printer's user manual for instructions.

You'll also need to know what size envelope you will be using in order to make the correct settings in Microsoft Word. The most popular size is the Number 10 envelope, which measures 4⅛ inches by 9½ inches. A variety of other envelope sizes are also supported.

There are several options for printing envelopes:

- You can access the envelope feature in Word and type in the address.

- You can highlight an address in a letter and print an envelope of the address.

- You can print multiple envelopes using the mail-merge feature and an existing address list.

A New Envelope

Follow this procedure whenever you want to print an envelope in Microsoft Word and you don't already have the address available in a Word document:

1. Open a blank Word document by clicking FILE > NEW, then double-click BLANK DOCUMENT.

2. Click the Mailings tab.

3. In the Create group on the Mailing tab, click ENVELOPES. The Envelopes and Labels dialog box will display with the Envelopes tab active.

4. Click the OPTIONS button. The Envelope Options dialog box will display.

5. Select the correct envelope size by clicking the Envelope Size drop-down arrow.

6. Click the Feed Options tab on the Envelope Options dialog box.

7. Select the correct feed method and whether the envelope is inserted face up or face down, based on your printer manual's recommendation. Also, select the correct printer tray by clicking the Feed From drop-down arrow. (If you don't know, leave the default setting and if the envelope does not print correctly the first time, make changes to these settings.)

8. Click the OK button. This returns you to the Envelopes and Labels dialog box.

9. Type the address for the person who will receive the letter in the Delivery Address text box.
   a. To change the font, right-click in the Delivery Address text box. The Font dialog box will display.
   b. Make any changes you want to the font, font style, and size. When you are finished, click the OK button.

10. Enter your return address in the Return Address text box. You will have the option of saving your current return address as the default address for future envelopes. You also have the option of omitting the return address by clicking the OMIT checkbox.
    a. To change the font, right-click in the Return Address text box. The Font dialog box will display.
    b. Make any changes you want to the font, font size, font style, color, and layout. When you are finished, click the OK button.

11. Insert the envelope in your printer according to your printer's specifications.

12. Click the PRINT button. Depending on your printer, you may be prompted to manually insert the envelope.

An Envelope for an Existing Letter

Follow this procedure whenever you already have the address available in a Word document, which will often be the case if you have just finished writing a letter:

1. Select the address in the letter or other Word document.

2. Click the Mailings tab.

3. In the Create group on the Mailings tab, click ENVELOPES. The Envelopes and Labels dialog box will display with the Envelopes tab active.

4. Click the OPTIONS button. The Envelope Options dialog box will display.

5. Select the correct envelope size by clicking the Envelope Size drop-down arrow.

6. Click the Feed Options tab on the Envelope Options dialog box. You can adjust the fonts for the delivery address and return address by clicking the appropriate

font button. Make any changes you want to the font, font size, font style, color, and layout. When you are finished, click the OK button.

7. Select the correct feed method and whether the envelope is inserted face up or face down, based on your printer manual's recommendation. Also select the correct printer tray by clicking the Feed From drop-down arrow. (If you don't know, use the default setting and if the envelope does not print correctly the first time, make changes to these settings.)

8. Click the OK button. This returns you to the Envelopes and Labels dialog box.

9. Confirm the address in the Delivery Address text box.

10. Enter your return address in the Return Address text box. You will have the option of saving your current return address as the default address for future envelopes. You also have the option of omitting the return address by clicking the OMIT checkbox.

11. Insert the envelope in your printer according to your printer's specifications.

12. Click the PRINT button. Depending on your printer, you may be prompted to manually insert the envelope.

Mail-Merge Envelopes

Whenever you have a list of addresses as a file in Word or Excel, you can use the mail-merge feature in Word to set up an envelope and print one for each address in the file. You can also use this same feature to print mail-merge labels (see Mail-Merge Labels, earlier in the chapter). Before you begin this procedure, you must first create your address list (see Creating an Address List, earlier in the chapter):

1. Open a blank Word document by clicking FILE > NEW, then double-click BLANK DOCUMENT.

2. Click the Mailings tab.

3. In the Start Mail Merge group on the Mailings tab, click START MAIL MERGE. The Start Mail Merge submenu will display.

4. Select ENVELOPES from the submenu. The Envelope Options dialog box will display.

5. Select the correct envelope size by clicking the Envelope Size drop-down arrow.

6. To set the typeface for the delivery address, click the FONT button for the delivery address. Make any changes you want to the font, font size, font style, color, and layout. Click the OK button when you are finished.

7. To set the typeface for the return address, click the FONT button for the return address. Make any changes you want to the font, font size, font style, color, and layout. Click the OK button when you are finished.

8. Click the OK button on the Envelope Options dialog box. The envelope is now formatted and ready for the mail merge.

9. In the Start Mail Merge group on the Mailings tab, click SELECT RECIPIENTS. From the submenu, click USE EXISTING LIST. The Select Data Source dialog box will display.

10. Click the Look In down arrow to locate and find the address list file on your computer. Select the file, and then click the OPEN button.

11. To select the names and addresses to use for the envelope mail merge, in the Start Mail Merge group on the Mailings tab, click EDIT RECIPIENT LIST. The Mail Merge Recipients dialog box will display.

12. Select the recipients for which you want to print an envelope by making sure the checkbox next to the name and address is selected. Click the OK button to continue.

13. To insert the merge fields, click your cursor in the first line of the blank document.

14. In the Write and Insert Fields group on the Mailings tab, click INSERT MERGE FIELD, then select the correct field from the submenu. For example, select FIRST NAME. Add a space on your document to separate fields such as first name and last name. Add any additional fields. Press ENTER on your keyboard to move to the next line in your document to add other fields, such as the company name or address. Press ENTER again and repeat the process to add fields for the city, state, and zip. You will need to add the comma in your document between the city and state fields.

15. When you are finished adding all the necessary fields to the address, click PREVIEW RESULTS. You will see a preview of the first recipient's envelope.

16. When you are ready to print, in the Finish group, click FINISH & MERGE. From the submenu, click PRINT DOCUMENTS. The small Merge to Printer dialog box displays.

17. To print envelopes for all the recipients, click ALL. To print an envelope only for the record currently selected, click CURRENT RECORD. To print the envelopes in batches, enter a range in the text boxes. Click the OK button when you are finished. The Print dialog box will display.

18. Make any necessary adjustments on the Print dialog box.

19. Load an envelope into your printer.

20. Click the OK button on the Print dialog box. Depending on your printer, you may need to load each envelope one at a time as they are printed.

Printing and Emailing Mail-Merge Letters

The mail-merge feature in Microsoft Word allows you to create one letter and customize it for each record in a database or table. For example, you could create a form letter with places for adding a person's name and address, then create a list of names and addresses, and merge the two to create a customized letter for each person on the list. This is a great timesaver whenever you need to send a similar letter to many different people.

Before you start this procedure, you should first create your address list (see Creating an Address List, earlier in the chapter, for more information). You should also create your form letter in Microsoft Word, leaving spaces for where customized information needs to be inserted during the merge, such as the person's name and address, and "Dear" followed by a blank for where the person's name will be placed.

The mail-merge process consists of six steps:

1. Select the type of document (in this case a form letter).

2. Select the recipients (your address list).

3. Insert fields from the recipient list into the letter.

4. Preview the document.

5. Merge the letter and the address list.

6. Print the customized mail-merge letters.

Because your address list can be created in Microsoft Word, Excel, or Outlook, and because you can create and print paper-based letters or send emails, we have included the following tutorials for this topic:

- Generating mail-merge form letters from an address list

- Using Outlook contacts for a mail merge

- Creating an email merge

Generating Mail-Merge Form Letters from an Address List

Whenever you have a list of addresses as a file in Word or Excel, you can use the mail-merge feature in Word to create a form letter and then merge content from the address list to create customized letters for each person in the list. You may also want to combine this process with the creation of mail-merge mailing labels (see Mail-Merge Labels, earlier in the chapter, for more information).

1. Open the form letter you have created.

2. Click the Mailings tab.

3. In the Start Mail Merge group on the Mailings tab, click START MAIL MERGE. The Start Mail Merge submenu will display.

4. Select LETTERS from the submenu.

5. In the Start Mail Merge group on the Mailings tab, click SELECT RECIPIENTS. From the submenu, click USE EXISTING LIST. The Select Data Source dialog box will display.

6. Click the Look In down arrow to locate and find the address list file on your computer. Select the file, and then click the OPEN button.

7. To select the names and addresses to use for the mail merge, in the Start Mail Merge group on the Mailings tab, click EDIT RECIPIENT LIST. The Mail Merge Recipients dialog box will display.

8. Select the recipients you want to print by making sure the checkbox next to the name and address is selected. Click the OK button to continue.

9. To insert the merge fields, position and click your cursor where the first item of merged content from the address list should appear. For example, if you want to insert a person's name after the word "Dear," click your mouse one space after the word.

10. In the Write and Insert Fields group on the Mailings tab, click INSERT MERGE FIELD, then select the correct field from the submenu. For example, select FIRST NAME. Add any additional fields by repeating steps 9 and 10.

11. When you are finished adding all the necessary fields to the address, click PREVIEW RESULTS. You will see a preview of the first recipient's letter.

12. When you are ready to print, in the Finish group, click FINISH & MERGE. From the submenu, click PRINT DOCUMENTS. The small Merge to Printer dialog box displays.

13. To print letters for all the recipients, click ALL. To print a letter only for the record currently selected, click CURRENT RECORD. To print the letters in batches, enter a range in the text boxes. Click the OK button when you are finished. The Print dialog box will display.

14. Make any necessary adjustments on the Print dialog box.

15. Click the OK button on the Print dialog box. The letters will be printed.

Using Outlook Contacts for a Mail Merge

Whenever you have a contact list in Outlook, you can use the mail-merge feature in Word to create a form letter and then merge content from the Outlook contact list to create customized letters for each person in the list. Before you begin this procedure, you must first create your address list and your form letter (see Creating an Address List, earlier in the chapter). You may also want to combine this process with the creation of mail-merge mailing labels (see Mail-Merge Labels, earlier in the chapter).

1. Open the form letter you have created.

2. Click the Mailings tab.

3. In the Start Mail Merge group on the Mailings tab, click START MAIL MERGE. The Start Mail Merge submenu will display.

4. Select LETTERS from the submenu.

5. In the Start Mail Merge group on the Mailings tab, click SELECT RECIPIENTS. From the submenu, click SELECT FROM OUTLOOK CONTACTS. The Select Contacts dialog box will display.

6. Click the OK button on the Select Contacts dialog box. The Mail Merge Recipients dialog box will display.

7. Select the recipients you want to print by making sure the checkbox next to the name and address is selected. Click the OK button to continue.

8. To insert the merge fields, position and click your cursor where the first item of merged content from the address list should appear. For example, if you want to insert a person's name after the word "Dear," click your mouse one space after the word.

9. In the Write and Insert Fields group on the Mailings tab, click INSERT MERGE FIELD, then select the correct field from the submenu. For example, select FIRST NAME. Add any additional fields by repeating steps 8 and 9.

10. When you are finished adding all the necessary fields to the address, click PREVIEW RESULTS. You will see a preview of the first recipient's letter.

11. When you are ready to print, in the Finish group, click FINISH & MERGE. From the submenu, click PRINT DOCUMENTS. The small Merge to Printer dialog box displays.

Using Microsoft Word

12. To print letters for all the recipients, click ALL. To print a letter only for the record currently selected, click CURRENT RECORD. To print the letters in batches, enter a range in the text boxes. Click the OK button when you are finished. The Print dialog box will display.

13. Make any necessary adjustments on the Print dialog box.

14. Click the OK button on the Print dialog box. The letters will be printed.

Creating an Email Merge

Rather than creating paper-based letters for your mail merge, you can create an email merge. You'll be able to combine a form letter you create in Microsoft Word with an address list or a contact list from Outlook and produce customized emails for each person on the list.

Before you begin this procedure, you must first have your address list or contact list and your form letter:

1. Open the form letter you have created.

2. Click the Mailings tab.

3. In the Start Mail Merge group on the Mailings tab, click START MAIL MERGE. The Start Mail Merge submenu will display.

4. Select EMAIL MESSAGES from the submenu.

5. In the Start Mail Merge group on the Mailings tab, click SELECT RECIPIENTS. From the submenu, click USE EXISTING LIST. The Select Data Source dialog box will display. (If you want to use your Outlook contact list, see Using Outlook Contacts for a Mail Merge, above.)

6. Click the Look In down arrow to locate and find the address list file on your computer. Select the file, and then click the OPEN button.

7. To select the names and addresses to use for the mail merge, in the Start Mail Merge group on the Mailings tab, click EDIT RECIPIENT LIST. The Mail Merge Recipients dialog box will display.

8. Select the recipients you want to print by making sure the checkbox next to the name and address is selected. Click the OK button to continue.

9. To insert the merge fields, position and click your cursor where the first item of merged content from the address list should appear. For example, if you want to insert a person's name after the word "Dear," click your mouse one space after the word.

10. In the Write and Insert Fields group on the Mailings tab, click INSERT MERGE FIELD, then select the correct field from the submenu. For example, select FIRST NAME. Add any additional fields by repeating steps 9 and 10.

11. When you are finished adding all the necessary fields to the address, click PREVIEW RESULTS. You will see a preview of the first recipient's letter.

12. When you are ready to print, in the Finish group, click FINISH & MERGE. From the submenu, click SEND EMAIL MESSAGES. The small Merge to Email dialog box displays.

13. Click the To drop-down list and select the field that contains the email addresses.

14. Type a subject in the Subject Line field.

15. Select HTML in the Mail Format field.

16. To send emails to all the recipients, click ALL. To send an email only for the record currently selected, click CURRENT RECORD. To send the emails in batches, enter a range in the text boxes.

17. Click the OK button and your email messages will be sent.

Working with Templates

Templates are sample documents available in Microsoft Word. Templates can save you time in creating commonly used business documents such as forms. Instead of having to take the time to create the form yourself, you can open a template, customize it, and then fill in the necessary information.

Some templates are installed when Word is installed on your computer. Others are available for download from Microsoft's website. You can also create your own templates for business forms that you use the most often in your work. When you save a document as a template, it is available when you start a new document within Word.

In the following tutorials, we explore some of the most common templates that are used by administrative assistants and secretaries:

- Telephone message forms

- Meeting agendas

- Meeting minutes

- Calendars

- Résumés

- Fax cover sheets

- Business letters

- Memos

- Status reports

- Invoices

- Time sheets

Figure 20-6 shows the templates available when clicking the File tab and then clicking NEW.

Telephone Message Form Template

Often, an administrative assistant will take telephone calls on behalf of his or her manager, rather than sending those calls to voice mail. Printed telephone message forms are useful for making notes about the calls received.

While preprinted telephone information forms are available, you can print your own from the templates available within Microsoft Word. The template can also be customized to add additional information that your manager may require. Follow these steps to create a telephone message form in Microsoft Word:

1. Open a blank Word document by clicking FILE > NEW. The New Document window will appear.

FIGURE 20-6 Templates available in Microsoft Word.

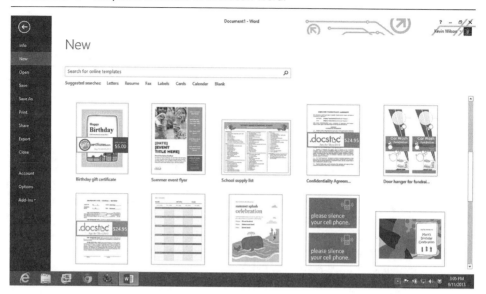

Screen shot used with permission from Microsoft.

2. A list of templates is available in the New Document window. In the search box at the top of the window, type "Telephone," then press ENTER on your keyboard. A list of templates related to "telephone" will be displayed.

3. Locate the template titled "Telephone Message Slip" and select it. Then, click the CREATE button. The template will be loaded into Word.

4. You can then print the template for your use.

Meeting Agenda Template

Many administrative assistants coordinate meetings on behalf of their managers. In addition to scheduling the meeting, reserving a room, and inviting the meeting participants, they sometimes have to create an agenda for the meeting. Consult with your manager about creating a meeting agenda. In most cases, it is a good idea to distribute the meeting agenda in advance to the participants via email attachment. You should also have paper copies available for distribution at the meeting.

Follow these steps to create a meeting agenda using Microsoft Word:

1. Open a blank Word document by clicking FILE > NEW. The New Document window will appear.

2. A list of templates is available in the New Document window. In the search box at the top of the window, type "Agendas," then press ENTER on your keyboard. A list of templates related to "agendas" will be displayed.

3. There are several meeting agenda templates available. You should open and review each of them to find one that fits your need. For the purpose of this tutorial, locate the template titled "Agenda." Then, click the CREATE button. The template will be loaded into Word.

4. You can then print the template for your use.

Meeting Minutes Template

During a meeting, administrative assistants are often required to take meeting minutes. This is usually done by taking notes on a notepad in addition to recording the meeting with a digital audio recorder and transcribing the details later.

A summary of the meeting is documented in the meeting minutes. The minutes should include the date and time, location, who attended the meeting, what was discussed, and any action items that were decided during the meeting. Follow these steps to use a meeting minutes template in Microsoft Word:

1. Open a blank Word document by clicking FILE > NEW. The New Document window will appear.

2. A list of templates is available in the New Document window. In the search box at the top of the window, type "Minutes," then press ENTER on your keyboard. A list of templates related to "minutes" will be displayed.

3. There are several meeting minute templates available. You should open and review each of them to find one that fits your need. For the purpose of this tutorial, locate the template titled "Meeting Minutes." Then click the CREATE button. The template will be loaded into Word.

4. You can then use the document to write the meeting minutes.

Calendar Template

Calendars can be created for posting on your wall or for keeping track of a specific project. You can schedule milestones and to-do items on the calendar, color-code certain dates, and print the calendar on paper for your own use or for distribution to a team. Follow these steps to create a calendar in Microsoft Word:

1. Open a blank Word document by clicking FILE > NEW. The New Document window will appear.

2. A list of templates is available in the New Document window. In the list of searches, click CALENDAR.

3. There are several calendar templates available. You should open and review each of them to find one that fits your need. Locate the template titled "20XX Calendar" (with the XX being the current year).

4. Then, click the CREATE button. The template will be loaded into Word.

5. You can then print the template for your use.

Résumé Template

Several templates are available in Word that allow you to easily format a professional-looking résumé. Follow these steps to use a resume template in Microsoft Word:

1. Open a blank Word document by clicking FILE > NEW. The New Document window will appear.

2. A list of templates is available in the New Document window. In the list of searches, click RESUME.

3. There are several résumé templates available. You should open and review each of them to find one that fits your need. For the purposes of this tutorial, locate the template titled "Resume."

4. Click the CREATE button. The template will be loaded into Word.

5. You can then use the template as a guide when adding your own work history and personal information to the résumé.

Fax Cover Sheet Template

You can quickly create a fax cover sheet from the many templates available in Word. Follow these steps to create a fax cover sheet in Microsoft Word:

1. Open a blank Word document by clicking FILE > NEW. The New Document window will appear.

2. A list of templates is available in the New Document window. In the list of searches, click FAX.

3. There are several fax templates available. You should open and review each of them to find one that fits your need. Locate the template titled "Fax Cover Sheet (Professional Design)."

4. Click the CREATE button. The template will be loaded into Word.

5. You can then enter specific information for the fax, print a copy, and include it as the cover sheet for your fax.

Business Letter Template

There are many sample business letter templates that will help you quickly create and customize commonly used correspondence. Follow these steps to use a business letter in Microsoft Word:

1. Open a blank Word document by clicking FILE > NEW. The New Document window will appear.

2. A list of templates is available in the New Document window. In the list of suggested searches, click LETTERS.

3. There are several letter template categories available. You should open and review each of them to find one that fits your need. Click the template category titled "Business." A list of subcategories is displayed.

4. You should review the many different business letters available by clicking each of the subcategories. For the purposes of this tutorial, click "Thank You."

5. A variety of thank-you letter templates will be available in this category. For the purposes of this tutorial, select the template named "Thank You to New Customer." Then, click the CREATE button. The letter template will be loaded into Word.

6. You can then customize the letter as needed for your purposes.

Status Report Template

Your manager may ask you to prepare status reports for various projects the department manages. There are several status report templates available in Word that can help you get started. Follow these steps to use a status report template in Microsoft Word:

1. Open a blank Word document by clicking FILE > NEW. The New Document window will appear.

2. A list of templates is available in the New Document window. In the search box, type "status report" then press ENTER.

3. You should review the many different status report templates available. For the purposes of this tutorial, click the template titled "Project Status."

4. Click the CREATE button. The template will be loaded into Word.

5. You can then customize the status report as needed for your purposes.

Invoice Template

In small businesses, administrative assistants and secretaries may assist their managers with billing customers. If your business does not use preprinted invoices, you can easily create and customize one of the invoice templates available in Word.

Follow these steps to use an invoice template in Microsoft Word:

1. Open a blank Word document by clicking FILE > NEW. The New Document window will appear.

2. A list of templates is available in the New Document window. In the search box, type "invoice" then press ENTER.

3. You should review the many different invoice templates available. For the purposes of this tutorial, click the template titled "Sales Invoice."

4. Click the CREATE button. The template will be loaded into Word.

5. You can then customize the invoice as needed for your purposes.

Time Sheets Template

In small businesses, administrative assistants and secretaries may assist their managers with payroll and keeping track of employee time sheets. You can easily create timesheets for use by employees using one of the time sheet templates in Word.

Follow these steps to use a time sheet template in Microsoft Word:

1. Open a blank Word document by clicking FILE > NEW. The New Document window will appear.

2. A list of templates is available in the New Document window. In the search box, type "time sheet" then press ENTER.

3. You should review the many different time sheet templates available. For the purposes of this tutorial, click the template titled "Time Sheet."

4. Click the CREATE button. The template will be loaded into Word.

5. You can then customize the time sheet as needed for your purposes.

Tracking of Changes and Revisions in Documents

Successive changes and revisions made to Word documents can be tracked, or recorded, thereby showing all modifications to a document along with who made the changes. By turning on Word's tracking feature, you highlight any corrections or alterations to the document and these changes remain in a contrasting color until they are "accepted."

Turning on the Tracking Function

The button for turning on this editing feature can be found on the Review tab, as shown in Figure 20-7.

FIGURE 20-7 Track Changes button on the Review tab.

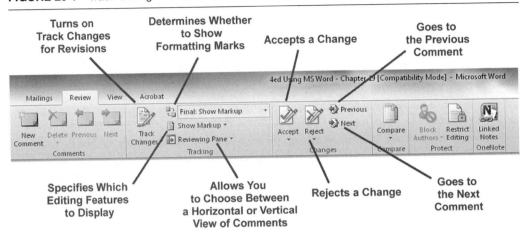

Screen shot used with permission from Microsoft.

To use the tracking feature when you want to review a document, follow these steps:

1. Open the document to be reviewed.

2. Click the Review tab.

3. In the Tracking group, click TRACK CHANGES.

4. From the Track Changes menu, click TRACK CHANGES.

Accepting or Rejecting Tracked Revisions

If someone has tracked his or her changes to a document you have created, you will need to review those changes and decide whether to accept or reject them. To accept or reject revisions, follow these steps:

1. Open the document to be revised.

2. Click the Review tab.

3. In the Changes group, click the NEXT button to see the first revision in the document.

4. To accept the revision, click the ACCEPT button.

5. Click the NEXT button to move to the next revision in the document.

6. Continue these steps until you have accepted or rejected all the revisions in the document.

7. To accept all the changes in the document at one time, click the down arrow on the Accept button and select ACCEPT ALL CHANGES IN DOCUMENT.

8. To reject the change, click the REJECT button.

9. To reject all the changes in a document at one time, click the down arrow on the Reject button and select REJECT ALL CHANGES IN DOCUMENT.

Inserting Comments in a Word Document

It is possible to insert comments within a document, as a feature of the Review function in Microsoft Word. Comments enable you to give advice or ask questions regarding things in the document without making changes in the document. To insert a comment in a document, follow these steps:

1. Select the text where you would like to insert the comment.
2. Click the Review tab.
3. In the Comments group, click NEW COMMENT.
4. In the Comment box, type your comment.
5. When you are finished, click anywhere outside of the Comment box.

Editing or Deleting Comments

To make changes to comments or to delete them, follow these steps:

1. Select the comment you want to edit or delete.
2. In the Comment box, enter any changes.
3. When finished, click anywhere outside of the Comment box.
4. To delete a comment, select the comment, and then on the Review tab, click DELETE.

Adding and Removing Draft Watermarks

A watermark is an image or text that appears behind the main text of a document. The most common watermark use is for designating draft or confidential documents.

To add a watermark to a document, follow these steps:

1. Open the document.
2. Click the Design tab.
3. In the Page Background group, click WATERMARK.
4. From the Watermark submenu, select one of the watermark options.

To remove a watermark from a document, follow these steps:

1. Open the document.
2. Click the Design tab.
3. In the Page Background group, click WATERMARK.
4. From the Watermark submenu, select REMOVE WATERMARK.

Using Microsoft Word

21

Using Microsoft PowerPoint

Microsoft PowerPoint is included as part of Microsoft Office and is used for creating slide show and multimedia presentations. PowerPoint presentations are commonly used in meetings, sales presentations, for training classes, and for webinars.

PowerPoint Views

The PowerPoint software allows you to view your presentation in several different ways. You can select different views using the View menu:

- *Normal View* is used for designing the look of the slides. Here you can work with the various fonts, colors, backgrounds, drop shadows, and so on (Figure 21-1).

- *Outline View* is best for working with text only. You can see your presentation in context, since you see the text of a number of slides at once. Also, Outline View gives you a sense of the relative importance of the various points you're making. Finally, you can easily add, rearrange, or delete slides in this view.

- *Slide Sorter View* allows you to see all the slides in reduced size. This view is used for arranging slides in the sequence you want as well as setting transitions, builds, hidden slides, and other features (see Figure 21-5, later in chapter).

- *Notes Page View* allows you to compose notes about each slide. The notes can be used to print a script for yourself or handouts for your audience.

To view your slide show, use the Slide Show menu. This is the view you use to present your presentation if you are going to do so on a computer screen or computer projector. In this view, since there are no toolbars or menus available, you primarily use keys to operate the show. For example, use the SPACEBAR to move to the next slide. After reaching the final slide in a presentation, the program exits from Slide Show View and the screen returns to the view you had before running the slide show.

Normal View

When you are in Normal View (where you'll likely be most of the time when you are creating a presentation), you can move through the slides by using the scroll bar on the right. You can click on the small slide images along the left side of the screen.

FIGURE 21-1   Microsoft PowerPoint in Normal View.

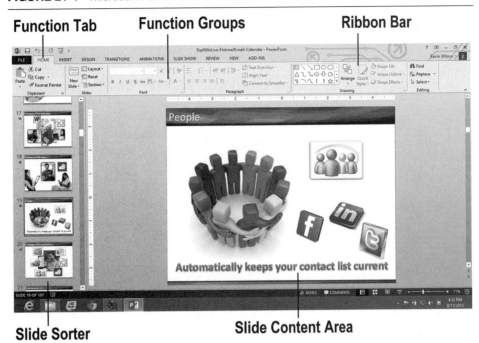

Function Tab   **Function Groups**   **Ribbon Bar**

Slide Sorter   **Slide Content Area**

Screen shot used with permission from Microsoft.

Using Zoom

While working with slides in Normal View, you can change the size of the image to make it more convenient to work with. The Zoom icon is located on the View ribbon bar and looks like a magnifying glass. When you click the Zoom icon, you are presented with a small menu that allows you to select the amount of magnification. To return to the Normal View after zooming, click the FIT TO WINDOW icon on the View menu ribbon bar.

Working with Multiple Presentations

Like many Windows programs, PowerPoint permits you to work with more than one file at a time. You can open several presentation files at once in PowerPoint, and copy and paste information between them. Each presentation opens in its own instance of PowerPoint. You can switch between presentations by clicking the PowerPoint icon on the Windows taskbar, and then select the presentation you want from the small preview images that appear.

Notes Page View

In Notes Page View, you can create notes about each slide in your presentation. These notes can be printed to serve as a script or as a handout for the audience. To switch into Notes Page View, click the Notes Page View button (Figure 21-2).

The slide appears on a representation of a sheet of paper, with an area below it for notes. To type a note, you can click inside the notes box to make a cursor appear. How-

FIGURE 21-2   Notes Page View in Microsoft PowerPoint.

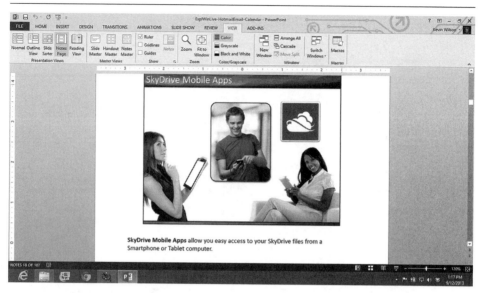

Screen shot used with permission from Microsoft.

ever, at this size it will be difficult to read your note as you type it. To solve that problem, you can use the Zoom icon on the View tab.

Outline View

You can access the Outline View on the View menu by clicking the Outline tab on the left just under the Presentation Views group. From Outline View, you can focus on the text of your presentation and work quickly from slide to slide (Figure 21-3).

Slide Sorter View

In Outline View, you can concentrate on the content of the presentation—the text and arrangement. To work with the appearance of the presentation, you'll use Slide Sorter View. To switch to Slide Sorter View, click on the Slides tab just below the ribbon bar on either the Home menu or View menu.

This view shows you the appearance of the slide, permitting your visual inspection. From here you can see if the colors are what you want, and if the general look and feel of the slide is proper.

PowerPoint Templates

A *template* is a presentation whose color schemes and layout formats can be applied to a slide presentation. PowerPoint comes with dozens of professionally designed, prebuilt templates you can use when creating your own slide shows (Figure 21-4). In fact, new presentations can be patterned after a default template called "Blank Presentation. pot," or you can select from a variety of templates.

FIGURE 21-3   Outline View in Microsoft PowerPoint.

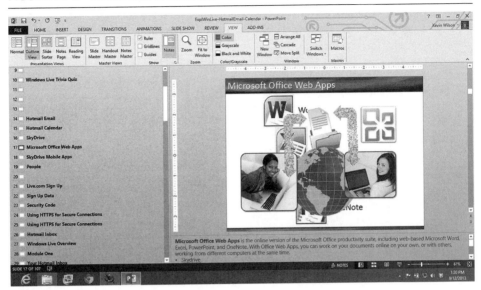

Screen shot used with permission from Microsoft.

FIGURE 21-4   Microsoft PowerPoint templates.

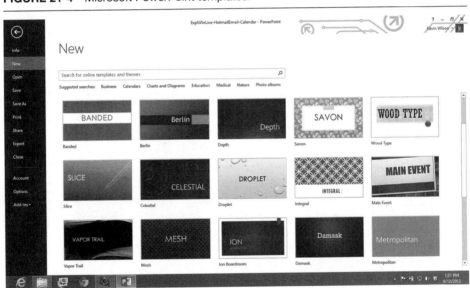

Screen shot used with permission from Microsoft.

After creating your presentation, you can even save its look and feel and use it again in another presentation by applying the template to the new file.

Changing a Template

Changing a PowerPoint template that you have chosen is a powerful way to instantly reformat your entire presentation. When you change templates, all formatting revisions you've made to the Slide Master, including font types and sizes, colors, and text position, are reset. However, changes that you made on individual slides will remain intact. Again, any formatting changes you made to individual slides will remain even though you changed templates.

Working with Slides in PowerPoint

After creating your slides, you can easily change the order of the slides in the presentation, copy information from one side to another, reformat text on a slides, and add or delete slides.

Adding a New Slide

You can add a new slide by selecting where you want the new slide to be and clicking on the NEW SLIDE button on the Home tab ribbon bar. Another way to create a new slide is to begin a new line in the outline at the top level. You begin a new line by pressing ENTER at the end of the previous line. The first text you type will be the title of the slide. When you press ENTER, you will start a new line of text.

Moving Text for Slides

If you need to move text from one slide to another, you can easily do it by selecting the text and dragging to another slide in the Outline View. When you release the mouse button, the text will be pasted into the second slide.

In Normal View, you can move text between slides by using the copy and paste feature on the Home tab.

Adding More Text to a Slide

If you need to add some text to an existing slide while in Outline View, the easiest way to do that is to press CTRL and ENTER at the end of the title line. This will automatically make a bullet appear and allow you to enter the next line.

Demoting and Promoting Text Lines

One of the most common features of a PowerPoint presentation is the bulleted text or numbered lists that accompany the slides. You can also have lines of text that are indented below another line. Indenting text is called *demoting*. Moving indented text out to be even with the rest of the lines or the bulleted list is called *promoting*. For example, if you need to demote a new line to become an item under the title, you can do that by clicking on the DEMOTE button.

As you might guess, you can promote items using similar methods (except you use the PROMOTE button, of course). If you promote an item all the way to the top level, it creates a new slide and becomes the title of the slide.

The Promote and Demote icons are available on the Home tab in the Paragraph group.

Rearranging Slides

To change the sequence of a slide, you should switch to Slide Sorter View. You can do this by clicking the View menu and then clicking SLIDE SORTER. This gives you a thumb-

FIGURE 21-5   Slide Sorter View in Microsoft PowerPoint.

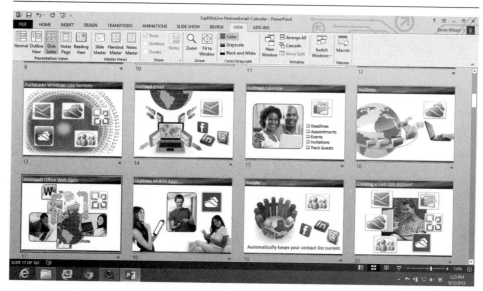

Screen shot used with permission from Microsoft.

nail view of the various slides in your presentation. To rearrange the order of your slides, you simply drag a slide icon to the new position. For example, if you wanted to move slide number 3 to the second position, you would click on the icon for slide number 3 and drag it until a horizontal line appears beneath slide 1 (Figure 21-5).

Deleting Slides

To delete a slide in Slide Sorter View, you select it and press the DELETE key. As with most Windows applications, you can undo a deletion (or any action) by using the Undo button in the top left corner of the screen. It looks like a curved arrow.

Using Transitions and Animation

The Transitions menu allows you to create transitions between the slides in your presentation. These transitions can take the form of fades, or dissolves and wipes, and are applied to the "incoming" (next) slide in a sequence.

Animation can be applied to the elements within a slide by selecting the element and then clicking the Animation menu.

For both transitions between slides and animations of elements within a slide, you can select an option from the ribbon bar. The Timing group of icons allows you to control the speed of the transition or animation.

Using Build Effects

In PowerPoint terminology, a *build* is a sequence of slides that displays each point, one at a time, in a bulleted list. While you could create each slide individually, using a build effect allows you to concentrate on other aspects of your presentation.

To reveal a series of bulleted text items one at a time during your presentation, select the text box, then click the Animations menu. Select one of the animations on the ribbon bar, then click the Effect Options icon and from the Sequence list, select BY PARAGRAPH.

Saving a Presentation

Once you've created a presentation, you'll want to save it. If you've used any Windows applications before, you already know how. You click the Save icon in the top left corner of the screen or you can click the File menu and then click SAVE or SAVE AS.

Previewing the Slide Show

One nice feature about PowerPoint is that you can run your slide show at any time while you're in the process of creating it. It's so simple to preview the show at any time that you may find yourself running the slide show often just to be certain that the effects come out right and the look is just what you want.

To run your slide show, click the Slide Show menu and then select one of the icons on the toolbar to start the presentation either from the beginning or from the currently selected slide. Your screen will go blank for a few moments while PowerPoint prepares to run the slide show. To move from slide to slide, use the space bar. Because different computer systems work at different speeds, you may experience a slight delay in getting to the first slide. Just be patient.

Here is a list of keyboard commands you can use while in the Slide Show. This table is taken from the online help screen, which you can display by searching for "keyboard shortcuts."

TABLE 21-1   Slide Show Keyboard Commands

To do this...	Press...
Start a presentation from the beginning	F5
Perform the next animation or advance to the next slide	enter
Perform the previous animation or return to the previous slide	backspace
Go to slide number __	Type the number, then press ENTER
Display a blank slide or return from a blank slide	Letter B or period
Display a white slide or return from a white slide	Letter W or comma
Start or restart an automatic presentation	Letter S
End a presentation	esc
Erase on-screen annotations	Letter E
Advance to a hidden slide	Letter H
Return to slide 1	Hold both mouse buttons for 2 seconds
Show or hide arrow pointer	=

Using Fonts and Color in Your Presentations

Fonts are usually thought of as the specific typeface designs for letters, numbers, and other characters that make up the text of a presentation. Windows supports an almost unlimited array of fonts, so using the correct one for the job is a fairly important matter.

Picture the front page of a typical newspaper for a moment. Headlines appear in larger, bolder fonts than the text that follows, designed to catch your eye as you read. Smaller subheads may punctuate sections of an article, allowing the reader to browse the piece quickly and grasp the meaning at a glance. The text of the presentation is in a smaller, less dramatic font so that reading the article won't become tiring on the eyes.

The point is that fonts should be used as a design element to make your presentation more easily absorbed by the audience. When you make presentations with a tool like PowerPoint, you want your material to be both easily understood and have enough pizzazz to keep everyone's attention. Fonts can go a long way toward getting your point across to an audience.

Changing Fonts

When you choose a template, an appropriate font is selected for you. But you can easily change the font for the entire presentation by making the change on the Slide Master, which we'll discuss later in the chapter. As a general design rule, though, you should stay with one font for all of the presentation. A single font will give your work a cleaner, more consistent look. If you mix fonts, you may end up with tacky-looking slides.

Although there are many different styles of fonts available, they fall into two basic categories, called serif and sans serif. A *serif* is a short line or stem at the end of the strokes of individual letters. This little "tail" lends a particular flair or style to the typeface design. *Sans serif* means "without the serif." A sans serif font has letters with no end strokes.

Studies show that serifs help guide the eyes and make text easier to follow. For this reason, publications with dense text, such as books, magazines, and newspapers, almost always use serif fonts. Typical examples of serif fonts include Times Roman, Times New Roman, New Century Schoolbook, Bookman, Palatino, and Courier (typewriter font).

For screen design, where text is kept to a minimum, a sans serif font may provide a cleaner look to your presentation. This is why television commercials and magazine ads frequently use sans serif fonts. Examples of sans serif fonts include Helvetica, Swiss, Arial, Avant Garde, and Modern. At least a few, if not all, of these fonts should be available on your particular computer system.

For presentations, you might use either a serif or a sans serif font, but you should avoid mixing them.

Changing the Font Size and Color

Each font style is available in a number of sizes, measured in units called *points*. The title of the slide is usually in a larger point size than the body text. To see the point measurement for the font size, simply look at the ribbon bar on the Home menu.

To increase or decrease the size of the text, simply click on one of the font size buttons until you get the font size you want. Each time you click the font size button, the text will become a bit smaller, shrinking to the next smaller point size available on your system. The other button will do just the opposite—that is, it will make the selected text get just a bit larger.

Color is an important aspect of character formatting. Here you have to be careful. The chosen template uses appropriately coordinated colors. To help protect you from choosing an inappropriate color, the template uses a color scheme. A small drop-down box appears with several colors shown. There's a reason so few colors are shown—these are colors matched to the color scheme you're using for the current slide, and they will blend in easily. Other colors are available, in case you need them, from the MORE FONT COLORS option.

Changing Alignments

With PowerPoint, you can use various paragraph alignments to reposition text. You can change the alignment for any text area, or for any individual paragraph, to centered, left, right, or justified.

While text is an undeniably important aspect of your presentation, the way your text is presented is also very important. PowerPoint allows you to modify the background to use a wide variety of colors and gradients, or fill patterns, to make your presentation as visually appealing as possible.

Changing the Slide Background

Shading means displaying a color that ranges from lighter to darker. Sometimes, shading is performed by adding what is called a *gradient*, which means a gradually changing range of colors. Gradients can display a color from light to dark, or one color to another, and in general add to the visual depth of your presentation.

You can change the background by selecting the Design menu and then selecting BACKGROUND STYLES.

Changing the Color Theme

Changing the color theme can dramatically influence the look of your presentation. Unlike a template, a color theme can be applied to individual slides as well as to the entire presentation.

You can change the color theme by selecting the Design menu. A list of various color themes is available on the ribbon bar as small preview icons. Holding your mouse over one of the icons will automatically change the color theme of your current page.

If you right-click one of the themes, a pop-up menu will allow you to choose whether you want to apply the theme to a single slide or all the slides in your presentation.

There may be instances when you want to use different schemes for different slides as a sort of color coding. In the absence of careful planning, however, varying schemes may cause problems with visual consistency, which may in turn annoy or distract your audience.

Using the PowerPoint Masters

PowerPoint lets you look at different masters that correspond with different ways of viewing your work. There's a Slide Master, a Notes Master, and a Handout Master.

The master shows you sample text to indicate the area size and placement of the title and body text. This helps you eye the layout of the template and gives you a way to reformat text on the master level.

Slide Master

The Slide Master controls the format for each slide in your presentation. For instance, when you want to change the size of the title on each slide, you simply change the title area one time on the Slide Master. You can access the Slide Master by clicking the View menu and then click the Slide Master icon.

Notes Master

The Notes Master gives you the ability to format your speaker notes. You can see your slide and type notes into the area shown to help remind you of important items to be covered in that slide, and any other related issues that may not be shown on the slide. You can access the Notes Master by clicking the View menu and then click the Notes Master icon.

Handout Master

The Handout Master is used to add text and artwork to your audience handouts. You can access the Handout Master by clicking the View menu and then clicking the Handout Master icon.

Inserting Visuals

Visual media, which include graphics, photographs, movies, and animations, can be added to multimedia productions in a wide variety of ways. These can come from commercial sources, such as computer clip art, or CDs or DVDs of images, or from photographic or computer supply companies. Clip art is one of the most commonly used sources of images for PowerPoint.

Clip Art

When PowerPoint is first installed, the clip art files are placed in a subdirectory on your hard drive. To open any of these files, click the Insert menu and then select CLIP ART. PowerPoint may take a few moments to compile available images the first time you use the INSERT > CLIP ART command. The Clip Art Menu will display. Enter search criteria that best describe what you are looking for, then click the GO button.

Each clip art category contains a number of images related by subject, as suggested by the titles. The Microsoft Clip Gallery is actually a miniature application within PowerPoint. You'll be able to add your own images and create your own categories, to better organize your clip art collection.

You can use the Clip Gallery program to preview clip art you wish to use in a presentation. Each image is represented by a *thumbnail*, or tiny version of the real thing. You might not be able to see all the detail in each picture, but you can get an overall idea about content, layout, and colors used from the thumbnail.

Once you've found the clip art that complements your presentation, you may find that a small amount of tweaking is needed to get it just right. PowerPoint allows you, like many other Windows-based drawing programs, to resize and move your graphics in almost any way you need.

Once a clip art image is pasted onto your slide, you can manipulate it by moving it or resizing it to fit your needs. Also, as a general rule, you should avoid using more than one image per slide. Too many images can clutter a slide and detract from your message.

Charts and Tables

Since your presentations cannot be dependent on clip art alone, it's nice to know that you can insert other types of graphic images into your slides. Charts and tables can communicate mathematical relationships in a visual way. PowerPoint actually has a graphing module built into the program. Just select the Insert menu and then click CHART.

When the datasheet is on the screen, you're actually using Microsoft Chart, a program included with PowerPoint. You could think of it as a (much) scaled-down version of Excel, or some other Windows-based spreadsheet application.

Smart Art

Another type of visual you can add to your PowerPoint presentation is Smart Art—colorful graphs and charts that you can customize with your own text for displaying bulleted text, conceptual diagrams, and organizational charts. You can access the Smart Art by clicking the Insert menu and then selecting SMARTART.

Original Artwork

In addition to using clip art, you can create graphics from scratch on the computer by using simple paint programs, such as Microsoft Paint, or more complicated drawing programs, such as Adobe Photoshop. Art can also be created outside the realm of the computer by way of pen, pencil, paint, crayons, photography, or any other medium, and then brought into the computer for editing and incorporation. You can digitize images with a scanner, shoot photos with a digital still camera, or have your camera film processed and the images digitized.

Drawings with Shapes

Another special tool, called Shapes, gives you the ability to create less conventional shapes, such as stars and arrows. You'll find this tool on the Insert menu of the ribbon bar.

The Shapes tool can be handy when you need something other than a simple rectangle or oval, and PowerPoint treats the shape as it does any other object. You can move and resize the shapes, type text onto them, or copy them for use elsewhere in your presentation. Using the SHIFT key will constrain your drawings—rectangles will become squares, ovals will become circles, and so on. Use the SHIFT key whenever you want symmetrical images.

Videos

You can incorporate videos into your presentations as simply as you can place graphics on the screen. Videos can be shot with a digital camcorder and transferred to the computer using a special cable or a video capture card. You can then edit the video using a program such as Windows Movie Maker and export it for use in the PowerPoint presentation.

Sound Media

In addition to still images and video, sound is another powerful medium. Audio in a multimedia presentation, just as graphics, can originate from a wide variety of sources, from commercial prerecorded music or historical speeches, to stand-alone sounds or part of a video, to narration recorded with a microphone connected to your computer.

Planning a Presentation

Consider the following as you plan your PowerPoint presentation.

- *Determine your goals and objectives.* Begin by defining your goals. What do you hope to accomplish? Is your goal to persuade or merely to inform? Persuasion may require getting your audience emotionally involved in your argument—getting them to care. On the other hand, if you are simply making a report, you may want your audience to remain objective, clear-headed, and somewhat emotionally detached. Define your objectives. What topics will support your thesis?

- *Consider the subject matter.* Are you presenting a training seminar, a presentation to managers or employees, or a sales presentation? This will determine the scope of your presentation and the tone you want to set.

- *Consider your audience.* Will it be employees, customers, business people, professionals, or mixed? Conservative or progressive? Formal or informal? Are they people you know personally or total strangers? Consider the audience's familiarity with the subject matter. If they are unfamiliar, or if the subject is somewhat technical, present one concept at a time and move in progression. Both subject matter and audience should help you determine the tone of your presentation. Do you want a lot of humor, or a more subdued approach?

- *Consider the size of your audience.* Larger audiences may dictate the need for more structure and formality. A smaller audience may be less formal, giving you more room for improvisation and one-on-one interaction.

- *Consider the environment.* Where will your presentation be viewed? Is it an office, small conference room, or hotel meeting room? How visible is the screen from each part of the room? If visibility is questionable, you may want to include handouts with printed versions of each slide. If you're not familiar with the equipment, try to arrange time for setting up and rehearsing your presentation before delivering the real thing.

- *Keep it simple.* Regardless of the purpose of your presentation, always keep it simple and focused. A simple, clear message can be delivered with greater impact and is more likely to achieve results. A complicated or muddled message will leave your audience confused and frustrated, which may hinder your chances for success. Keep the number of topics to a minimum. When expounding on each topic, make sure the information on each slide is clear and easy to understand.

- *Design for flow.* Outline your content in a topical format, with a beginning, middle, and end. Keep your ideas focused, organized, and directed toward reaching a logical conclusion. While sound reasoning and logic are not the only ways to effectively communicate or persuade, they are tried-and-true methods.

- *Design for drama.* Timing is everything. Design your presentation with a dramatic curve in mind. That is, build anticipation until you pique your audience's interest toward the end and deliver the central conclusion.

- *Think and plan ahead.* Do you need to prepare slides, overheads, or handouts? If you plan to distribute handouts, consider whether you want to give them out before or after the presentation. If before, the audience can follow along, write notes on the handouts, and have an immediate reference, should they have trouble seeing the screen. Yet, saving the handouts until the end may help you avoid giving away any surprises you may have planned.

- *Practice.* Practice delivering the presentation to a coworker or friend. Your friends can offer helpful critiques by letting you know if your presentation is clear and focused, if your style and manner are tasteful, and if your treatment is interesting enough. They can also help you smooth over some of the rough spots.

Making Your Presentation

When the day arrives for your presentation, there is a set of steps you might follow to ensure success. These guidelines will help you become a better developer and presenter. It's really true—practice does make perfect in the world of multimedia development. And post-presentation follow-up is an essential part of this process.

Step 1: *Set up.* The first step is to set up the necessary equipment.

Step 2: *Test run.* Make a test run through the presentation. This is especially necessary if the presentation was prepared on a different computer.

Step 3: *Backup plan.* Develop a plan B. If the computer breaks or does not make it to the room in which the presentation will take place, what will you do? Having a backup plan is always a good idea!

Step 4: *Deliver.* Deliver the presentation. This may seem obvious, but don't be afraid to just do it! If everything goes perfect, you will be lucky. If not, relax, smile, and work through the problems.

Step 5: *Evaluate.* Take time to reflect on the experience now that the presentation is over:

- What went well?

- What needs to be improved?

- What was frustrating?

- What was exciting?

- What did you learn from the process?

22

Using Microsoft Excel

What Is a Spreadsheet?

Many administrative assistants use computerized spreadsheet software to handle accounting chores, assist with budgets, and perform similar tasks. Spreadsheet software takes the place of the columnar pad that was so popular in the past. A columnar pad is divided into columns across the top and rows that run down the side. The rows and columns intersect in small boxes. Altogether, there are hundreds of these small boxes on each page. Similarly, an electronic spreadsheet is a large grid of columns and rows. A box where a column and row intersect is called a *cell*. Each cell has a unique *address*. Most spreadsheets label columns using letters, and rows using numbers. Therefore, the cell at the intersection of column C and row 5 is cell C5.

The largest spreadsheet can contain millions of cells depending on the memory size of the computer running the software. However, most of the applications you'll be working with use only 500 to 1,000 cells.

The most commonly used spreadsheet program is Microsoft Excel. Figure 22-1 shows a screen image of Microsoft Excel.

Navigating Around a Spreadsheet

When you are using a spreadsheet, one cell is always active—that is, ready for you to input data. This cell is designated by a cell pointer, highlighted area, or flashing cursor. To make another cell active, you use the arrow keys, numeric keypad, or mouse to move to another location. Owing to the limits on screen size, only a small group of cells can be displayed at any one time. If you wish to view additional cells, use a mouse or the arrow keys to move even farther on the spreadsheet.

Navigating around on a spreadsheet to view additional cells is called *scrolling*. There are also special commands that will take you to predefined locations on a spreadsheet, such as the bottom or top.

To make using Excel as simple as possible, designers used menus and ribbon bars with icons for various built-in functions. Table 22-1 shows a list of menus and some of the functions on each menu.

Spreadsheet Data

Any entry into a cell can be one of three possible items: a label, number, or formula. A *label* is a word used to describe information in your spreadsheet. For example, you

247

FIGURE 22-1   Microsoft Excel features and functions.

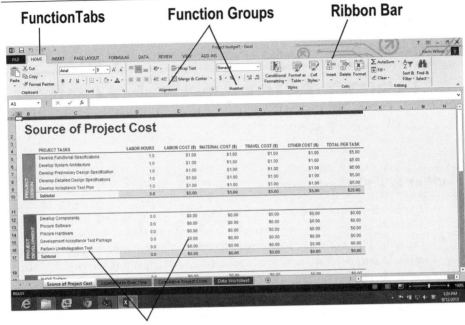

Screen shot used with permission from Microsoft.

TABLE 22-1   Excel Menus and Functions

Menu	Functions Available
File	save, save as, open, close, new, print
Home	cut, copy, paste, fonts, alignments, cell formatting, cell colors, inserting and deleting, sorting, find and select
Insert	pictures, graphs, smartart, pivot tables, text boxes, symbols
Page layout	themes, page setup, scaling, sheet options, arranging objects
Formulas	functions, formulas, calculations
Data	importing data, sorting, filtering, data tools
Review	spelling, comments, worksheet protection
View	views, showing features, zooming, windows

might want to calculate a budget for office expenses. Therefore, you would create a list of those expenses: paper, pens, computer supplies, stamps, and so forth. These words describe the numbers in another column or row, which is why they're called labels.

The actual expenses for the office supplies are the *numbers*. In order to calculate a total of all the expenses at the bottom of the list, you need to enter a *formula*, which is a combination of cell addresses connected by mathematical symbols—for instance, A1 + A2 + A3.

To enter a label, number, or formula into a cell, click the cursor on the cell you want to make active, then begin typing. As you type, the information you enter will be displayed in the control panel. When you are ready to put that information in the active cell, you either click the mouse or press ENTER/RETURN on the keyboard.

Formulas

A formula will work correctly only with numbers. Therefore, in order for a spreadsheet to distinguish labels, numbers, and formulas, most spreadsheet software programs use special predefined characters so that a user can specify the difference. For example, if the first character you type in a cell is a number, the spreadsheet will assume that entry is a number. If the first character you type is a letter, the spreadsheet will assume the entry is a label. And if you type in a special software-defined character such as "=", the spreadsheet will assume your entry is a formula.

Spreadsheet formulas can get complicated. Formulas can link information from one area to another so that totals from one group or section can be added to an overall summary. For example, an accounting system could be set up that allows you to enter expenses into various accounts. One formula would calculate the total expenses for each account; another would be used to link the total of a particular account to an over-all profit-and-loss statement.

The simplest formula is one that moves the data from one cell to another. If you entered the following formula in cell A1, "=Sum(A2)," whatever amount appeared in cell A2 would automatically also appear in A1.

The use of parentheses is an important aspect of formulas. For example, a formula such as "=Sum(A1:A10)" would provide a total of all the numbers in cells A1 through A10. When combined with other mathematical symbols for division, multiplication, and subtraction, a formula containing multiple sets of nested parentheses could be created, for example, "=Sum(((A1:A10) * A20) – A30)."

In order to create a formula correctly, you must know the order in which the mathematical operations will be performed by the computer. The natural order is to perform any calculation involving exponents first, followed by multiplication and division, and then addition and subtraction. For example, to solve the formula = Sum(($2^2 \times 10$) + ((144/12) – (5 + 6))), the computer would do the following:

2^2: First square the 2 to get 4 = Sum((4×10) + ((144/12) – (5+6)))

4×10: Multiply 4 by 10 to get 40 = Sum(40 + ((144/12) – (5+6)))

144/12: Next, divide 144 by 12 to get 12 = Sum(40 + (12 – (5+6)))

Then, do the addition and subtraction, starting inside the parentheses:

5 plus 6 equals 11 = Sum(40 + (12 – 11))

12 minus 11 equals 1 = Sum(40 + 1)

To finish, 40 plus 1 equals 41 = Sum(41)

Whenever a continuous group of cells is involved in a formula such as a row or column or block of numbers, rather than type in each individual cell address, a *range* is specified instead. For example, A1:A10 specifies a range of cells from cell A1 to cell A10 including all cells in between. A range can be as small as two cells or as large as the entire spreadsheet. It can be a row, a column, part of a row or column, or a block of several rows and columns. Most often a range is specified by identifying the beginning cell, followed by a colon or an ellipsis, followed by the ending cell.

Automatic Recalculations

One of the nice features of Excel is the ability to recalculate formulas automatically if you change any of the numbers in the cells included in the formula. If you have formulas that link various columns, rows, or sections, changing one number in a cell can cause numbers to change throughout the entire spreadsheet as each formula automatically recalculates. This recalculation feature is extremely useful for performing a "what if" analysis.

If you want to see the effect of a change on one particular area on a spreadsheet, enter the new number and see what it does to the overall total. This feature allows you to build what are sometimes called *spreadsheet templates*. For example, if you create a spreadsheet to keep track of petty cash or a project budget, once you create the spreadsheet and the formulas, you can go back and change the labels and the numbers and have a whole new spreadsheet with a lot less work. By saving the new spreadsheet with a new name, both the old version and the new version will be stored for future use.

Functions

Excel has a variety of built-in functions that can replace complicated formulas. One of the simplest is the *sum function*. It allows you to calculate the total of a range of cells. Functions are identified by first typing either "=" or "@" and then the function name. This lets Excel know that the entry is a function and not a label. The Formulas menu offers many different mathematical, statistical, and financial formulas.

Editing Your Spreadsheet

Another feature that can save you much time is Excel's ability to copy labels, numbers, and formulas from one location to another. For example, you might want to list your petty cash expenses by months, with each month in a separate column. Rather than re-creating the labels and formulas for each month, you could copy the entire first month's information and paste it into the next column or the next group of columns. Excel automatically compensates for the differences in cell labels from column to column and row to row and adjusts the new column so that the formula calculates the numbers in the new column, not in the original month column. The commands for selecting, copying, and pasting can all be found on the Home menu ribbon bar.

Arranging Layout

Arranging your layout to look the way you want is another useful feature of Excel. You can change the contents of any cell; add or delete rows or columns; and copy, cut, and paste data from one cell, row, column, or block to another similar area. All of these functions are available on the Home menu or by right-clicking a cell, row, or column on the spreadsheet and making a selection from the pop-up menu.

Editing Commands

The simplest editing feature is to access the contents of a single cell and to alter the data there. When you make a cell active by selecting it with the cursor or mouse, its contents appear in the control panel. There you can insert text, type in completely new text, or change a number.

You create new cells by inserting a new row or column. The INSERT command or CREATE NEW COLUMN OR ROW command allows you to do this easily. You select a column to the left of where you want to insert a new column, right-click, and then select the INSERT command from the pop-up menu. For inserting rows, you select the row where you want the new row to appear. Pointing to the very top of a column or the extreme left of a row with a mouse will allow you to select it.

To delete a row or column, select the entire row or column, right-click, and choose DELETE from the pop-up menu.

Whenever you insert or delete a row, it's important to note that some cells and formulas will move in the spreadsheet to a new cell address. Excel will automatically adjust to compensate for these moves, so that you don't have to go back and make changes. Therefore, if you have a formula that adds up the total of a column of ten cells, and you insert five new rows in the middle, the formula will automatically be changed to add up a total of fifteen cells instead.

Formatting features help you align the numbers and text to make your spreadsheet look good when printed out on paper. Formatting commands that are found on the Home menu allow you to justify the text in a document, center text or numbers, or make them flush left or flush right. You can format individual cells or rows to specify how many decimal points will be displayed or to create dates, dollar signs, commas, percentages, and scientific notations. You can change the width of a cell or column in order to display more information, such as a long label or a very large number.

Other Spreadsheet Functions

Saving and Printing

When you have formatted your spreadsheet to look the way you want, you may print it or save it. Printing and saving are commands you can select from the File menu. If you select SAVE, you'll be asked where you want to save your spreadsheet and to give it a name. You choose the drive where you want to save the file and then type in the name. Whenever you work with a spreadsheet that has been saved previously and you wish to save it again, it will automatically be saved under the same name in the same location. If you want to save two or more versions of a spreadsheet, you will need to change the name slightly. This can be accomplished by selecting SAVE AS from the File menu.

When you wish to print a spreadsheet, you'll be given an opportunity to determine how much of your spreadsheet you want printed, whether you want a header or footer, if you want borders or a grid, column and row numbers, and so forth.

Templates

To help get you started, Excel has built-in *templates*, which are pre-built spreadsheet models for common applications in business such as budgets and financial analysis. By loading a template, you can edit the spreadsheet to customize it to your particular business. This can be a great time-saver. You can access templates by selecting FILE > NEW, and then selecting one of the Office.com templates.

Spreadsheet Macros

Spreadsheet macros are another great time-saver. As you may already know from your word processing work, a *macro* is a way to minimize repetitive keystrokes. You can create a macro by selecting MACRO from the Developer tab.

The Developer tab is a special tab that must be added manually by customizing the ribbon bars. You can do this by right-clicking any of the ribbon bars and then select CUSTOMIZE THE RIBBON.

When you create a macro, you will be asked to type in the keystrokes you want to record. Once these are recorded, you'll be asked to assign a simple keyboard command to trigger the macro. Excel comes with built-in macros that you can customize and access with special keyboard commands.

Creating Charts and Graphs

It is easy to create charts and graphs with Excel. Follow these steps to create a chart or graph:

1. Create a spreadsheet and add the data that you want to use for creating the chart.

2. Use your mouse to select the data from the spreadsheet to be used for the chart.

3. Click the Insert menu, and in the Charts group, select the type of chart you want to create. For example, select BAR to create a bar chart.

4. From the drop-down menu, select the specific chart you want.

5. The chart will display in your spreadsheet. It can be moved and positioned anywhere on the sheet, as well as copied and pasted into a Microsoft Word document.

6. If the information on the axes of the chart is incorrect, click the Design menu, and click SWITCH ROW/COLUMN.

Modifying an Existing Chart

To modify an existing chart, follow these steps:

1. Right-click on the chart and from the pop-up menu, select CHANGE CHART TYPE. The Create Chart dialog box will display.

2. Select the kind of chart you want and click OK.

3. To change the data used to create the chart, edit the original spreadsheet that was used to create the chart.

Creating an Organizational Chart

The SmartArt function in Excel, Word, or PowerPoint can be used to create an organizational chart (Figure 22-2). To create the chart, follow these steps:

1. Create a new spreadsheet.

2. Click the Insert menu, and select SMARTART.

3. From the Choose a SmartArt Graphic dialog box, select HIERARCHY. A list of chart styles is displayed.

Using Microsoft Excel

FIGURE 22-2 Organization chart created using Excel SmartArt.

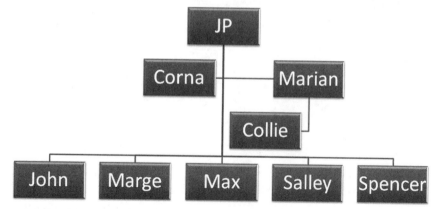

Screen shot used with permission from Microsoft.

4. Click the chart style you want from the list, and click OK. A blank hierarchy chart will appear on the spreadsheet.

5. Click the tab to the left with the small left and right arrows to expand the text entry box.

6. Enter the appropriate text for the organizational chart in the outline. Indenting items using the TAB key on your keyboard will create another level in the hierarchy.

7. As you fill up the chart, the text will get smaller and smaller. You can expand the size of the chart by clicking and dragging one of the corners of the chart.

8. You can change the look of the chart by clicking the Design Tab.

9. Select one of the SmartArt Styles to see the various possibilities. In addition, you can select one of the styles in the Layout group to modify the chart. One of the options even allows you to insert photos of each person listed in the chart.

23

Using Microsoft Publisher

Overview of Microsoft Publisher

Microsoft Publisher is an application used for creating documents with complex formatting, such as brochures, newsletters, flyers, and websites. Publisher allows you to change such things as page size, text, graphics, and border to create professional-looking documents.

The process for creating a document includes adding and positioning blocks of text, adding images and other graphic elements, and then positioning these elements on the page to create a layout.

Like all Microsoft Office applications, Publisher features Command tabs with ribbon bars, along with a page layout area that takes up most of the screen. There are Command tabs for File, Home, Insert, Page Design, Mailings, Review, and View. To the left is a Page Navigation pane that makes it easy to switch between pages in a multipage document. Figure 23-1 shows the Publisher screen. Most of the screen is dedicated to creating your layout.

Creating a New Document

To create a new blank document in Publisher, start by clicking the File menu and then select NEW. From the Available Templates pane, click BLANK 8.5 × 11. You have the option to select a blank page in a portrait or landscape layout depending on which icon you select. A blank page will be displayed that is ready for you to begin work.

Opening an Existing Document

To open an existing Publisher document from the File menu, click OPEN. Navigate using the Open Publication dialog to find the document and select it. Then, click OPEN. The document will be loaded into Publisher.

Working with Publisher Tools

Rulers and Guides

Microsoft Publisher includes rulers and ruler guides that help you position and align text and graphics in your layout. *Rulers* appear across the top and left side of the layout pane. Ruler *guides* are straight lines that can be positioned anywhere on your document to assist with layout; however, they do not print. Ruler guides are often use-

FIGURE 23-1   Microsoft Publisher features and functions.

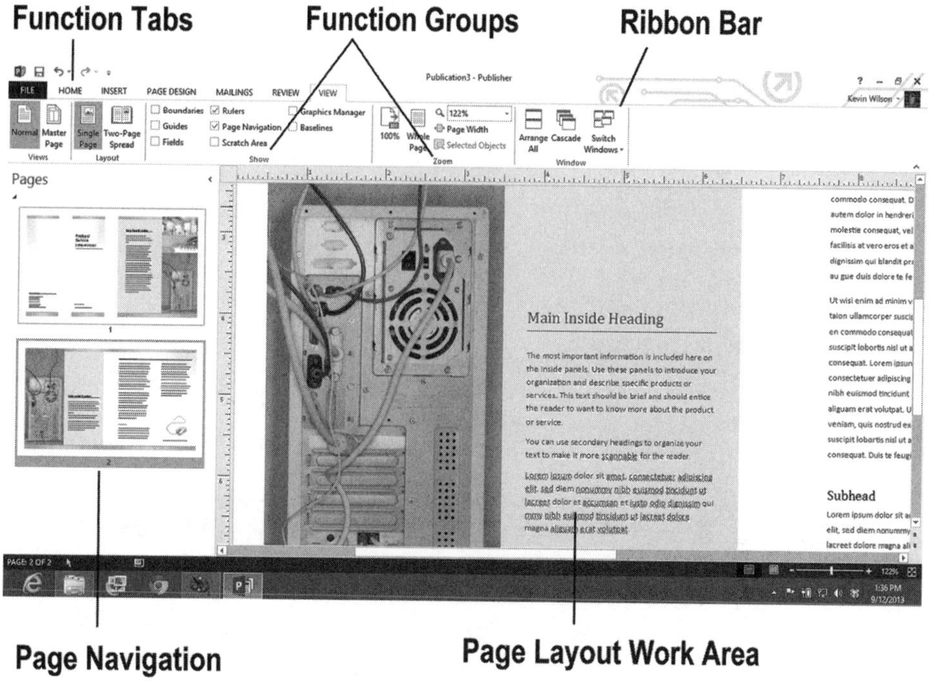

Function Tabs   **Function Groups**   **Ribbon Bar**

Page Navigation   **Page Layout Work Area**

Screen shot used with permission from Microsoft.

ful to mark where a brochure will fold, so you can balance other design elements on the panels.

To display the rulers and guides, click the View tab and click the checkbox for RULERS and the checkbox for GUIDES.

To position the ruler guides, place your mouse over the guide until the cursor becomes a double-sided arrow. You can then click and drag the mouse to move the guide.

Text and Text Boxes

Working with text in Publisher is similar to working with text in Microsoft Word. The main difference is that all text in your Publisher layout is contained within a text box. The text within a text box can easily be moved and positioned anywhere on the page. Before you begin typing, though, you must first create a text box.

To create a text box, click the Insert tab and then click DRAW TEXT BOX. Then click anywhere on the layout and the text box will appear. In addition, the Text Box Tools tab will appear as a new tab that offers a wide variety of text-related functions (Figure 23-2).

Click inside the text box to begin entering your text. You can also write your text in Microsoft Word and copy and paste it into a text box in Publisher.

After entering your text, you can change the font, font size, color, alignment, and add special effects using the functions available on the Text Box Tools tab. To make changes to a previously created text box, just click the text box. You can then edit the text to make formatting changes from the Text Box Tools tab functions.

FIGURE 23-2   Text Box Tools tab in Microsoft Publisher.

Screen shot used with permission from Microsoft.

Setting Up Columns

Layouts for brochures and newsletters often feature columns of text, just like a newspaper. You can create columns by creating multiple text boxes or by dividing a text box into columns.

To create column guides in your layout, click the Page Design tab, and then click GUIDES. From the list of guides, select the one of the predefined layouts. If none of the predefined layouts are appropriate, you can manually add column guides by clicking either ADD HORIZONTAL RULER GUIDE or ADD VERTICAL RULER GUIDE.

To divide an existing textbox into two columns, click the text box to select it, and then on the Text Box Tools tab, click COLUMNS. Click the number of columns you want from the drop-down list. Figure 23-3 shows a column layout sample.

Adjusting Line and Character Spacing

Publisher allows you to adjust the spacing between lines and paragraphs, as well as between words and characters. The amount of space between lines is called *leading*. To adjust the space between lines of text, select the text, and then click the Home tab and select the Line Spacing icon in the Paragraph group. You can then select whether you want your lines single-spaced, double-spaced, and so forth.

The amount of space between paragraphs is called *paragraph spacing*. You can adjust the amount of space before or after a paragraph by selecting the paragraph and then click the Home tab. Click the Line Spacing icon in the Paragraph group, and from the menu select LINE SPACING OPTIONS. The Paragraph dialog box will display. In the Line Spacing section, click the up or down arrows to increase or decrease the amount of space before or after the paragraph.

FIGURE 23-3   Microsoft Publisher layout with multiple columns.

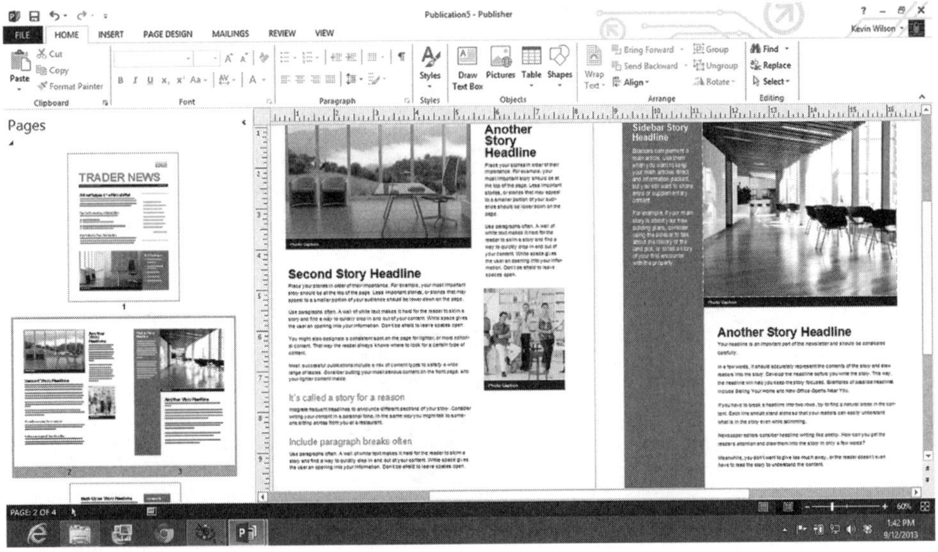

Screen shot used with permission from Microsoft.

The amount of space between characters is called *kerning*, and the amount of spacing between blocks of text is called *tracking*. A kerning adjustment is made between two characters within a word. To adjust the kerning, select the two characters you want to kern, and then on the Format tab, click the Character Spacing icon (it looks like a double-sided arrow with AV above it). From the Character Spacing drop-down list, make a selection. Tracking is essentially a kerning adjustment applied to an entire line of text. Select the line of text, and click the Format tab. Then click the Character Spacing icon and make a selection from the drop-down list.

Adding Pages

To add additional blank pages to your document, right-click in the Page Navigation pane and click INSERT BLANK PAGE. A new blank page will be inserted in the Page Navigation pane and a blank layout will display ready for you to begin work.

Using Master Pages

Master pages are templates that save time when creating multipage documents. Information that appears on the master page then also appears on all other pages in the document. The most common reason for using master pages is to include the same layout grid on each page, or to add headers or footers, page numbers, and graphics that appear in the same place on every page, as well as column guides.

To create a master page, click the View tab, and then click MASTER PAGE. The master page layout will be displayed along with the Master Page tab and ribbon bar. Any text, graphics, or other design elements that you place on the master page layout can

FIGURE 23-4   Master page in Microsoft Publisher.

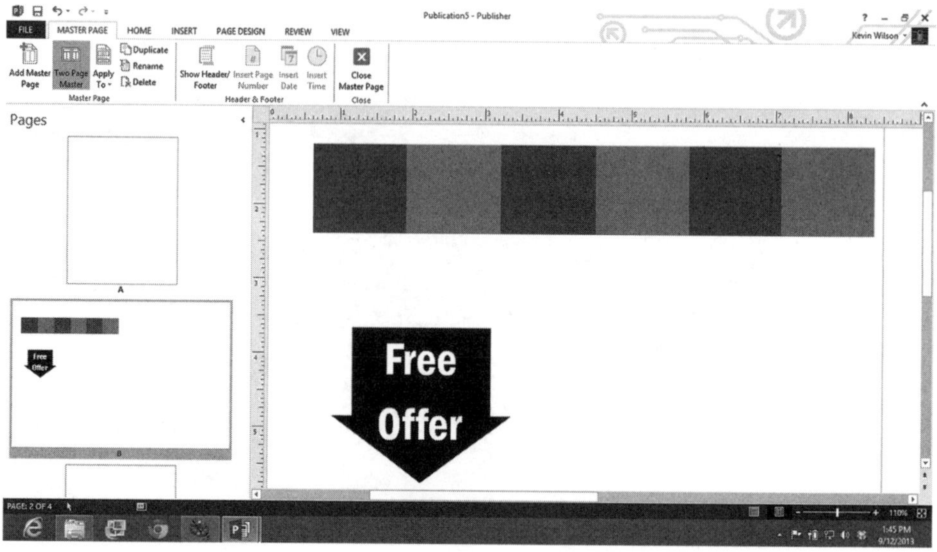

Screen shot used with permission from Microsoft.

be applied to all the pages in your document or to specific pages. Figure 23-4 shows a master page set up to repeat on other pages in the document.

Working with Graphics

Art and photographs can be inserted into your layout and positioned anywhere on the page. To insert a graphic, click the Insert tab and then click PICTURE. Navigate using the Insert Picture dialog box to the location on your computer where you have stored the graphic. Select the image, and then click the INSERT button. The graphic will then appear in your layout. Click and drag the graphic to position it in your layout.

You can insert clip art, graphic shapes, and WordArt also using the icons available on the Insert tab's ribbon bar.

To resize a graphic, select the graphic and click and drag one of the sizing handles that surround the image to change the height and width.

Graphics may be copied and pasted between pages just like text. Select the graphic, and then click the Copy icon on the Home tab. Click the page in the Page Navigation pane, and click the Paste icon to paste the graphic onto the new page.

Setting Up Styles

Styles are definitions of the text, font, font style, and alignment settings for a particular type of text in your document. Creating and using styles in your document will allow you to have consistent-looking elements, such as titles, topic headings, and body text.

The easiest way to create a style is to format a particular piece of text exactly the way you want it. Then you highlight the text and click the Styles icon on the Home tab ribbon bar. From the drop-down list, click NEW STYLE. The New Style dialog box will

FIGURE 23-5   Templates in Microsoft Publisher.

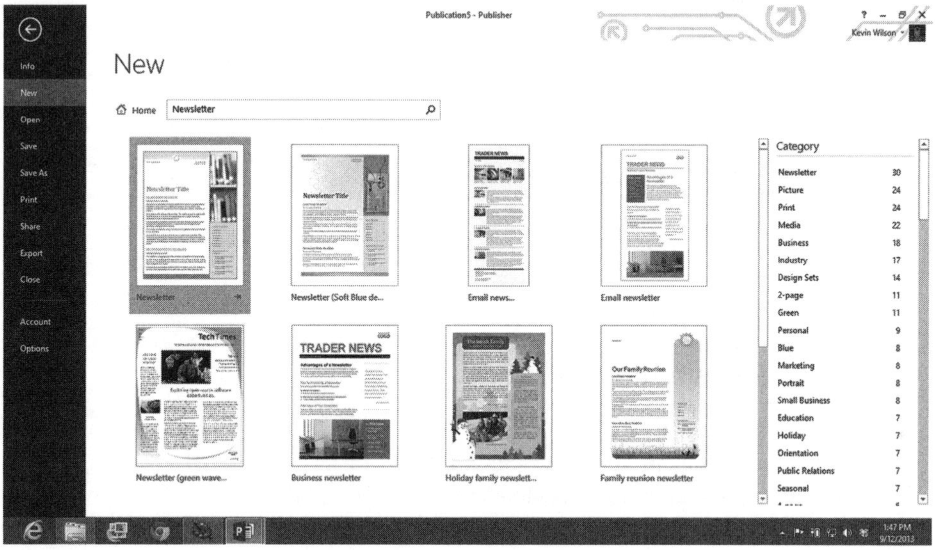

Screen shot used with permission from Microsoft.

be displayed. Enter a name for the new style. You have the option of setting the style for the next paragraph. This can be useful for the body text in your document, so that you can start a new paragraph and continue with the same style you were using.

To apply a previously defined style or to use one of the standard styles that are available with Publisher, first select the text in your document where you want the style applied, click the Styles icon on the Home tab ribbon bar, and from the drop-down list, click the style you want to apply.

Using Templates

There are a variety of templates available in Publisher that can give you design and layout ideas. You can start with a template and customize it as needed.

To use a template, click the File tab and then click NEW. On the Available Templates pane, select one of the templates listed (Figure 23-5). You can view additional templates by clicking the More Categories folder.

Each template icon will display a wide variety of individual templates within that category. For example, if you click "Flyers," dozens of sample flyer templates are displayed. Double-click the template you would like to use and it will be downloaded and displayed in the Publisher layout pane.

24

Using Microsoft OneNote

What Is Microsoft OneNote?

Microsoft OneNote is a powerful note-taking tool that provides you with a digital notebook for storing all your notes and information. It can be extremely useful to an administrative assistant who takes notes at meetings and then needs to be able to quickly find those notes again in the future. OneNote has a powerful search capability that makes it easy to quickly find your information.

Unlike a word processor like Microsoft Word, or an email system like Microsoft Outlook, OneNote lets you gather and organize text, pictures, digital handwriting, audio, video, and websites. All of your notes and information are organized into digital notebooks.

For example, you could use OneNote to store scanned images of handwritten notes taken during a meeting along with an audio file you record at the meeting using a digital recorder. You can also type your notes directly into OneNote and create separate notebooks for each project. Figure 24-1 shows the features of a page in OneNote.

When OneNote is installed, it links with both your other Microsoft Office applications and Internet Explorer. Documents you have created in Word or Excel can easily be imported into OneNote. If you find a website that you need to store in your notes, you can quickly save it by clicking the OneNote icon on Internet Explorer's toolbar.

Creating a Notebook

To create a new OneNote notebook, follow these steps:

1. Open OneNote and click the File menu.

2. From the File menu, select NEW.

3. In the Store Notebook On section, select the place where you would like to store the notebook. Normally, you will store your notes on your computer, but you can also store your notes in your SkyDrive.

4. In the Name box, give your notebook a name.

5. In the Location box, browse to the location on your computer where you would like to store your notes.

6. Click CREATE NOTEBOOK.

FIGURE 24-1   Microsoft OneNote features and functions.

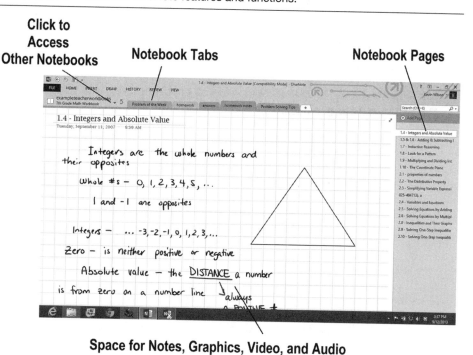

Screen shot used with permission from Microsoft.

Using OneNote Templates

Microsoft OneNote has a variety of built-in templates that you can use to get started. To find and apply a template to a new page in OneNote, follow these steps:

1. Open OneNote and open a notebook or section where you want to add a page.

2. Click the INSERT tab.

3. Select PAGE TEMPLATES from the Insert ribbon bar, then click PAGE TEMPLATES from the menu.

4. In the Templates pane, expand the template category for the type of template you want. For example, select BUSINESS.

5. Select one of the templates from the list and view the changes automatically on the notebook page. If you don't like the look of a particular template, click another one until you are satisfied.

Adding Pages or Notes

To insert a new page, in the pages tabs list, just click NEW PAGE.

   To add notes to a page, click anywhere on the page and just start typing. OneNote creates a textbox for each block of text you type. You move the textboxes around to organize your notes as if they were sticky notes on your desktop.

Saving a Notebook

Microsoft OneNote will automatically save your work as you take notes whenever you switch to another page or another section or close a page or section. There is no need to save your notes manually.

Printing a Page of Notes

To print a page of notes, click the File menu and then select PRINT. You can see what your notes will look like on paper if you select PRINT PREVIEW.

Microsoft OneNote

25

Using Microsoft Outlook

Microsoft Outlook is the most commonly used email and scheduling program in business today. Like all Windows-based programs, Outlook includes tabs and ribbon bars that display available functions. Outlook also includes a folder list, navigation pane, email message views, calendar, and tasks.

Figure 25-1 shows the various parts of Microsoft Outlook.

Tabs and Ribbon Bars

The tabs and ribbon bars in Outlook include buttons that are grouped together by function. The tabs include:

- File
- Home
- Send/receive
- Folder
- View

Each tab includes a ribbon bar with icon groups for various functions.

Navigation Pane

The Navigation pane is located along the left side of the Outlook window in Outlook 2010 and along the bottom of the screen in Outlook 2013. It contains the folder list as well as a customizable menu that allows you to easily select different Outlook features. As an example, MAIL takes you to your inbox for managing your email. CALENDAR takes you to the calendar for scheduling appointments.

Folder List

Outlook uses folders for you to store messages from your inbox, sent mail, deleted mail, and outbox. You can also create your own folders for organizing and archiving email messages you have received or written.

The Folder list displays all of your folders. Folders can be nested inside of one another for those who want a more detailed filing system.

FIGURE 25-1 Microsoft Outlook features and functions.

Create New Email Message   Tabs   Email Messages   Ribbon Bar

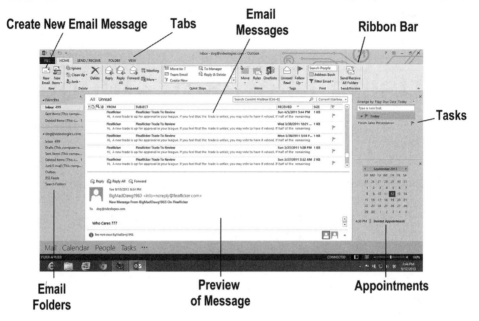

Tasks

Email Folders   Preview of Message   Appointments

Screen shot used with permission from Microsoft.

Search Field

Outlook includes a Search field that allows you to find any message stored anywhere within your folders. The default search searches only the currently viewed folder. You can also set the Search field to search all of your other folders.

Project Window

If you create a new mail message, appointment for the calendar, or task, a new window will open. This new window includes its own, unique tabs and buttons that are appropriate for your particular document.

Using Email with Outlook

The most common uses for Outlook include sending messages, reading messages, deleting messages, and printing them.

Sending a New Email

Follow these steps to send a new email message:

1. On the Home tab, click NEW EMAIL. An untitled message window displays.
2. In the To field, type the email address of the person to whom you are sending a message.
   a. An alternative is to the search for recipients already in your contact list.
   b. If you need to send a message to more than one person, use a semicolon to separate the email addresses.

3. In the Subject field, type the subject of the message.

4. Click in the body of the message and then type your message.

5. When you are finished and have reviewed your work, click the SEND button.

Reading Email Messages

Follow these steps to read an email message:

1. In the Folder list, select the INBOX.

2. Double-click the message you want to read.

Deleting Email Messages

Follow these steps to delete an email message:

1. In the Folder list, select the INBOX.

2. Select the message you want to delete, then press DELETE on your keyboard or click the DELETE icon on the ribbon bar.

Printing Email Messages

Follow these steps to print an email message:

1. In the Folder list, select the INBOX.

2. Double-click the message you want to print to open it in a new window.

3. Click the File Tab, then click PRINT.

4. On the Print window, click PRINT.

Using the Calendar with Outlook

The calendar within Microsoft Outlook has its own set of features and gives you the ability to schedule meetings and create reminders. You can share your calendar with your coworkers, so they'll know when you are not available. You can access the calendar by clicking CALENDAR in the Navigation pane (Outlook 2010) or Navigation bar (Outlook 2013). Figure 25-2 shows the calendar in Microsoft Outlook.

Selecting a Calendar View

Adjustable calendar views allow you to view your calendar by day, week, or month. To adjust your calendar view, follow these steps:

1. Click CALENDAR in the Navigation pane (Outlook 2010) or Navigation bar (Outlook 2013).

2. On the Home tab, click the desired view in the Arrange group.

Scheduling an Appointment

When you need to block time for a project, you can schedule an appointment in Outlook. Follow these steps to schedule an appointment using Outlook's calendar.

1. Click CALENDAR in the Navigation pane (Outlook 2010) or Navigation bar (Outlook 2013).

2. On the Home tab, click NEW APPOINTMENT.

FIGURE 25-2   Calendar features in Microsoft Outlook.

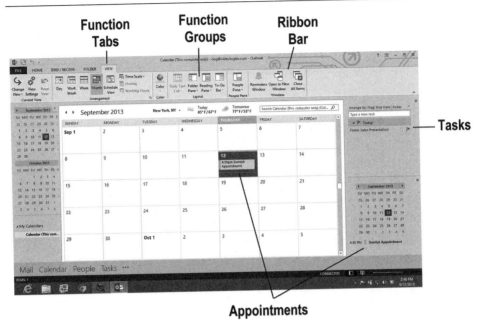

Screen shot used with permission from Microsoft.

3. On the Untitled Appointment window, enter information in the Subject and Location fields.

4. To add a desired start and end date and time, adjust the times using the down arrows and make selections from the list of dates and times.

5. To receive a reminder, in the Options group, click the down arrow for the REMINDER list and select how much time before the appointment you would like the reminder to appear.

6. In the body of the message, enter any other information you deem necessary.

7. Click SAVE & CLOSE.

Scheduling a Meeting

You can schedule a meeting with one or more people using the Scheduling Assistant tool in Outlook. This feature allows you to send one meeting request to a group of people rather than having to send separate emails to each one. Follow these steps to schedule a meeting:

1. Click CALENDAR in the Navigation pane (Outlook 2010) or Navigation bar (Outlook 2013).

2. On the Home tab, click NEW MEETING.

3. On the Untitled Meeting window, click SCHEDULING. The Scheduling Assistant will display.

4. To select meeting attendees from your address book, click SCHEDULING.
   a.   Select the attendees and click either the REQUIRED or OPTIONAL button.
   b.   When you are finished, click OK.

5. Click APPOINTMENT on the Meeting tab.

6. Enter the subject of the meeting in the Subject field.

7. Enter the location of the meeting in the Location field.

8. Set the time for the meeting using the Start Time and End Time fields.

9. In the body of the appointment message, enter information about the purpose of the meeting. If you have a meeting agenda, copy and paste it in the body of the meeting message.

10. When you are finished, click SEND.

Contact and Distribution Lists

Contact information can be stored in Outlook for the individuals with whom you regularly communicate. You can store names, addresses, phone numbers, and email addresses. Anyone who sends you an email can quickly be added to your contact list. You can also manually enter information about your contacts.

Adding Contacts

You can add contacts from the File menu or from an existing email message. To add a contact manually from the File menu, follow these steps:

1. Click CONTACTS in the Navigation pane (Outlook 2010) or PEOPLE on the Navigation bar (Outlook 2013).

2. On the Home tab, click NEW CONTACT. The Contact window displays.

3. Enter the information you have in the appropriate field, such as full name, company, email address, and so forth.

4. When you are finished, click SAVE & CLOSE.

To add a contact from an existing email message, follow these steps:

1. Open the email message.

2. Right-click the person's email address.

3. From the pop-up menu, click ADD TO OUTLOOK CONTACTS.

Making Distribution Lists

A distribution list is a group of email addresses for people who are generally related in some way. For example, you might want a distribution list for everyone in your workgroup or all of the team members for a particular project. To create a distribution list, follow these steps:

1. Click CONTACTS in the Navigation pane (Outlook 2010) or PEOPLE on the Navigation bar (Outlook 2013).

2. Click NEW CONTACT GROUP on the Home tab.

3. In the Name field, enter a name for the distribution list.

4. Click ADD MEMBERS.

5. From the drop-down list, click FROM OUTLOOK CONTACTS.

6. A list of your Outlook contacts displays. Select the members you want to add, then click the MEMBERS button.

7. Click OK when you are finished.

8. Click SAVE & CLOSE.

9. The distribution list will be available as one of your Outlook contacts. Select it when sending a message just like any other entry in your contact list.

Using the Tasks Feature in Outlook

A day in the life of a typical administrative assistant is filled with to-do lists, telephone messages, and emails. Rather than letting your desk pile up with Post-it notes, bombarding your boss with telephone message slips, or letting your email inbox fill up with hundreds, or even thousands, of messages, consider using the Tasks feature in Microsoft Outlook to organize your life.

If you learn to use the Tasks feature, you can plan your work effort and be more effective and productive. Tasks can also help you avoid feeling overwhelmed, when too much work gets piled upon you at one time. If you combine the Tasks feature with scheduling appointments in Outlook, you can prioritize your assignments and more effectively communicate delivery times with individuals who are expecting information from you.

If you and your manager both agree to use Outlook tasks, your manager can assign tasks to you electronically. When you complete a task, your manager will be updated automatically.

Using Tasks in Outlook involves the following:

- Viewing tasks
- Creating a new task
- Creating recurring tasks
- Assigning tasks
- Accepting a task
- Updating the status of a task
- Marking a task complete

Viewing Tasks in Outlook

Outlook's Task feature creates an electronic to-do list. It is also fully integrated with Outlook's calendar. Follow these steps to view Tasks in Outlook:

1. Click TASKS from the Outlook Navigation pane along the left sidebar (Outlook 2010) or Tasks on the Navigation bar (Outlook 2013).

2. You can view tasks in several different ways by clicking the appropriate radio button in the Navigation pane.

3. The Task Timeline view is useful when planning projects.

4. When you view email, if you maximize the right sidebar, you will see the to-do bar with a list of your tasks.

Creating a New Task in Outlook

Follow these steps to create a new task in Outlook:

1. While viewing tasks, click the NEW TASK icon on the far left of the Outlook toolbar.

2. An Untitled Task window will open.

3. Enter the description of the task in the Subject field. Also enter the Start Date and the Due Date.

4. Use the Status field to select the level of progress you've made on this task.

5. Use the % Complete field to list how much of the task has been completed.

6. Use the Priority field to set the priority.

7. Back on the Untitled Task window, you can put notes and other information about the task in the box below the reminder line.

8. You can set a reminder by clicking the REMINDER checkbox, and then selecting the time when you want to be reminded. At the appropriate time, a pop-up window will appear on your screen to remind you about the task.

9. You can group your tasks into color-coded categories by clicking CATEGORIES on the ribbon bar of the new Task window and then selecting one of the categories from the list.

10. To rename or add new categories, click ALL CATEGORIES from the Category menu.

11. Select a category and click the RENAME button to rename it.

12. Click the NEW button to add a new category to the list.

13. When you are finished click the OK button.

14. As an option, you can flag a task to follow up at a particular time by clicking the FOLLOW-UP icon on the ribbon bar of the new Task window and then selecting one of the items from the list.

15. To save your task and allow it to show up on your to-do list, click the SAVE & CLOSE icon on the ribbon bar of the new Task window. You should now see the new task on your to-do list.

Creating a Recurring Task

A *recurring* task is one that happens on a regular basis. For example, you might want to create a recurring task for your weekly status report. To create a recurring task, follow the same steps for creating a task. After entering the necessary information about the task, click the RECURRENCE button on the Task window toolbar. On the Task Recurrence dialog box, change the settings so the task will automatically recur based on the timing you select.

Assigning a Task

If you and your boss agree to use Outlook tasks as a way to assign work, your boss may create tasks and assign them to you. You would also be able to assign tasks to your boss, such as asking for reviews of material, or as a way to give your boss telephone messages. Follow these steps to assign a task:

1. To assign a task to someone else, start by creating a new task as previously described. After filling out the appropriate information on the New Task window, click the ASSIGN icon on the Ribbon Bar.

2. Enter the email address of the person to whom you want to assign the task in the To field. You can also check the box to indicate whether you want the task to appear on your own to-do list.

3. There is also a checkbox to indicate whether you would like to receive an email report when the task has been completed.

4. Click the SEND button to email the task request.

Accepting an Assigned Task

You may receive task assignments from your manager or colleagues as email messages in Outlook. Follow these steps to accept an assigned task:

1. To view the task, double-click the message in your Inbox.

2. To accept the task, click the green ACCEPT checkmark on the Ribbon Bar. Your to-do list will be updated with the task automatically.

Updating the Status of a Task

If a task has been assigned to you, when you update the status, the person who assigned it to you will be automatically notified of your status change. Follow these steps to update the status on a task:

1. Click TASKS from the Outlook Navigation pane along the left sidebar (Outlook 2010) or Tasks on the Navigation bar (Outlook 2013).

2. Double-click the task you want to update from the list. The Task window will display.

3. Click the Status field and update the status.

4. Click the up or down arrows for the % COMPLETE field to update the completion status.

5. Click SAVE & CLOSE.

Marking a Task as Completed

When you finish a task, you should mark it as completed. If the task was assigned to you by someone else, when you mark it as completed, the person who created the task for you will be notified. To complete a task, follow these steps:

1. Click TASKS from the Outlook Navigation pane along the left sidebar (Outlook 2010) or Tasks on the Navigation bar (Outlook 2013).

2. Double-click the task you want to complete from the list. The Task window will display.

3. Click MARK COMPLETE. The Task window will automatically close.

26

Using Microsoft Web Applications

Microsoft Web applications are Web versions of popular Microsoft Office programs like Word, Excel, PowerPoint, and OneNote. These scaled-back online versions are not only free but they also allow for collaboration because the documents can be shared by a work team.

To access Microsoft Web applications, first register for a free Windows Live account at http://www.live.com. In addition to giving you access to the Microsoft applications, Windows Live provides you with an email account, links to Skype, a photo-sharing service, an instant messaging program, and SkyDrive. After registration, use your ID and password to sign into Windows live, then click the link at the top for OFFICE.

Creating an Online Document with Microsoft Web Applications

Clicking any of the icons for Word, Excel, PowerPoint, or OneNote will allow you to create a new online document. You'll be asked to give the document a name and determine with whom it should be shared. After clicking the SAVE button, a Web version of the application will open in your Web browser (Figure 26-1).

Working with a Microsoft Word Web Application

If you already use Microsoft Office applications, you'll notice that the Web versions don't have all the same menu options. For example, the Web version of Word has only the File, Home, Insert, and View menus. Each menu has a limited ribbon bar with icons for common features like the clipboard, fonts, paragraph, styles, and spell-checking.

To save your work, click the Diskette icon or click the File menu and then select SAVE. You can also print your work using the PRINT option on the File menu.

The Open in Word option will open a copy of your document in your regular full version of Microsoft Word.

To share your document with others, click the File menu and then select SHARE. The Edit Permissions window will display, allowing you to determine who gets access to the document (Figure 26-2). You can enter specific email addresses, determine whether the person can view or edit the document, and then send a notification to the person giving the individual a link to the document. Everyone who shares a document and works collaboratively must have a Windows Live account.

FIGURE 26-1   Web version of Microsoft Word.

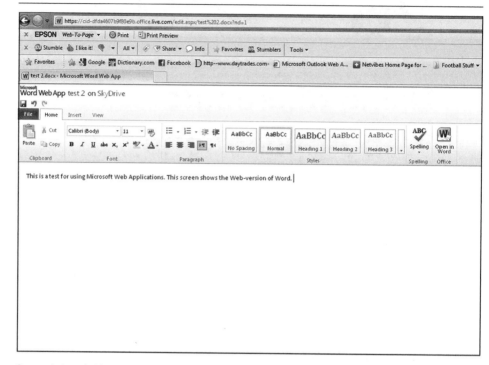

Screen shot used with permission from Microsoft.

FIGURE 26-2   Email notification with link to shared document.

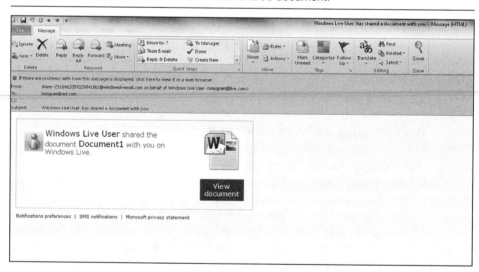

Screen shot used with permission from Microsoft.

Working with a Microsoft Excel Web Application

The Microsoft Excel Web application is limited to the File, Home, and Insert menus. The File menu offers the same options as just discussed for the Web version of Word, including the ability to save, print, and share. The Home menu offers the clipboard functions, font, alignment, number formatting options, table controls, sorting, inserting and deleting cells, data connections, search, and Open in Excel. The Insert menu offers the ability to create a table, chart or graph, or hyperlink.

Working with a Microsoft PowerPoint Web Application

The Microsoft PowerPoint Web application offers the ability to create simple presentations that include text and graphics. Menus are limited to File, Home, Insert, and View.

Like the other Web applications, when you click the PowerPoint Web application you'll be asked to name your presentation and determine with whom you will share your presentation. You are given the opportunity to select a theme for your presentation or begin with no theme. You can then begin creating slides. Icons on the Home menu ribbon bar allow you to create new slides, delete, duplicate, or hide. The clipboard and font groups give you similar functionality to the regular version of Microsoft PowerPoint.

Working with a Microsoft OneNote Web Application

The Microsoft OneNote Web application offers the ability to take notes online and open and organize them later in Microsoft OneNote. Menus are limited to File, Home, Insert, and View.

You can build a basic notebook with multiple pages using the OneNote Web application. The Insert menu allows you to insert a new page or section, as well as add tables, graphics, and hyperlinks to your notes.

Managing Your Microsoft Web Application Documents

After creating and saving a Microsoft Web application document, you can close the document by selecting FILE > CLOSE or by clicking the X in the top right corner of the Web application window (not the CLOSE button for the browser). The All Documents window displays a list of all your personal and shared documents (Figure 26-3). This window can be accessed after signing into Windows Live by clicking OFFICE > YOUR DOCUMENTS from the Home page

If you hold your mouse over any of the documents in the list, a pop-up menu displays the options. You can edit the document in your browser, open the document in your regular Microsoft Office application, share the document, rename it, download it, or delete it.

Using SkyDrive to Share Files

All of the documents you create using Microsoft Web applications are automatically stored on your Windows SkyDrive. You can access the SkyDrive from the Windows Live Home page by clicking WINDOWS LIVE > SKYDRIVE. Figure 26-4 shows the folders and files stored in Windows Live SkyDrive.

FIGURE 26-3   Microsoft Web application documents.

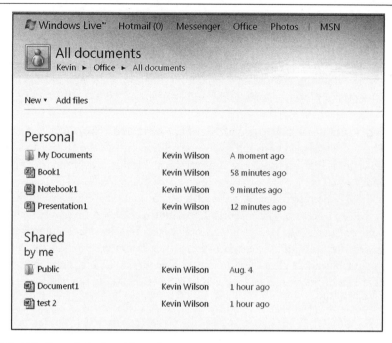

Screen shot used with permission from Microsoft.

FIGURE 26-4   Windows Live SkyDrive.

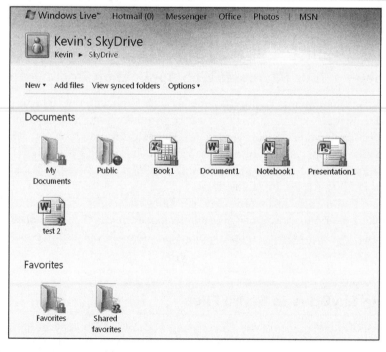

Screen shot used with permission from Microsoft.

SkyDrive displays icons for your saved Web application document as well as any documents you upload to the SkyDrive. To upload a file from your computer, click the ADD FILES link. You can move files to the SkyDrive by dragging and dropping them.

Like the Web applications, you can use SkyDrive to share files with other people. It is a great way to collaborate in a work team. For example, a report that many people need to review or comment on could be uploaded to the SkyDrive, with view or edit access given to the team members. Another good use for SkyDrive would be creating a project plan using a Microsoft Excel Web application spreadsheet. As team members finish their tasks, they could go online and update the spreadsheet.

SkyDrive for PC and Macintosh

To sync files that you want to keep both on SkyDrive and on your computer, you can install SkyDrive for Windows or SkyDrive for Mac on your computer. There, a folder is created where you keep your desktop copies of files that are also on your SkyDrive. Changes that you make to a file in one location will automatically update in the other location so that all copies remain in sync.

Even if you're away from your computer and forgot to put something into your computer's SkyDrive folder, you can still access it because SkyDrive gives you the ability to remotely access all of your computer's contents through SkyDrive.com.

To install SkyDrive on a Windows computer, click PCs on your SkyDrive homepage. Then click DOWNLOAD SKYDRIVE FOR WINDOWS and follow the standard installation instructions.

To install SkyDrive for Mac, you'll need a Mac OS X 10.7 (Lion) operating system or higher. From your SkyDrive page, you'll click GET SKYDRIVE APPS at the bottom left of your screen. Then click on the MAC Tile to go to the download page. Click DOWNLOAD NOW, and follow the online instructions.

After you complete the installation process, the SkyDrive folder on your computer displays, duplicating the default folders and any new folders you've created. The checkmarks next to these folders mean they are in sync with SkyDrive.com, and any updates you make to a document in these folders will be automatically updated in all locations.

To add a file or photo, simply navigate to the file on your computer, then click and drag, or copy and paste them into your SkyDrive folder.

Once SkyDrive is installed, if you're away from your computer and realize you forgot to move a file into your SkyDrive folder, you can still access it through SkyDrive .com as long as your computer is connected to the Internet.

The first time you use SkyDrive to remotely connect to your computer, Windows Live, for added security, provides a code that you will use to complete the sign in. This will help protect your computer from unauthorized access. After you click to sign in, Windows Live sends the security code to the phone or alternate email address you entered when registering for a live.com account. Check your phone or email, then enter the code. Now click to check the box next to I TRUST THIS PC. Use it to verify my account in the future. Add a name to identify the computer, then click SUBMIT.

Your computer's folders, libraries, and connected drives appear as tiles on SkyDrive .com. Click on a tile to open it and navigate to your file.

You'll hover your cursor over the file to bring up the checkbox on the tile. Then click to check the box.

Uploading Files to SkyDrive

Click UPLOAD TO SKYDRIVE at the top of your screen to upload a file, then choose where you want to save the file. When the upload is complete, you will find the uploaded file in the folder where you saved it.

SkyDrive Mobile App

If you have a Smartphone or tablet, you can access SkyDrive while you're out and about. The SkyDrive Mobile app is available for the iPhone, iPad, Android phone, Android tablets, and the Windows Surface. Once installed, you'll be able to access your Office Web app documents on your mobile device.

To install the SkyDrive app on your iPhone or iPad, go to the Apple Apps store and search for SkyDrive.

To install the SkyDrive app on your Android phone or tablet, go to the Google Play Store and search for SkyDrive.

Once the app is installed, when you first access the app, you'll need to sign into your Windows Live account. You'll then see the contents of your SkyDrive. To open a file or folder, just select it.

To open a file or folder, just select it. The SkyDrive mobile app does not provide the capability to edit your documents; however, if you have another app that can handle word processing, spreadsheets, or presentations, you can open your file in the companion app.

The SkyDrive mobile app does give you the ability to share a document with someone else and edit the permissions for who can see it.

27

Gmail and Google Docs

Google apps are an excellent free resource for businesses. Imagine having an email account that is yours for life, that doesn't change when you change jobs or change Internet providers. And this email account has instant messaging and video calls built in. What if it came with an online calendar where you could share your schedule with anyone you wanted anywhere in the world? What if you could easily send invitations to meetings, create word processing documents, spreadsheets, and presentations without having to purchase expensive desktop software? Imagine having access to your files from any computer in the world and being able to access your files from your phone or tablet. Imagine being able to share those files with anyone you choose—coworkers, family, and friends—and collaborating without ever being in the same room. Imagine publishing anything you want on the Internet, and creating free websites for your office, your club, or your family. With Google Apps, all of these things are possible and, what's more, they're all free.

The Google Account

To access all the free services available to you through Google, you'll first create a Google account. There's no fee for this account, and it's simple to set up. Your Google account is like a portal into many popular Google services, including Gmail, Google Plus, Google Calendar, Google Drive, Google Sites, and YouTube.

Gmail is Google's Internet-based email service. With Gmail, you can send and receive messages from any computer that has Internet access. You can also attach photos and videos to your email, and even use Gmail Chat to converse live over the Internet via text, voice, or video just by clicking a few buttons.

Google Plus is a new social networking platform similar to Facebook.

Google Calendar is a scheduling tool that integrates with Gmail to help you keep track of appointments and events, organize your to-do list, and invite people to meetings and gatherings.

Google Drive gives you free access to word processing, spreadsheet, presentation, forms, and drawing software, delivered to you through the Internet. It can be accessed from any Internet-ready computer.

Google Sites gives you the tools to create your own free website. The simple design makes it easy to share with a group, keeping the group members posted on upcoming events and updating them on news and assignments.

Access to all of these free services and more are available to you, once you create a Google account.

You do that on Google's sign-up page. You'll fill in the simple online form, and make up a user name and password that you'll use to access your account. You will also be required to fill in your birthday and gender. Phone and current email address are optional. From there you'll be guided to the Create Your Photo page, where you can add a picture of yourself that will appear on your Gmail page. Or you can skip this step and add a photo at another time. Then on the welcome page, you'll see your new email address.

Google Chrome

Google services can be accessed from many popular web browsers. But for speed and performance enhancements, its best to use Google Chrome. To install Google Chrome on a PC with Windows 7, Vista, or XP, go to www.google.com/chrome and follow the online instructions. To install it on a Mac with Mac OSX 10.5 or later, go to www .google.com/mac.

Gmail

Gmail is the free email program that comes with your Google account. With Gmail, everything is just a matter of a few clicks.

When you sign into your Gmail page, you'll find everything you need to send and receive emails. You'll see your Inbox here, where you'll receive messages (Figure 27-1). The first time you sign in, a few emails will already be listed, sent to you from the Gmail team. New, unread emails will be listed in bold font. You'll click on an email to open the message.

You'll click the red COMPOSE button to send emails. This will take you to a blank email page where you'll fill in the recipient's email address and the subject, and type your message.

The Sent Mail tab enables you to see messages you've already sent. The Drafts tab saves messages that you're working on, but haven't sent yet.

The Circles tab integrates with Google Plus to create circles of family, friends, and colleagues.

The Chat tab is the starting point for conversing live over the Internet through text, voice, and video calls.

Sending and Receiving Email with Gmail

To send and receive email with Gmail, follow these steps:

1. To access your Gmail page, go to www.gmail.com and enter your user name and password to sign in. Click the SIGN IN button.

2. This takes you to your Gmail page. New messages are in bold font.

3. Click on an email message to open it. The message opens so you can read it.

4. To send a message, click the red COMPOSE button.

5. The cursor defaults to the To window. Type in the email address then click on the SUBJECT line.

6. Type in the topic of your message.

FIGURE 27-1   The Gmail Inbox.

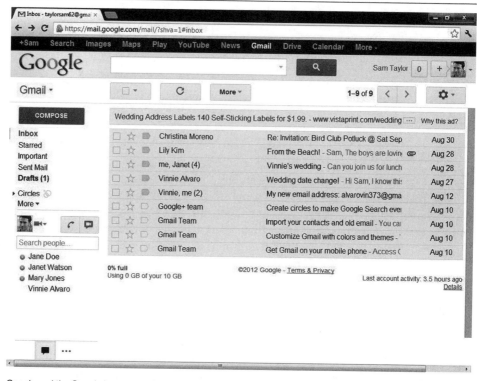

Google and the Google logo are registered trademarks of Google Inc., used with permission.

Gmail and Google Docs

7. Then click on the MESSAGE field.

8. Type your message.

9. Then click the red SEND button.

10. Your message has been sent, and you will be returned to the Inbox on your Gmail page.

11. To check your sent message, click SENT MAIL.

12. Your sent mail appears with the name and subject line.

Printing a Gmail Message

If you want to print a paper copy of an email message, just click the small printer icon. This will take you to your printer's onscreen directions. When you're finished printing, you may need to close the print window to get back to your message.

Replying to and Forwarding Messages

To reply to or forward a Gmail message, follow these steps:

1. Click to open a message in your Inbox.

2. To reply to the message, click the REPLY button.

3. The email is set to reply back to the person and your cursor will be positioned at the top of the message field above the previous message.

4. Enter your reply.

5. Click the SEND button.

6. To forward a message you've opened, click the FORWARD button.

7. The cursor defaults to the To field. Enter the person's email address.

8. Click at the top of the message field and enter your own message.

9. When you are finished, click the SEND button.

Attachments

You can "attach" other files, such as pictures or documents that are stored on your computer, to your email messages using Gmail. To add an attachment to a message you're composing, click ATTACH A FILE. Then browse to the file you want to attach. Click on the file, then click the OPEN button. This adds the attachment to your message.

If you see that an attachment has been added to a message you've received, click VIEW, under the Attachment listing. This opens the attachment.

Contact Manager

To keep track of your contacts, Gmail provides an online address book, called the Contact Manager. The names of your contacts will be listed here in alphabetical order. You can add people to your contacts yourself, or when people email you, you can add them to the list. Google also automatically stores the twenty most frequently used email addresses. You can also organize your contacts into groups for ease in sending group emails.

To access Contact Manager, after signing into Gmail, click the GMAIL tab. Then click CONTACTS from the drop-down list. You can select people who have emailed you and then click ADD TO MY CONTACTS. You can also enter people who haven't emailed you yet by clicking the NEW CONTACT button and then entering the person's contact information.

Text, Voice, and Video Calls

Making text, voice, and video calls through your computer is easy with Gmail Chat. Typing quick text messages back and forth with another Gmail user, called Instant Messaging, is available as soon as you set up your Gmail account. To make voice and video calls, you'll need a microphone and webcam attached to your computer. Then all you need to do is download and install the voice and video plugin. You can get to this download by clicking the down arrow that pops up when you hover your cursor over the Chat tab. Click Voice and Video Plugin. Then follow the online instructions. It's quick and easy. After you've downloaded and installed the plugin, you're ready to chat by text, voice, or video.

First you'll need to invite someone to chat. The person will need either to have a Gmail account or to sign up for Gmail Chat through Google Talk at www.google.com/talk.

To send the invitation, hover your cursor over the name in your contacts list to open the contact's profile. Then click INVITE TO CHAT.

A small pop-up window informs you that your invitation has been sent successfully. You'll see the name now listed in the Chat section, indicating that the person has been invited. If you don't see the person's name, try hovering your cursor over the chat section and then scroll down through the names.

When your contact accepts the invitation, a ball or video camera icon appears next to the contact's name in the Chat section. If the person is not logged in to Gmail at the time, the icon is gray. If he or she is available to chat, you'll see a green icon. If the icon is yellow, this indicates that the person is logged-in to Google but is away from his or her computer. If the icon is red, this means your Contact has set his or her status to "Busy" and is not available to chat.

You can set your own status to "Busy" by clicking the down arrow under your name in the Chat section, then click BUSY.

When you're ready to change your status back to available, click AVAILABLE.

If there's a green ball or camera icon by a person's name, you can try sending an Instant Message. Hover your cursor over the name and click CHAT from the person's profile window. A chat window pops up. Type your message and click enter. A small chat window will pop up on your recipient's screen with your message. If he or she has time to chat, you'll see a notification in your screen that the person is typing. When he or she is done, the return message will pop up on your screen, ready for your reply.

When you're ready to end the conversation, just click the x at the top of the window. Or if you decide to continue your conversation by voice rather than text, you can click the phone button at the top of the chat window.

If the person you're calling has voice and video enabled on his or her computer, you'll see an option to call the computer. If you have a phone number entered with the contact information, you'll have the option of calling his or her phone. Click on your choice and your computer will place the call.

If you don't have the Contact's phone number entered with the person's contact information, you can click the CALL PHONE tab on the left of your Gmail page in the Chat section. A phone pad pops up. Enter your contact's phone number, area code first. Then click the blue CALL button. You'll see a dollar amount at the top right of the phone pad, indicating the charge to be billed for the call. Calls within the U.S. and Canada are free, but if you're calling another country, there will be a low cost per minute charge for the call.

When you're calling a phone, the recipient will see a phone number on his or her Caller ID, indicating the call is from your state. So the recipient may need to be alerted to pick up. If you call the computer, it will go directly to whichever computer your contact is using for Gmail. You'll hear a ring tone, and then the person's voice when they answer. When you're done with your phone conversation, just click the END button in the chat window.

To Video Chat with someone who has a green camera icon by his or her name, it's best to first send an Instant Message inviting the person to Video Chat. If the person accepts, click the camera icon at the top of the chat window to start the call.

When the person answers, you'll see him or her in a small video window on your screen, and the person will be able to see you.

To make the video screen larger, hover your cursor over the screen, then click the FULL SCREEN button that pops up.

Gmail and Google Docs

FIGURE 27-2   Google Calendar.

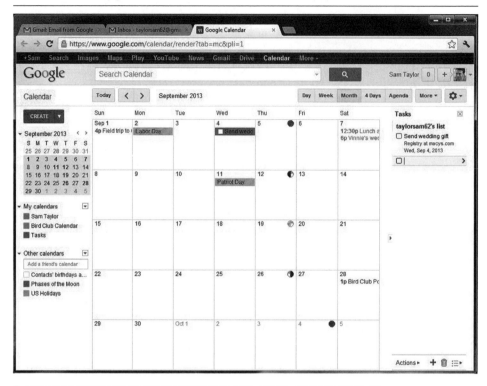

Google and the Google logo are registered trademarks of Google Inc., used with permission.

When you're finished with Gmail and want to sign out of your account, click your name or photo at the top right of your screen to open your profile window. Then click SIGN OUT.

Google Calendar

To access Google Calendar, click on the CALENDAR link at the top of your Gmail page. Your first calendar is automatically created, ready for your input (Figure 27-2)

There are different calendar views possible including the daily, weekly, monthly, four days, or agenda view. You can add events to your calendar to keep track of meetings or to plan your day. To add an event to your calendar, follow these steps:

1. When viewing the daily view, click a particular timeslot.

2. The cursor defaults to the What field in the pop-up window. Enter the event name, then click CREATE EVENT.

3. Click in the WHERE field, then enter the location for the event.

Scheduling Meetings

Another great feature of Google Calendar is the ability to create an event and invite other people. If they accept the invitation, the event will appear on their calendars too. Follow these steps to schedule an event and invite other people:

1. To add your special event, start by clicking the red CREATE button.
2. The cursor defaults to the title field. Enter a name for the event or meeting.
3. Click on the DATE.
4. Enter the date.
5. Click on the START TIME.
6. Enter the start time for the event.
7. Click on the ENDING TIME.
8. Enter the ending time for the event.
9. Click in the WHERE field.
10. Enter the location for the event.
11. Click in the DESCRIPTION field.
12. Enter a description for the event.
13. Click in the email field under ADD GUESTS.
14. Enter the email addresses for the people you want to invite.
15. The names of your guests appear in the Guest section.
16. Click the red SAVE button at the top.
17. Click SEND to send the invitations.
18. The event appears on the Calendar.

Receiving an Event Invitation

If you receive an event invitation created through Gmail, all you have to do is open the email and click Yes, Maybe, or No. The sender will automatically receive your reply. If you then go to your calendar page, you'll see that the event has been automatically added to your schedule.

Checking Replies to a Special Event

To check the replies to an invitation you've sent, double click on the event in your calendar to quickly bring up the full Event window. The guest status is listed under Guests. It updates automatically as people send their replies. Written responses will go directly to your Gmail.

Printing a Calendar

To print a copy of your schedule, first select the calendar view: a day, a week, a month, or another view. Then click the MORE tab, and select PRINT from the drop-down window. From here, you'll follow your printer's online instructions.

Creating Additional Calendars

You can create many different calendars for various purposes with Google Calendar. You can also share your calendar with select people, such as all the employees and vendors working on a particular project.

To create and share a calendar, follow these steps:

1. Click the down arrow next to the MY CALENDARS tab.
2. Click CREATE NEW CALENDAR from the drop-down list.

3. The cursor defaults to the CALENDAR NAME field. Enter a name for the new calendar.

4. Click in the DESCRIPTION field, then enter a description for the calendar.

5. The rest of the form is optional, but make sure you select the correct time zone.

6. To enable others to see this calendar, click the email address field under SHARE WITH SPECIFIC PEOPLE. Enter email addresses for people with whom you want to share the calendar.

7. Click the CREATE CALENDAR button.

8. A window pops up asking if you want to invite people who don't use Google Calendar to use this service. This is optional.

9. Click the INVITE button.

Task List

You can also have a to-do list that is part of your calendar. By adding tasks that have a specific due date, you can set reminders. Your task list pops up to the right of your calendar. To create a task list, follow these steps:

1. To open your Task list, click the TASKS tab under MY CALENDARS.

2. Now click on the blank task field.

3. Enter a description of the task, then click the right arrow.

4. Click on the DUE DATE window.

5. Enter the due date on the pop-up calendar.

6. The date appears in the field. It also appears above the date on your calendar.

7. Click in the NOTES field.

8. Enter any notes about the task, then click BACK TO LIST.

9. Click on the task to see your details.

Completing Tasks

After you've finished a task, you can mark it as completed by clicking the box to the left of the item in the task list. A line marks through the task to show it as completed.

To clear completed tasks from your task list, click the ACTIONS tab at the bottom right of your screen. Then click CLEAR COMPLETED TASKS.

The completed tasks disappear. To see your completed tasks, click the ACTION tab and click VIEW COMPLETED TASKS from the pop-up window. A listing of completed tasks appears in the task list window. They also appear by date in the calendar.

To go back to your task list, click the ACTIONS tab and again click CLEAR COMPLETED Tasks.

Google Drive

Google Drive gives you free access to word processing, spreadsheet, presentation, forms, and drawing software, delivered to you through the Internet. Because your Google Drive files are online rather than on one computer, you can pull up your files from any computer with Internet access and a recent web browser, anywhere in the world.

FIGURE 27-3   Google Drive.

Google and the Google logo are registered trademarks of Google Inc., used with permission.

Google Drive is an online storage system. It gives you access to all the files, folders, and Google Docs you've stored in Google Drive (Figure 27-3). You'll have five gigabytes of free storage space, with the capability of upgrading to twenty-five gigabytes for less than $2.50 per month.

You can also give access to selected individuals to view or collaborate on documents stored in your Google Drive by using the Share feature.

You can collaborate on the same online document, at the same time, from different computers anywhere in the world. Rather than sending a copy of the document to each collaborator to work on individually and send back to you, everyone's input is together in the one online document. All your feedback and changes are in one place.

Google Docs are the free web-based applications available from Google. They include word document, spreadsheet, presentation, forms, and drawing apps. They are similar to Microsoft Office applications, but with the added online collaboration feature.

Google Documents is a word processing app used to create text documents, similar to Microsoft Word. It has many of the same basic tools. You can import Microsoft Word and other word processing documents, as well as export back to them.

Google Spreadsheets allows you to create spreadsheets, charts, and graphs. You can import spreadsheets from other software apps like Excel, and convert them to a Google Spreadsheet. You can also export a Google Spreadsheet to Excel and other formats.

Google Presentations lets you create visual presentations using text, images, and video; it is somewhat similar to PowerPoint. You can also import and convert PowerPoint presentations, or export to PowerPoint if needed.

Google Forms gives you access to simple forms to help collect RSVPs, send out a survey or quiz, or collect other information. The forms are connected to a spreadsheet that automatically collects and organizes the responses.

Google Drawings gives you the tools to create charts and diagrams and add them to your documents, presentations, and websites.

Google Drive works with many popular web browsers, but for speed and compatibility, it's best to use Google Chrome. The new, improved Google Drive is replacing what used to be called the Google Documents List. As Google makes this transition, you may see either Documents or Drive on the tab at the top of your Gmail and calendar pages.

To install Google Drive, click the DOCUMENTS or DRIVE tab on your Gmail page. Then follow the online instructions. It's quick and easy. You should be ready to go in minutes. Once you've installed Google Drive, the tab should now read Drive. Click on it anytime you want to access Google Drive. This takes you to your Google Drive page. Your Google Docs are listed there under My Drive, along with any other computer files and folders you move there.

There are some basic features common to all Google Docs applications. To create a new document, click the red CREATE button. Click on the app you want to open from the drop-down window and it takes you to a blank page, ready for your input.

If you want to upload files from your computer into your Google Drive, you do this by clicking the UPLOAD icon, just to the right of the Create button. On an uploaded file, you can choose to export to an editable format by clicking the FILE tab and choosing EXPORT TO GOOGLE DOCUMENT to convert the file. Now on your My Drive page, you'll see both the original, view-only document, and the editable Google Docs version of the document.

Within the Google Docs applications, many of the tabs are the same. Under the File tab, you can quickly start a new app by clicking the right arrow next to NEW and selecting the desired application.

You can rename a document you're working on by clicking rename here, or just by clicking on the title to access the Rename window.

Click DOWNLOAD to export to other applications, and PRINT to access your printer.

You can also access the Share feature under the File tab, to share the document with others. There is also a separate Share button at the top right of your document.

There's no Save button, because Google Docs are saved automatically in your online files.

Under Edit are familiar features like Undo, Cut, Paste, and Delete.

Under the Format tab are common formatting tools. Some of these are also accessible from the Formatting Palette at the top. There is also a printer icon here for quick access.

Sharing Files with Google Drive

Once you've created a document you want to share, you can access the Share feature within the document. Or you can access it from your Google Drive page by clicking on the box next to the document you want to share, then clicking the SHARE icon that pops up near the top of the page.

This takes you to a pop-up window where you can enter email addresses for people with whom you want to share your document. As you begin entering email addresses, you'll select what kind of access you want for each contact. You can choose for a person to be able to change and edit the document, or to comment on a document but not edit, or to just be able to view the document.

Each collaborator's changes and comments will then be shown in a separate color on the original document. No more confusion about which version of the document each person is working on because everyone is working on the same online file.

Google Mobile Apps

If you have a Smartphone or a tablet, you can access your Gmail and your Google Drive documents while you're out and about.

Gmail, Google Drive, and the Google app are available for the iPhone, iPad, Android phones, and Android tablets. And like the Web-based versions, they are all available for free.

To install these apps on your iPhone or iPad, go to the Apple Apps store and search for Gmail, Google Drive, and Google. To install them on your Android phone or tablet, go to the Google Play Store and search for Gmail and Google Drive. Once the apps are installed, when you first access the app, you'll need to sign into your Google account.

In the case of the Gmail app, after signing in, you can access your email on your mobile device (Figure 27-4). You can then read your messages; however, the interface for Gmail is a bit different from what you see in the Web-based version.

The icons at the bottom of each message allow you to reply or forward the message to someone else. The pencil icon on the toolbar will take you to a new message screen, where you can compose an email message. The magnifying glass icon allows you to search your mail for specific words or phrases. The trash can icon allows you to delete messages from your inbox. The menu icon which looks like three horizontal lines gives you access to the same folder structure you'll see in the web-based version of Gmail.

FIGURE 27-4   The Gmail App.

FIGURE 27-5   The Google Drive App.

Google and the Google logo are registered trademarks of Google Inc., used with permission.

The Google Drive mobile app gives you a way to access the files stored in your Google Drive using your smartphone or tablet (Figure 27-5). The first time you access the Google Drive app, you'll also have to sign in using your Google account. Once you've signed in, you'll then have access to all the files stored in your Google Drive account. You can add people who can view shared documents, and you can read your documents here. On some versions of Google Drive, you can create new Google Drive documents.

FIGURE 27-6   The Google App for an iPad.

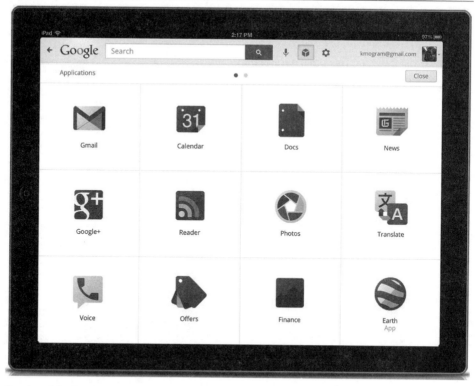

Google and the Google logo are registered trademarks of Google Inc., used with permission.

A third useful app is the Google app for the iPad (Figure 27-6). After signing into your account, the Applications choice on the Home screen gives you access to Gmail, your Google Calendar, as well as Google Drive documents. In this version, the mobile version of Gmail offers the same features but has a slightly different interface. The Calendar option allows you to view your schedule as well as create new calendar events. The Google Docs application allows you to view all the files in your Google Drive as well as create new word processing documents and spreadsheets.

Business Documents

28

The Business Letter

Appearance

Despite constantly improving forms of communication such as email, the business letter still exerts enormous influence and deserves your close attention. Business letters are more formal and personal than email. They are also more private.

Very few customers of a business ever see the home office or a branch office; this is often true even of small businesses. What customers do see is company correspondence. An untidy or ungrammatical letter gives the instant impression that the company's product or service is equally flawed. On the other hand, upon receiving a handsomely spaced, well-constructed, and well-organized letter, a customer unconsciously assumes it has come from an up-to-date, well-organized, and successful business.

Letter and email writing occupies at least one third of all office work, and good writing is the most effective advertisement of your capability. Any skills you can acquire or improve in this area do double duty: they help you work more quickly and effectively while advancing your career.

Besides the skills you need for your own writing, you need to learn techniques of letter writing to handle your boss's correspondence. Most successful businesspeople have already mastered the mechanics of language, but many in authoritative positions lack such skills. They rely on their administrative assistants to see that their letters are satisfactory.

Any letter that comes from your keyboard—whether composed by you or your employer—must have a businesslike appearance that does not distract from the message it has to convey. The letter must be neat and symmetrical, and it must not have any typographical, grammatical, or spelling errors. Its language should clearly and simply go to the heart of the matter discussed. Its language and appearance should also be within the conventions of the commercial world. That is the reason each company selects its own style for presentation to its public.

The way in which a company is known to its customers, its good name, its reputation, and the quality of its products or services all constitute the corporate image. Image is very important, and many companies spend fortunes to have the image instantly recognized by the consumer, so no matter what style the company uses, use it consistently. This helps make the company's correspondence characteristically its own. That consistency also translates into dependability in the customer's mind.

293

Paragraphing

If you are new to the company, it's not likely you'll be invited to decide on which style of letter to use. A certain style may have already been selected long ago after various experiments. In accordance with that style, you'll be instructed to indent paragraphs or to block them and to put a double space between paragraphs that are single-spaced. Your boss will no doubt also tell you his or her way of closing a letter, perhaps with the company's name and his or her signature with title below. You should conform to your employer's preference without question.

At the same time, you'll be told about *open punctuation* (no marks at the end of each line that appears above or below the text of the letter) or *closed punctuation* (marks after the date line, after each line of the addressee's name and address, after the complimentary close, and after the signature). Closed punctuation is usually used with blocked paragraphs.

Parts of a Business Letter

The various parts of a business letter (Figure 28-1) include:

- *Date line*—two to six lines below the last line of the printed letterhead. The date should be written out in this form: January 1, 2015.

- *Reference line*—a numerical file number, invoice number, policy number, or order number should appear on a new line below the date.

- *Special mailing notations*—special notations such as "confidential" should appear two lines below the date.

- *Inside address*—should include the addressee's title and full name, business title, business name, and full address.

- *Attention line*—if the letter is not addressed to a specific person, skip one space after the inside address and add, "Attention: _____." You can make the letter go to the attention of a department.

- *Salutation*—one line after the attention line or the inside address. Examples include: Dear ———— , Ladies and Gentlemen, Dear Sir or Madam, Dear [company name].

- *Subject line*—gives an overview of what the letter is about. Can be used in place of a salutation or reference line.

- *Message*—the body of your letter with paragraph breaks; optional indentations for paragraphs, bullet lists, and number lists.

- *Complimentary close*—appears two lines below the last line of the message. Either left justified or five spaces to the right of center.

- *Signature block*—justified with the complimentary close with options of typed name and title, signature, or just signature.

- *Identification initials*—the initials of the typist appears left-justified two spaces below the signature block.

- *Enclosure notation*—located with the identification initials or in place of them with a notation such as: enc, encl, enclosures (3), 3 encs.

FIGURE 28-1   Parts of a business letter.

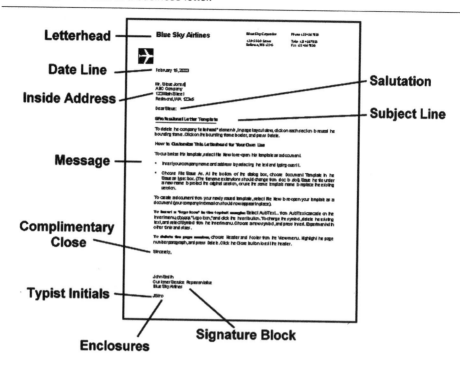

- *Copy notation*—left-justified two lines below identification initials with the notation: cc: [person's full name or initials].
- *Postscript*—two spaces below the last text on the page with a P.S. and then a short sentence.

Beginning the Letter

The Date Line

Some offices show the *standard date line* near the body of the letter, ending at the right margin two spaces above the name of the addressee, which is written flush with the left margin. If the *centered date line* is chosen, it is placed two spaces below the letterhead as though it's part of the letterhead and centered exactly. This is an effective and well-balanced look if the company name and address in the letterhead fall in the center. If the letterhead is spread out across the whole top of the page ending at the right margin, then the standard date line seems more graceful and more balanced. When paper without a letterhead is used, the date line must be standard and must be a part of the three-line heading. This consists of the address of the writer and the date of the letter:

1501 Guadalupe Street
Austin, Texas 78702
May 28, 2015

Never place the name of the writer in the typewritten heading of the letter, for that belongs only at the end of the letter.

In typing the date line, never abbreviate the name of the month or use figures for it. Also, use numerals only for the day of the month; never add *nd*, *d*, *rd*, *st*, or *th* to the numerals. These sounds are heard but are never written.

Wrong	Right
May 28th, 2015	May 28, 2015
June 22d, 2015	June 22, 2015

The Inside Address

The name and address of the addressee should be exactly as typed on the envelope.

If a street address is long enough to require two lines, place the less important of the two above:

Student Union Building
Northwestern State Teachers College
Alva, Oklahoma 76021

If an individual in a company is addressed, show the individual's name (and title) with the company's name below that, single spaced. If there is a long address that must be carried over to a second line, indent the second line three spaces:

Mr. Rick Ritenour, President
San Francisco National Bank and
   Mortgage Association
1200 Market Street
San Francisco, California 99001

Never abbreviate part of the company name unless the company's registered name uses an abbreviation (Co., Inc., or &) and such abbreviation is shown on the company's official letterhead.

Figures are used for all house numbers except "one" (which is spelled out). If there is a numerical street number, separate the house number and street number by a dash:

3780-87th Street

Names of cities are never abbreviated; the names of states are also never abbreviated. There is one exception: use the official U.S. Postal Service postal state abbreviations on the envelope address.

Never use an abbreviation such as a percentage mark for "care of"; always spell the words out. Never use "care of" before a hotel name if the addressee is a guest there, and never use it before a company name if the addressee is employed there. However, if the addressee is temporarily receiving mail at the office of the company, "care of" may be used before the company name:

Mr. Steve Eichman
Care of The Rockwell Corporation
60 Wall Street
New York, New York 10022

Titles

An individual's name is always preceded by a title—for example, Mr., Ms., Mrs., Miss, Dr., or Col. It's permissible to place initials denoting a degree after the name of an addressee; in that case, always omit the beginning title:

Wrong	**Right**
Dr. Gary K. Wilson, Ph.D.	Gary K. Wilson, Ph.D.

Reverend and *Honorable* are titles of respect and are preceded by the word *The.* The *Mr.* is omitted:

Wrong	**Right**
Rev. John Wilson	The Rev. John Wilson
Reverend Jim Seckman	The Reverend Jim Seckman

Women and Men

In addressing a woman, it's useful to refer to previous correspondence from the individual to see whether she included a courtesy title when she typed or signed her name. If you have no previous correspondence, use these general guidelines: *Miss* is used for an unmarried woman; *Mrs.* is used with her husband's full name (if known) for a married woman or a widow. If a divorcee retains her married name, use *Mrs.* plus her own name, not her husband's. *Ms.* is used in any of the above cases if the woman prefers it; it's also used if you do not know the woman's marital status or if you're addressing a divorcee who has resumed her maiden name.

Address a professional woman by her title, followed by her given and last name:

Dr. Bernice Wilson

The previous custom was to use *Mr.* as the title when the gender of the addressee was in doubt. The current custom, to avoid giving offense, is more likely to use the addressee's full name without a title, in both the address and the salutation:

Dear Toby Wilson

However, if the letter has some importance, it's worth making a quick call to the other party to get the proper title. Simply say to whoever answers the telephone: "I'm addressing a letter to Pat Richardson. Is that Mr. Richardson or Ms.?" This can save you and your employer much embarrassment later on.

Business Titles

Business titles are never abbreviated:

Wrong	**Right**
Mr. Mark Giddens, Sr. Ed.	Mr. Mark Giddens, Senior Editor
Ms. Julie Seckman, Asst. Mgr.	Ms. Julie Seckman, Assistant Manager

When you are writing to a person holding more than one office within a company, use the highest title unless you are replying to a specific letter signed by him or her under another title, as applying to the subject covered. When you are writing to a department of a company, rather than to a person within the company, place the company name on the first line and the department on the second line:

MB's Department Store
Electronics Department
120 Irving Mall
Irving, Texas 76022

Attention Line

An *attention line* refers the letter to the person or department in charge of the situation covered. The word *Attention* is followed by the name of the individual or department. Do not abbreviate the word *Attention* or follow it with a colon.

The attention line is placed two spaces below the last line of the name and address of the addressee, either flush with the left margin of the letter or in the center of the page when paragraphs are blocked. When paragraphs are indented, the attention line is placed in the center of the page.

The attention line is never used in a letter to an individual; it is used only in a letter having a plural addressee, in which case the letter is written to the entire company and not to the person named in the attention line. The salutation must always agree (singular or plural) with the name of the addressee, not with the name on the attention line. For example:

Johnson Smith & Company, Inc.
1500 Main Street
Greenville, Texas 75401

Attention Mr. Horace Wauson

Gentlemen:

Salutation

The salutation is typed two spaces below the addressee's address or the attention line, flush with the left margin. The first word of the salutation begins with a capital, as does the name of the addressee. In business letters, the salutation is followed by a colon. In personal letters, the salutation is followed by a comma:

Dear Governor Thompson:

My Dear Mrs. Thomas:

Dear Jane,

Sometimes you'll be required to write a letter addressed to no particular person or company (such as a letter of recommendation); then you use capitals for the salutation:

TO WHOM IT MAY CONCERN:

Subject Line

The *subject line* of a letter is an informal way of categorizing or titling the letter. Many letters in business must begin with a subject line after the salutation, a valuable aid in the distribution of mail that also facilitates filing. The subject line can be centered, but when the paragraphs are blocked, it is flush with the left margin.

The Business Letter

Do not type "Re" or "Subject" before the subject line. Underline the subject line, but if it occupies more than one line, underline only the bottom line, letting the line extend the length of the longest line in the subject.

Be sure to word the subject line so that it is helpful. If the letter is about an order of silk, a subject line reading simply "Silk" would contribute nothing; instead, the subject line should read:

Silk Returned, Our Shipping Order 8939

The clerk opening the letter could promptly route it to the person within the organization best able to reply.

Contents

With the body of the letter, first consider its appearance. You must judge how long the letter will be and how much space it will occupy in order to place it on the page as within a picture frame—never too high, never too low, always with proper side margins. If you create the letter with word processing software, you can add spaces to the top of the letter or change the page margins after you have written the letter.

The body of the letter should be brief and straightforward. The letter should have the same ease as a personal conversation. Although you must write whatever your boss dictates, many times while typing you can ease the language a bit to improve its impression on the reader; it's possible to do this with just a word or two more or less that won't call attention to any change. Of course, you should always have your boss approve your revisions. It's your responsibility to see that the letter going forth is creditable in every way to your employer's interests.

The length of the letter should be in accordance with its importance. If the letter is too short, it may have a curt tone and may seem to slight the recipient. If the letter is too long, the recipient's attention may wander after the first page, and he or she may not read the letter in its entirety.

Closing the Letter

Complimentary Close

When the salutation has been "Dear Sir" or "My Dear Sir," no personal connection exists between the writer and the recipient. Thus, the complimentary closing can be "Yours truly" or "Very truly yours." "Sincerely" or "Sincerely yours" is appropriate when there is an established personal as well as a business relationship, but it is used only in letters to individuals, never to a company. "Respectfully yours" appears only on letters addressed to a person of acknowledged authority or in letters of great formality.

Avoid the use of such complimentary closes as "Yours for lower prices" or "I remain" and other hanging phrases. In addition, "Cordially yours" is not suitable in a business letter. It is often used but this is incorrect since the phrase is too familiar for business. Avoid it.

The Signature

If in the body of the letter the writer has referred to *we, us,* or *ours,* the company—and not an individual in the company—is writing the letter. Consequently, the signature would then consist of the typed name of the company under the complimentary close, the space for the writer's signature, and the typed name of the writer with his or her title. The whole signature is typed in block form beginning under the first letter of the complimentary close. In some blocked paragraph letters, the complimentary close begins at the left margin; then the signature also begins at the left margin.

Very truly yours,
GRAM'S QUILT COMPANY

Evelyn Wauson, President

Never put a line for the writer's signature. This is a superfluous and old-fashioned practice.

When the writer has referred within the letter to *I, me, my,* or *mine,* this means that he or she—not the company—is writing the letter. Therefore, the writer's name is typed with his or her title, omitting the company name entirely.

Very truly yours,

Evelyn Wauson, President

A woman may include a courtesy title in her typed signature, so as to allow the recipient of the letter to reply appropriately. Parentheses may be used:

(Miss) Louise A. Scott

Ms. Tina Anderson-Tate

Mrs. Pat Brueck

The courtesy title is blocked with the complimentary close, not extended to the left of it. For a married woman, the signature may consist of either the woman's first name and her surname or her husband's name preceded by Mrs. (no parentheses).

Sincerely yours,

Mrs. Ruth Wilson

A widow may sign as though her husband were living. A divorced woman no longer uses the given name or initial of her former husband. She may use whatever courtesy title she wishes, whether or not she keeps her married surname.

Other Elements

Reference Initials   It's no longer considered necessary to type reference initials—the initials of the letter writer and the typist. However, if the company requires identification of this kind for its files, show these on the file copy only and not on the original. The writer's initials are typed in capitals, the typist's in lowercase. To separate the two, use a colon or a slash. Many companies require only the typist's initials since the writer's initials are obvious from the signature of the letter.

When using a word processor, write the initials or name of the person dictating the letter on the office file copy.

Enclosures   Mention of enclosures should be placed two lines below the reference initials. It may seem to serve no purpose to add "Enc. 2" if the body of the letter mentions the enclosure of two papers. However, the mailing department may find this notation helpful to sort outgoing mail. In addition, as the recipient of such mail, this helps you keep the contents of letters together as you prepare to distribute them without having to read every line.

Postscript   Sometimes the letter writer will take advantage of the postscript—following the initials, with "P.S." typed two spaces below the signature or reference initials—to dramatize some bit of information. This is acceptable. However, you should never use the postscript to add something that was forgotten during the writing of the letter. Instead, rewrite the letter.

A Last Look

Before you consider the letter finished, decide if it looks like a picture on the page; that is, have you centered the whole thing? Ask yourself: If you received this letter, would you be favorably impressed? Then check your grammar, spelling, and punctuation again.

A business letter should be folded neatly and precisely. The side edges must match, the text of the letter should be inside the folded letter rather than on the outside, and only the fewest folds for the perfect fit into the envelope must be used. Upon taking the letter from the envelope, the recipient should be able to begin reading the letter immediately and should find it attractive. Remember that this is the reader's first impression of your organization.

Letters Written by the Administrative Assistant

Letters written over your own signature usually are acknowledgments of correspondence received while your boss is away, letters requesting appointments, follow-up letters, and letters requesting information that another administrative assistant can furnish. While these letters are an excellent opportunity to show your capability and initiative, always keep in mind that service to your boss and the company is the main factor in deciding which letters to write without dictation.

Many of the routine letters described in this chapter may be handled electronically through email. However, because business letters are more formal, personal, and usually generate results better than email, many executives prefer them over email for certain types of correspondence. Regardless of whether the document is printed on paper or transmitted as an email or fax, you should follow the same guidelines.

Planning the Letter

Good ideas can be clouded by verbosity, while clear and forceful words make for quick understanding. Therefore, plan your letters before you write a word. You'll save yourself precious time and effort and add to the company's bottom line because the time element is the greatest cost connected with writing a letter.

To begin, ask yourself: Is this letter supposed to serve the writer, the reader, or both? Will the letter give information, or will it request information? Will it ask for action? What data must it contain? Before you write, be sure that you have all necessary information on the subject, so you can readily refer to previous correspondence or double-check your information. If you're hazy about the subject of the letter, the reader will be, too.

In the first sentence, mention your purpose in writing so that the reader immediately knows what the letter is about. Then follow with whatever explanation is necessary, using a positive tone at all times—that is, words chosen to evoke a positive response. Speak directly to the reader from his or her own point of view, not from yours. The reader must see the advantages of replying favorably.

Use concise language, but be as natural as possible, as though you were speaking to the other person. Reserve the last sentence to request a response if there is to be further correspondence on the subject. Always make that last sentence complete, never hanging. A hanging statement is one that leads into the signature, such as "Hoping this meets with your approval, I am . . ." If that's the thought you wish to express, state it instead as, "I hope this meets with your approval."

In a business letter, there's no place for cute or clever remarks or for slang. Your use of slang may be misinterpreted as your not knowing the correct English equivalent. Also avoid exaggeration, sarcasm, or any remarks derogatory to any person or to any product—even competitors.

Letters Written for the Employer's Signature

Your boss may prefer that all letters be written over his or her name rather than having some letters written over yours. This may be true even if you compose the letters and have permission to sign the boss's name yourself.

When you're composing such a letter, use the boss's characteristic language and style. If your employer usually dictates in a short, concise manner, word the letter in the same way. If your boss usually goes into detail, do the same. And when you sign your employer's name, try to duplicate his or her handwriting as nearly as possible. In other words, make the reader think that your employer took the time to dictate the letter and sign it. To do less is an insult to the recipient.

Never write "Dictated but not read" or "Signed in Mr. Wilson's absence." It's insulting to the recipient, implying that your employer either didn't have the time or didn't take the time to read and sign the letter personally. It also hints that you could not be trusted to write what your employer asked you to write.

For the same reasons, don't sign the boss's name and then add your initials beside it. If you find it useful to show the true writer and true signer, make a notation on only the file copy for future reference.

When you write a letter on your employer's behalf but in your own name, sign it, but do not type your name below the signature line. Instead, type:

Sincerely yours,

Secretary to Mr. Wilson

Routine Letters

Encourage your boss to trust you with routine correspondence by emphasizing the enormous time savings it will produce. Then, when the boss discovers you can prepare such letters for signature without dictation, he or she may reward you with more challenging correspondence. Following are the types of routine letters you should be able to handle with ease.

Appointments and Acknowledgments

You may write letters that request an appointment for your boss or acknowledge letters requesting an appointment with him or her. In each letter, always refer to the reason for the appointment and the suggested time. Always request a confirmation.

If a certain time has been requested and your employer approves, confirm the appointment accordingly. If your boss will be occupied at the requested time, suggest another and ask for confirmation. Be sure to keep a record of appointments suggested and not yet confirmed. If there is ever a disagreement over whether your employer broke an appointment, you will have proof otherwise in writing. For this reason, if the back-and-forth process of setting an appointment moves from the letter to the telephone, always send a letter to confirm it in writing.

Follow Up

In some offices, secretaries use a follow-up file (or a tickler file) to check on delayed replies after a certain lapse of time. When you write a follow-up letter, refer to the previous correspondence, identifying the last letter by date as well as content, and perhaps enclosing a copy if it contains a great deal of detail that could be useful should the original not be available to the addressee.

If you have many follow-up letters to write, instead of composing separate reminders, prepare a form request that can be duplicated on the copier machine or in your word processor. When follow-ups are sent outside the company, often the enclosure of a stamped return envelope will speed a reply.

Sample Model Letters

When a letter is typical of ones you send out frequently, make an extra copy and place it in a special binder, and keep an electronic copy on your computer's hard drive in a folder named "Sample Letters" so you can refer to it as a model when you have to write that sort of letter again.

Personal Letters

You'll find that many of the letters in this "letter bank" will be from your boss to another businessperson, yet the subject will be personal in nature. These letters are among the most difficult to write, since they must display sincerity in a variety of situations: sending congratulations, declining invitations, offering condolences, and the like.

Figures 28-2 through 28-4 are samples of personal letters to business associates that you may adapt for your own use. Such letters should use the salutation that your boss would normally use for the recipient. For the signature, use the name the employer is called by that recipient.

Personal Service and Hospitality

When a person has done your employer a personal service or has entertained the boss without financial remuneration when he or she is out of town, that person should be thanked in a letter that can be written by you (Figure 28-5).

FIGURE 28-2   Sample letters of congratulations and acknowledgments.

> Dear John:
>
>   I have just read in *The Wall Street Journal* of your promotion to General Sales Manager. I don't think that Smith and Company could have chosen a better person for the job.
>
>   Sincerely yours,
>
>   [signed] Phil

> Dear John:
>
>   I appreciate your generous letter about my promotion to Executive Vice President. Such good wishes and kind words will help me do a better job, I'm sure.
>   Thanks for your note and for your valued friendship.
>
>   Sincerely yours,
>
>   [signed] Phil

FIGURE 28-3   Sample letters of condolences.

> Dear Mrs. Wilson:
>
>   It is with great regret that I just read of your son's passing.
>   I know no words of mine can console you in this sorrowful time, but I do want you to know of my deepest sympathy. You have many friends who are thinking of you.
>
>   Sincerely yours,
>
>   Philip Brown, President

> Dear Mr. Crenshaw:
>
>   All of us at Thorne and Sons were saddened to learn of your wife's death. We know there is nothing we can say to help you in this time of grief, but we do want you to know that we extend to you our very deep sympathy.
>
>   Sincerely yours,
>
>   Philip Brown, President

The Business Letter

FIGURE 28-3   Sample letters of condolences (*continued*).

Dear Mrs. Holmes:

We at Liberty Oil Company were sorry to read of the tornado that struck your Denison factory. We know the loss was very great, but we know also that you will rise and go ahead with rebuilding.

If we can be of service in helping you overcome your present problems, please call on us. We have enjoyed doing business with R. G. Holmes Corporation and look forward to resuming our enjoyable relationship in the near future.

Sincerely yours,

Philip Brown, President

FIGURE 28-4   Sample letter of thanks.

Dear Henry:

Your card and beautiful bouquet of roses helped a great deal to make last week bearable.

I am back at the office and feel I shall be good as ever very soon. The accident was a shock, but with good friends like you, I know the days ahead will be brighter.

You may be sure that I appreciate your friendship all the more at a time like this.

Sincerely yours,

[signature only]

FIGURE 28-5   Sample letter of personal service and hospitality.

Dear Janet:

If it hadn't been for your keen mind and able assistance, our recent sales meeting might have been a complete flop. Because I had never before conducted such a meeting, I certainly was lucky to have your help.

Thank you for your good judgment and wise suggestions.

Sincerely yours,

[signature only]

Introductions

Letters of introduction written by you for the boss's signature may be mailed or prepared for delivery in person. Such letters should contain the name of the introduced person, the reason for the introduction, the personal or business qualifications of the person, and a courtesy statement (Figures 28-6 and 28-7).

Invitations

Letters of invitation should be gracious without undue formality. Always tell when, where, and why the event will take place (Figures 28-8 and 28-9).

FIGURE 28-6   Sample letter of introduction to a business associate.

> Dear Mr. Fielding:
>
> This will introduce a good friend of mine, John August, who is associated with our state's Department of Commerce. He has heard of the fine work you are doing in Ohio and hopes he will have a chance to talk with you for a few minutes when he visits Cincinnati next Tuesday, March 22.
>
> I have asked Mr. August to telephone you upon his arrival in Cincinnati to learn whether you can see him on that day. If you can, I shall appreciate it. I think you will enjoy meeting him.
>
> It was great to see you at the Boston convention, and I look forward to the Buffalo convention in September.
>
> > Sincerely yours,
> >
> > Philip Brown, President

FIGURE 28-7   Sample letter of introduction to a personal friend.

> Dear Tom:
>
> A very good friend of mine, John August, will be passing through Nashville on his way to Boston next Tuesday, and I have asked him to stop by your office. John is a fellow you will enjoy meeting.
>
> I shall appreciate any courtesy you may extend to him while he is in Nashville—his first visit to your great city, by the way.
>
> > Sincerely yours,
> >
> > [signature only]

The Business Letter

FIGURE 28-8   Sample invitations to attend a luncheon or dinner.

Dear Mr. Brueck:

The American Consolidated Life Insurance Company is holding a dinner next Thursday evening honoring its million-dollar-a-year salespeople. Will you join us as our honored guest?

Since you would be seated at the head table, we are asking you to join us in Room 200 of the Waldorf Hotel at seven-thirty, so that we may arrive at the banquet room in a group.

Sincerely yours,

Nora Drake, President

Dear Roger:

Arthur Whitfield is coming to town next Friday, and Mary Smith and I are entertaining him at a luncheon at the Ritz. We hope you can set aside a couple of hours so as to join us. I am sure Arthur will be happy to see you, as Mary and I shall also.

The luncheon will be held in the Persian Room at twelve-fifteen.

Sincerely yours,

[signature only]

FIGURE 28-9   Sample invitation to give an address.

Dear Mr. Lee:

As President of the Chicago Rotary Club, I have been asked to arrange the program for our next Thursday noon meeting. I know that all of our Chicago Rotarians would like to hear the address you gave in Detroit last week (I was privileged to be in attendance there) on the subject of "The International Situation."

Next Thursday's meeting will be held in the Venetian Room of the Drake Hotel. I hope you will be with us to give our members the same treat you afforded the Detroit Rotarians.

Sincerely yours,

Philip Brown, President

Acceptance of Invitations

Letters of acceptance should be brief, appreciative, and enthusiastic. If the letter of invitation failed to include complete details, the letter of acceptance should ask for specific information (Figure 28-10).

Declinations

Letters declining an invitation should express appreciation and enthusiasm, with an assurance of regret or an explanation (Figures 28-11 and 28-12).

Because this cancellation comes so close to the date of the speech, this letter would immediately be delivered by messenger or would be faxed or emailed if the addressee is in another city. It is wise to follow up with a phone call.

Interoffice Memorandums and Emails

If the company you work for is large, much of your correspondence will be with other departments or perhaps with branch offices scattered throughout the company. The office memorandum, commonly called a memo, is a popular and inexpensive method of communicating with these fellow employees.

FIGURE 28-10   Sample acceptances of an invitation.

Dear Ms. Drake:

It is a pleasure to accept your invitation to attend the dinner next Thursday evening honoring your million-dollar-a-year salespeople.

I shall be in Room 200 of the Waldorf Hotel promptly at seven-thirty, as you request.

Thank you very much for your invitation.

Sincerely yours,

Philip Brown

Dear Mr. Stroman:

I shall be delighted to speak to the Chicago Rotary Club next Thursday. Thank you for inviting me.

Your suggestion that I repeat my Detroit address means that I won't have to prepare a new one.

I shall look forward to seeing you in the Venetian Room at noon.

Sincerely yours,

Barry Lee

The Business Letter

FIGURE 28-11   Sample letters of declination.

Dear Miss Drake:

Only yesterday, I accepted an invitation to speak in Boston on July 12, the date of your dinner meeting honoring your million-dollar-a-year salespeople. This will make it impossible for me to be your guest that evening.

It was kind of you to invite me, and I regret my inability to attend. I hope the occasion will be a very successful one.

Sincerely yours,

Steve Wauson

My Dear Mrs. Scott:

In reply to your letter of May 3 inviting me to participate in your association's fund-raising campaign, I appreciate your thoughtfulness in writing to me.

I am familiar with your association's good work, and in the past it has been my pleasure to contribute to it. It is with regret, therefore, that I must tell you that all my available funds for purposes of this nature have been pledged. It is not possible for me to be a party to your worthy program at this time.

You have my best wishes for a highly successful campaign.

Sincerely yours,

Mrs. Susan Wilson

FIGURE 28-12   Sample letter of declination.

Dear Mr. Bryson:

I dislike writing a letter that will cause someone inconvenience, but this one falls within that category, to my regret.

This morning, I was advised that a close relative had passed away in Denver, and I shall be leaving this afternoon to attend the service tomorrow, the day of your meeting.

I am sorry that I shall not be able to speak to your group and especially that you will have to find a speaker to replace me at this late date. I hope you understand that I am helpless to avoid this trip.

I hope your meeting will be successful in every way.

Sincerely yours,

Nora Drake, President

FIGURE 28-13 Sample interoffice memorandum.

TO: Mary Anne Scott, Shipping Department Manager
FROM: Bob Brueck, President
DATE: May 12, 2016
SUBJECT: Meeting to discuss various overseas carriers

A meeting has been scheduled for Tuesday, May 12, in my office to discuss with several carrier representatives suggested methods and costs to deliver our products to international markets. Your attendance is requested.

Distribution:

Tom Alberton
Martha Reeves

In most offices, paper memos have been replaced by emails. However, there are many types of communication that are inappropriate for email. For example, confidential information or information that should not be forwarded should be printed on paper and not sent as email.

Memos should be directed only to persons within the organization and should be signed or initialed by the sender. If a memorandum is confidential in nature, enclose it in a sealed envelope. If copies are sent to individuals other than the person or persons addressed, a notation to that effect should be made at the lower left corner of the form. Figure 28-13 contains an example.

Paper Selection

Paper selection is important for some written communications. Paper and envelopes come in various sizes, colors, and qualities. One way to rate a particular paper is by its basis weight. For example, 20-lb paper is often used in copy machines and laser printers, while 100-lb paper can be used for report covers.

Paper with rag content and cotton is more expensive than other varieties and is often a choice for letterhead. The standard size for letterhead is 8½ × 11 inches.

Envelopes

Envelopes come in a variety of sizes. Security envelopes have extra thickness so that documents cannot be read through the envelope by holding it up to a light source. Windowed envelopes have a clear plastic window that allows an address to show through. Typical envelope sizes include:

- No. 6¾—3⅝ inches × 6½ inches
- No. 9—3⅞ inches × 8⅞ inches
- No. 10—4½ inches × 9½ inches

29

Other Written Communications

Reports

As an administrative assistant, you may be asked to create a variety of reports for your boss. Some of the reports will be routine and will be created from various sources already available. Other, more formal, reports will require input from your boss in the form of dictation, supplied documents, and a series of reviews and revisions.

There are four general types of reports that will be created by administrative assistants:

1. Memorandum report
2. Letter report
3. Short report
4. Formal report

Memorandum Report
The memorandum report is a routine and informal report that might be prepared on a weekly basis to, for example, report the status of projects to upper management. This report is objective and impersonal in tone. There may be some introductory comments; however, they are very brief. Headings and subheadings are used for quick reference and to highlight certain aspects of the report. Usually, the memorandum report is single-spaced and printed on plain paper; however, in some businesses, this report may be sent as an email or email attachment.

Letter Report
The letter report is normally a one-page letter that is printed on company letterhead. Letterhead second sheets are used for continuation pages. The letter report is most often sent outside the company to consultants, clients, or the board of directors. The report should have headings and subheadings to organize the content.

Short Report
The short report differs from the memorandum and letter reports because it has a title page, a preliminary summary with conclusions and recommendations, authorization information, and a statement of the problem, findings, conclusions, and recommendations.

311

The short report may contain tables and graphs and can be either single or double spaced. Headings and subheadings are used to organize the content and to emphasize certain aspects.

The title page has the name, title, and address of the person or company to whom the report is being submitted. In addition, the title page includes the preparer's name, title, and address. Long report titles are divided and centered.

Formal Report

The formal report is more complex and has a greater length compared to the short report. Included in the formal report are the following:

- Report cover
- Flyleaf
- Title fly
- Title page
- Letter of authorization
- Letter of transmittal
- Foreword or preface
- Acknowledgments
- Table of contents
- List of tables
- List of figures
- Synopsis
- Report body
- Endnotes or footnotes
- Appendix
- Glossary
- Bibliography
- Index

There are specific margin settings for a formal report. The top margin for the first page should be 2 inches, and the top margin for subsequent pages should be 1 inch. Bottom margins on all pages are 1 inch. The left and right margins on all pages are 1 inch. For bound reports, the left margin should be 1½ inches to allow extra room for the binding.

Spacing for the body of the report can be single or double. Set-off quotations should be single spaced, as are footnotes.

Paragraph indentations should be five spaces. Long quotations should be indented five spaces in from body. Numbered and bullet lists should also be indented five spaces in from body. Footnotes should match paragraph margins.

Primary headings should be left justified, bold, with additional space above and below. A 20- to 24-point sans serif font such as Helvetica should be used. Secondary headings should be left justified, bold, with a 16- to 18-point sans serif font. Third-level headings should also be left justified, bold, with a 12- to 14-point sans serif font.

FIGURE 29-1   Heading numbering systems.

1.   Main heading
    1.1   Subheading
    1.2   Subheading
       1.2.1   Third-level heading
       1.2.2   Third-level heading
	I. Main heading
	    A. Subheading
	    B. Subheading
	       1. Third-level heading
	       2. Third-level leading

There should be no page number on the title page, although a page number should be assigned for numbering purposes. The front matter should use lower-case roman numerals for numbering. The body of the report should use Arabic numerals starting with 1. Page numbers should be either centered or in the right margin, ½ inch to 1 inch from the top, or ½ inch from the bottom.

Headings and Subheadings   You should use a numbering system for headings. You can use numbers or a combination of numbers and letters. Figure 29-1 shows two alternative heading numbering systems.

Headings and subheadings should be parallel in structure. The following are examples of nonparallel and parallel structure:

Nonparallel

1. Reading the Manual

2. The Instructions

3. How to Install the Software

Parallel

1. Reading the Manual

2. Following the Instructions

3. Installing the Software

Report Cover   The cover should have the title and author's name. The title should be in all capital letters. The cover optionally may be printed on card stock.

Flyleaf   The flyleaf is a blank page that is inserted after the cover. A flyleaf is also sometimes added to the end of the report just before the back cover.

Title Fly   The title fly is a single page with just the report title in all caps, centered on the upper third of the page.

Title Page   The title page should include the title of the report in all caps, followed by the subtitle if there is one. It should also contain the recipient's name, corporate title, department, company name, and address. The page should also include the preparer's name, corporate title, department, company name, and address. The date the report is submitted should be included on the title page as well.

Letter of Authorization   The letter of authorization should be printed on letterhead and should explain who authorized the report and any specific details regarding the authorization.

Letter of Transmittal   The letter of transmittal is a cover letter for the report. It explains the purpose of the report, its scope, limitations, research used, special comments, and acknowledgments. The letter of transmittal may take the place of a foreword or preface.

Foreword or Preface   The foreword or preface contains an author's statement about the purpose of the report. This is an optional section that is used to provide background on the project or to thank individuals who supported the project.

Acknowledgments   The acknowledgments page should list individuals, companies, or institutions that assisted in creating the report.

Table of Contents   The table of contents should include headings, subheadings, and third-level headings with page numbers. You can use an outline style with a heading numbering system. If you are using a word processor, you can automatically generate a table of contents based on the heading styles.

List of Tables   If tables are used in the report, you should include a list of tables in the front matter. The list should include table numbers, page numbers, and the descriptions that are used as table titles in the body of the report.

List of Figures   If illustrations are used in the report, you should include a list of figures in the front matter. The list should include figure numbers, page numbers, and the captions that are used with the figures in the body of the report.

Synopsis or Abstract   The synopsis or abstract is a brief summary that presents the main points to be covered later in the report.

Report Body   The body of the report should include an introduction to the report, an introduction to the major sections (headings, subheadings, and third-level headings), and a summary at the end of major sections. The body should include normal paragraph breaks, bullet lists, numbered lists, illustrations, and tables.

Endnotes and Footnotes   A footnote is a note of text written at the bottom of a page in a report in order to site a reference or to make additional comments on content in the main body of the text. A footnote is normally labeled with a superscript number.

Endnotes are similar to footnotes, but rather than being written at the bottom of a page, they are listed at the end of a section or at the end of the report.

Appendix   If there are supplementary reference materials or sources of research, you can include them at the end of the report in a separate section, the appendix.

Glossary   The glossary should include technical terms with definitions along with any abbreviations. Abbreviations should be spelled out the first time they are used in the body of the report.

Bibliography   The bibliography should list all sources of information that were used to compile the report.

Index   An index is optional for many reports. If you are using a word processing program such as Microsoft Word, an index can be generated automatically similar to the way a table of contents is created. However, you will need to mark index entries throughout your document before you ask the program to create the index.

Indexes are an alphabetical listing. The first word of each entry has an initial capital letter. The rest of the words are lowercase. Subentries in the index are like subheadings and are indented one or two spaces. Cross-references direct the reader to another location in the index. Punctuation is kept to a minimum.

Documenting Sources of Information

You should always acknowledge the work of other writers to allow the reader to judge the quality of the information based on the quality of the source, and to enable the reader to verify information. Some writers use parenthetical references within the text to document sources; others include footnotes or endnotes.

Footnotes and Endnotes

Footnotes are short notes set at the bottom of the page. Endnotes are placed at the end of the report. In one common method for documenting sources, both footnotes and endnotes are numbered, with a small number inserted at the end of the text being referred to. The corresponding footnote appears at the bottom of the page; the corresponding endnote appears at the end of the report.

Footnotes and endnotes should include the author's name (or authors' names), the title of the source, the place of publication and publisher, the date, and the page reference. For example:

James Stroman, Kevin Wilson, and Jennifer Wauson, *The Administrative Assistant's and Secretary's Handbook* (New York, AMACOM Books, 2014), page 201.

You can also document sources by inserting parenthetical references within the text. The parenthetical references generally include only author names and the page being cited, for example: (Stroman, Wilson, and Wauson, p. 201). Full publication information appears in a bibliography at the end of the report.

Bibliographies

Bibliographies list all works citied in the report footnotes/endnotes or parenthetical references. You may also include research that was not cited as a specific reference but was used to create the report. The bibliography listings are ordered alphabetically by author's last name. If there is no main author, then the book title is used. The author's surname comes first. Additional authors are listed first name, last name. For example:

Stroman, James, Kevin Wilson, and Jennifer Wauson. *The Administrative Assistant's and Secretary's Handbook.* New York, AMACOM Books, 2014.

Report Templates

If you are using a word processing program such as Microsoft Word, you can create a report by using one of the report templates that are available. By clicking FILE, NEW, and then clicking the Reports tab, you will see three default reports that you can choose from:

1. Contemporary report

2. Elegant report

3. Professional report

Press Releases

When writing a press release, start with the main idea, followed by major details related to the idea, followed by minor details, and then finally supplemental information. The major elements to include are the five W's: who, what, when, where, and why. Also, don't forget to explain how.

A press release should be factual, interesting, and informative. All the details should be carefully verified and proofread.

Press releases should be printed on normal-size office paper and be double spaced. All margins should be 1 inch.

The top of the press release should include contact information, with name, address, phone number, and email. The words *Press Release* and *For Immediate Release* or *For Release* (and then the date) should also be included.

If a press release is longer than one page, *MORE* is typed at the bottom of the first page in all capital letters, centered or on the right side. Subsequent pages are numbered and should include a short title caption, left justified.

At the conclusion of the press release, type five number signs ##### or *-end-* or *(END)*.

Tables

Tables are a good way to organize information into a compact, easy-to-read form. Word processing software programs, such as Microsoft Word, have features for creating and formatting tables.

The default table has horizontal and vertical grid lines. You can determine the number of rows and columns as you create the table. You can also add additional rows or columns as needed. The table grid will be the same width as regular paragraphs (Table 29-1).

You can click within a table cell and move the column spacers in the ruler to make columns wider or smaller.

Column headings are usually added at the top of each column. The first row of each column can be merged to form a single row. This is where the title should be listed. The table title should be bold, often in all capital letters (Table 29-2).

TABLE 29-1 A Table Grid

TABLE 29-2   Sample Table with Data

Sales by Region			
North	**South**	**East**	**West**
$123,000	$145,221	$132,010	$90,321
$133,210	$111,301	$112,101	$99,781
$141,210	$98,989	$156,297	$101,341

TABLE 29-3   Table with Formatting Features

Sales by Region			
North	**South**	**East**	**West**
$123,000	$145,221	$132,010	$90,321
$133,210	$111,301	$112,101	$99,781
$141,210	$98,989	$156,297	$101,341

Other table cells can be merged to create cross-headings that span several columns or several rows. To do this, select the cells, then click the Table menu, then click MERGE CELLS.

Data in a default table will be left justified. You can select a row and then click on a different justification using the icons on the toolbar. Some types of data—such as money—are often presented right justified.

Heading text, as well as other text, can be made bold, italics, or both. You can change the color of the text and add shading to rows or columns.

You can change the height above and below the text within the table by selecting the table, then clicking FORMAT, PARAGRAPH, and then adjusting the settings for Spacing Before and After.

Using the borders and shading feature in the Format menu, you can select the entire table or parts of the table and change the size or style of the grid lines. You can also remove the grid lines completely if you want. Table 29-3 is an example of changing the format of a table.

You should capitalize the first word of each item in a table, plus any proper nouns or proper adjectives. Table text can include numbered lists and bullets, just like regular document text.

When placing tables within a report, the table should appear as soon as possible after it is mentioned in the text. Tables should always be introduced in the text. Avoid breaking a table at the end of a page and running it onto the next page. Start the table at the beginning of a new page if necessary.

Add two spaces after the last normal paragraph text before inserting the table. Leave two spaces after the table before resuming with the next paragraph.

Editing and Proofreading

Editing a document requires checking for the following:

- Grammar
- Spelling
- Punctuation
- Accuracy
- Style

The traditional lines between copyediting and proofreading have blurred with the use of computers in business. Many administrative assistants must edit and proofread their own documents before they are distributed. In some large offices, a technical writer or documentation specialist may edit reports that will be distributed to wide audiences within the company or communications destined for outside the company.

Sometimes a boss edits and proofreads documents and then sends them back with corrections. Depending on who is performing these tasks, an administrative assistant may need to make corrections to documents that contain proofreading symbols and abbreviations (Tables 29-4 and 29-5).

TABLE 29-4   Common Proofreading Symbols

Symbol	Meaning
⌃	Insert a comma
⌄	Insert an apostrophe or single quotation mark
⋀	Insert something
⌄ ⌄	Use double quotation marks
⊙	Use a period here
℘	Delete
∼	Transpose elements
⌒	Close up this space
#	A space is needed here
¶	Begin new paragraph
No¶	No paragraph

TABLE 29-5   Common Proofreading Abbreviations

Abbreviation	Meaning
Ab	A faulty abbreviation
AgrS/V or P/A	Agreement problem: subject/verb *or* pronoun/antecedent
Awk	Awkward expression or construction
Cap	Faulty capitalization
CS	Comma splice
Dgl	Dangling construction
DICT	Faulty diction
- ed	Problem with final -*ed*
Frag	Fragment
||	Problem in parallel form
P/A	Problem with pronoun/antecedent agreement
Pron	Problem with pronoun
Rep	Unnecessary repetition
R-O	Run-on sentence
Sp	Spelling error
- s	Problem with final -*s*
STET	Let it stand
S/V	Problem with subject/verb agreement
T	Verb tense problem
Wdy	Wordy
WW	Wrong word

Copyediting

Use the following checklist when copyediting a document or manuscript:

- Are the headings and subheadings consistently used?
- Is the spelling correct?
- Are all proper names accurate?
- Are all lists parallel in structure?
- Do all nouns and verbs agree?
- Are numbered lists correctly numbered?
- Are all dates correct?
- Are all alphabetical lists in alphabetical order?
- Is all punctuation correct and consistent?
- Is all capitalization correct and consistent?
- Are all bibliographical references accurate and consistent?

FIGURE 29-2   Revisions in a Microsoft Word document.

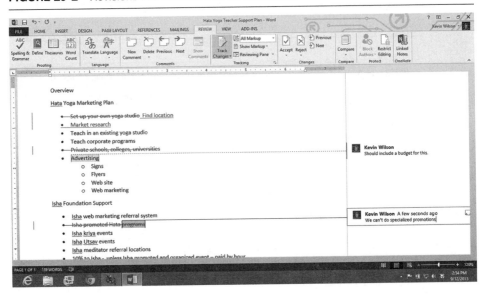

Screen shot used with permission from Microsoft.

Proofreading

Use the following checklist when proofreading a document or manuscript:

- Are all headings and other text elements consistent in style and layout?
- For letters, are the dateline, reference line, initials, enclosure, and carbon-copy notation accurate?
- Are all cross-references accurate?
- Are all margins consistent and proper?
- Are all tables aligned correctly and consistently?
- Have any footnotes been omitted?
- Are all end-of-line word divisions accurate?
- Are there any accidentally repeated words in the document?
- Are the page numbers correct?
- Are all headings and captions separate?

Electronic Revisions

Rather than make edits on paper, you can make edits electronically on a word processing document. By using the Track Changes feature (Figure 29-2) in a program like Microsoft Word, you can allow multiple people to add revisions and comments. Revisions show up in different color fonts for each person's changes. After you have reviewed the revisions, you can accept them or reject them, either one at a time or all at once.

30

Forms of Address

Using the correct form of address helps to create a favorable impression, whether you are communicating in an email, in a letter, by telephone, or in person. This chapter provides a list of the correct forms in alphabetical order by the title of the person being addressed.

Handy Reference Chart

Chart Code

EA	Envelope address
S	Salutation of a letter
C	Complimentary closing of a letter
SP	Speaking to
WR	Writing about

Abbot

EA	The Right Reverend Jackson Thomasson, O.S.B., Abbot of _____
S	Dear Father Abbot
C	Respectfully yours
SP	Abbot Thomasson *or* Father Abbot
WR	Father Thomasson

Alderman or Selectman

EA	The Honorable Horace Wauson, The Honorable Julie Seckman
S	Dear Mr./Mrs./Miss/Ms. Wauson
C	Very truly yours *or* Sincerely yours
SP	Mr./Mrs./Miss/Ms. Wauson
WR	Mr./Mrs./Miss/Ms. Wauson

Ambassador (United States)

EA	The Honorable Regina A. Strauss, American Ambassador (*but in Central or South America:* The Ambassador of the United States of America)
S	Sir/Madam *or* Dear Mr./Madam Ambassador
C	Sincerely yours *or* Very truly yours
SP	Mr. /Madam Ambassador
WR	the American Ambassador *or* the Ambassador of the United States

Ambassador (foreign)

EA	His Excellency Tom Jowers, Her Excellency Rosemary Boyd
S	Excellency *or* Dear Mr. /Madam Ambassador
C	Respectfully yours *or* Sincerely yours
SP	Mr. /Madam Ambassador
WR	the Ambassador of Spain *or* the Ambassador

Archbishop (Roman Catholic)

EA	The Most Reverend Archbishop of New York *or* The Most Reverend John C. Terrell, Archbishop of New York
S	Your Excellency *or* Dear Archbishop Terrell
C	Respectfully yours *or* Sincerely yours
SP	Your Excellency
WR	the Archbishop of New York *or* Archbishop Terrell

Archdeacon

EA	The Venerable Paul A. Morgan
S	Venerable Sir *or* My dear Archdeacon
C	Respectfully yours *or* Sincerely yours
SP	Archdeacon Morgan
WR	the Archdeacon of Los Angeles

Assembly Representative (see Representative, State)

Attorney General (of the United States)

EA	The Honorable Daniel Jones, Attorney General, Washington, DC 20503
S	Dear Mr./Madam Attorney General
C	Sincerely yours *or* Very truly yours
SP	Mr./Madam Attorney General *or* Attorney General Jones
WR	the Attorney General *or* Mr./Mrs./Miss/Ms. Jones

Attorney General *(of a state)*

EA	The Honorable Marsha Smith *or* Attorney General of the State of Kansas
S	Sir/Madam *or* Dear Mr./Madam Attorney General
C	Sincerely yours *or* Very truly yours
SP	Attorney General Smith
WR	the Attorney General *or* the State Attorney General *or* Mr./ Mrs. Miss/ Ms. Smith

Bishop *(Roman Catholic)*

EA	The Most Reverend Phillip Johnson, Bishop of _____
S	Your Excellency *or* Dear Bishop Johnson
C	Respectfully yours *or* Sincerely yours
SP	Bishop Johnson
WR	Bishop Johnson

Bishop *(Episcopal, not presiding)*

EA	The Right Reverend Mark Lessing, Bishop of _____
S	Right Reverend Sir *or* Dear Bishop Lessing
C	Respectfully yours
SP	Bishop Lessing
WR	the Episcopal Bishop of _____

Bishop *(Episcopal, presiding)*

EA	The Most Reverend Peter Brown, Presiding Bishop
S	Most Reverend Sir *or* Dear Bishop Brown
C	Respectfully yours *or* Sincerely yours
SP	Bishop Brown
WR	Bishop Brown

Bishop *(Methodist)*

EA	The Reverend Andrew Carter
S	Reverend Sir *or* Dear Bishop Carter
C	Respectfully yours *or* Sincerely yours
SP	Bishop Carter
WR	Bishop Carter

Brother *(of a religious order)*

EA	Brother Robert, S.J.
S	Dear Brother Robert
C	Respectfully yours *or* Sincerely yours

SP	Brother Robert
WR	Brother Robert, S.J.

Brother *(superior of a religious order)*

EA	Brother Thomas, S.J., Superior
S	Dear Brother Thomas
C	Respectfully yours *or* Sincerely yours
SP	Brother Thomas
WR	Brother Thomas

Cabinet Officer of the United States *(current; addressed as "Secretary")*

EA	The Honorable Timothy Dutton, Secretary of State, Washington, DC 20044
S	Sir/Madam *or* Dear Mr./Madam Secretary
C	Very truly yours *or* Sincerely yours
SP	Mr. /Madam Secretary
WR	the Secretary of State, Timothy Dutton

Cabinet Officer of the United States *(former)*

EA	The Honorable James Barker
S	Dear Mr./Mrs./Miss/Ms. Barker
C	Very truly yours *or* Sincerely yours
SP	Mr./Mrs./Miss/Ms. Barker
WR	Mr./Mrs./Miss/Ms. Barker

Canon

EA	The Reverend Thomas R. Milford
S	Dear Canon Milford
C	Respectfully yours *or* Sincerely yours
SP	Canon Milford
WR	Canon Milford

Cardinal *(Roman Catholic)*

EA	His Eminence John Cardinal Simonton, Archbishop of Chicago, (plus address)
S	Your Eminence *or* My dear Cardinal Simonton *or* Dear Cardinal Simonton
C	Respectfully yours *or* Sincerely yours
SP	Your Eminence *or* Cardinal Simonton
WR	His Eminence Cardinal Simonton *or* Cardinal Simonton

Chairperson of a Committee, U.S. Congress

EA	The Honorable John Brown, Chairman, Committee of the United States Senate/House
S	Dear Mr. Chairman/Madam Chairwoman
C	Sincerely yours *or* Very truly yours
SP	Senator/Congressman/Congresswoman Brown *or* Mr. Chairman/Madam Chairwoman
WR	Senator Brown *or* Congressman/Congresswoman Brown *or* the Chairman/Chairwoman of the Senate/House Committee on _____

Chancellor of a University *(see University Chancellor)*

Chaplain *(of a college or university)*

EA	The Reverend Dean A. Augustine, Chaplain
S	Dear Chaplain Augustine
C	Respectfully yours *or* Sincerely yours
SP	Chaplain Augustine
WR	Chaplain Augustine

Charge d'Affaires ad interim, United States

EA	Gary K. Wilson, Esq., American Charge d'Affaires ad Interim (*or in Central or South America:* United States Charge d'Affaires ad Interim)
S	Dear Mr./Mrs./Miss/Ms. Wilson
C	Sincerely yours
SP	Mr./Mrs./Miss/Ms. Wilson
WR	the American Charge d'Affaires in France (*or in Central or South America:* the United States Charge d'Affaires in France)

Clergy, Lutheran

EA	The Reverend Arthur Anderson (*plus* address of church)
S	Dear Pastor Anderson
C	Respectfully yours
SP	Pastor Anderson
WR	Pastor Anderson

Clergy, Protestant *(no degree, excluding Episcopal)*

EA	The Reverend Donald Reese (*plus* address of church)
S	Dear Mr./Mrs./Miss/Ms. Reese
C	Respectfully yours
SP	Mr./Mrs./Miss/Ms. Reese
WR	The Reverend Mr. Reese

Clergy, Protestant *(with degree)*

EA	The Reverend Dr. William Johnson
S	Dear Dr. Johnson
C	Respectfully yours
SP	Dr. Johnson
WR	The Reverend Dr. Johnson

Clerk of a Court

EA	Elizabeth Pym, Esq. *or* Clerk of the Court of _____
S	Dear Mr./Mrs./Miss/Ms. Pym
C	Sincerely yours *or* Very truly yours
SP	Mr./Mrs./Miss/Ms. Pym
WR	Mr./Mrs./Miss/Ms. Pym

Congressperson *(see Representative, Congress)*

Consul *(United States or other)*

EA	John Robert Henderson, Esquire, American (*or other*) Consul
S	Dear Sir/Madam
C	Very truly yours
SP	Mr./Mrs./Miss/Ms. Henderson
WR	The American Consul in Brazil

Dean *(of a cathedral)*

EA	The Very Reverend John C. Majors *or* Dean John C. Majors
S	Dear Dean Majors
C	Sincerely yours *or* Respectfully yours
SP	Dean Majors
WR	Dean Majors

Dean of a University or College *(see University or College Dean)*

Doctor of Dentistry/Divinity/Medicine/Philosophy

EA	Deana Fate, D.D.S. *or* Deana Fate, D.Div. *or* Deana Fate, M.D. *or* Deana Fate, Ph.D.
S	Dear Dr. Fate
C	Sincerely yours *or* Very truly yours
SP	Dr. Fate
WR	Dr. Fate

Governor *(of a state)*

EA	The Honorable Penny Corson, Governor of New York
S	Dear Governor Corson
C	Respectfully yours
SP	Governor *or* Governor Corson
WR	Governor Corson

Governor-elect *(of a state)*

EA	The Honorable Diane Jennings, Governor-elect of Ohio
S	Dear Mr./Mrs./Miss/Ms. Jennings
C	Respectfully yours
SP	Mr./Mrs./Miss/Ms. Jennings
WR	Mr./Mrs./Miss/Ms. Jennings

Governor *(of a state, former)*

EA	The Honorable Elizabeth Rietz
S	Dear Mr./Mrs./Miss/Ms. Rietz
C	Sincerely yours
SP	Mr./Mrs./Miss/Ms. Rietz
WR	Mrs. Elizabeth Rietz, Former Governor of Ohio

Judge

EA	The Honorable George Smithers, Justice (*plus name of court*)
S	Sir/Madam
C	Sincerely yours *or* Very truly yours
SP	Judge Smithers
WR	Judge Smithers

King

EA	His Most Gracious Majesty, King Philip
S	May it please Your Majesty
C	Respectfully
SP	Your Majesty (*initially; thereafter:* Sir)
WR	His Majesty *or* King Philip

Lawyer

EA	James Robert Judd, Esq. *or* Mr./Mrs./Miss/Ms. Judd
S	Dear Mr./Mrs./Miss/Ms. Judd
C	Very truly yours *or* Sincerely yours

Forms of Address

SP	Mr./Mrs./Miss/Ms. Judd
WR	Mr./Mrs./Miss/Ms. Judd

Lieutenant Governor *(of a state)*

EA	The Honorable Mary Brown, Lieutenant Governor of Maine
S	Madam/Sir *or* Dear Mr./Mrs./Miss/Ms. Brown
C	Respectfully yours *or* Sincerely yours
SP	Mr./Mrs./Miss/Ms. Brown
WR	Lieutenant Governor Brown

Mayor

EA	His/Her Honor the Mayor *or* The Honorable Alison Starnes, City Hall (*plus city, state*)
S	Sir/Madam
C	Very truly yours *or* Sincerely yours
SP	Mayor Starnes
WR	Mayor Starnes *or* Mayor of Raleigh

Military Enlisted Personnel *(United States)*

EA	rank, full name, address
S	Sir/Madam *or* Dear Sir/Madam
C	Very truly yours
SP	Sergeant Smith, Airman Jones, Private Jackson
WR	Sergeant Smith, Airman Jones, Private Jackson

Military Officer *(United States)*

EA	rank, full name, address
S	Sir/Madam *or* Lieutenant Banks, Admiral Banks
C	Very truly yours
SP	Lieutenant Banks, Admiral Banks
WR	Lieutenant Banks, Admiral Banks

Minister, Protestant *(no degree)*

EA	The Reverend Richard W. Fate
S	Dear Mr./Mrs./Miss/Ms. Fate/Reverend Fate
C	Respectfully yours *or* Very truly yours
SP	Mr./Mrs./Miss/Ms./Reverend Fate
WR	Mr./Mrs./Miss/Ms./Reverend Fate

Minister, Protestant *(with degree)*

EA	The Reverend Robert R. Foley, D.D.
S	Dear Dr. Foley
C	Respectfully yours *or* Very truly yours
SP	Dr. Foley
WR	Dr. Foley

Monsignor, Roman Catholic

EA	The Right Reverend Monsignor Johnson
S	Right Reverend Monsignor Johnson
C	Respectfully yours
SP	Monsignor Johnson
WR	Monsignor Johnson

Pope

EA	His Holiness the Pope, Vatican City, Italy
S	Your Holiness *or* Most Holy Father
C	Respectfully yours
SP	Your Holiness
WR	His Holiness *or* the Pope

Premier

EA	His/Her Excellency (full name), Premier of _____
S	Dear Mr./Madam Premier
C	Sincerely yours
SP	Your Excellency
WR	The Premier of _____ *or* The Premier

President of the United States *(current)*

EA	The President, The White House, Washington, DC 20500
S	Mr. /Madam President *or* Dear President Jackson
C	Respectfully yours
SP	Mr./Madam President *or* Sir/Madam
WR	The President *or* President Jackson

President of the United States *(former)*

EA	The Honorable Leslie Crespie
S	Sir/Madam *or* Dear Mr./Mrs./Miss/Ms. Crespie
C	Respectfully yours

SP	Mr./Mrs./Miss/Ms. Crespie
WR	Former President Crespie *or* Mr./Mrs./Miss/Ms. Crespie

President of a University or College *(see University or College President)*

Priest, Episcopal

EA	The Reverend Ann Thomason *or if degreed:* The Reverend Dr. Ann Thomason
S	Dear Mr./Mrs./Miss/Ms. Thomason *or* Dr. Thomason *or* Reverend Thomason
C	Respectfully yours
SP	Mr./Mrs./Miss/Ms. Thomason *or* Dr. Thomason *or* Father/Mother Thomason
WR	Father/Mother Thomason *or* Dr. Thomason

Priest, Roman Catholic

EA	The Reverend Leland Smith (*plus initials of his order*)
S	Reverend Father (*formal*) *or* Dear Father (*less formal*)
C	Respectfully yours
SP	Father Smith
WR	Father Smith

Prime Minister

EA	His/Her Excellency, Prime Minister of _____
S	Excellency *or* Dear Mr./Madam Prime Minister
C	Respectfully yours
SP	Mr./Madam Prime Minister
WR	The Prime Minister of _____

Prince

EA	His Royal Highness
S	Sir *or* Your Royal Highness
C	Respectfully
SP	Your Royal Highness
WR	His Royal Highness *or* Prince George

Princess

EA	Her Royal Highness
S	Madam *or* Your Royal Highness
C	Respectfully

Forms of Address

SP   Your Royal Highness

WR   Her Royal Highness *or* Princess Mary

Professor

EA   Professor *or* Dr. *(if Ph.D.)* Gary Keith Wilson, Department of Chemistry, Vanderbilt University, Nashville, Tennessee 37235

S   Dear Professor Wilson

C   Very truly yours *or* Sincerely yours

SP   Professor *or* Dr. Wilson

WR   Professor *or* Dr. Wilson

Queen

EA   Her Most Gracious Majesty Queen Anne

S   May it please Your Majesty

C   Respectfully

SP   Your Majesty *(initially; thereafter:* Ma'am)

WR   Her Majesty, Queen Anne

Rabbi

EA   Rabbi David L. Fader *or if degreed:* Rabbi David L. Fader, D.D.

S   Dear Rabbi Fader *or* Dear Dr. Fader

C   Respectfully yours *or* Sincerely yours

SP   Rabbi Fader

WR   Rabbi Fader

Representative, Congress *(current)*

EA   The Honorable Douglas Scrimshaw, United States House of Representatives, Washington, DC 20515

S   Dear Sir/Madam *or* Dear Representative Scrimshaw

C   Very truly yours *or* Sincerely yours

SP   Mr./Mrs./Miss/Ms. Scrimshaw

WR   Douglas Scrimshaw, U.S. Representative from _____ *or* Congressman Douglas Scrimshaw

Representative, Congress *(former)*

EA   The Honorable Greg Linton *(plus local address)*

S   Dear Mr./Mrs./Miss/Ms. Linton

C   Very truly yours *or* Sincerely yours

SP   Mr./Mrs./Miss/Ms. Linton

WR   Mr./Mrs./Miss/Ms. Linton

Representative, State (including Assemblyperson, Delegate)

EA	The Honorable Nancy Northcutt, The State Assembly *or* House of Representatives *or* The House of Delegates
S	Dear Mr./Mrs./Miss/Ms. Northcutt
C	Sincerely yours *or* Very truly yours
SP	Mr./Mrs./Miss/Ms. Northcutt
WR	Mr./Mrs./Miss/Ms. Northcutt, the State Representative *or* Assemblyperson *or* Delegate

Secretary of State (of a state)

EA	The Honorable James Cobb *or* The Secretary of State of _____
S	Dear Mr./Madam Secretary
C	Sincerely yours *or* Very truly yours
SP	Mr./Mrs./Miss/Ms. Cobb
WR	Mr./Mrs./Miss/Ms. Cobb

Senator, U.S.

EA	The Honorable Larry Zezula, United States Senate, Washington, DC 20510
S	Dear Senator Zezula
C	Sincerely yours *or* Very truly yours
SP	Senator Zezula *or* Senator
WR	Senator Zezula *or* The Senator from _____ *or* The Senator

Senator (state legislature)

EA	The Honorable Martin Allen, The Senator of _____
S	Dear Senator Allen
C	Sincerely yours *or* Very truly yours
SP	Senator Allen
WR	Senator Allen

Senator-elect

EA	The Honorable Mary Branson, Senator-elect (*plus local address*)
S	Dear Mr./Mrs./Miss/Ms. Branson
C	Sincerely yours *or* Very truly yours
SP	Mr./Mrs./Miss/Ms. Branson
WR	Senator-elect Branson

Sister (member of a religious order)

EA	Sister Mary Martha, S.C.
S	Dear Sister *or* Dear Sister Mary Martha

C Respectfully yours *or* Sincerely yours

SP Sister Mary Martha

WR Sister Mary Martha

Sister (superior of a religious order)

EA The Reverend Mother Superior, S.C.

S Reverend Mother *or* Dear Reverend Mother

C Respectfully yours

SP Reverend Mother

WR The Reverend Mother Superior *or* The Reverend Mother

Speaker, U.S. House of Representatives

EA The Speaker of the House of Representatives *or* The Honorable Allan Carl, Speaker of the House of Representatives

S Dear Mr./Madam Speaker

C Sincerely yours *or* Very truly yours

SP Mr./Madam Speaker *or* Mr./Mrs./Miss/Ms. Carl

WR The Speaker *or* Mr./Mrs./Miss/Ms. Carl

Supreme Court Justice (United States, Associate Justice)

EA Mr. Anthony Barrett, The Supreme Court, Washington, DC 20543

S Dear Mr./Madam Justice *or* Dear Justice Barrett

C Sincerely yours *or* Very truly yours

SP Mr./Madam Justice Barrett

WR Mr./Madam Justice Barrett

Supreme Court Justice (United States, Chief Justice)

EA The Chief Justice of the United States (*never:* The Chief Justice of the Supreme Court)

S Dear Mr./Madam Chief Justice

C Respectfully *or* Respectfully yours

SP Mr./Madam Chief Justice

WR The Chief Justice of the United States *or* The Chief Justice

Supreme Court Justice (State, Associate Justice)

EA The Honorable Lewis Ritenour, Associate Justice of the Supreme Court of _____

S Dear Justice Ritenour

C Sincerely yours *or* Very truly yours

SP Mr. /Madam Justice

WR Mr. /Madam Justice Ritenour *or* Judge Ritenour

Supreme Court Justice *(State, Chief Justice)*

EA	The Honorable Margaret W. Smoot, Chief Justice of the Supreme Court of _____
S	Dear Mr./Madam Chief Justice
C	Sincerely yours *or* Very truly yours
SP	Mr. /Madam Chief Justice *or* Chief Justice Smoot
WR	Mr./ Madam Chief Justice

United Nations Delegate *(United States)*

EA	The Honorable Edwin L. Rutherford, United States Permanent Representative to the United Nations, United Nations, New York, NY 10017
S	Dear Mr./Madam Ambassador
C	Respectfully *or* Sincerely yours
SP	Mr./Madam Ambassador
WR	The United States Representative to the United Nations

United Nations Delegate *(foreign)*

EA	His Excellency Charles Turner/Her Excellency Allison Turner
S	My dear Mr. /Madam Ambassador
C	Respectfully *or* Sincerely yours
SP	Mr. /Madam Ambassador
WR	The Representative of Canada to the United Nations

United Nations Secretary-General

EA	His Excellency Juan Perez/Her Excellency Juanita Perez, Secretary General of the United Nations, United Nations, New York, NY 10017
S	Dear Mr. /Madam Secretary-General *or* Your Excellency
C	Respectfully
SP	Sir/Madam *or* Mr./Mrs./Miss/Ms. Perez
WR	The Secretary-General of the United Nations

University Chancellor

EA	Dr. Barbara R. Rodgers, Chancellor *(plus name and address of university)*
S	Dear Dr. Rodgers
C	Sincerely yours *or* Very truly yours
SP	Dr. Rodgers
WR	Dr. Barbara R. Rodgers, Chancellor of *(name or university)*

University or College Dean

EA	Dean Hamilton Smythe *or* Dr. Hamilton Smythe, Dean (*plus name and address of university*)
S	Dear Dr.Smythe *or* Dear Dean Smythe
C	Very truly yours *or* Sincerely yours
SP	Dean Smythe *or* Dr. Smythe
WR	Dr.Smythe, Dean of (name of university)

University or College President

EA	Dr. Thomas A. Harmon, President *or* President Thomas A. Harmon (*plus name and address of university*)
S	Dear President Harmon *or* Dear Dr. Harmon
C	Sincerely yours *or* Very truly yours
SP	Dr. Harmon
WR	Dr. Harmon

Vice President of the United States

EA	The Vice President, United States Senate, Washington, DC 20510
S	Dear Mr./Madam Vice President
C	Respectfully
SP	Mr./Madam Vice President
WR	The Vice President

Warrant Officer

EA	Warrant Officer John C. Calhoun, Jr. *or* Chief Warrant Officer John Smith
S	Dear Mr./Mrs./Miss/Ms. Calhoun
C	Very truly yours
SP	Mr./Mrs./Miss/Ms. Calhoun
WR	Warrant Officer Calhoun *or* Mr./Mrs./Miss/Ms. Calhoun

Some Additional Guidelines

The Honorable and The Reverend

"The Honorable" is a title of distinction reserved for appointed or elected government officials such as congressional representatives, judges, justices, and cabinet officers. "The Honorable" is never used before a surname alone—for example, The Honorable Thomas Jones, *not* The Honorable Jones. Also, do not combine "The Honorable" with a common courtesy title, such as "Mr." or "Ms."—for example, *not* The Honorable Mr. Thomas Jones. Never abbreviate "The Honorable" in either forms of address or formal writing.

"The Reverend" should be used in official or formal writing. "The Reverend" is often abbreviated to "The Rev." or just "Rev." in informal and unofficial writing. However, when used in conjunction with a full name, "The Reverend" must be used—for example, The Reverend John Reeves or The Reverend Dr. Louise A. McGinnis. Notice that both titles are used with the full name on the envelope address but not in the salutation of the letter. Also note that "The" always precedes these titles.

Esquire

When the title "Esquire" is used, it is always abbreviated after the full name, and no other title is used before the name—for example, James Rogers, Esq. Although the abbreviation "Esq." is most commonly seen after the surnames of attorneys, it may also be used after the surnames of other professionals—engineers, consuls, architects, court clerks, and justices of the peace. "Esquire" is written in signature lines and addresses but is never used in salutations. It is commonly used regardless of sex, but there are some who object to using "Esquire" as a title for a woman professional.

Women Clergy

The issue of addressing women clergy reflects the problem of our ever-changing vocabulary. In many instances, "Reverend" or "Doctor" will suffice for both men and women, but some denominations address their ordained male members as "Father." The natural tendency then is to address the female counterpart as "Mother," but there may be strong resistance to this title from both the individual and the group. Whenever possible in such a situation, try to discover the preference of the individual.

Retired Military

When military officers retire from active duty, they retain their highest rank, and this rank is always used when they are addressed.

31

Legal Documents

Grammalogues

Business secretaries will probably not be called upon to take legal dictation, but it's helpful to have a brief knowledge of legal *grammalogues*. A grammalogue is a shorthand shortcut for full expressions used. When taking dictation, it's useful to be able to write in one stroke the representation for "time is of the essence," "writ of habeas corpus," "denied certiorari," and other phrases. You can have your notes complete before the person dictating has finished a sentence because you know what he or she means to say and how to record it quickly.

Document Formats

When you are asked to type or print a legal document, use plain white legal paper, 8½ × 14 inches, or legal cap paper, which is the same size but has a wide ruled margin at the left and a narrow ruled margin at the right. The text must be kept within these ruled margins. Wills are written on heavy noncorrectable paper of legal size without ruled margins.

Always double-space legal papers and reports, with triple spaces between paragraphs. Retain a 2-inch margin at the top and a 1-inch margin at the bottom of the page. If plain paper is used rather than ruled, leave a 1½-inch margin on the left and a ¾-inch margin on the right.

Indent paragraphs ten spaces; for land descriptions or quotations that are single spaced, indent an additional five spaces.

If copies are to be signed (called duplicate originals), they are printed on the same kind of paper as the original.

Number the pages in the center of the bottom of the page (¾ inch from the bottom edge), except for briefs, which are numbered in the upper right corner. The first page number is not marked.

Legal documents are bound with a sheet of heavy backing paper (9 × 15 inches). The backing sheet should be folded to provide four sections of the sheet 9 inches long. On one of these sections, type an endorsement, and label to briefly describe what the document represents. Following is an example of an endorsed mortgage backing:

No. A-31075

RELEASE OFOIL AND GAS LEASE

FROM

WILLIAM P. ALLEN

TO

FIRST CITY BANK OF NEW YORK

Printed legal forms of many kinds, referred to as "law blanks," can be obtained at stationery and office supply stores and at legal stationers. They are easily filled in with a pen and are quickly read. They may sometimes serve as a guide in drafting a document on your computer.

When writing numbers in legal documents, write them in words, and repeat them immediately in numerals inside parentheses; for example, "ten thousand five hundred and seventy-five (10,575)," or "ten thousand five hundred and seventy-five dollars ($10,575)". Dates may be spelled out, or you may express the day and the year in numerals, with the month always spelled out.

The following words and phrases often used in legal documents are customarily written in full capitals, usually followed by a comma, a colon, or no punctuation:

THIS AGREEMENT, made this second day of . . .

KNOW ALL MEN BY THESE PRESENT, that . . .

IN WITNESS WHEREOF, I have this day . . .

MEMORANDUM OF AGREEMENT made this twenty-fifth day of . . .

Case titles are always underscored, followed by a comma, the volume and page numbers, and date:

Johnson v. Smith, 201 Okla. 433, 32 Am. Rep. 168 (1901).

Notary Public Forms

In a small office and even in many larger offices, the administrative assistant is probably also a notary public. Figure 31-1 shows commonly used forms of notary public acknowledgments on legal documents.

Codicils to a Will

Additions to and changes to a will are made by an instrument known as a codicil, sometimes written on the last page of the will. It must be dated, formally executed, signed, witnessed, and probated with the will (Figure 31-2).

Legal Documents

FIGURE 31-1   Commonly used forms of notary public acknowledgments.

For an individual

State of _____

County of _____

On the _____ day of _____, 20___, before me came _____ known to me to be the individual described in and who executed the foregoing instrument and acknowledged that he (or she) executed the same.

_____
Notary Public

[Stamp and Seal]

For a corporation

State of _____

County of _____

On the _____ day of _____, 20___, before me personally appeared _____ to me known, who, being by me duly sworn, did depose and say that he (or she) resides at _____; that he (or she) is _____ (title) of _____ (Company), the corporation described in and which executed the foregoing instrument; that he knows the seal of said corporation; that the seal affixed to said instrument is such corporate seal; that it was so affixed by order of the (title) of said corporation; and that he (or she) signed his (or her) name thereto by like order.

_____
Notary Public

[Seal]

For a partnership

State of _____

County of _____

On the _____ day of _____, 20___, before me personally appeared _____ to me known, and known to me to be a member of _____ (name of partnership), and the person described in and who executed the foregoing instru-ment in the firm name of _____, and he (or she) duly acknowledged to me that he (or she) executed the same as and for the act and deed of said firm of _____ (repeat name of partnership).

_____
Notary Public

[Seal]

FIGURE 31-2   Sample of a codicil to a last will and testament.

I, JOHN PHILIP MOORE, a resident of the City of Chicago, County of Cook, State of Illinois, do hereby make, publish, and declare the following as and for a codicil to the Will and Testament heretofore by me executed, bearing date of the _____th day of _____, 20_____.

FIRST: [state provisions]

SECOND: [state provisions]

In all other respects and except as hereinbefore set forth, I hereby republish, ratify, and confirm my said Will, dated the _____th day of _____, 20_____. WITNESS MY HAND AND SEAL this _____ day of _____, 20_____.

_____

[Seal]

Sample of attestation

The foregoing Codicil, consisting of one-half page, containing no interlineations or erasures, was on the date thereof signed by the above-named Testator and at the same time published and declared by him (or her) to be a Codicil to his (or her) Last Will and Testament. The said Testator signed this instrument in the presence of the undersigned, who acted as attesting witnesses at his (or her) request. Each of the undersigned signed as a witness in the presence of the Testator and in the presence of each other. At the time of the execution of this Codicil the said Testator was of sound mind and memory and under no undue influence of restraint.

NAME *_____   ADDRESS: *_____

_____

_____

*The secretary usually types the name and address of each witness beneath these lines.

Agreements and Contracts

Agreements or contracts should state the obligations of each party (Figure 31-3).

Proxy

A proxy is a form of power of attorney given by one person to another, authorizing the second person to vote in lieu of the first person at a meeting of a corporation (Figure 31-4).

FIGURE 31-3 Sample contract.

THIS AGREEMENT, made this _____ day of _____, 20____, between _____ of _____, First Party (hereinafter called the Seller), and _____ a corporation under the laws of the State of _____, with principal place of business in _____, _____ (city and state), Second Party (hereinafter called the Purchaser),

WITNESSETH:

WHEREAS the Seller has this day agreed to _____; and WHEREAS the Purchaser is willing to _____; and WHEREAS_____; NOW, THEREFORE, it is agreed that _____. WITNESS the signatures of the parties hereto on the date aforesaid.

_____
Seller

_____
Purchaser

By_____
President

[Corporate Seal]

FIGURE 31-4 Sample proxy.

[Corporate Seal]

I, JOHN WILLIAM SMITH, do hereby constitute and appoint HAROLD JACKSON attorney and agent for me, to vote as my proxy at a meeting of the stockholders of THE JOHN SMITH CORPORATION, according to the number of votes I should be entitled to cast if personally present.

Date: _____   _____

Language Usage

32

Grammar

The Parts of Speech

There are nine parts of speech in the English language:

1. Nouns
2. Verbs
3. Adjectives
4. Adverbs
5. Pronouns
6. Prepositions
7. Conjunctions
8. Articles, determiners, and quantifiers
9. Interjections

This chapter examines the correct use of these parts of speech.

Nouns

A *noun* is the name of a person, place, thing, or idea. A *proper noun*, which names a specific person, place, or thing (Kevin, Atlanta, God, English, Jennifer), is usually capitalized. A proper noun used as someone's name is called a *noun of address*. The remaining nouns for everything else are called *common nouns* and are not usually capitalized.

A group of related words can act like a noun within a sentence. This is called a *noun clause*, and it contains a subject and a verb. Here is an example of a noun clause:

What he did for the country was unbelievable.

In this example, "What he did for the country" is the noun clause.

A *noun phrase* consists of a noun with several modifiers that act as a single noun. The following are examples of noun phrases:

Professional football team

Money market account

Grossly exaggerated totals

345

Abnormally long fingers

Real estate investment trust

There are also groups of words that can form *compound nouns*. Some examples include:

Son-in-law

Stick-in-the-mud

Other Noun Categories

There are additional categories of nouns:

- *Count nouns*—used for anything that can be counted, such as five dollars, a dozen, and seven continents.

- *Mass nouns*—used for naming things that can't be counted, like water, air, energy, and data.

- *Collective nouns*—used for naming groups of individuals or things, such as team, class, or jury.

- *Abstract nouns*—used for naming intangible things, such as love, peace, justice, hope, hatred, and friendship.

Some words can be a count noun or a non-count noun, depending on how they are used. Whether a noun is a count or non-count noun determines whether it can be used with articles and determiners. For example:

- *Non-count*: "The team got into trouble."

- *Count:* "The team had many troubles."

Noun Case

Nouns can be in the subjective, possessive, and objective case. The case tells you the role of a noun in a sentence. Here are some examples:

The football player (*subject*) runs very fast.

He selected a car (*object*).

The football player's (*possessive*) jersey was torn.

Nouns in the subjective and objective case are identical. Nouns in the possessive usually require an apostrophe followed by the letter *s* or *es*.

Verbs

Verbs are used in a sentence to describe an action or the idea of being. Consider the following:

- *Idea of being:* I *am* an administrative assistant.

- *Action:* The assistant *worked* late.

There are many different ways to classify verbs. *Transitive* verbs require an object; for example, "Will you *lay* the book on the desk?" In this example, "the book" is the object. *Intransitive* verbs do not require an object, for example: "The dog *lies* down every day after lunch." Some verbs can be both transitive and intransitive depending on how they are used in a sentence. Others can be used only one way.

Verbs are also classified as either *finite* or *nonfinite*. A finite verb can stand alone as the main verb of a sentence. A nonfinite verb cannot. For example:

- *Finite:* The car *destroyed* the mailbox.

- *Nonfinite:* The *broken* mailbox . . .

Verb Forms

There are four basic forms of verb inflections (endings):

1. Base form

2. Past form

3. Present participle

4. Past participle

These are used to help determine the tense of the verb. Tense tells you whether an action is happening now, is going to happen in the future, or has already happened in the past. Unlike some languages, English verbs do not form their tense just with the endings. Instead, they use auxiliary words. For example:

- *Base form:* I write.

- *Past form:* I wrote.

- *Present participle:* I am writing.

- *Past participle:* I have written.

Linking Verbs

A linking verb is used to connect a subject and its complement (a noun or adjective that describes the subject). These are often forms of the verb *to be*, but they sometimes include verbs related to the five senses (sight, sound, smell, feel, taste) and verbs that relate to a state of being (appear, seem, become, grow, turn, prove, remain). Here are some examples of linking verbs:

These children *are* all students.

Those clouds *look* dark.

Rain *seems* likely.

Mood

Mood in verbs refers to the attitude of the speaker or writer. There are three attitudes that can accompany a verb. The first is *indicative mood*, which is used to make a statement or ask a question. These are the most common verb moods. The second attitude is *imperative mood*, which is used to give directions, give orders, or make a strong suggestion. Verbs used in the imperative mood do not need a subject since it is understood to be "you." For example:

Get out of here.

Go to the store before you come home.

The third attitude is *subjunctive mood*, which is used (1) with dependent clauses to express a wish, (2) with "if" and a condition, (3) with "as if" or "as though" along with a speculation, or (4) with expressions that begin with "that" and express a demand. For example:

He wishes she were here.

We would have won the game if we played harder.

They acted as if they were hungry.

The letter demanded that membership dues be paid on time.

One of the most important things about a verb's mood is the ability it gives to distinguish between factual statements and hypothetical statements. Hypothetical statements often use the words *could, would,* or *might.*

Phrasal Verbs

Phrasal verbs consist of a verb along with another word or phrase. Usually phrasal verbs are accompanied by a preposition. They are usually casual conversational phrases that are accepted into mainstream language usage. Here are some examples:

The old people were *sitting around* doing nothing.

He *looked up* his old teacher in the phone book.

In each case, the word that is joined with the verb is called a *particle*. The problem with phrasal verbs is that their meaning is often unclear. They can be used in conversation, but it is best to avoid them in formal business writing.

Causative Verbs

Causative verbs are used to describe an action that is necessary to cause another action; for example, "The devil *made* me *do* it." In this example, "made" causes the "do" to happen. There are many other causative verbs, including *let, make, help, allow, have, require, motivate, get, convince, hire, assist, encourage, permit, employ,* and *force.* Most causative verbs are followed by an object (a noun or pronoun) and an infinitive ("to" plus a verb). For example:

He *allows his dog to sleep* all day.

There are three causative verbs that do not follow this pattern: *have, make,* and *let.* These verbs are usually followed by an object and the base form of the verb. For example:

She *made her associates read* the entire report.

Factitive Verbs

Verbs like *make, choose, judge, elect, select,* and *name* are called *factitive verbs.* These verbs can take two objects. For example:

The people elected Mike Jackson president of the homeowners association.

"Mike Jackson" is the object and "president of the homeowners association" is the second complement.

Grammar

Verb Tenses

A *tense* shows the time of an action or state of being. There are three tenses that change the endings of verbs. The *present tense* means that something is happening now, for example: "He is an executive. He wears nice suits." The *simple past tense* indicates that something happened in the past: "He was an executive. He wore nice suits." The *past participle* is combined with an auxiliary verb to indicate that something happened in the past prior to another action: "He had been an executive. He had worn nice suits."

Unlike other languages, English does not have a future tense. Instead, future verb forms are created with the use of auxiliaries: "He will be an executive. He will wear nice suits."

Progressive Verbs

Progressive verbs, which indicate something being or happening, are formed by the present participle form (ending in "-ing") along with an auxiliary. Here are some examples:

> She is crying.
>
> She was crying.
>
> She will be crying.
>
> She has been crying.
>
> She had been crying.
>
> She will have been crying.

The progressive form occurs only with dynamic verbs (verbs that show the ability to change). *Stative verbs*, on the other hand, are those that describe a quality that is incapable of change. For example, you wouldn't say, "She is being tall."

There are a variety of *dynamic verbs*: activity verbs, process verbs, verbs of bodily sensation, transitional events verbs, and momentary verbs. Following are some examples:

- *Activity verbs*—ask, play, work, write, say, listen, call, eat
- *Process verbs*—change, grow, mature, widen
- *Verbs of bodily sensation*—hurt, itch, ache, feel
- *Transitional events verbs*—arrive, die, land, leave, lose
- *Momentary verbs*—hit, jump, throw, kick

There are two classifications of stative verbs: verbs of inert perception and cognition, and relational verbs. Following are some examples:

- *Verbs of inert perception and cognition*—guess, hate, hear, please, satisfy
- *Relational verbs*—equal, possess, own, include, cost, concern, contain

Irregular Verbs

Most verbs form the simple past and past participle by adding "ed" to the base verb; for example: "He walked." "He has walked." There are some irregular verbs that do not follow this pattern. For example, common verbs such as "to be" and "to have" have irregular forms.

Grammar

Sequence of Tenses

There is a relationship between verbs in a main clause and verbs in a dependent clause. The verb tenses do not have to be the same as long as they are accurate about time and order. For example: "My father *will have returned*, before I *leave*."

Verbals

Verbals are words that seem to mean an action or a state of being but do not function as a real verb. They are sometimes called *nonfinite verbs*. Verbals are frequently used with other words in what is called a *verbal phrase*.

Participles

A participle is a verb that acts like an adjective; for example, "The *running* dog chased the *speeding* car." A present participle describes a present condition; a past participle describes something that has already happened. For example: "The *burned* tree fell down in the storm."

The Infinitive

An infinitive is formed with the root of a verb and the word "to"; for example, "To be, or not to be." A *present infinitive* describes a present condition, for example: "I like to dream." The *perfect infinitive* describes a time earlier than that described by the verb; for example, "I would like to have slept until nine."

Gerunds

A gerund is a verb form ending in "-ing" that acts as a noun; for example, "Walking in the street after dark can be dangerous." Gerunds are usually accompanied by other words that make up a gerund phrase. In the example given, "walking in the street after dark" is a gerund phrase.

Because gerunds and gerund phrases are nouns, they can be used just like nouns. For example:

- *As a subject*—"*Being president* is a difficult job."
- *As objective of a verb*—"He didn't really like *being poor*."
- *As objective of a preposition*—"He read a book about *being careful*."

Problems with Split Infinitives

One of the most common grammar mistakes is the *split infinitive*. An infinitive is said to be split when a word (usually an adverb) is placed between the "to" of the infinitive and the root of verb; for example, "To boldly go where no man has gone before."

The argument against split infinitives is based on the idea that an infinitive is a single unit and should not be divided. Because it is so easy to spot, many writers try to avoid this construction. However, many dictionaries and word usage books now say that the rule against splitting infinitives can be ignored. To avoid the argument, it is a good rule to avoid split infinitives in business writing.

Infinitives, Gerunds, and Sequence

Although infinitives and gerunds are not really verbs, they describe action. When combined with auxiliary verb forms, infinitives and gerunds can also express concepts of time (Table 32-1).

Grammar

TABLE 32-1 Infinitives, Gerunds, and Sequence

Simple forms	• We had planned *to watch* the Super Bowl. • *Seeing* the Cowboys win is always a great thrill.
Perfect forms	• The Cowboys hoped *to have won* the Super Bowl. • I was thrilled about their *having been* in the big game.
Passive forms	• *To be chosen* as an NFL player must be the biggest thrill in any football player's life. • *Being chosen*, however, doesn't mean you get to play.
Perfective passive forms	• The men did not seem satisfied simply *to have been selected* as players. • *Having been honored* this way, they went out and earned it by winning the Super Bowl.
Perfective progressive infinitive	• *To have been competing* at this level was quite an accomplishment.

Passive and Active Voices

Verbs can either be *active* ("The assistant *used* the computer") or *passive* ("The computer *was used* by the assistant") in voice. In the active voice, the subject and verb relationship is easy to understand. The subject is the do-er or be-er and the verb describes an action. In the passive voice, the subject is not a do-er or be-er. Instead, the subject is being acted upon by something else.

Computerized grammar checkers, such as the one built into Microsoft Word, can detect passive voice construction and suggest a revision. There is nothing incorrect about using passive-voice verbs; however, if you can say the same thing using the active voice, you should do so. Your writing will be easier to understand.

The passive voice does have its uses. When it is more important to draw attention to the person or thing that was acted on, the passive voice can be used; for example, "George *was killed* while riding a bicycle." Another situation where the passive voice is more appropriate is when the subject is not important; for example, "The meteor shower *can be observed* just after dark."

The passive voice is sometimes required for technical writing, where the do-er or be-er can be anyone, and the process being described is more important. Instead of writing, "I developed a computer program that can print checks," you would write, "A computer program was developed that can print checks."

The passive voice is created by combining a form of the "to be" verb with the past participle of the main verb. Other helping verbs are sometimes used.

Only transitive verbs (those that are objects) can be transformed into passive voice. However, some transitive verbs cannot be transformed into passive voice. "To have" is an example. You can say or write, "She has a new computer," but you can't say, "A new computer is had by her." Some other examples of verbs that cannot be used with the passive voice include *resemble, look like, equal, agree with, mean, contain, hold, comprise, lack, suit, fit,* and *become.*

Verbals can also be used in the passive voice. An infinitive phrase in the passive voice can perform a variety of functions in a sentence. The same is true for passive gerunds and passive participles.

Adjectives

Adjectives are words that describe or modify a person, place, or thing. Articles such as *a*, *an*, and *the* are adjectives. So are words like *tall*, *solid*, and *cold*.

A group of words containing a subject and verb may act as an adjective. These are called an *adjective clause;* for example, "My brother, *who is much older than I am*, is a psychologist." If the subject and verb are removed from an adjective clause, an *adjective phrase* results; for example, "He is the man ~~who is~~ *keeping my family fed*."

One thing to keep in mind about adjectives is that you should not ask too much of them. Use nouns and verbs to describe something. Sometimes adjectives don't add much to a sentence in the first place. For example, what do *interesting*, *beautiful*, *lovely*, and *exciting* really do for a sentence?

Adjective Position in a Sentence

Unlike adverbs, which can go almost anywhere in a sentence, adjectives almost always appear immediately before a noun or noun phrase that they modify. Sometimes adjectives appear in a string, and when they do, they must appear in a particular order according to category. When indefinite pronouns—such as *something*, *someone*, and *anybody*—are modified by an adjective, the adjective comes after the pronoun.

The order in which adjectives are arranged in a sentence is difficult for people learning English. They wonder why we wouldn't say "red big barn" instead of "big red barn." Adjectives are ordered as follows:

- *Determiners*—articles and other limiters, such as a, an, five, her, our, those, that, several, and some
- *Observation*—post-determiners and limiter adjectives and adjectives subject to subjective measure, such as beautiful, expensive, gorgeous, dilapidated, and delicious
- *Size and Shape*—adjectives subject to objective measure, such as big, little, enormous, long, short, and square
- *Age*—adjectives describing age, such as old, antique, new, and young
- *Color*—adjectives denoting color, such as red, white, and black
- *Origin*—adjectives denoting the source of the noun, such as American, French, and Canadian
- *Material*—adjectives that describe what something is made of, such as silk, wooden, silver, and metallic
- *Qualifier*—final limiter that is often part of the noun, such as rocking chair, hunting cabin, passenger car, or book cover

Sentences that run two or three adjectives together can be laborious to read. In addition, when adjectives belong to the same class, they are called *coordinated adjectives* and require a comma between them in a sentence. One good rule is to consider whether you could have inserted *and* or *but* between the adjectives. If so, then use a

Grammar

TABLE 32-2 Degrees of Adjectives

Positive	Comparative	Superlative
Rich	Richer	Richest
Lovely	Lovelier	Loveliest
Beautiful	More beautiful	Most beautiful

TABLE 32-3 Irregular Forms in the Comparative and Superlative Degree

Positive	Comparative	Superlative
Good	Better	Best
Bad	Worse	Worst
Little	Less	Least
Much, many, some	More	Most
Far	Further	Furthest

comma between them. For example, you could say "inexpensive but comfortable house." If the *but* is not in the sentence, you would punctuate it as "inexpensive, comfortable house."

Degrees of Adjectives

Adjectives can express degrees of modification: positive, comparative, and superlative. We use the comparative for comparing two things and the superlative for comparing three or more things. Sometimes the word *than* accompanies the comparative adjective and the word *the* precedes the superlative adjective. The inflected suffixes "-er" and "-est" are used to form most comparative and superlatives. Sometimes "-ier" and "-iest" are added when a two-syllable adjective ends in *y*. Table 32-2 gives some examples.

Some adjectives have irregular forms in the comparative and superlative degree, as shown in Table 32-3.

You should be careful not to form comparative or superlative adjectives that already describe a unique condition or extreme of comparison. *Perfect* and *pregnant* are good examples; a person cannot be *more* perfect or *more* pregnant.

Also be careful not to use the word *more* along with a comparative adjective formed with the "-er" suffix, or the word *most* along with a superlative adjective formed with the "-est" suffix. You'll end up with phrases such as *more larger* and *most largest*.

Less and Fewer

When making a comparison of quantities, we often have to make a choice between the adjectives *less* and *fewer*. When you are talking about countable things, you should use the word *fewer*. When you are talking about measurable quantities that cannot be counted, you should use the word *less;* for example, "He has fewer assets, but less worries."

Grammar

Than I or Me

When making a comparison between yourself and something else, you'll often end with a subject form or object form like "taller than I/she." In the sentence "He is taller than I am," or "He is taller than she is," normally we leave out the verb in the second clause (*am* or *is*).

Be careful with comparisons such as "I like him better than she" or "I like him better than her." In the first case, you are saying that you like him better than she likes him. In the second case, you are saying that you like the male person better than you like the female person. To avoid confusion with the word *than*, you should write, "I like him better than she does" or "I like him better than I like her."

Capitalizing Proper Adjectives

When an adjective's origin is a proper noun, it should be capitalized, for example: Christian music, Nixon era, Victorian poet, and Jeffersonian democracy.

Collective Adjectives

When the article *the* is combined with an adjective describing a class or group of people, the resulting phrase can act as a noun: the meek, the rich, the poor. The difference between a collective noun and a collective adjective is that the collective adjective is always plural and requires a plural verb; for example, "The *meek will* inherit the earth."

Adjectival Opposites

The opposite of an adjective can be formed in a number of different ways. One way is to find an adjective antonym. For example, the opposite of cold is hot. A thesaurus can help you find an appropriate antonym. Another way to form a negative adjective is through use of a prefix. Consider the following pairs:

- Fortunate—unfortunate
- Prudent—imprudent
- Considerate—inconsiderate
- Honorable—dishonorable
- Alcoholic—nonalcoholic
- Filed—misfiled

A third way to form an adjectival opposite is to combine the adjective with *less* or *least*. In fact, this method allows for tact and a smoother tone in some cases. For example, "That is the least beautiful girl in the class" is somewhat more tactful than "That is the ugliest girl in the class."

Good Versus Well

Frequently we have to choose between using *well* and *good* in our sentences. *Good* is an adjective and *well* is an adverb. Therefore, when describing an action verb, the only choice is the adverb *well*, for example: "He speaks well."

When using a linking verb or a verb that has to do with the five human senses, you'll want to use the adjective *good* instead, for example: "You smell good today." Many writers use *well* after linking verbs related to health, since *well* is related to wellness. For example: "How are you doing? I am well, thank you."

Grammar

Bad Versus Badly

The same rule that applies to *well* and *good* also applies to *bad* and *badly*. *Bad* is an adjective and *badly* is an adverb. Use the adjective *bad* when referring to human feeling: "I felt bad." If you said, "I felt badly," this would imply that there was something wrong with your sense of touch.

A- Adjectives

There are a group of adjectives that follow their own, unique rules. These so-called a- adjectives are *ablaze, afloat, afraid, aghast, alert, alike, alive, alone, aloof, ashamed, asleep, averse, awake*, and *aware*. These adjectives are used after a linking verb, for example: "The man was ashamed."

Sometimes you can use an a- adjective before the word it modifies; for example, "the alert driver." A- adjectives are sometimes modified with "very much," for example: "The man was very much ashamed."

Adverbs

Adverbs are words that modify verbs, adjectives, or another adverb. Adverbs often describe when, where, why, or under what circumstances something happened. Adverbs often end in "-ly"; however, there are many words not ending in "-ly" that serve as adverbs. There are also words ending in "-ly" that are not adverbs. For example, the words *lovely, lonely, motherly*, and *friendly* are adjectives.

When a group of words containing a subject and a verb act as an adverb (modifying another verb in the sentence), it is called an *adverb clause*. Here is an example: "*When this game is over*, we're going home for dinner." When a group of words not containing a subject and a verb act as an adverb, it is called an *adverbial phrase*. Prepositional phrases frequently have the function of an adverb; for example, "She works *on weekends*."

An infinitive phrase can also act as an adverb; for example, "The assistant ran *to catch the bus*."

Adjectives cannot modify adverbs, but adverbs can modify adjectives; for example, "The executive showed a *wonderfully* casual attitude." Like adjectives, adverbs can have comparative and superlative forms; for example, "You should walk *faster* if you want to get some exercise." "The candidate who types *fastest* gets the job." Sometimes words like *more* and *most, less* and *least* are used to show an amount; for example, "The house was the *most beautifully* decorated home on the tour."

Another construction used to create adverbs is use of *as . . . as*, for example: "He can't read *as* fast *as* his sister."

A small group of adverbs have two forms, one that ends in "-ly" and one that doesn't. In some cases, the two forms have different meanings. For example: "They departed *late*." "*Lately*, they can't seem to be on time." In most cases, the form without the "-ly" should be reserved for casual conversation and not business writing; for example, "He did her wrong."

Adverbs are often used as *intensifiers* in order to convey a greater or lesser meaning. Intensifiers have three different functions. They can emphasize, amplify, or tone down a verb. The following are some examples of each type:

- *Emphasize*—"I *really* don't like him." "He *simply* ignores me."
- *Amplify*—"He *completely* wrecked his new car." "I *absolutely* love fresh fruit."

American Management Association • www.amanet.org

■ *Tone down*—"I *kind of* like this restaurant's food." "She *mildly* disapproved of his smoking."

Types of Adverbs
There are five main types of adverbs:

1. *Adverbs of manner*—"He spoke *slowly* and walked *quietly*."
2. *Adverbs of place*—"He lives *there* now."
3. *Adverbs of frequency*—"He drives to work *every morning*."
4. *Adverbs of time*—"He slept *late*."
5. *Adverbs of purpose*—"He drives his car slowly *to avoid getting a ticket*."

Adverbs in a Numbered List
Within normal text, it is usually best not to number items beyond three or four. Anything more than that should be formatted in a vertical numbered list. When you create a numbered list, do not use adverbs with an "-ly" ending (secondly, thirdly, etc). Instead, use first, second, third, and so on.

Adverbs to Avoid
Adverbs like *very*, *extremely*, and *really* don't intensify anything. They are often too imprecise for business writing. You should avoid using such adverbs.

Positions of Adverbs
Adverbs have a unique ability to be placed in different places within a sentence. Adverbs of manner are unusually flexible in this regard. For example:

Solemnly, the president returned the salute.

The president solemnly returned the salute.

The president returned the salute solemnly.

Adverbs of frequency can appear at the following places within a sentence:

■ *Before the main verb*—"He *never* gets up before noon."

■ *Between the auxiliary verb and the main verb*—"I have *rarely* called my sister without a good reason."

■ *Before the verb "used to"*—"I *always* used to talk to him at the bus stop."

Indefinite adverbs of time can appear either before the verb or between the auxiliary and the main verb:

He *finally* showed up for the date.

He has *recently* traveled to France.

Order of Adverbs
There is a basic order in which adverbs can appear in a sentence when there is more than one (Table 32-4).

As a general rule, shorter adverbial phrases precede longer ones, regardless of content. For example: "Mike takes a short swim *before breakfast every morning in the*

Grammar

TABLE 32-4   Order of Adverbs

Verb	Manner	Place	Frequency	Time	Purpose
John jogs	enthusiastically	in the park	every morning	before sunrise	to keep in shape
Mary drives	hurriedly	into town	every afternoon	before dinner	to do her shopping

summer." Among similar adverbial phrases of kind (manner, place, frequency), the more specific adverbial phrase goes first; for example, "He promised to meet her *for coffee sometime next week.*" If you move an adverbial modifier to the beginning of a sentence, additional emphasis will be placed on that modifier. This is especially useful with adverbs of manner; for example, "*Slowly, ever so carefully*, the little boy crept into his parents' bedroom."

Inappropriate Adverb Order   Modifiers can sometimes attach themselves to the wrong word; for example, "They reported that Leslie Fiedler, a famous literary critic, had won the lottery *on the evening news.*" It would be better to move the modifier immediately after the verb it is modifying ("reported") or to the beginning of the sentence: "They reported on the evening news that Leslie Fiedler, a famous literary critic, had won the lottery."

The adverbs *only* and *barely* are often misplaced modifiers; for example, "He *only grew* to be five feet tall." This would be better stated as follows: "He grew to be *only five feet tall.*"

Adjuncts, Disjuncts, and Conjuncts

Adverbs are usually neatly integrated into the flow of a sentence. When this is true, the adverb is called an *adjunct*. When an adverb does not fit into the sentence flow, it is called a *disjunct* or *conjunct* and is usually set off by a comma or a series of commas. A disjunct acts as if it is evaluating the rest of the sentence. Rather than modify the verb, it modifies the entire clause; for example, "*Honestly*, Bill, I don't really care." Conjuncts serve as a connector within the flow of the text, signaling a transition; for example, "If they start talking politics, *then* I'm leaving." One variation is the adverbial conjunction. These are words like *however* and *nevertheless*. For example: "I love this job; *however*, I don't think I can afford to stay."

Special Adverbial Clauses

Some adverbs have special rules for their placement. For instance, the adverbs *enough* and *not enough* usually take a post-modifier position; for example, "Is your food *hot enough*? This food is *not hot enough.*" *Enough* can also be an adjective. When it is used as an adjective, it comes before the noun; for example, "The teacher didn't give us *enough time.*" The adverb *enough* is often followed by an infinitive verb; for example, "They didn't play hard *enough to win.*"

The adverb *too* usually comes before adjectives and other adverbs; for example, "He ate *too fast.*" "He eats *too quickly.*" When *too* appears in a sentence after an adverb, it is a disjunct adverb and is set apart with a comma, for example: "John works hard. He works *quickly, too.*" The adverb *too* is sometimes followed by an infinitive verb; for example, "He talks *too slowly to keep* my attention." The adverb *too* can also be followed by the prepositional phrase *for* plus the objective of the preposition plus an infinitive. For example: "This food is *too spicy for Grandma to eat*."

Relative Adverbs

Adjectival clauses can be introduced by *relative adverbs*: *where, when,* and *why*. Although each of these is an adjectival clause and modifies a noun, the relative word itself serves in an adverbial function, modifying the verb within the clause. The relative adverb *where* begins a clause that modifies a noun of place; for example, "My family now lives in the *town where* my grandfather used to be sheriff." The relative pronoun *where* modifies the verb *used to be*, but the entire clause modifies the noun *town*.

A *when* clause modifies nouns of time; for example, "My favorite day of the week is *Friday, when* the weekend is about to begin."

A *why* clause modifies the noun *reason;* for example, "Do you know the *reason why* school is out today?" Sometimes the relative adverb is left out of these clauses and the writer substitutes *that* instead; for example, "Do you know the *reason that* school it out today?"

Viewpoint Adverbs

A viewpoint adverb usually comes after a noun and is related to an adjective that precedes the noun; for example, "Investing all our money in technology stocks was probably not a *good idea financially*."

Focus Adverbs

A focus adverb is used to limit a specific aspect of the sentence; for example, "He got a promotion *just* for being there."

Negative Adverbs

Negative adverbs can create a negative meaning in a sentence without the use of words like *no, not, neither, nor,* or *never*. Here are some examples: "He *seldom* smiles." "He *hardly* eats anything since he got sick." "After the team lost so many key players, *rarely* did anyone attend the games."

Pronouns

Usually, pronouns refer to a noun, an individual or a group, or a thing whose identity has been made clear previously. The word a pronoun substitutes for is called its *antecedent*. "Jeanne accepted Carmelo's proposal. She knew *he* was the right guy for *her*." Not all pronouns refer to an antecedent. For example, in the sentence "Everyone on this floor charges over one hundred dollars an hour," the pronoun *everyone* does not have an antecedent.

Types of Pronouns

There are different kinds of pronouns, which are discussed in the following sections:

■   Personal

■   Demonstrative

- Relative
- Indefinite
- Intensive
- Reflexive
- Interrogative
- Reciprocal

Personal Pronouns   Personal pronouns change form according to their various uses within a sentence. The pronoun *I* is used as the subject of a sentence, for example: "I am tall." The pronoun *me* is used as an object in various ways; for example, "He gave me a car." The pronoun *my* is used for the possessive form; for example, "That's my house." The same is true for other personal pronouns: the singular *you* and *he/she/it* and the plurals *we*, *you*, and *they*. These forms are called *cases* (Table 32-5).

When a personal pronoun is connected by a conjunction to another noun or pronoun, it does not change case; for example, "I am taking a course in Latin." "John and I are taking a course in Latin." You'll notice in the second example that "John" is listed before "I." The same is true when the object form is used: "The professor gave the Latin books to me." "The professor gave the Latin books to John and me."

When a pronoun and a noun are combined, you must choose the case of the pronoun that would be appropriate if the noun were not there; for example: "*We* teachers are demanding a raise." With the second person, there's not as much confusion because the pronoun *you* is the same for both subject and object form: "*You* teachers are demanding too much money."

Among the possessive pronoun forms, there are nominative possessives such as *mine*, *yours*, *ours*, and *theirs*. Here are some examples: "This new house is mine." "Look at those houses. Theirs needs work. Ours is in good shape." "Mine is newer than yours."

Demonstrative Pronouns   The demonstrative pronouns—*this*, *that*, *these*, *those*, and *such*—can be used as either pronouns or as determiners. As pronouns, the demonstra-

TABLE 32-5 Various Cases for Pronouns

	Subjective	**Possessive**	**Objective**
Singular first person	I	My, mine	Me
Singular second person	You	Your, yours	You
Singular third person	He, she, it	His, her, hers, its	Him, her, it
Plural first person	We	Our, ours	Us
Plural second person	You	Your, yours	You
Plural third person	They	Their, theirs	Them
Relative and interrogative pronouns	Who, whoever, which, that, what	Whose	Whom, whomever, which, that, what
Indefinite pronouns	Everybody	Everybody's	Everybody

tive pronouns identify a noun: "*That* is marvelous!" "I will never forget *this*." "*Such* is life."

As determiners, the demonstrative pronouns adjectivally modify a noun that follows. They are used to convey a sense of time and distance. For example: "*These* [strawberries that are in front of me] look delicious. *Those* [that are farther away] look even better."

A sense of emotional distance can also be conveyed through the use of demonstrative pronouns; for example, "You're going to eat *that*?" Pronouns used in this way receive special emphasis in a spoken sentence.

When used as subjects, demonstrative pronouns can refer to objects as well as persons, for example: "This is my mother." "This is my book."

Relative Pronouns   The relative pronouns—*who, whoever, which,* and *that*—relate to groups of words, nouns, and other pronouns. The pronoun *who* connects the subject to the verb within a dependent clause. Choosing between *which* and *that* and between *who* and *whom* is difficult for many people. Generally, we use *which* to introduce clauses that are parenthetical in nature. That means they can be removed from the sentence without changing the meaning of the sentence. For that reason, a *which* clause is often set apart with a comma or a pair of commas. We use *that* to introduce clauses that are indispensable for the meaning of the sentence. *That* clauses are not set apart with commas. The pronoun *which* refers to things, *who* refers to people, and *that* usually refers to things but also refers to people in a general way.

The expanded relative pronouns *whoever, whomever,* and *whatever* are known as indefinite relative pronouns. They do not define a thing or person in particular; for example, "The company will hire *whomever* it pleases." "She seemed to say *whatever* came to mind." "*Whoever* took the money will be punished." *What* can be an indefinite relative pronoun when used in the following way: "He will give you *what* you need for the trip."

Indefinite Pronouns   The indefinite pronouns—*everybody, anybody, somebody, all, each, every, some, none,* and *one*—do not substitute for specific nouns but act as nouns themselves.

One of the problems with the indefinite pronoun *everybody* is that it seems to be plural but takes a singular verb, for example: "*Everybody* is coming." The indefinite pronoun *none* can be either singular or plural. It is usually always plural except when something else in the sentence forces it to be singular. *Some* can be singular or plural depending on whether it refers to something countable or not countable.

Some indefinite pronouns also double as determiners, such as *enough, few, fewer, less, little, many, much, several, more, most, all, both, every, each, any, either, neither, none,* and *some.*

Intensive Pronouns   The intensive pronouns—*myself, yourself, herself, ourselves,* and *themselves*—consist of a personal pronoun plus the suffix *-self* or *-selves.* They are used to emphasize a noun; for example, "I *myself* didn't play baseball."

Reflexive Pronouns   Reflexive pronouns indicate that the subject in a sentence also receives the action of the verb: "People who cheat on their taxes are only hurting *themselves.*" Whenever there is a reflexive pronoun in a sentence, there must be a person to whom the pronoun can reflect. For example, "Please give the food to *myself*" is incorrect because there is no other subject such as "I" in the sentence.

There is a tendency to use reflexive and intensive pronouns (those ending in "-self") when they are not appropriate. For example, "These books will be read by *myself*" should be "These books will be read by *me*."

The indefinite pronoun *one* has its own reflexive form; for example, "One must trust oneself." Other indefinite pronouns use either *himself* or *themselves* as reflexives.

Interrogative Pronouns   Interrogative pronouns are used to introduce questions, for example: "*What* is that?" "*Who* is coming?" "*Which* dog do you like best?" *Which* is used for specific reference rather than *what*. For example, in the sentence "Which dogs do you like best?" you are referring to specific dogs. "What dogs do you like best?" refers to general dog breeds you like best.

Interrogative pronouns can also act as determiners; for example, "It doesn't matter which road you take." In this role, the pronouns are called *interrogative adjectives.*

Interrogative pronouns are used to introduce noun clauses. Like relative pronouns, the interrogative pronouns play a subject role in the clause they introduce; for example, "I already told the salesman *what I thought about it.*"

Reciprocal Pronouns   The reciprocal pronouns—*each other* and *one another*—are used for combining ideas; for example, "My brother and I give *each other* a hard time." If more than two people are involved, you would use *one another*.

Reciprocal pronouns can also take the possessive form; for example, "They borrowed *each other's* clothes."

Pronouns and Antecedent Agreement

A pronoun usually refers to its antecedent, and the two must agree in number. Therefore, if the antecedent is plural, the pronoun must be plural. The same is true if the antecedent is singular; the pronoun must then be singular.

Certain pronouns like *anyone, anybody, everyone, everybody, someone, somebody, no one,* and *nobody* are always singular. This is perplexing for some people, because they feel that *everyone* and *everybody* refer to more than one person. The same is also true for *either* and *neither*. Even though they seem to be referring to two things, they are singular.

One of the most frequently asked grammar questions is regarding the pronoun *who* (*who, whose, whom, whoever,* and *whomever*). The choice of singular or plural is determined by what the pronoun refers to. It can refer to a single person or a group. For example: "*The person who* broke my window should confess." "*The people who* have been without power should complain." One good way to understand the uses for *who* is to compare it with the pronouns *he* and *they*. (See Table 32-6.)

So one good way to choose between the various forms of *who* is to think of the sentence in terms of the choice between *he* and *him*. If *him* feels right, choose *whom*. If *he* sounds better, pick *who*. For example:

Who do you think is coming? (Do you think *he* is coming?)

Whom shall we invite to the movie? (Shall we invite *him* to the movie?)

Give the money to *whomever* you please. (Give the money to *him*.)

Give the money to *whoever* wants it most. (*He* seems to want it most).

Whoever guesses my age will win the prize. (*He* guesses my age.)

TABLE 32-6   The Pronoun *Who* Compared to *He* and *They*

	Subject Form	Possessive Form	Object Form
Singular	He	His	Him
	Who	Whose	Whom
Plural	They	Their	Them
	Who	Whose	Whom

Another related problem is confusing *whose* with *who's*. *Who's* looks like it is possessive; however, it is really a contraction of "who is."

Prepositions

Prepositions are used to describe relationships between other words in a sentence. Prepositions like *in*, *on*, or *between* are good examples because they describe the spatial nature of things.

Prepositions are almost always combined with other words to become prepositional phrases. Prepositional phrases consist of a preposition plus a determiner, along with an adjective or two, followed by a pronoun or noun that is called the object of the preposition. The prepositional phrase takes on a modifying role of its own, acting as either an adjective or adverb to locate something in time and space, or explaining when or where, or understanding under what circumstances something occurred.

Types of Prepositions

Prepositions can be divided into four types: (1) prepositions of time, (2) prepositions of place, (3) prepositions of location, and (4) prepositions of movement.

Prepositions of Time: *At, On, In, For*, and *Since*   *At, on*, and *in* often serve as prepositions of time. We use *at* to designate specific times; for example, "Meet me *at* five o'clock." We use *on* to designate days and dates; for example, "I work all day *on* Saturdays." We use *in* for nonspecific times; for example, "He likes to read *in* the evenings."

The preposition *for* is used to measure time; for example, "He worked *for* twenty years." The preposition *since* is used with a specific date or time; for example, "I have known him *since* January 2003."

Prepositions of Place: *At, On*, and *In*   *At, on*, and *in* can also serve as prepositions of place. We use *at* for specific addresses: "I live *at* 5203 Legendary Lane." We use *on* to designate streets: "I live *on* Legendary Lane." We use *in* for the names of towns, states, and countries: "I live *in* Acworth."

Prepositions of Location: *At, On*, and *In*   *At, on*, and *in* can also be used as prepositions of location. Their usage is specific to certain places. For example, we say: "in the bed," "in the bedroom," "in the car," "in the class," "in the library," "in the room," and "in the school." We also say "at class," "at home," "at the library," "at the office," "at school," or "at work." Depending on the specific situation, we can say: "on the bed," "on the ceiling," "on the floor," "on the horse," "on the plane," or "on the train."

Grammar

Prepositions of Movement: *To* and Toward   The preposition *to* is used to express movement to a place; for example, "I am driving to work."

Toward and *towards* are also used to express movement; for example, "We were working towards a common goal." They are both the same word with a spelling variation; however, *toward* is the preferred spelling in the United States while *towards* is common in British usage.

Preposition Combinations

Some prepositions are so commonly used with particular nouns, adjectives, and verbs that they have almost become one word. The following is a list of nouns and preposition combinations:

- Approval of
- Awareness of
- Belief in
- Concern for
- Confusion about
- Desire for
- Fondness for
- Grasp of
- Hatred of

- Hope for
- Interest in
- Love of
- Need for
- Participation in
- Reason for
- Respect for
- Success in
- Understanding of

The following is a list of adjectives and preposition combinations:

- Afraid of
- Angry at
- Aware of
- Capable of
- Careless about
- Familiar with
- Fond of
- Happy about
- Interested in

- Jealous of
- Made of
- Married to
- Proud of
- Similar to
- Sorry for
- Sure of
- Tired of
- Worried about

A combination of a verb and preposition is called a *phrasal verb*. The word that is joined with the verb is called a *particle*. The following is a list of verb and preposition combinations:

- Apologize for
- Ask about
- Ask for
- Belong to
- Bring up
- Care for
- Find out

- Give up
- Grow up
- Look for
- Look forward to
- Look up
- Make up
- Pay for

- Prepare for
- Study for
- Talk about
- Think about

- Trust in
- Work for
- Worry about

Conjunctions

Conjunctions are words that connect parts of a sentence. The simplest conjunctions are called *coordinating conjunctions*. They include *and, but, or, yet, for, nor,* and *so.*

When a coordinating conjunction connects two independent clauses, it is often accompanied by a comma; for example, "John wants to play football for Texas, *but* he has had trouble with his grades." It is also correct to use a comma with *and* when used to attach the list item in a list; for example: "John needs to study harder in math, history, physics, *and* economics." When a coordinating conjunction is used to connect all the elements in a series, a comma is not used, for example: "Math *and* history *and* physics are the subjects that give John the most trouble." Commas are also used with *but* when a sentence expresses a contrast; for example, "John is a great player, *but* not very smart."

The most common coordinating conjunctions are *and*, *but*, and *or*. Each has its own unique uses.

Coordinating Conjunction: **And**

The coordinating conjunction *and* can be used in the following ways:

- To suggest that one idea is sequential to another; for example, "Steve sent in his application *and* waited for the response in the mail."

- To suggest that an idea is the result of another; for example, "Linda heard the thunder *and* quickly took shelter inside the house."

- To suggest that one idea is in contrast to another; for example, "Lori is an artist, *and* her sister is a doctor." Frequently, the conjunction *but* is used for this purpose.

- To suggest an element of surprise; for example, "Atlanta is a beautiful city *and* has symptoms of urban blight." Frequently, the conjunction *yet* is used for this purpose.

- To suggest that one clause is dependent; for example, "Drink too much water before the trip *and* you'll soon find yourself stopping at every rest area."

- To make a comment on the first clause; for example, "Horace became addicted to gambling—*and* that's why he moved to Las Vegas."

Coordinating Conjunction: **But**

The coordinating conjunction *but* can be used in the following ways:

- To suggest an unexpected contrast; for example, "Tom lost money in his investments, *but* he still maintained a comfortable lifestyle."

- To express positively what the first part of the sentence implies negatively; for example, "Tom never invested foolishly *but* listened carefully to the advice of investment newsletters."

■ To connect two ideas with the meaning "with the exception of"; for example, "Everyone *but* Tom is making money in the stock market."

Coordinating Conjunction: Or

The coordinating conjunction *or* can be used in the following ways:

■ To suggest that only one possibility is realistic and excludes the other; for example, "You can sell your investment now *or* you can lose all your money."

■ To suggest alternatives; for example, "We can go out to eat and to a movie, *or* we can just stay home and see what's on TV."

■ To suggest a refinement of the first clause; for example, "The University of Texas is the best school in the state, *or* so it seems to every UT alumni."

■ To suggest a correction to the first part of the sentence; for example, "There's no way you can lose money in this investment, *or* so Eric told himself."

■ To suggest a negative condition; for example, "You have two choices: pay taxes *or* die."

Other Conjunctions

The conjunction *nor* is used occasionally by itself; however, it is most commonly used in a correlative pair with *neither;* for example, "He is *neither* rich *nor* poor." Nor can also be used with negative expressions; for example, "This is not how I normally dress, *nor* should you get the idea I have no taste in clothes."

The word *yet* sometimes functions as an adverb and has various meanings such as *in addition*, *even*, *still*, and *eventually*. It also functions as a coordinating conjunction with a meaning of *nevertheless* or *but;* for example, "Rosemary is an expert in computer programming, *yet* her real passion is poetry."

The word *for* is often used as a preposition, but it does sometimes act as a coordinating conjunction. When it is used as a coordinating conjunction, it has a meaning of *because* or *since;* for example, "For he's a jolly good fellow."

The conjunction *so* can be used to connect two independent clauses along with a comma. It has the meaning of *as well* or *in addition*. Many writers would eliminate the *so* and use a semicolon between the two clauses.

Subordinating Conjunctions

A subordinating conjunction comes at the beginning of a dependent clause and establishes the relationship between the clause and the rest of the sentence; for example, "He spoke Spanish *as if* he had been born in Mexico."

Many subordinating conjunctions also serve as prepositions. When they serve as subordinating conjunctions, they introduce the dependent clause (Table 32-7).

Correlative Conjunctions

Correlative conjunctions combine with other words to form grammatically equal pairs. The following is a list of correlative conjunctions.

■ Both . . . and

■ Not only . . . but also

■ Not . . . but

TABLE 32-7 Common Surrounding Conjunctions

After	If	Though
Although	If only	Till
As	In order that	Unless
As if	Now that	Until
As long as	Once	When
As though	Rather than	Whenever
Because	Since	Where
Before	So that	Whereas
Even if	Than	Wherever
Even though	That	While

- Either . . . or
- Neither . . . nor
- Whether . . . or
- As . . . as

Articles, Determiners, and Quantifiers

Articles, determiners, and quantifiers are little words that precede and modify nouns; for example, "*the* dog," "*a* cat," "*those* people," "*whatever* purpose," "*either* way," "*your* choice." Sometimes these words tell you whether the subject is something specific or more general. Sometimes they tell you how much or how many.

The choice of the proper article or determiner is usually not a problem for the native English speaker. The following is a list of determiner categories:

- Articles—*an, a, the*
- Determiners—articles and other limiters such as *a, an, five, her, our, those, that, several,* and *some*
- Possessive nouns—*Kevin's, the worker's, my mother's*
- Possessive pronouns—*his, your, their, whose*
- Numbers—*one, two, three,* etc.
- Demonstrative pronouns—*this, that, these, those, such*

Articles

The three articles *a, an,* and *the* are a type of adjective. *The* is called the *definite article* because it tends to name something specific. *A* and *an* are called *indefinite articles* because they refer to things in a less specific way.

The is used with specific nouns and is required when the noun refers to something that is unique; for example, "*The* earth orbits *the* sun." *The* is also used for abstract nouns; for example, "The city of Atlanta has encouraged *the* use of mass transit."

A is used before singular nouns that begin with consonants; for example, "A dog, *a* cat, *a* mountain." *An* is used before singular nouns that begin with vowels or vowel-like sounds; for example, "*An* apple, *an* eagle, *an* invitation."

Grammar

Predeterminers

Predeterminers occur prior to other determiners and include multipliers (*double, twice, two/three times*, etc.); fractional expressions (*one-half, one-third*, etc.); the words *both, half*, and *all*; and the intensifiers *quite, rather,* and *such*.

Multipliers precede plural count and mass nouns and with singular count nouns denoting numbers or an amount; for example, "This classroom holds *three times* the students as my old room."

Fractional expressions have a similar construction as multipliers and optionally include *of;* for example, "*One-half of* the voters favored lower taxes."

Intensifiers occur primarily in casual speech and are more common in British English than in American English; for example, "This food is *rather* bland, isn't it?" "The voters made *quite a* fuss over the debate."

Quantifiers

Quantifiers are words that also precede and modify nouns. They are used to communicate how many or how much. Selecting the correct quantifier depends on whether it is used with a count or non-count noun. For example, the following quantifiers can be used with count nouns: *many* people, a *few* people, *several* people, *a couple of* people, *none of the* people. The following quantifiers can be used with non-count nouns: *not much* eating, *a little* eating, *little* eating, *a bit of* eating, *a good deal of* eating, *a great deal of* eating, *no* eating.

Interjections

Interjections are words or phrases used to communicate excitement, orders, or protests. Sometimes they can be used by themselves, but often they are contained within more complex sentence structures; for example, "*Wow*, I can't believe it." "*Oh*, I didn't realize you were here." "*No*, you shouldn't have done that."

Most interjections are treated as parenthetical elements and are set apart from the rest of the sentence by commas or a set of commas. If the interjection is more forceful, it is followed with an exclamation point.

Chapter 33

Language Usage and Style

Subject and Verb

The *subject* of a sentence is the person, place, or thing that is the main focus of the sentence. To find the subject of a sentence, first locate the verb. Then answer the question: "What or who is being 'verbed'?" For instance, in the sentence "The monkeys in the treetops must be observed," the verb is *must be observed*. So, what must be observed? The answer is *monkeys*. A *simple subject* is the subject without any modifiers. For example, the simple subject of the following sentence is *event*: "The upcoming event, stripped of all the hype, is nothing but a fund-raiser."

Sometimes a simple subject can be more than one word or even an entire clause. Consider the following: "*What he had forgotten about the law* was amazing considering how many years he spent in law school." The simple subject is the entire clause printed in italics.

Usually, when the subject of a sentence is *you* and the sentence is a suggestion, order, or command, the *you* is left out. For example, in the sentence "Get out of the way!" *you* is understood to be the subject.

For sentence analysis, the person who initiates an action is called the *agent* of a sentence. When the active voice is used, the subject is the agent; for example, "The class failed the test." When the passive voice is used, the agent is not the subject. In fact, some passive sentences don't contain an agent.

Subject-Verb Inversion

Normally, a sentence contains a subject and then a verb, in that order. This pattern is disturbed in only a few instances. Here are a few examples:

- In questions—"Have you read that book?"

- *In expletive constructions*—"Here is your book."

- *To put focus on a particular word*—"What's more important is his reluctance to find a job."

- *When a sentence begins with an adverb, adverbial phrase, or clause*—"Rarely have so many been eaten in just one meal."

- *After the word "so"*—"I believe him; so do the people."

Subject-Verb Agreement

The basic rule of subject-verb agreement is that a singular subject needs a singular verb. Likewise, plural subjects need plural verbs. For example: "My *brother is* a psychologist. My *brothers are* psychologists."

Indefinite pronouns like *anyone, everyone, someone, no one,* and *nobody* are singular subjects and, thus, require singular verbs. For example: "Everyone *is* studying hard."

Some indefinite pronouns, such as *all* and *some*, can be singular or plural depending on whether the thing they're referring to is countable or not. For example: "Some of the candy *is* missing. Some of the dogs *are* barking."

There is one indefinite pronoun, *none*, that can be either singular or plural, and it doesn't matter whether you use a singular or plural verb—that is, unless something in the sentence specifies its number. For example: "None of you *write* poetry." "None of the cars *are* speeding."

Some indefinite pronouns like *everyone* and *everybody* sound like they are talking about more than one person; however, they are both singular. For example: "Everyone *is* working hard." The pronoun *each* is often followed by a prepositional phrase ending in a plural word: "Each of the monkeys . . . " *Each*, however, is also singular. For example: "Each of the monkeys *is* eating a banana."

Don't confuse the word *and* with the phrases *together with, as well as,* and *along with*. They do not mean the same and do not create compound subjects the same way *and* does. For example: "The boy, as well as his brother, *is* going to school." "The boy and his brother *are* going to school."

The pronouns *neither* and *either* are singular even though they appear to be referring to two things; for example, "Neither of the two computers *is* obsolete. Either *is* a good choice for a student." Sometimes *neither* and *either* take a plural verb when they are followed by a prepositional phrase that begins with *of;* for example, "*Have* either of you two kids seen my dog?" "*Are* either of you listening to me?"

When the conjunctions *or* and *nor* are used, the subject closest to the verb determines whether the verb is singular or plural; for example, "Neither the bear nor the monkeys *were* awake when we visited the zoo." It's also a good idea to put the plural subject closest to the verb since the following version of the same sentence would be incorrect: "Neither the monkeys nor the bear were awake when we visited the zoo."

The words *there* and *here* can never be subjects in a sentence. For example: "Here *are* my two books. There better *be* a good reason you have them." These are called *expletive constructions*, and the subject follows the verb and determines whether the verb is singular or plural.

Verbs for third-person singular subjects like *he, she,* and *it* have -s endings; for example, "He loves to eat."

Sometimes modifiers will slip between a subject and a verb. When this happens, don't let them confuse the subject-verb agreement. For example: "The *workers*, who always seem to be standing around taking a break, gathered around in a circle like a football huddle, *are* being fired."

Sometimes nouns take peculiar forms that make it confusing to tell whether they are singular or plural. Words such as *glasses, gloves, pliers,* and *scissors* are thought of as plural unless they're preceded by the phrase *pair of*—in which case *pair* becomes the subject. For example: "My glasses *are* on the desk." "The pair of glasses *is* on the desk."

Some words that end in -*s* seem to be plural but are really singular and thus require singular verbs. For example: "The evening news *is* full of disasters." There are other words that end in –*s* that refer to a single thing but are actually plural and require a plural verb. For example: "His assets *were* totally wiped out by the bankruptcy."

Fractional expressions such as *half of* and *a percentage of* can be either singular or plural. The same is true when words like *some, all*, and *any* serve as subjects. For example: "One-half of the population *is* over sixty-five." "One-quarter of the students *were* absent." "Some of the houses *are* painted white." "Some of the money *is* missing."

Finally, when you have a sentence that combines a positive and a negative subject and one is plural and the other singular, the verb should agree with the positive subject. For example: "It's the teacher not the students who *decides* what to teach."

Predicates

Predicates are used to complete a sentence. While the subject names the person, place, or thing that is doing something, a simple predicate consists of a verb, verb string, or a compound verb. For example: "The flower *bloomed.*" "The flowers *have been blooming.*" "The bulbs *opened, blossomed, and then closed for the night.*"

A *compound predicate* consists of two or more predicates connected; for example, "The mountain biker *began to ride down the trail* and *eventually entered one of the most beautiful valleys in the area.*"

A *complete predicate* consists of a transitive verb and all modifiers and other words that complete its meaning; for example, "The slowly moving thunderstorm *flashed lightning across the dark foreboding sky.*"

A *predicate adjective* follows a linking verb and describes the subject of the sentence; for example, "The minerals in the water taste *bad.*"

A *predicate nominative* follows a linking verb and describes what the subject is; for example, "Dylan Wilson is *president* of the firm."

Objects

Objects are the part of a sentence that receives actions. In the sentence "He threw *the ball,*" "the ball" is a *direct object.*

An *object complement* renames or describes a direct object. Take the sentence "He took his monkey, Meep, to the beach." In this example, "his monkey" is the direct object; "Meep" is the object complement.

An *indirect object* identifies to what or to whom the action of a verb is directed. Take the sentence "He sold me his car." In this example, "me" is the indirect object; "his car" is the direct object. The word *me*—along with other pronouns such as *him, us*, and *them*—is not always an indirect object; it can also serve as a direct object, for example: "Save me!"

Complements

A complement is any word (or phrase) that completes a subject, object, or verb. A *subject complement* follows a linking verb and is used to rename or define the subject; for example, "A tarn is a small glacial *lake.*"

An *object complement* follows or modifies a direct object and can be a noun or adjective. In the sentence "The players named Logan *captain* to keep him *happy*," the noun "captain" complements the direct object "Logan"; the adjective "happy" complements the object "him."

A *verb complement* is either a direct or an indirect object of a verb; for example, "Mark gave *Terry* [indirect object] all his old *albums* [direct object]."

Modifiers

Modifiers are words that limit certain aspects of a sentence. Some modifiers—such as *only, just, nearly*, and *barely*—can easily end up in the wrong place in a sentence. Compare these two sentences: "He only threw the ball ten feet." "He threw the ball only ten feet." The best rule is to place these modifiers immediately before the word they modify. When a modifier improperly modifies something, it is called a *dangling modifier*. One common example is starting a sentence with a prepositional phrase; for example, "Cleaning the windows every six months, the building seemed to look better." Buildings can't clean their own windows. This example could be rewritten as: "Cleaning the windows every six months, the maintenance staff made the building look better."

If you have a sentence where a participial phrase is followed by an expletive construction, you will often have a *dangling participle*. For example: "Cleaning the windows every six months, there is a simple way to keep a building looking better." This example could be rewritten as: "If you clean the windows every six months, you can keep a building looking better."

Another situation where dangling participles can occur is when you have a participial phrase followed by a passive verb. This happens because the real subject of the sentence is disguised. For example: "Cleaning the windows ever six months, the building was kept in beautiful condition." This example could be rewritten as: "Cleaning the windows every six months, the workmen kept the building in beautiful condition."

Infinitive phrases can also end up as dangling modifiers; for example, "To keep the employees interested in their health, a fitness center was set up in the basement." In this example, the infinitive phrase *To keep the employees interested in their health* should probably modify the person who set up the fitness center. Thus, this example could be rewritten as: "To keep the employees interested in their heath, the manager set up a fitness center in the basement."

Finally, one additional misplaced modifier problem involves adverbs. Adverbs can be placed almost anywhere in a sentence, but their placement can sometimes obscure their meaning; for example, "The people who listen to public radio often like classical music." Does this mean that anyone who listens to public radio even for a few minutes likes classical music? By moving the placement of the adverb *often*, this example could be rewritten as: "The people who often listen to public radio like classical music."

Phrases

A phrase is a group of related words that does not include a subject and verb. If a subject and verb are present, it is considered to be a *clause*.

Noun Phrases

A noun phrase includes a noun and its modifiers, for example: "The tall dark man." The modifiers that are included in the noun phrase can be any of the following:

- *Adjectives*—"tall dark man"

- *Participial phrase*—"the bushes following the edge of the sidewalk"

- *Infinitive phrase*—"the first woman to fly around the world"

- *Modifying clause*—"the mistakes he had made the day before"

- *Prepositional phrase*—"the trail next to the lake, over by the dam"

Usually, all the words in a noun phrase are together; however, occasionally they can be broken up into what is called a *discontinuous noun phrase*. For example: "*Several burglaries* have been reported *involving people who were gone for the weekend*." There is nothing wrong with a discontinuous noun phrase. They are sometimes useful for balancing a subject and predicate. Otherwise, we end up with a ten-word subject and a three-word verb.

One common problem to avoid involves a long string of compound noun phrases. This often happens when the string also involves a group of compound nouns, such as *student body*, *book cover*, or *meeting place*. If you put together a long string of these phrases, the result can be a very difficult sentence.

An addressed person's name or substitute name is called a *vocative*. These sometimes take the form of a noun phrase. A vocative is treated as a parenthetical element and is set apart from the rest of the sentence by a pair of commas if it appears within the flow of a sentence; for example, "Mike, stop the car." You do not need to add commas every time someone's name is mentioned in a sentence. Commas are used only when the name refers to someone who is being addressed in the sentence. Overall, there are four types of vocatives:

- Single names, with or without a title

- The personal pronoun *you*

- Appellatives of endearment, such as *darling, my dear, sweetheart,* and *sir*

- Nominal clauses, such as in the sentence "Whoever is singing, stop it now."

Prepositional Phrases

A prepositional phrase consists of a preposition, a noun or pronoun that serves as the object of the preposition, and an adjective or two that modifies the object. Prepositional phrases usually tell us when or where something is happening; for example, "in a half hour."

A prepositional phrase used at the beginning of a sentence is called an *introductory modifier*. You can set apart an introductory modifier with a comma; however, it is optional unless the introductory modifier is long.

You have probably heard the rule regarding not ending a sentence with a preposition. Although you can easily revise sentences that do this, sometimes the revision results in a very clumsy sentence.

Appositive Phrases

An appositive phrase involves renaming or amplifying a word that immediately precedes it; for example, "My favorite professor, *a world famous author*, just won a prestigious literary award."

Absolute Phrases

An absolute phrase is a group of words consisting of a noun or pronoun, a participle, and any modifiers. Absolute phrases do not connect to or modify any other word in a sentence; instead, they modify the entire sentence. Absolute phrases are often treated as parenthetical elements set off from the rest of the sentence with a comma or pair of commas; for example, "*National champions three out of four years*, the university's football team were treated as gods."

Infinitive Phrases

An infinitive phrase consists of a infinitive—the root verb preceded by *to*—along with modifiers or complements. Infinitive phrases can act as adjectives, adverbs, or nouns. Consider the following examples:

- His plan *to eliminate smoking* was widely popular. (*To eliminate smoking* serves as an adjective that modifies *plan*.)

- *To watch him eat ribs* is something you have to see. (*To watch him eat ribs* serves as the noun-subject of the sentence.)

- Eric went to college *to study to be an engineer*. (*To study to be an engineer* tells us why he went, so it's an adverb.)

Gerund Phrases

Gerund phrases consist of verbals that end in *-ing* but act as nouns, along with modifiers and complements. These phrases can do anything a noun can do; for example, "*Walking after dark* is not very safe."

Participial Phrases

Present participles (verbals ending in *-ing*) and past participles (verbals ending in *-ed*) or other irregular verbs can be combined with complements and modifiers to create a *participial phrase*. They always act as adjectives. When they begin a sentence, they are set apart by a comma just like an introductory modifier. If they appear within the middle of a sentence, they are set apart with a pair of commas. For example: "*Working around the clock*, the workers repaired the airport runway in less than a week. The concrete, *having been damaged by the crash landing of the airliner*, needed to be replaced."

Clauses

A clause is a group of words that contains a subject and a verb. As discussed earlier, a clause is different from a phrase because a phrase does not include a subject and a verb.

Independent Clauses

An independent clause could stand by itself as a sentence. However, if it did, it would be a sentence and not a clause. When an independent clause is included in a sentence, it is usually separated from the rest of the sentence by a comma. Being able to recognize when a clause is acting as an independent clause is essential to knowing when to use commas in avoiding sentence fragments and run-on sentences.

Two independent clauses can be combined into a single thought; for example, "Charlie didn't mean to run away, but he did it because he was angry." In this example, two independent clauses are separated by a comma and the coordinating conjunction *but*. If the word *but* was missing, this example would be a comma splice.

Clauses can be combined three different ways:

1. With coordination

2. With subordination

3. By using a semicolon

Coordination involves using coordinating conjunctions such as *and, but, or, nor, for, yet,* and sometimes *so*. By using a coordinating conjunction, you avoid monotony and what is often called "primer language"—simple sentence constructions. Your sentences are also balanced.

Subordination involves turning one of the independent clauses into a subordinate element using a subordinating conjunction or a relative pronoun. When the clause begins with a subordinating word, it transforms into a dependent clause; for example, "Linda never liked to fly in airplanes, because she was afraid of heights."

Semicolons can be used to connect two independent clauses with or without the help of a conjunctive adverb. However, semicolons should be used only when the two independent clauses are very closely related and nicely balanced in length and content; for example, "Sheena is a very pretty girl; she looks like an angel."

Dependent Clauses

A dependent clause cannot stand by itself like an independent clause. It must be combined with an independent clause in order to become a sentence.

Dependent clauses can perform a variety of different functions within a sentence. They can be noun clauses, adverb clauses, or adjective clauses. Noun clauses can do anything a noun can do in a sentence; for example, "*What he knows about boxing* is not important to me." Adverb clauses tell us about what is going on in the independent clause: where, when, or why. For example: "*When the game is over*, we'll go get some burgers." Adjective clauses function just like multiword adjectives to modify a noun; for example, "My wife, *who is a video producer*, has just completed an award-winning documentary about music."

Sentence Fragments

A sentence fragment fails to be a sentence because it cannot stand by itself. It does not contain at least one independent clause. There are several reasons a group of words may appear to be a sentence but turn out instead to be a sentence fragment. The sentence fragment may contain a series of prepositional phrases without a proper subject-verb relationship; for example, "In Texas, sometime in early April, just before the bluebonnets appear." The sentence fragment may be a verbal phrase that wants to modify something, but that something is missing; for example, "Working deep into the night in an effort to get his taxes completed." Finally, the sentence fragment may have a subject-verb relationship, but it has been subordinated to another idea or word so it cannot stand by itself; for example, "Although he was taller than his older brother."

Sentence Variety

A *sentence* is a group of words containing a subject and a predicate. There are many different types of sentences, and the way they are used in your writing, the order they are used in, and the way they are combined and punctuated determines your writing style.

It is relatively easy to write short sentences. However, if you use only short sentences, your writing will appear to be primer style and give your reader a poor impression of your level of professionalism.

To write more complicated sentences, you have to create constructions of clauses and phrases. Long sentences and run-on sentences are not the same thing. Combing too long a series of clauses may cause the reader to get confused. However, many writers are afraid they'll create run-on sentences and tend to lean toward the shorter variety.

By coordinating the use of clauses and punctuation, you can allow the complexity of a sentence to develop after the verb, not before it. The key is to make the subject-verb connection and then allow the sentence to paint a picture of the world surrounding that subject and verb. As you allow a sentence to develop, be careful to keep your structures in the predicate in parallel form.

One issue that is difficult for many business writers is the need to repeat key terms in long sentences. It feels awkward. When properly handled, though, repeated phrases can create a rhythm that helps to emphasize the meaning of the sentence.

Another way to enhance sentence variety and complexity is to avoid clumsy "which clauses" and replace them with dependent clauses. Take the following sentence: "Atlanta continues to grow in every direction, which means that homes are rapidly replacing the fields and forests in outlying areas." An alternative would be: "Atlanta continues to grow in every direction, as homes are rapidly replacing the fields and forests in outlying areas."

When used sparingly, you can create an interesting twist to a sentence by ending it with a set of prepositional phrases, each beginning with a present or past participle. For example: "You'll find working with Videologies to be an excellent experience, one that will develop into a lasting relationship, into a partnership, winning future business for us all."

Resumptive and Summative Modifiers

By adding modifying phrases to the end of a sentence, you take a sentence in an unexpected direction. A *resumptive modifier* takes a word from a sentence that appears to be ending and adds additional information. For example: "You'll find working with Videologies to be both enlightening and rewarding—enlightening due to the many innovations we'll introduce to your company, rewarding because of the enhancements to productivity your company will experience."

A *summative modifier* renames or summarizes what has been going on earlier in the sentence and adds new information. For example: "The email etiquette seminar promises to show employees how to write effective emails, emails that get results, and emails that result in a positive image for your business—three benefits that can enhance the productivity of any business."

Modifier Placement

You can add variety to your sentences by the way you place modifiers. This section gives four different strategies for modifier placement.

Using Initial Modifiers

- *Dependent clause:* "Although he was tired, Bob wrote the report."
- *Infinitive phrase:* "To please his boss, Bob wrote the report."
- *Adverb:* "Slowly and laboriously, Bob wrote the report."
- *Participial phrase:* "Hoping to be promoted, Bob wrote the report."

Using Mid-Sentence Modifiers

- *Appositive:* "Bob, an expert on regulations, wrote the report."
- *Participial phrase:* "Bob, hoping to catch up on his work, worked late."

Using Terminal Modifiers

- *Present participial phrase:* "Bob worked on the report, hoping to please his boss."
- *Past participial phrase/adjectival phrase:* "Bob worked on the report, pushed by ambition."

Combining Modifiers

- "Slowly and laboriously, Bob, an expert on regulations, worked on the report, hoping to please his boss."

Other Ideas on Sentence Variety

Remember to throw an occasional question, exclamation, or command into your writing. Questions can be useful at the beginning of a paragraph to summarize the content that follows. Commands provide direction and energy by telling your readers what to do.

Occasionally, try to begin sentences with something other than the normal subject-verb combo. Try starting with a modifying clause or participial phrase. Consider beginning a sentence with a coordinating conjunction (*and, but, nor, for, yet,* or *so*). Many people think they should never begin a sentence with *but.* Instead, it should be linked to the previous sentence into a compound structure. But a sentence like this calls attention to itself and can be a useful device.

Sentence Types

There are a variety of basic sentence structures:

- *Simple*—one independent clause
- *Compound*—more than one independent clause
- *Complex*—one independent clause and at least one dependent clause
- *Compound complex*—more than one independent clause and at least one dependent clause
- *Periodic*—begin with modifying phrases and clauses and end with an independent clause
- *Cumulative*—begin with an independent clause and end with a series of modifying constructions

Compound Sentences

A compound sentence consists of two or more independent clauses. Thus, there are two thoughts within the sentence and either can stand alone. The clauses of a compound sentence are separated either by a semicolon or by a comma and a coordinating conjunction. The most common coordinating conjunction is *and*; it simply links the two ideas. Other coordinating conjunctions, such as *but, or, for, yet,* and *so,* establish a relationship between the two clauses.

Compounding Sentence Elements   You can combine various sentence elements to create compound sentences:

- *Subjects*—Two or more subjects doing parallel things can be combined as a compound subject; for example, "Working together, *IBM and Apple Computer* developed the Power PC processor."

- *Objects*—When the subjects are acting on two or more things in parallel, the objects can be combined; for example, "The company president believed *that* the partnership between the two companies might help them increase sales *and that* he could eventually force a merger."

- *Verbs and verbals*—When the subjects are doing two things simultaneously, the elements can be combined by compounding verbs and verbals; for example, "He *studied* sentence structure and grammar *and learned* how to speak and write effectively."

- *Modifiers*—When appropriate, modifiers and prepositional phrases can be compounded; for example, "The company recruited its programmers *from universities across the country and various competing companies.*"

Transitions

As you compound sentences and vary your sentence structures to add variety to your writing, you will want to consider using transitions between ideas. Transitions help guide a reader from one idea to the next.

There are four general ways to add transitions between ideas:

1. Using transitional expressions
2. Repeating key words and phrases
3. Using pronoun reference
4. Using parallel forms

Transitional Expressions

In addition to coordinating conjunctions—*and, but, nor, for, yet, or,* and *so*—you can use conjunctive adverbs and transitional expressions such as *however, moreover,* and *nevertheless* to transition your sentences from one thought to the next. The key is to avoid using the same transitional elements, as it becomes boring. The following is a list of some conjunctive adverbs that can add spice to your transitions.

- Addition—*again, also, and, and then, besides, equally important, finally, first, further, furthermore, in addition, in the first place, last, moreover, next, second, still, too*

- Comparison—*also, in the same way, likewise, similarly*
- Concession—*granted, naturally, of course*
- Contrast—*although, and yet, at the same time, but at the same time, despite that, even so, even though, for all that, however, in contrast, in spite of, instead, nevertheless, on the contrary, on the other hand, otherwise, regardless, still, though, yet*
- Emphasis—*certainly, indeed, in fact*
- Example—*after all, as an illustration, even, for example, for instance, in conclusion, in short, it is true, namely, specifically, that is, to illustrate, thus*
- Summary—*all in all, altogether, as has been said, finally, in brief, in conclusion, in other words, in particular, in short, in simpler terms, in summary, on the whole, that is, therefore, to put it differently, to summarize*
- Time sequence—*after a while, afterward, again, also, and then, as long as, at last, at length, at that time, before, besides, earlier, eventually, finally, formerly, further, furthermore, in addition, in the first place, in the past, last, lately, meanwhile, moreover, next, now, presently, second, shortly, simultaneously, since, so far, soon, still, subsequently, then, thereafter, too, until, until now, when*

Repeating Key Words

By repeating a key word or phrase, you can establish its importance in the mind of the reader.

Pronoun Reference

Pronouns can be used to refer the reader to something earlier in the text. A pronoun such as *this* causes the reader to summarize what has been said so for. For example: "There has been increase in the number of earthquakes in California in the past ten years. *This* is true because we have geological records that go back almost 150 years and *they* show a clear trend."

Parallelism

Parallel constructions are expressions with similar content and function. Their similarity enables the reader to more easily recognize the content and understand the message.

An article such as *the, a,* and *an* must either be used only before the first term in a group, or it must be repeated before each term. For example: "At the World's Fair, we saw all the latest model automobiles, including the new Hondas, Toyotas, and Nissans." "We left on Sunday for vacation with the Wilsons, the Wausons, and the Bruecks."

Correlative expressions (*both, and; not, but; not only, but also; either, or; first, second*) should be followed by the same grammatical construction. For example: "It was not only the blowing wind, but also the freezing temperatures that made travel so treacherous."

When making comparisons, the things compared should be in parallel form.

Paragraph Construction

Paragraphs are groups of sentences that focus on a single topic. If that single topic gets too long or the focus shifts to another topic, it is time to start a new paragraph. The elements of a paragraph include the use of topic sentences, transitions between sentences and paragraphs, and signposts that signal the reader where the rest of the document is going.

Within every paragraph there should be a topic sentence that indicates what the paragraph is about. For most business writing, you should introduce the topic using a topic sentence. That makes it easier for your reader to get the point quickly.

After writing that first topic sentence, the rest of the paragraph is used to develop and defend that initial statement. You can do that by doing any of the following:

- Use examples and illustrations.
- Provide details, statistics, and evidence.
- Provide quotes and paraphrases from other people.
- Tell a story.
- Define terms.
- Compare and contrast ideas.
- Evaluate causes and effects.
- Offer a chronological summary.

Avoiding Redundancies

While a well-rounded writing style includes compound and complex sentences, it is important to avoid redundancies. Avoid saying the same thing twice. The following is a list of some of the most common redundant phrases:

- 12 midnight
- 12 noon
- 1 a.m. in the morning
- Circle around
- Close proximity
- Completely unanimous
- Cooperate together
- Each and every
- Enclosed herewith
- End result
- Exactly the same
- Final completion
- Free gift
- In spite of the fact that
- In the field of
- In the event of
- New innovations

- One and the same
- Particular interest
- Period of X days
- Personally, I think
- Personal opinion
- Refer back
- Repeat again
- Return again
- Revert back
- Shorter in length
- Small in size
- Summarize briefly
- Surrounded on all sides
- The future to come
- There is no doubt but
- We are in receipt of

Language Usage and Style

Phrases and Words to Omit

The following is a list of words that are usually not necessary in a sentence. They don't add anything and can be omitted without changing the meaning.

- Really
- Very
- Quite
- Extremely
- Severely
- All things considered
- As a matter of fact
- As far as I'm concerned
- At the present time
- Because of the fact that
- By means of
- By virtue of the fact
- Due to the fact
- For all intents and purposes
- For the most part

- For the purpose of
- Have a tendency to
- In a manner of speaking
- In a very real sense
- In my opinion
- In the case of
- In the final analysis
- In the event that
- In the nature of
- In the process of
- It seems that
- The point I am trying to make
- Type of
- What I mean to say is

Clichés

Clichés are overused expressions that have become trite and even annoying. The following is a list of clichés that should be avoided:

- Acid test
- At loose ends
- Babe in the woods
- Better that than never
- Black as night
- Blind as a bat
- Bolt from the blue
- Brought back to reality
- Busy as a bee (or beaver)
- Cat's meow
- Cool as a cucumber
- Cool, calm, and collected
- Crack of dawn
- Crushing blow
- Cry over split milk

- Dead as a doornail
- Dog-eat-dog world
- Don't count your chickens
- Dyed in the wool
- Easier said than done
- Easy as pie
- Face the music
- Feathered friends
- Flash in the pan
- Flat as a pancake
- Gentle as a lamb
- Go at it tooth and nail
- Good time was had by all
- Greased lightning
- Happy as a lark

- Head over heels
- Heavy as lead
- Horns of a dilemma
- Hour of need
- Keep a stiff upper lip
- Ladder of success
- Last but not least
- Looking a gift horse in the mouth
- Meaningful dialogue
- Moving experience
- Needle in a haystack
- Open-and-shut case
- Pain in the ass
- Point with pride
- Pretty as a picture
- Put it in a nutshell
- Quick as a flash (or wink)
- Rat race
- Ripe old age
- Ruled the roost
- Sad but true
- Sadder but wiser
- Set the world on fire

- Sick as a dog
- Sigh of relief
- Slow as molasses
- Smart as a whip
- Sneaking suspicion
- Spread like wildfire
- Straight as an arrow
- Straw that broke the camel's back
- Strong as an ox
- Take the bull by the horns
- Thin as a rail
- Through thick and thin
- Tired but happy
- To coin a phrase
- To make a long story short
- Trial and error
- Tried and true
- Under the weather
- White as a sheet
- Wise as an owl
- Work like a dog
- Worth its weight in gold

Unbiased Language

Most gender problems can be avoided without the use of *he/she*, *he or she*, *him or her*, or *him/her* constructions. Plural pronouns such as *they* can be very helpful in this regard. An occasional he or she is okay, but after a while it becomes distracting. When a singular pronoun is necessary, use either *he* or *she* consistently to avoid confusion.

Sexist Language

There are a variety of words and phrases that make demeaning assumptions about gender role. However, in some cases people go out of their way to be politically correct and try awkward alternatives. Substitutes should be reasonable and appropriate. Try not to highlight the fact you are trying to avoid sexist language.

The following is a list of words to avoid and their alternatives:

- Actress—use *actor*
- Anchorman—use *anchor*
- Businessman—use *businessperson*

- Chairman—use *chairperson* or *chair*
- Coed—use *student*
- Forefathers—use *ancestors*
- Foreman—use *supervisor*
- Freshman—use *first-year student*
- Mailman—use *mail carrier*
- Male nurse—use *nurse*
- Man (meaning human being)—use *person, people*
- Managers and their wives—use *managers and their spouses*
- Mankind—use *humanity, people*
- Poetess—use *poet*
- Policeman—use *police officer*
- Salesman—use *sales representative*
- Stewardess—use *flight attendant*
- Waiter/waitress—use *server*

Colloquialisms

Colloquialisms are words or phrases that are often used in informal conversation; however, they should be avoided in your written communications. The following is a list of colloquialisms you should edit out of every first draft:

- A lot
- A whole lot
- Ahold
- All about
- And while we're at it
- Back in the day
- Being that
- Being there for
- Came time
- Come to find out
- Come up missing
- Could of, should of, would of
- Get/got
- Gone bad
- Hassle
- Keep on
- Mess up
- Might could
- More so
- Nice and easy
- Out there
- Somewhat
- Stuff
- Things
- Thru
- Where . . . at
- Without a hitch

Jargon and Buzzwords

Buzzwords are popular overused words that are common to business environments. Buzzwords are often pretentious and difficult to understand. Avoid them in your business writing. Common buzzwords to avoid include:

- Accountability
- Action items
- Architect
- Ballpark
- Benchmarking
- Best of breed
- Best practice
- Big picture
- Bleeding edge
- Bottom line
- Business case
- Buy-in
- Champion
- Cross-platform
- Customer-focused
- Deliverables
- Downsize
- Drill down
- Empowerment
- Enterprise-wide
- Fast track
- Front-end
- Game plan
- Globalize
- Goal-oriented
- Going forward
- Heads up
- Heavy lifting
- Herding cats
- Ideation
- In the loop
- In-market for
- Info superhighway
- Intellectual capital
- Key player
- Knowledge base
- Leading-edge
- Lean and mean
- Level-set
- Leverage
- Long-term
- Low-risk high-yield
- Matrix
- Methodology
- Mindset
- Mission-critical
- Mission statement
- Monetize
- Multitasking
- Networking
- On the same page
- Out-of-the-loop
- Out-of-the-box
- Outside the box
- Oxymoron
- Paradigm shift
- Partner
- Peel the onion
- Performance-based
- Play hardball
- Power shift
- Push the envelope
- Ramp up
- Reality check
- Re-engineer
- Resource constrained
- Results-drive
- Right-size
- Risk management
- ROI (short for "return on investment")
- Rubber stamp
- Scalable
- Service organization

- Stand-alone
- Synergize
- Take that off-line
- Talking points
- Task force
- Think outside the box
- Tip of the iceberg
- Total quality
- Touch base

- Touch points
- Train wreck
- Turn-key
- 24/7
- User-centric
- Value-added
- Whiteboard
- Win-win
- World class

Global Communications

When writing for an international audience, it is easy to run into problems with clarity and miscommunication. To overcome this problem, you need to avoid using slang or words with double meanings that can be misunderstood by nonnative English speakers. To revise your writing for an international audience, consider the following:

- Use both the active and passive voice, since some cultures—such as in Japan and China—consider the active voice to be condescending and prefer the passive voice instead.

- Use a more direct rather than indirect style, since the indirect style can be confusing.

- Avoid using abbreviations and brand names, unless you are writing about a specific brand name.

- Use short sentences and simple sentence constructions.

- Avoid phrasal verbs like *call up, put up, drop down*, and so forth that can easily be said as a single word and mean the same thing.

- Be extremely clear when using pronouns.

- Avoid clichés and slang.

- Be careful with humor, since it may not be understood by a non–English-speaking person.

- Don't use contractions, since they make translation more difficult.

- Avoid cultural metaphors that are recognized in the U.S. but would be meaningless to an international audience, for example: Big Apple, pigskin, brown-bagging.

- When using graphics in your document, avoid using human hands, animals, or religious symbols.

- Use androgynous figures for humans.

- Make sure you use "which" and "that" correctly.

- Write out dates by spelling the month (September 22, 2012), rather than writing 09/22/2012.

- If you must refer to gender, use the terms *man* and *woman* rather than *male* and *female*.

- Do not use the word *domestic* to refer to the U.S.
- Avoid using symbols and special characters such as # for pound, $ for currency, " for ditto, " for inches, ' for feet, or ? for help.
- When your document will be translated, keep in mind that the same content may expand by 15% or more in the new language.

34

Common English Usage Problems

Language: Key to Your Success

Give careful attention to your use of the English language. The ability to write and speak correctly is so important to a business career that you'll find the following to be almost always true: As you improve your speech, you will also naturally improve your business success.

Words, phrases, and sentences that are outworn should not be used in a business letter. Stock phrases, like slang, give the impression that the writer has not thought the idea through and has not chosen the best language for expressing those ideas. It's necessary first to understand thoroughly what you want to say and then to say it forcefully with words as natural to you as those of a conversation. This will help you accomplish the purpose of communication.

To help yourself write naturally, consider how you would respond to a luncheon invitation from an acquaintance. Would you say, "In accordance with your request that I have lunch with you, I beg to advise that I shall be happy to do so"? No. You would be more likely to say, "Thanks. I'll be glad to have lunch with you."

Verbose Expressions

You should be alert to everything you write. Beware of words that do not mean exactly what you want to say. Also beware of phrases that are careless, vague, or wordy. Table 34-1 gives examples of such pitfalls. After studying this list, protect yourself from similar mistakes. As a famous company once said in its ads, "The audience is listening!"

Correct Usage

In addition to being verbose, many letter writers frequently misuse parts of speech. The examples in the following subsections are given to alert you to these errors. Some of the examples are grammatically correct for colloquial use but not for formal speech and writing—which is the only kind you should use in business.

American Management Association • www.amanet.org

TABLE 34-1 The Real Meaning Behind Verbose Expressions

Verbose Expressions	What You Really Mean
I beg to be advised	Please tell me
Thank you kindly	Thank you
I feel that you are able to appreciate	You can appreciate
Which you will remember is in connection with	Regarding
I am not at present in a position to	I am unable to
I would, therefore, ask that you kindly write	Please write
We would appreciate it if you would investigate the matter and inform us and report	Please check the matter
You have my permission to	You may
I am in receipt of a complaint from John Smith	John Smith complains
You have not, I believe, favored us with a reply	You have not replied
I acknowledge receipt of your letter	I received your letter

Affect, Effect

Affect is most commonly used as a verb, meaning "to influence." It is used as a noun only as a psychological term, meaning "feeling or emotion." *Effect* is a verb meaning "to bring about." It is also used as a noun, meaning "a result or consequence, or a mental impression."

> *Wrong:*   The light effects my vision.
>
> *Right:*   The light affects my vision.
>
> *Wrong:*   Can you affect a change in the operation?
>
> *Right:*   Can you effect a change in the operation?

All Right

Always spell *all right* as two words, never one.

> *Wrong:*   It will be alright if you wish to go.
>
> *Right:*   It will be all right if you wish to go.

Already, All Ready

Already denotes time; *all ready* denotes preparation.

> *Right:*   She had already arrived.
>
> *Right:*   We are all ready to leave.

Altogether, All Together

Altogether means "quite" or "in all." *All together* means "in one place."

> *Right:*   She is altogether pleasant.
>
> *Right:*   His bills came to fifty-seven dollars altogether.
>
> *Right:*   The books were all together on one shelf.

Any, Either

Any refers to one of several. *Either* refers to one of two.

    Right: You may have any of the six books.

    Right: Either of those two cars will be acceptable.

Awful, Awfully

Never use *awful* or *awfully* as a synonym for "very."

    Wrong: She performed an awful hard task.

    Right: She performed a very difficult task.

    Wrong: Bill is awfully smart.

    Right: Bill is unusually smart.

A While, Awhile

Awhile is an adverb and should never be used as the object of a preposition (which can only be a noun or pronoun).

    Wrong: Please come to my home for awhile before you start your journey.

    Right: Please come to my home for a while before you start your journey.

    Right: Relax awhile before you begin the task.

Badly

Badly is an adverb, but it is often mistakenly used as an adjective.

    Wrong: He wanted badly to go with them.

    Right: He wanted very much to go with them.

    Wrong: She felt badly after her operation.

    Right: She did not feel well after her operation.

Because

Because is not to be used in place of *that.*

    Wrong: The reason he did not attend the party is because he was in Chicago.

    Right: The reason he did not attend the party is that he was in Chicago.

    Right: He did not attend the party because he was in Chicago.

Between, Among

Between is used to differentiate two, and only two, objects. *Among* is used to differentiate more than two.

    Right: The dog was sitting between John and me.

    Right: There were three good books among the many he gave me.

Both, Alike

It's illogical to use the combination *both alike* since two items can't be alike if one is not.

    Wrong: The cars are both alike.

    Right: The two cars are alike. They are both the latest model.

Both, Each

Both is used to describe a condition that applies to two entities. *Each* is used to describe a single entity.

Wrong: There is a picture on both sides of the mantel.

Right: There is a picture on each side of the mantel.

Bring, Take

Bring is used to denote movement toward someone or something, while *take* is used to denote movement from someone or something.

Right: Bring me the book.

Right: Take the book to him.

Bushel

Add an *s* when referring to more than one bushel.

Wrong: Eight bushel of oats.

Right: Eight bushels of oats.

Business

Don't use *business* when you really mean *right.*

Wrong: What business is it of theirs to question my action?

Right: What right have they to question my action?

Came By

Came by is a colloquial phrase that you should not use.

Wrong: He came by to see me.

Right: He came to see me.

Can't Seem

Seem is a verb that means "look" or "appear." Using *can't* with *seem* is awkward.

Wrong: I can't seem to make the journey in an hour.

Right: It seems impossible for me to make the journey in one hour.

Combination

Don't confuse *combine*—normally a verb unless referring to farm equipment—with *combination,* which is a noun referring to a group of entities.

Wrong: That combine will be a large one.

Right: That combination will be a large one.

Cooperate

Cooperate is a verb that means "to work together." Therefore, *cooperate together* is redundant.

Wrong: If they cooperate together, their purpose will be accomplished.

Right: If they cooperate, their purpose will be accomplished.

Council, Counsel, Consul

A *council* is a group of persons convened for advisory purposes. *Counsel* is advice; the word sometimes means "attorney." A *consul* is an official appointed by a government to report on matters that the official observes while residing in a foreign land.

Credible, Credulous

Credible means "believable" or "worthy of being believed." *Credulous* means "inclined to believe too readily."

Right:	He related the incident in a credible manner.
Right:	She is too credulous for her own good.

Data

Data is can be singular or plural.

Right:	This data proves that our business is growing.
Right:	These data prove that our business is growing.

Deal

Deal should not be used informally to refer to a business agreement.

Wrong:	She made a deal to buy the house.
Right:	She made an agreement to buy the house.

Different From, Different Than

Different from takes an object; *different than* is used to introduce a clause.

Wrong:	That coat is different than mine.
Right:	That coat is different from mine.
Right:	He was different than I remembered.

Don't, Doesn't

Don't means "do not"; *doesn't* means "does not."

Wrong:	He don't care to go with us.
Right:	He doesn't care to go with us.

Each, Their

Pronouns must agree in number and person with the words to which they refer.

Wrong:	Each drives their own car.
Right:	Each drives his own car.
Right:	Each of the women listed her needs. (The singular pronoun *each* is the subject.)

Either, Neither

Either and *neither* refer to two.

Wrong:	Neither of the four books suited him.
Right:	None of the four books suited him.

Wrong:	Either of the three books is the one I want.
Right:	Either of the two books will do.
Right:	Any of the three books will suit me.

Enthuse, Enthusiastic

Enthuse is used only as a colloquialism. For the formal language needed for business writing, use *to be enthusiastic*.

Wrong:	He was enthused over winning the award.
Right:	He was enthusiastic about winning the award.

Except, Unless

Except is a preposition used to introduce a prepositional phrase. *Unless* is an adverbial conjunction used to introduce a subordinate clause. They are not interchangeable. *Except* may be used as a conjunction only when it's followed by the word *that*; however, that construction, although correct, is often awkward, and *unless* is preferable.

Wrong:	The horse cannot be entered in the race except the judges permit.
Right:	The horse cannot be entered in the race unless the judges permit.

Expect

Don't use *expect* to mean *think* or *suppose*.

Wrong:	I expect she was well received.
Right:	I suppose she was well received.
Right:	I expect you to be there at 8 a.m.

Farther, Further

Farther shows a specific, quantifiable distance. *Further* shows degree or extent.

Right:	I walked farther than he did.
Right:	He will go further with your help than without it.

Fix

Fix means to repair. Don't use it to mean a bad situation.

Wrong:	She is in a desperate fix.
Right:	She is desperate because of her present situation.

Foot, Feet

Foot is singular, *feet* is plural.

Wrong:	The room is twelve foot long.
Right:	The room is twelve feet long.

Got

Don't use *got* when you could use *have, has,* or *must*.

Wrong:	I have got a new car.
Right:	I have a new car.

Right: He has a new job.

Wrong: I've got to stop at his house. [Colloquial]

Right: I must stop at his house *or* I have to stop at his house.

Gotten

This is an obsolete word. Do not use; replace with *got*.

Guess

Don't use *guess* when you really mean *think*.

Wrong: I guess you are right.

Right: I think you are right.

Right: In the word game, Marcus was the first to guess correctly.

Inaugurate

Don't use *inaugurate* in place of *started or began*.

Wrong: The program was inaugurated on August 1.

Right: The program was begun on August 1.

Right: The president of the United States was inaugurated on January 4.

Inside Of, Within

Don't use *inside of* where you could use *within*.

Wrong: He will visit us inside of a week.

Right: He will visit us within a week.

Invite

Don't confuse *invite* (a verb) with *invitation* (a noun).

Wrong: I have an invite to the party.

Right: I have an invitation to the party.

Its, It's

Its (without an apostrophe) is a possessive pronoun. *It's* (with an apostrophe) is a contraction meaning "it is."

Right: It's getting dark (meaning "it is getting dark").

Right: The ship was flying its flag at half-mast.

Kind

Kind is singular; *kinds* is plural.

Wrong: She asked for those kind of flowers.

Right: She asked for those kinds of flowers.

Right: She asked for that kind of flower.

Kind Of, Sort Of

Kind of and *sort of* are unclear. Be definite when speaking or writing.

Wrong:	He appeared to be kind of ill.
Right:	He appeared to be rather ill.
Wrong:	She was sort of ill at ease.
Right:	She was somewhat ill at ease.

Learn, Teach

Before you can *learn*, someone must first *teach* you.

Wrong:	She learned me how to type.
Right:	She taught me how to type.
Right:	If I teach him correctly, he will learn quickly.

Less, Fewer

Less refers to a smaller amount, degree, or value. *Fewer* refers to a quantifiable number.

Right:	This mine contains less gold than the Jackass Mine.
Right:	This city has fewer people today than it had a year ago.

Let, Leave

Let means "to permit." *Leave* means "to depart," "to bequeath," or "to allow, to remain."

Right:	Leave her alone.
Right:	Let her go with us.

Liable, Likely

Liable should be used when referring to legal responsibility.

Right:	The landlord is liable for damages.
Right:	That horse is likely to win the race.

Lie, Lay

Many people confuse these two words because the word *lay* is both the present tense of *lay* (*lay, lay, laid*) and the past tense of *lie* (*lie, lay, lain*). *Lie* means "to remain in position" or "to rest." It is intransitive, meaning no object ever accompanies it. *Lay* means "to place something somewhere." It is transitive, meaning an object always accompanies it.

Wrong:	He lays down after lunch every day.
Right:	He lies down after lunch every day.
Right:	Yesterday he lay on the couch for two hours.
Right:	Will you please lay the book on the table?
Right:	The pen lay on the desk all day.

Like, As

Like is a preposition always followed by a noun or pronoun in the objective case. *As* is an adverbial conjunction used to introduce a subordinate clause.

Wrong:	It appears like he isn't coming.
Right:	It appears as if he isn't coming.
Right:	Though he was such a little boy, he marched like a major.

Line

Line should not be used in place *of business*.

Wrong:	He is in the jewelry line.
Right:	He is in the jewelry business.

Loan

A *loan* should be used as a noun to refer to an agreement to borrow. To allow someone to borrow is *to lend*.

Wrong:	Loan me your pen.
Right:	Lend me your pen.
Right:	He went to the bank to receive a loan.

Lost

Don't use extra words—like *out*—that are not necessary for meaning.

Wrong:	He lost out.
Right:	He lost.

Lots

Don't use *lots* when referring to an amount of something.

Wrong:	She receives lots of fan mail.
Right:	She receives a great deal of fan mail.

Mad, Angry

Use *angry* rather than *mad*. Remember, dogs go mad, people get angry.

Wrong:	Mary was mad at Jane.
Right:	Mary was angry with Jane.

May, Can

May refers to permission. *Can* refers to ability.

Wrong:	Can I help you?
Right:	May I help you?
Right:	Can he drive a car?

Might Of, Would Of, Could Of

This construction is the result of poor pronunciation. The correct phrases are *might have, would have,* and *could have.*

Wrong: If you could of arranged it, I would of gone.

Right: If you could have arranged it, I would have gone.

Most, Almost

Most of all is a colloquial expression. Use *most of* or *almost* instead.

Wrong: We walked most of all the way.

Right: We walked most of the way.

Right: We walked almost all the way.

Never

Never means never; it does not refer to a limited period of time.

Wrong: We never saw your dog since yesterday.

Right: We have not seen your dog since yesterday.

Right: We never saw your dog. What breed was he?

Off

Off is always used alone and not with *of.*

Wrong: The ribbon was taken off of the package.

Right: The ribbon was taken off the package.

Only

Be careful of where you place this adverb; position determines which word you modify.

Wrong: I could only get him to play one piece.

Right: I could get him to play only one piece.

Open

Open should be used without *up.*

Wrong: We open up the doors promptly at noon.

Right: We open the doors promptly at noon.

Party

Party can be used to refer to a person in legal documents, but it is too formal for common use. A *party* can also be a celebration.

Wrong: The party I called was disturbed.

Right: The person I called was disturbed.

Right: (In legal documents): The party of the second part hereby agrees . . .

Right: He celebrated his birthday with a party.

English Usage Problems

People

People refers to a large group of individuals. When referring to people of a particular organization or place, it's better to use *people* before the name.

Wrong: The General Motors people.

Right: The people of General Motors; the people of Massachusetts.

Percent

This is one word, following an amount, never *per cent*.

Right: Six percent interest was charged.

Percentage

Use when no amount is given.

Right: What percentage of interest was charged?

Posted, Informed

Don't use *posted* in place of *informed*.

Wrong: You are well posted on the subject.

Right: You are well informed about Australia.

Raise, Rise

Raise is a transitive verb and must always take an object. *Rise* is an intransitive verb and never takes an object.

Right: They raise the question at every meeting.

Right: I rise to make a motion.

Real

Don't use *real* when you really mean *very*.

Wrong: He is real handsome.

Right: He is very handsome.

Run

When referring to a business or organization, don't use *run* in place of *manage*.

Wrong: He runs the bakery.

Right: He manages the bakery.

Same

Don't use *same* to refer to the subject of a sentence.

Wrong: Your letter arrived and I acknowledge same with thanks.

Right: Your letter arrived and I acknowledge it with thanks.

Shall, Will

Use *shall* to express a simple expected action with the first person. Use *will* with second and third persons. However, to express determination or command, reverse the order; use *will* for the first person and *shall* for the second and third.

Right:	I shall go tomorrow.
Right:	He will go, too.
Right:	You will be at school by the time we arrive.
Right:	I will go tomorrow, and no one can stop me.
Right:	He shall go with me even if I must force him.
Right:	You shall never do that again.

Shape (meaning tangible form)

Don't use *shape* to refer to the status of something.

Wrong:	The transaction was completed in good shape.
Right:	The transaction was completed to everyone's satisfaction.

Should, Would

Use *should* with the first person and *would* with the second and third persons to express expected action. However, using *should* and *would* instead of *shall* and *will* implies a doubt that the action will take place. *Should* and *would* may also be used with all persons, but in these instances, the meaning of the verbs is different. *Should* may be used with all persons to show obligation. *Would* may be used with all persons to show habit or determination.

Right:	A child should love his parents.
Right:	If I had enough money, I would buy a car.

Sit, Set

Sit is a an intransitive verb. *Set* is a transitive verb.

Right:	She sits near her husband at every meeting.
Right:	He sets the plates on the table in an orderly manner.

So

Avoid overuse of this adverbial conjunction. *Consequently, therefore,* and *inasmuch as* are good substitutes when you want to vary the style.

Avoid:	It had snowed over a foot that day, so we drove the jeep into town.
Right:	It had snowed over a foot that day; consequently, we drove the jeep into town.

Sometime, Some Time

Sometime means occasional. *Some time* means an amount of time.

Wrong:	I will go sometime this morning.
Right:	If I have some time this morning, I shall do the job for you.

To, At

Do not use either of these words with *where*.

Wrong:	Where are you at?
Right:	Where are you?

Wrong: Where did he go to?

Right: Where did he go?

Try And, Come And, Be Sure And

Don't use "and" in place of "to" if it is not necessary to convey your meaning.

Wrong: Try and be here at noon.

Right: Try to be here at noon.

Wrong: Come and see me tomorrow.

Right: Come to see me tomorrow.

Wrong: Be sure and watch out as you cross the street.

Right: Be sure to watch out as you cross the street.

Wait On

When *wait* refers to time, *on* is not needed. When it refers to the actions of a waiter or waitress, *wait on* is acceptable.

Wrong: Please do not wait on me if I am not at the station when you arrive.

Right: Please do not wait for me if I am not there when you arrive.

Right: The headwaiter assigned the red-haired woman to wait on me.

Where

Whether used as an adverb or a conjunction, *where* denotes position or place. It should never be used as a substitute for *that* when introducing a clause.

Wrong: Did you read in the paper where our mayor was honored at a banquet?

Right: Did you read in the paper that our mayor was honored at a banquet?

Which

When used to introduce a clause, *which* must refer to a specific noun or pronoun and not to a whole situation.

Wrong: He did not arrive in time for the meeting, which caused the president embarrassment.

Right: His failure to arrive in time for the meeting caused the president embarrassment.

Right: His failure to arrive, which caused the president embarrassment, was the reason for his dismissal.

Who, Which, That

Who is used to refer to people. *Which* and *that* refer to objects.

Right: She is the woman who smiled at him.

Right: She is the kind of person whom everyone likes.

Right: I read the book on bridges, which I found fascinating.

Problem Pronouns

I, We, He, She, They

Pronouns in the nominative case—*I, we, he, she, they*—serve as subjects of verbs but never objects of verbs or prepositions. You can often tell that the wrong case is being used because the sentence sounds odd. However, when compound subjects or compound objects are used, it may be difficult to hear the correct case.

To test such an instance, drop the other subject or object and repeat the sentence with only the pronoun in question.

I—nominative case, never an object

Wrong:	This is just between you and I.
Right:	This is just between you and me.
Wrong:	He asked that the money be given to you and I.
Test:	He asked that the money be given to I.
Right:	He asked that the money be given to you and me.
Test:	He asked that the money be given to me.

She, He—nominative case, never an object

Wrong:	If you stay there, the ball will hit you and she.
Test:	If you stay there, the ball will hit she.
Right:	If you stay there, the ball will hit you and her.
Test:	If you stay there, the ball will hit her.

They—nominative case, never an object

Wrong:	I will give the money to you and they.
Test:	I will give the money to they.
Right:	I will give the money to you and them.
Test:	I will give the money to them.
Wrong:	You and them are welcome to come.
Test:	Them are welcome to come.
Right:	You and they are welcome to come.
Test:	They are welcome to come.

We—nominative case, never an object

Wrong:	Us boys are ready to play the game.
Test:	Us are ready to play the game.
Right:	We boys are ready to play the game.
Test:	We are ready to play the game.

Me, Us, Her, Him, Them

Similarly, pronouns in the subjective case—*me, us, her, him, them*—are always used as objects, of either verbs or prepositions, and never as subjects. With a compound subject, use the same way of testing as above, changing the number of the verb as needed.

Me, Us—objective case, never a subject

Wrong: Jim and me went to the movies.

Test: Me went to the movies.

Right: Jim and I went to the movies.

Right: Jim went to the movies with me.

Test: I went to the movies.

Wrong: Julie and us sat on the top bleacher.

Test: Us sat on the top bleacher.

Right: Julie and we sat on the top bleacher. (Sounds awkward and should be rewritten.)

Test: We sat on the top bleacher.

Right: Julie sat on the top bleacher with us.

Her, Him, Them

Her, him, and *them* are used as objects. *She, he,* and *they* are the subjective case.

Wrong: Tommy and her [him, them] argued every day.

Test: Her [him, them] argued every day.

Right: Tommy and she [he, they] argued every day. (Sounds awkward and should be rewritten.)

Dangling Participles

A dangling participle modifies the noun or pronoun to which it refers. Since position determines the referent, how you construct the sentence determines the meaning.

Wrong: Walking down Main Street, the art museum is visible. (This implies the art museum is walking down Main Street.)

Right: Walking down Main Street, you can see the art museum.

35

Spelling

With easy access to spelling checkers in word processing programs, is there really a need for an administrative assistant to be concerned with spelling? For some people, running a spell-check on their document takes the place of a good proofread. Computerized spelling checkers are indeed useful to any writer. However, there are many words that may appear to be correctly spelled according to the word processor's spelling checker when in reality they are incorrectly spelled for the particular context, or the wrong word has been used entirely. For example, a spelling checker cannot tell the usage differences between *there, their*, and *they're*.

Thus, there is a need for basic spelling skills. This chapter focuses on the most common spelling rules that any good administrative assistant should know.

Dictionary Uses

The constant study of spelling and the exact meaning of words are an important aspect of every administrative assistant's career. Always keep a dictionary close at hand. Besides providing spelling and definitions, this invaluable aid also sets out such information as the following:

- Syllabication (useful when you want to split a word at the end of a typewritten line)
- Variant spellings, with the preferred spelling listed first
- Pronunciations, with the preferred form shown first
- Capitalization
- Hyphenation
- Italicization
- Part of speech
- Plural of nouns
- Cases of pronouns
- Verb tenses
- Comparative and superlative forms of irregular adverbs and adjectives
- Derivations of the word
- Synonyms and antonyms
- Status label (if a word is colloquial, obsolete, etc.)

401

Some words whose spelling frequently puzzles many of us are discussed in this chapter in order to sharpen your awareness of spelling in general.

Plurals

1. The general rule is to form the plural of a noun by adding *s*:
- book—books
- clock—clocks
- pen—pens

2. A noun ending in *o* preceded by a vowel takes an *s* for the plural:
- curio—curios
- folio—folios
- radio—radios
- ratio—ratios
- studio—studios

Some nouns ending in *o*, preceded by a consonant, take *es* to form the plural, while others take *s*:
- banjo—banjos
- buffalo—buffaloes
- cargo—cargoes
- Eskimo—Eskimos
- hero—heroes
- mosquito—mosquitoes
- motto—mottoes
- piano—pianos
- potato—potatoes
- soprano—sopranos
- tomato—tomatoes

3. A singular noun ending in *ch, sh, s, x,* or z takes *es* for the plural:
- bush—bushes
- chintz—chintzes
- dress—dresses
- inch—inches
- wax—waxes

4. A noun ending in *y* preceded by a consonant changes the *y* to *i* and adds *es* for the plural:

Spelling

- ability—abilities
- auxiliary—auxiliaries
- discrepancy—discrepancies
- facility—facilities
- industry—industries
- lady—ladies
- society—societies

5. A noun ending in *y* preceded by a vowel takes only an *s* for the plural:

- attorney—attorneys
- galley—galleys
- kidney—kidneys
- monkey—monkeys
- turkey—turkeys

6. Some plurals end in *en*:

- child—children
- man—men
- ox—oxen

7. Some nouns ending in *f* or *fe* change the *f* or *fe* to *v* and add *es* for the plural:

- calf—calves
- knife—knives
- leaf—leaves
- life—lives
- loaf—loaves
- shelf—shelves

But there are some exceptions:

- bailiff—bailiffs
- belief—beliefs
- chief—chiefs
- gulf—gulfs
- roof—roofs

8. Some nouns require a vowel change for the plural:

- foot—feet
- goose—geese
- mouse—mice
- tooth—teeth

9. The plural of numerals, signs, and letters is shown by adding an *s* (or an apostrophe and an *s* to avoid confusion):

- COD—CODs
- one B—four B's

10. To proper names ending in *s* or in an *s* sound, add *es* for the plural:

- Brooks—the Brookses
- Burns—the Burnses
- Jones—the Joneses

11. A compound noun, when hyphenated or when consisting of two separate words, shows the plural form in the most important element:

- attorney-in-fact—attorneys-in-fact
- brigadier general—brigadier generals
- brother-in-law—brothers-in-law
- notary public—notaries public
- passerby—passersby

12. The plural of solid compounds (a compound noun written as one word) is formed at the end of the solid compound:

- bookshelf—bookshelves
- cupful—cupfuls
- lumberman—lumbermen
- stepchild—stepchildren
- stepdaughter—stepdaughters

13. Some nouns have the same form for singular and plural:

- Chinese
- corps
- deer
- salmon
- sheep
- vermin
- wheat

14. Some nouns are always treated as singular:

- civics
- mathematics
- measles
- milk
- molasses
- music

- news
- statistics

15. Some nouns are always treated as plural:

- pants
- proceeds
- remains
- riches
- scissors
- thanks
- trousers
- tweezers

The Suffix

1. Words whose roots end with *ge* or *ce* generally retain the *e* when a suffix is added:

- change—changeable
- damage—damageable
- disadvantage—disadvantageous
- outrage—outrageous

2. A final silent *e* is usually dropped before a suffix that begins with a vowel:

- argue—arguing
- change—changing
- conceive—conceivable

3. A final silent *e* is usually retained before a suffix that begins with a consonant:

- achieve—achievement
- definite—definitely

4. In words ending in *c*, add *k* before a suffix beginning with *e*, *i*, or *y*, so that the hard sound of the original *c* is retained:

- frolic—frolicked—frolicking
- mimic—mimicked—mimicking
- picnic—picnicked—picnicking

5. A word ending in *ie* changes the *ie* to *y* when adding a suffix:

- die—dying
- lie—lying
- tie—tying
- vie—vying

Spelling

6. Words that end in *y* preceded by a vowel retain the *y* when adding the suffix:

■ survey—surveying—surveyor

7. Words that end with *y* preceded by a consonant change *y* to *i* when adding a suffix, except when the suffix is *ing*:

■ embody—embodying—embodied

■ rely—relying—relied

■ satisfy—satisfying—satisfied

8. A final consonant is usually doubled when it is preceded by a single vowel and takes a suffix:

■ mop—mopping

9. A final consonant is doubled when it is followed by a suffix, and the last syllable is accented when the suffix is added:

■ acquit—acquitted

10. The final consonant is not doubled when the accent is shifted to a preceding syllable when the suffix is added:

■ refer—referring—reference

Or when the final consonant is preceded by two vowels:

■ fooled—fooling

Irregular Spelling

1. Irregular spellings to watch closely:

■ acknowledgment

■ awful

■ judgment

■ ninth

■ truly

■ wholly

2. While they may sound the same, there are three ways to spell words ending in *ceed, cede*, and *sede*:

■ exceed

■ intercede

■ precede

■ proceed

■ recede

■ secede

- succeed
- supersede

Memorize: The only English word that ends in *sede* is *supersede*. The only English words that end in *ceed* are *exceed, proceed*, and *succeed*.

3. Watch for *ant* and *ent* endings:

- relevant
- correspondent
- eminent

4. Watch for *ance* and *ence* endings:

- occurrence
- perseverance

5. Watch for *able* and *ible* endings:

- deductible
- accessible
- compatible
- comfortable
- affordable

6. Don't omit silent letters:

- silhouette
- hemorrhage
- acquisition
- diaphragm
- abscess

7. Don't be confused over double consonants:

- accommodate
- commitment
- necessary
- occurrence

8. Some words are not spelled the way they are sometimes pronounced:

- asterisk
- separate
- auxiliary
- boundary
- prerogative

Capitalization

Proper nouns that denote the names of specific persons or places are capitalized, though names that are common to a group are not. Following are examples of words that are capitalized:

Acts of Congress

- Civil Rights Act
- Taft-Hartley Act
- Child Labor Amendment
- Eighteenth Amendment

Associations

- Society of Professional Engineers
- American Business Association
- Young Women's Christian Association
- American Heart Association

Cars of Railroads and Automobile Models

- Car 54, Train 93
- Prius
- Cadillac

Churches and Church Dignitaries

- Fifth Avenue Presbyterian Church
- the Archbishop of New York
- Bishop John Barnes

Cities

- Jefferson City, Missouri
- Los Angeles
- *BUT*—the city of Los Angeles

Clubs

- Possum Kingdom Club
- the Do-Gooders
- the Union League Club
- *BUT*—many Toastmasters clubs in the West

Codes

- the Code of Building Maintenance

- *BUT*—the building code
- Code VI

Compass Points Designating a Specific Region

- the Northeast (*section of the country*), the Pacific Northwest
- *BUT*—just drive north
- the West
- *BUT*—west of town

Constitutions

- the Constitution of Texas
- the Constitution of the United States
- *BUT*—the constitution of any nation

Corporations

- American Brake Corporation
- Container Corporation of America
- *BUT*—The corporation was dissolved.

Courts

- the Criminal Court of Appeals
- *BUT*—a court of appeals
- the Supreme Court
- the Magistrate's Court
- *BUT*—a county court

Decorations

- Purple Heart
- Good Conduct Medal
- Croix de Guerre
- *BUT*—Soldiers are given decorations to signal their acts of heroism.

Degrees (academic)

- B.A.
- D.D.S.
- M.D.
- Ph.D.

Districts

- First Congressional District
- *BUT*—a congressional district

Educational Courses

- English 101
- Spanish Grammar
- Mathematics Made Easy
- *BUT*—He is studying physics and chemistry.

Epithets

- First Lady of the State
- Alexander the Great

Fleets

- the Third Fleet
- *BUT*—The ship was part of the fleet.

Foundations

- Carnegie Foundation
- Ford Foundation
- *BUT*—He established a foundation.

Geographic Divisions and Designations

- Lone Star State
- Sooner State
- *BUT*—There are fifty states in our country.
- Northern Hemisphere
- South Pole
- Old World, Near East

Government Divisions

- Federal Reserve Board
- the Boston Fire Department
- *BUT*—The department was headed by Mr. Charles Bleeker.

Historical Terms

- Dark Ages
- Renaissance
- Christian Era
- World War II
- Battle of the Bulge
- Declaration of Independence
- Magna Carta

Holidays

- Thanksgiving Day
- Passover
- Easter Sunday
- New Year's Eve

Libraries

- Carnegie Library
- Albany Public Library
- *BUT*—The library is a source of information.

Localities

- Western Europe
- East Africa
- Wheat Belt
- West Side
- Mississippi Delta

Military Services

- United States Navy
- Signal Corps
- Second Battalion
- Company B
- Squadron 28

Nobility and Royalty

- Queen of Belgium
- *BUT*—Many queens were honored here.
- Duke of Windsor
- *BUT*—She was proud to have met a duke.

Oceans and Continents

- Pacific Ocean
- *BUT*—He was glad to be crossing the ocean.

Parks

- Greenleaf Park
- Lake Texoma State Park
- Yellowstone National Park
- *BUT*—The park was in a southern state.

People and Tribes

- Jews
- Christians
- Malay
- Chickasaw

Personification

- He sang about Summer in all its glory.
- *BUT*—In summer the days are longer.

Planets and Other Heavenly Bodies

- Mars
- Venus
- Big Dipper
- *EXCEPTIONS*: moon, sun, stars

Publication Titles and Their Subdivisions

- *The American Way,* Chapter VI
- *Remembrance of Things Past,* Volume 11
- *Forest Flower Magazine*
- *Wall Street Journal*

Rivers

- Mississippi River
- Wabash River
- *BUT*—The Mississippi and Wabash rivers were flooding after the torrential rains.

Sports Stadiums and Teams

- Dallas Cowboys
- Madison Square Garden
- Super Bowl
- Dodgers

Confusing Homonyms

Homonyms are words that are pronounced the same but have different meanings; for example, *brake* for *break* or *there* for *their*. The following is a list of commonly confused homonyms:

- altar—alter
- born—bourn
- breach—breech
- caret—carrot

- compliment—complement
- council—counsel
- cubicle—cubical
- deserts—desserts
- discrete—discreet
- dual—duel
- foreword—forward
- led—lead
- mettle—metal
- peace—piece

- piqued—peaked
- principal—principle
- rein—reign—rain
- ringer—wringer
- role—roll
- stationary—stationery
- tick—tic
- tow—toe
- waved—waived
- yoke—yolk

American English and British English Differences

There are differences between the way certain words are spelled in American English and the way they are spelled in British English. Table 35-1 provides a list of words that have this peculiar treatment.

Compound Words and Hyphenation

Compound words are two or more words that are used to mean a single concept. Some compound words are written as two separate words with a space between them. These are called *open compounds*. Some compound words are combined into a single word, called *closed compounds*. Another variation is compound words that are separated by a hyphen. These are called *hyphenated compounds*.

Open Compounds
The following is a list of commonly used open compounds:

- ad hoc
- bed wetter
- bona fide
- drop in
- half brother
- life cycle
- more or less

- side effects
- stick up
- T square
- time frame
- under way
- V neck
- vice versa

Closed Compounds
The following is a list of commonly used closed compounds:

- backslide
- carryover
- clearheaded

- coldcock
- crossbreed
- deadpan

TABLE 35-1 Words Spelled Differently in American English and British English

American English	British English
Acknowledgment	Acknowledgement
Aging	Ageing
Analyze	Analyse
Anesthetic	Anaesthetic
Burned	Burnt
Canceled	Cancelled
Catalog	Catalogue
Center	Centre
Check	Cheque
Dialog	Dialogue
Draft	Draught
Dreamed	Dreamt
Encyclopedia	Encyclopaedia
Endeavor	Endeavour
Fetus	Foetus
Fiber	Fibre
Honor	Honour
Humor	Humour
Maneuver	Manoeuvre
Paralyze	Paralyse
Plow	Plough
Program	Programme
Spoiled	Spoilt
Theater	Theatre
Usable	Useable
Worshiping	Worshipping

- handwrite
- layoffs
- lifeline
- longtime
- makeup
- ongoing
- sendoff

- shortlist
- sidecar
- standstill
- stickhandle
- twofold
- waterlogged

Hyphenated Compounds

The following is a list of commonly used hyphenated compounds:

- all-encompassing
- all-knowing
- anti-inflammatory
- back-check
- bed-wetting
- cold-shoulder
- community-wide
- cross-fertilize
- dead-on
- de-emphasize
- do-able
- ex-employee
- ex-husband
- multi-item
- nuclear-free
- off-color
- pre-engineered
- president-elect
- self-doubts
- self-esteem
- stand-in
- time-out
- water-resistant

Hyphenation with Numbers

You should include a hyphen when spelling out any two-word number or fraction:

- twenty-nine
- ninety-nine
- thirty-six

When a fraction includes more than two numbers, you should hyphenate only the two-word number:

- two and three-quarters
- one twenty-fifth

Negative Formations

Just as not all plurals are made by adding *s* to a word, not all negatives are made by adding *un* as a prefix. There are many other methods for creating negatives. The following is a list of common negative formation techniques.

A or An

A or *An* is often used before a vowel or words beginning with *h*:

- amoral
- asexual

Anti

Anti is added to a word to mean "the opposite of":

- antichrist
- antimatter

- antifreeze
- antibiotic

Counter
Counter is added to a word to mean "the opposite of or contrary to":

- counterculture
- counterclockwise

De
De is added to a word to mean "the reverse of":

- decompose
- demagnetize
- deforestation

Dis
Dis is added to a word to mean "the reverse of":

- disrespectful
- disarm
- discontented

Dys
Dys is added to a word to mean "abnormal or impaired":

- dysfunctional
- dyspeptic

Mal
Mal is added to mean "bad or incorrect":

- malformed
- malfunctioning

Mis
Mis is added to mean "bad or incorrect":

- misuse
- misinterpret
- misfortune

Non
Non is added to a word to reverse the meaning:

- nonexistent
- nonfattening
- nonintoxicating

Un, In, Il, Im, Ir

These are added to a word to reverse the meaning:

- undressed
- undrinkable
- incapable
- illegitimate
- imbalance
- implausible
- irrefutable
- irrevocable

Less

Less is added to the end of a word to mean "without":

- helpless
- motionless
- shoeless

Free

Free is added to a word to mean "without":

- caffeine-free
- crime-free
- sugar-free

Commonly Misspelled Words

A

absence	achievement	affect	appearance
abundance	acquaintance	alleged	arctic
accessible	acquire	amateur	argument
accidentally	acquitted	analysis	ascend
acclaim	across	analyze	atheist
accommodate	address	annual	athletic
accomplish	advertisement	apartment	attendance
accordion	advice	apparatus	auxiliary
accumulate	advise	apparent	

B

balloon	beggar	beneficial	business
barbecue	beginning	benefit	
bargain	belief	biscuit	
basically	believe	boundaries	

C

calendar	cigarette	competent	controversial
camouflage	climbed	completely	controversy
candidate	cloth	concede	convenient
Caribbean	clothes	conceivable	correlate
category	clothing	conceive	correspondence
cemetery	collectible	condemn	counselor
challenge	colonel	condescend	courteous
changeable	column	conscience	courtesy
changing	coming	conscientious	criticism
characteristic	commission	conscious	criticize
chief	committee	consistent	
choose	commitment	continuous	
chose	comparative	controlled	

D

deceive	describe	difference	disease
defendant	description	dilemma	dispensable
deferred	desirable	dining	dissatisfied
definitely	despair	disappearance	dominant
definition	desperate	disappoint	drunkenness
dependent	develop	disastrous	
descend	dictionary	discipline	

E

easily	embarrass	equivalent	expense
ecstasy	emperor	especially	experience
effect	encouragement	exaggerate	experiment
efficiency	encouraging	exceed	explanation
eighth	enemy	excellence	extremely
either	entirely	exhaust	exuberance
eligible	environment	existence	
eliminate	equipped	existent	

F

facsimile	February	forcibly	fourth
fallacious	fictitious	foreign	fueling
fallacy	fiery	forfeit	fulfill
familiar	finally	foresee	fundamentally
fascinating	financially	formerly	
feasible	fluorescent	forty	

G

gauge	governor	guardian
generally	grammar	guerrilla
genius	grievous	guidance
government	guarantee	

H

handkerchief	heinous	hindrance	hygiene
happily	hemorrhage	hoarse	hypocrisy
harass	heroes	hoping	hypocrite
height	hesitancy	humorous	

I

ideally	incidentally	inevitable	interference
idiosyncrasy	incredible	influential	interrupt
ignorance	independence	information	introduce
imaginary	independent	inoculate	irrelevant
immediately	indicted	insurance	irresistible
implement	indispensable	intelligence	island

J

jealousy	judicial

K

knowledge

L

laboratory	leisure	likelihood	losing
laid	length	likely	lovely
later	license	loneliness	luxury
latter	lieutenant	loose	
legitimate	lightning	lose	

M

magazine	marriage	minuscule	mortgage
maintain	mathematics	minutes	mosquito
maintenance	medicine	miscellaneous	mosquitoes
manageable	millennium	mischievous	murmur
maneuver	millionaire	missile	muscle
manufacture	miniature	misspelled	mysterious

N

narrative	necessity	ninety	nowadays
naturally	neighbor	ninth	nuisance
necessary	neutron	noticeable	

O

obedience	official	opportunity	origin
obstacle	omission	oppression	outrageous
occasion	omit	optimism	overrun
occasionally	omitted	optimistic	
occurred	opinion	orchestra	
occurrence	opponent	ordinarily	

P

pamphlets	personnel	potato	principle
parallel	perspiration	potatoes	privilege
particular	physical	practically	probably
pavilion	physician	prairie	procedure
peaceable	piece	precede	proceed
peculiar	pilgrimage	precedence	profession
penetrate	pitiful	preceding	professor
perceive	planning	preference	prominent
performance	pleasant	preferred	pronounce
permanent	portray	prejudice	pronunciation
permissible	possess	preparation	propaganda
permitted	possession	prescription	psychology
perseverance	possessive	prevalent	publicly
persistence	possibility	primitive	pursue
personal	possible	principal	

Q

quantity	quarantine	questionnaire	quizzes

R

realistically	recommend	reminiscence	rheumatism
realize	reference	repetition	rhythm
really	referring	representative	rhythmical
recede	relevant	resemblance	ridiculous
receipt	relieving	reservoir	roommate
receive	religious	resistance	
recognize	remembrance	restaurant	

S

sacrifice	separation	souvenir	succeed
sacrilegious	sergeant	specifically	success
safety	several	specimen	succession
salary	severely	sponsor	sufficient
satellite	shepherd	spontaneous	supersede
scary	shining	statistics	suppress
scenery	siege	stopped	surprise
schedule	similar	strategy	surround
secede	simile	strength	susceptible
secretary	simply	strenuous	suspicious
seize	simultaneous	stubbornness	syllable
sense	sincerely	studying	symmetrical
sentence	skiing	subordinate	synonymous
separate	sophomore	subtle	

Spelling

T

tangible	themselves	tomorrow	truly
technical	theories	tournament	twelfth
technique	therefore	toward	tyranny
temperamental	thorough	tragedy	
temperature	though	transferring	
tendency	through	tries	

U

unanimous	unique	usable	utilization
undoubtedly	unnecessary	usage	
unforgettable	until	usually	

V

vacuum	vigilant	violence	virtue
valuable	village	visible	volume
vengeance	villain	vision	

W

warrant	weird	wholly	worthwhile
warriors	wherever	withdrawal	writing
weather	whether	woman	
Wednesday	which	women	

Y

yacht	yield	young

36

Pronunciation

Perfecting Your Speech

How you pronounce the words you choose to say can dramatically support—or under-cut—the substance of what you're saying. Incorrect pronunciation or slurred enuncia-tion reflects poorly on one's intelligence and ability. While this judgment may be unfair, it's reality: First impressions count. To make a favorable impression, try to perfect your speech.

Begin by carefully listening to the speech of others and comparing it with your own. What are the differences, especially between your speech and that of the people you most admire? Consult the dictionary when you hear differences to see whether you or the other person has made a mistake. This moment of truth will quickly improve your pronunciation and help you enlarge your vocabulary. It is one of the finest steps toward cultivation of improved speech patterns. Go to www. dictionary.com to listen to the correct pronounciation.

Following is a partial list of words often mispronounced; perhaps a vowel or a con-sonant sound is mispronounced, or a syllable is commonly dropped, added, or slurred. Sometimes letters that should be silent are sounded, or vice versa. Study the correct pronunciation carefully. You may be accustomed to pronouncing several of these words differently, but remember: Colloquial pronunciation is not preferable for business standards.

Word List

abject	address
absolutely	admirable
abstemious	adult
absurd	aerial
accede	ally
accept	applicable
accession	architect
accessories	arctic
accidentally	area
acclimate	attack

attitude	dessert
attorney	detour
autopsy	diamond
avenue	distribute
aviation	divide
battery	doing
being	drowned
beneficent	duly
bicycle	duty
biography	edition
breadth	educate
casualty	elm
champion	envelop
chastisement	envelope
chauffeur	epitome
chestnut	equitable
chocolate	era
clique	err
comment	etiquette
compromise	every
concave	exigency
concentrate	exponent
concierge	exquisite
condolence	extant
conversant	extraordinary
convex	fact
corps	family
creek	fasten
cruel	favorite
data	figure
deaf	film
decade	finance
decisive	financial
defect	financier
deficit	forehead
demonstrable	forte
depot	formidable
depths	fragmentary

friendship	latent
genuine	length
gingham	library
glisten	lieu
gondola	lightning
government	long-lived
grievous	longevity
guardian	luxury
hasten	lyceum
height	manufacture
heinous	maturity
herculean	memorable
heroism	mischievous
homeopathy	municipal
horizon	museum
hostile	new
hundred	oblique
idea	office
ignoramus	often
immediate	on
impious	ordeal
incognito	osteopath
incomparable	osteopathy
indictment	overalls
industry	parade
inexorable	partner
inexplicable	patron
infamous	pecan
inquiry	pecuniary
Iowa	peremptory
irrevocable	piano
Italian	picture
italics	pique
judiciary	plumber
just	positively
knew	possess
lapel	precedence
large	preface

preferable

prescription

presentation

radiator

radio

rambling

realm

recognize

recourse

refutable

reputable

research

resources

respite

revocable

robust

romance

Roosevelt

route

sagacious

schism

simultaneous

short-lived

slippery

solace

solder

sphere

status

strictly

subpoena

subtle

suit

superfluous

surprise

telegrapher

temperament

tenet

theater

tract

trembling

tremendous

tribune

tube

Tuesday

tumult

umbrella

usurp

Utica

vagary

vehement

vehicle

verbose

was

water

what

wheel

whether

white

wrestle

37

Punctuation

Purpose of Punctuation

The sole purpose of punctuation is to make the text clear. If a mark of punctuation does not clarify the text, it should be omitted. Of course, you'll follow your boss's preference if he or she instructs you, for example, to insert more commas or semicolons than today's magazines and newspapers typically use. When public changes occur, not every person immediately approves. But if a matter is left to your discretion, remember that the old tried-and-true comma rule also applies for many other marks of punctuation: "When in doubt, leave it out."

Nevertheless, there are still standards and formalities in punctuation that you must fully grasp, not only to satisfy your boss but also to help promote your own career. Once it leaves the office, your work speaks for itself. You want it to be a source of pride for both your employer and you.

Following is a list of punctuation marks with usage rules and examples for each.

The Period

A period is used at the end of a declarative sentence to denote a full pause:

- I am going to town.
- You may go with me if you wish.

Use a period, not a question mark, when the sentence contains an indirect question:

- He could not understand why she was leaving.

Also use a period for a request phrased as a question:

- Will you please return the diskette when you are finished.

The period is used in decimals to separate a whole number from a decimal fraction:

- 5.6 percent
- $19.50

It is also used in abbreviations:

- Mrs.
- Ph.D.
- etc.

The Comma

The presence of a comma, or its absence, can cause different interpretations of a written sentence. It is thus of vast importance, particularly in legal documents. The comma tells the reader to pause. Some writers can tell where commas belong by reading their sentences aloud and inserting commas where there seems to be a natural pause. This only works, however, if you read a sentence carefully and accurately.

Series

Commas are used to separate nouns in a series or adjectives in a series of the same rank modifying the same noun:

- The workers picked cherries, peaches, and plums.
- We swam in cool, clear, fresh water.

Some bosses may prefer to omit the comma before the *and* in such sentences unless it's needed for clarity. The same applies to commas before *but* and *or*. Many writers believe these words take the place of the final comma in a series.

Sometimes a term consisting of years, months, and days is considered not a series but a single unit of time. No commas are used:

- Interest will be computed for 6 years 3 months and 2 days.

Compound and Complex Sentences

Two sentences are often connected with a comma and conjunction, such as *and* or *but*. A comma is used between the clauses of a compound sentence:

- John went to the theater, but he left before the play ended.

Do not confuse this with a compound predicate, which takes no comma:

- John went to the theater but left before the play ended.

An adverbial clause usually follows the independent clause, and no comma is used. But for emphasis, the order of the clauses is sometimes transposed. Then a comma is used.

Usual order: John was met by a large delegation when he came home.

Transposed order: When John came home, he was met by a large delegation.

Introductory Expressions

Introductory expressions, such as transitional words and phrases, mild exclamations, and other independent expressions, are set off by a comma when they occur alone at the beginning of a sentence:

- Yes, I will go.
- Well, perhaps she is right.
- Nevertheless, I wish he had waited for me.
- To tell the truth, I think you should go.
- As a rule, he arrives very early.

A few introductory expressions are more emphatic without punctuation, however, and need not be followed by a comma:

- Doubtless she just couldn't be here.
- At least you tried.
- Undoubtedly the plane's engines both failed.
- Indeed you may bring your friends with you.

To distinguish between the two, ask whether you naturally pause after the word or words in question. A comma is used to signal the natural pause.

Other Transitional Words

A comma is used to set off the transitional words *however, therefore*, and *moreover* when used within the sentence or as the first or last word of the sentence:

- Jean may not arrive until noon, however.
- Her problem, therefore, must be solved at once.
- I will be there, moreover, as soon as I can.

Sometimes *though* is used to mean *however* and should be set off with commas:

- I will be there, though, if at all possible.

Prepositional Phrases

No comma is used for prepositional phrases within a sentence unless the phrase comes between the subject and the predicate of the clause:

- I am sure that because of your generosity we will be able to build the new dormitory.
- The bag, in addition to a hatbox, will be sent to you today.

Contrasting Phrases

Contrasting expressions within a sentence are set off by commas:

- The lion, not the tiger, growled.
- We walk slowly, never quickly, to the garage.
- This letter was meant for you, not for me.
- *BUT*—This letter was meant for you but not for me.

Nonrestrictive Modifiers

Nonrestrictive modifiers are phrases or clauses that could be omitted without affecting the meaning of the main clause. These should be set off from the rest of the sentence by a comma or by parenthetical commas:

- John, my favorite friend, is visiting me.
- That car is, I believe, a new model.
- Mary Brown, who lives next door, is in the third grade.
- *BUT*—That is the girl who lives next door.

Infinitive Phrases

An infinitive phrase used independently is set off by commas:

- The color is too dark, to list one fault.

If the phrase is used as a modifier, it is not punctuated:

- The piano is too large to fit in the room.

Dialogue

A comma is used to separate a dialogue quotation from the main sentence:

- "Please go with me," the boy said.
- "What do you think," Mr. Bleeker asked, "the mayor will do next?"

Commas also separate the name of the person addressed in dialogue from the remainder of the sentence:

- "Will you come with me, John?"
- "But, Jane, how do you know that the plane is late?"

A confirming question within a sentence is set off by commas:

- "He left, did he not, on the noon plane?"

Repeated Words

A comma is used for clarity and to avoid confusion when the same word is repeated:

- Whoever goes, goes without my consent.

Omission

When words are omitted in one part of a sentence because they were used in a previous part, a comma is used to show where the words were omitted:

- Sam's first car was a Cadillac, and mine, a Ford.

Transposed Adjective Order

An adjective normally precedes the noun it modifies. When an adjective follows a noun, the adjective is set off by commas; when an adjective precedes a noun but also precedes the article before the noun, a comma follows the adjective:

- The physician, dignified and competent, told them the bad news.
- Dignified and competent, the physician told them the bad news.

Numbers

A comma is used in writing large numbers, separating the thousands digits from the hundreds, the millions digits from the thousands, and so forth:

- 249,586
- 1,345,000

A comma is used to separate two or more unrelated numbers:

- On August 1, 2015, the museum was visited by 437 people.
- Out of eighty, twenty were discarded.

Do not forget the second comma when the date occurs in the middle of the sentence:

- She left for England on June 22, 2016, and returned a month later.

However, it is acceptable if your boss prefers no commas at all:

- She left for England on June 22 2016 and returned a month later.

Addresses

Elements of an address are set off by commas:

- He lives at 410 Hawthorne Street, Chicago, Illinois, near the University of Chicago campus.

On an envelope address, there is no comma between the state and the zip code.

Titles

A comma is used to separate a name and a title:

- The letter was from Mrs. Masterson, our president, and contained a list of instructions.

Set off Jr. and Sr. from a proper name by a comma. A roman numeral is not set off by a comma:

- Philip W. Thompson, Sr.
- Philip W. Thompson III

Degrees are also set off by a comma:

- Jennifer Galt, M.D.

But descriptive titles are not:

- Attila the Hun

Company Names

Company names consisting of a series of names omit the last comma in the series:

- Pate, Tate and Waite

When *and Company* completes a series of names, the last comma is also omitted:

- Pate, Tate, Waite and Company

Set off *Incorporated* from the name of a company by a comma:

- Johnson Brothers, Incorporated

The Question Mark

A question mark closes a question:

- What time is it?

A question mark is used to express a doubt:

- He is older (?) than she.

If the question is indirect, no question mark is used:

- I wonder whether he will be here.

When a question is asked in the middle of a sentence, the question is enclosed by commas and the sentence ends with a question mark:

- They are arriving, aren't they, on the noon train?

When the question is enclosed in parentheses, the question mark is inside the parentheses, not at the end of the sentence:

- The magazine (did you see it?) describes the city in great detail.

If the question mark is part of a quotation, it is placed inside the closing quotation mark; if it is not a part of the quotation, it is placed outside the closing quotation mark:

- The statement ended, "And is that all?"
- What did she mean by "jobless years"?

If the last word in a question is an abbreviation and thus contains a period, the question mark is also used:

- Do you think he will arrive by 4 p.m.?

When it is desired to make a question of a statement, the question mark is used:

- He is arriving today?
- Really?

The Exclamation Point

An exclamation point is used when making extravagant claims or to express deep feeling:

- Here is the finest car on the market!
- The announcement was unbelievable!

An exclamation point is used after a word or phrase charged with emotion:

- Quick! We don't want to be late.

It is also used for double emphasis:

- Did you catch that innuendo!

Caution: Some people get into the habit of using exclamation points far too often to express strong emotion, and they end up blunting the very purpose of the punctuation. For effective writing, show emotion through the choice of words instead, and reserve exclamation points for only the strongest of feelings.

The Semicolon

A semicolon is used when the conjunction is omitted between parts of a compound sentence:

- I went with them; I should have stayed at home.

A semicolon precedes words such as *however, moreover,* or *otherwise* when they introduce the second of two connected full sentences:

■ She is arriving at noon; however, she will not stay long.

If parts of a series contain inner punctuation such as a comma, the parts are separated by a semicolon:

■ He came to see his mother, who was ill; his sister, who lived in the next town; and his old schoolmate.

The Colon

The colon generally follows a sentence introducing a tabulation or a long quotation:

■ The following quotation is from the *Detroit Free Press*: "Regardless of what may be accomplished, the company will still be involved."

■ During your first year, you will study such subjects as these: algebra, physics, chemistry, and psychology.

Exception: When the tabulated list is the object of a verb or a preposition, a colon is never used:

■ During your first year, you will study algebra, physics, chemistry, and psychology.

Emphasis or Anticipation
The colon is also used to stress a word, phrase, or clause that follows it or when a sentence creates anticipation for what immediately follows:

■ The newspaper published a startling statement: the city had been completely destroyed by fire.

Time
The colon is used to separate hours and minutes in expressions of time:

■ 4:15 a.m. CST

Titles
The colon is used to separate a title from a subtitle:

■ *Gone With the Wind: A Story of the Old South*

Quotation Marks

Double quotation marks are used to set off any material quoted within a sentence or paragraph. If the quoted material consists of several paragraphs, the opening quotation mark is used at the beginning of the quotation and at the beginning of each paragraph within the quotation; a closing quotation mark, however, is used only at the conclusion of the quotation. It is not used at the end of each paragraph within the quotation, as many people mistakenly think. For example:

> The passage he read aloud was from the first chapter: "The discovery of this energy brings us to the problem of how to allow it to be used. The use of atomic

power throws us back to the Greek legend of Prometheus and the age-old question of whether force should be exerted against law.

"The man of today must decide whether he will use this power for destruction or for peaceful purposes." When he had finished the reading, there was loud applause.

Quotations Within Quotations

Single quotation marks indicate a quotation within the quotation:

- He said, "Did you hear John make the statement, 'I will not go with her,' or were you not present at the time he spoke?"

Titles

In printed text, the titles of essays, articles, poems, stories, or chapters are set off within quotation marks; titles of plays, books, and periodical publications are italicized:

- The name of the article is "I Believe."
- The *Eternal Echos* CD contains the poem "Tread Gently."
- The title of the book is *Journey Into Night*.
- It was first published in *Harper's Magazine*.

Quotation Marks and Punctuation

Place quotation marks outside the comma and the period:

- "Don't stop now," he said, "when you have so little left to finish."

Place quotation marks inside the colon and the semicolon:

- He called her a "little witch"; that was right after she broke his model plane.

Place quotation marks outside an exclamation point or a question mark when the quoted material alone is an exclamation or a question:

- "I passed my test!"

Place quotation marks inside an exclamation point or a question mark when the quoted material alone is not an exclamation or a question:

- Didn't he claim to be "too tired"?

Italics

Italics are sometimes used for emphasis:

- Notice where you are, not where you *have been*.

But the best writing avoids italics for this purpose, depending on choice of language to bring out the emphasis. As mentioned earlier, italics are used for the names of books, pamphlets, and periodicals:

- *Saturday Evening Post*
- *Black Beauty*
- *Washington Daily News*

The names of ships are italicized but not abbreviations in front of them.

- *Sea Witch*
- USS *Heinz*

Note: When using a typewriter and not a word processor or computer, indicate italics by underlining:

- <u>Sea Witch</u>
- USS <u>Heinz</u>
- <u>Washington Daily News</u>

The Apostrophe

As a mark of omission, the apostrophe may denote that a word has been contracted intentionally:

- It's time to go.
- Haven't you finished the task?

Possession

To show possession, use an apostrophe followed by an *s* after a singular noun:

- the city's founder

Use it alone after plural nouns ending in *s*:

- the books' titles

Plural nouns not ending in *s* form the possessive by adding an apostrophe and an *s*:

- men's clubs
- sheep's clothing

The plural of compound nouns and joint possessive nouns is formed by adding an apostrophe followed by an *s* to the second word only:

- the Secretary-Treasurer's decision
- Mary and John's cassette player

But if the items are separately owned, the compound nouns each add an apostrophe followed by an *s*:

- Mary's and John's coats

No apostrophe is used with possessive pronouns:

- his
- yours
- hers
- ours
- its
- theirs

The apostrophe is used to express duration of time:

- a day's traveling time
- twelve months' duration

For a proper name ending in *s*, use an apostrophe followed by an *s*:

- Lewis's hat
- Miss Bliss's book

Two proper names are traditionally observed as exceptions:

- Moses' robe
- Jesus' parable

For proper names ending in *s*, use an apostrophe only:

- The Joneses' boots were left in the hall.

The Em Dash

The em dash (in typing, indicated by two hyphens) is used to introduce an added thought:

- I shall go with you—you don't mind, do you?

The em dash also breaks the continuity of a thought as a digression:

- "The Scherzo Sonata" by Tolstoy is a sad story—but the writing is magnificent.

It is sometimes used before and after a parenthetical expression in place of commas:

- Henry Higgins—bareheaded and without a coat—left the house and ran down the road.

Sometimes you can think of an em dash as a super comma. When a sentence already contains a series separated by commas, a dash is a good tool for separating a clause that might otherwise look like it was part of the series. Consider the following:

- The Mississippi River weaves among Tennessee, Arkansas, and Louisiana—a state famous for its French culture—before emptying into the Gulf of Mexico.

Ellipses

To show omission of words in quoted material, three spaced dots (ellipses) are used if material is deleted within the sentence. When the last part of a quoted sentence is omitted, it is followed by three spaced dots plus its punctuation. At the end of the quotation, only the punctuation is used:

- "Five hundred firemen . . . attended the ball . . . ."
- Mr. Brown went on to say: "The shoe department functions smoothly. Many salespeople have won prizes for efficiency."

Ellipsis dots may also be used to mark a thought expressed hesitantly:

- He said, "If . . . if I do go with you, will you return early?"

Parentheses

Parentheses are used to enclose matter that is introduced by way of explanation:

- If the lessor (the person owning the property) agrees, the lessee (the person renting the property) may have a dog on the premises.

Parentheses are used to enclose figures that enumerate items:

■ The book contained chapters on (1) capitalization, (2) spelling rules, (3) troublesome verbs, and (4) punctuation.

They are also used to enclose citations of authority:

■ The definition of action is "the process or state of being active" (*American College Dictionary*).

And they are used to enclose figures repeated for clarity, as in legal documents:

■ He was willed five thousand dollars ($5,000) by his uncle.

■ You will be paid twenty (20) percent interest.

Brackets

Brackets and parentheses are sometimes used interchangeably; however, brackets have two common uses:

■ They identify changes to quoted material.

■ They enclose digressions within parentheses.

Changes to Quoted Material

If you are quoting someone but make a change to the quote in order to clarify something, you should put your change within brackets. Consider the following:

■ Original quote—"Everyone knew it was about to break any day now."

■ Revised quote—"Everyone knew it [the dam] was about to break any day now."

Digressions Within Parentheses

Sometimes you will find situations where you need an extra set of parentheses nested within a previous pair. Consider the following:

■ The computer's memory (Random Access Memory [RAM] and Read Only Memory [ROM]) is where software is loaded.

The Hyphen

Hyphens are used both in spelling and in punctuation. When it is used as punctuation, it is not part of a word or phrase. There are four general ways the hyphen can be used as punctuation:

1. Breaking a word at the end of a line

2. Combining words that form a compound adjective

3. Acting as a substitute for a repeated word

4. Indicating special pronunciations

Line Breaks

Most word processing programs, such as Microsoft Word, have a built-in hyphenation feature that you can turn on and off. This feature automatically adds hyphens to long words that won't fit on the end of a line. Sometimes the computer's idea of where to put a hyphen can cause the hyphenated word to look ridiculous. Therefore, it's important for you to know the general rules regarding line break hyphenation. Here are some of those rules:

- Don't break one-syllable words.
- Don't break a word if just one letter is left on a line.
- Break hyphenated compound words at the hyphen.
- Break closed compound words between the words.

Compound Adjectives

Compound adjectives are groups of words or phrases used in a sentence to describe a noun. Consider the following:

- It was a once-in-a-lifetime opportunity.
- I wouldn't touch that line with a ten-foot pole.
- The computer's processor has a 512 single-byte bus.
- Eight-month-old kittens were given away.
- Eight month-old kittens were given away.

Do not use hyphens when the first word of a compound adjective ends in *-ly*. The following examples are *incorrect*:

- It was a highly-motivated student body.
- It was a beautifully-made sweater.

Hyphens as Substitute Words

If a word repeats with a different modifier in a sentence, it can make the sentence sound long and difficult. One way to solve this problem is to use a hyphen. Consider the following examples:

- We both over- and underestimated the amount of driving time for the trip.
- The Dallas Cowboys used a three-, four-, and five-man line.
- Most computers today have either a 32- or 64-bit processor.

Hyphens for Pronunciation

You can use hyphens when writing dialogue in order to achieve a particular pronunciation in the reader's mind:

- "S-s-s-s," said the snake.
- "Mr. S-s-smith," he stuttered, "May I p-p-please have some w-w-water?"

The Slash

The slash is often used as shorthand or when the choice between outcomes is nebulous. Since the slash is often ambiguous, it should be used with caution.

The slash is used for the following:

- With and/or combinations
- To indicate other relationships between words

And/Or Combinations

The slash can be used to indicate options that are available, to indicate equal possibilities, or to show that something has more than one function. For example:

- The potter worked alone in the cold garage/studio.
- Dear Sir/Madam:
- The ingredients of the drink are: ice, rum, lime/lemon, and cola.

Indicating Other Relationships

The slash can be used to separate elements that are being compared, to separate origins and destinations, to separate the numerals in a date, to indicate a period that spans two or more calendar years, in place of the word *per*, and to write fractions.

- The Redskins/Cowboys rivalry has a long history.
- The Dallas/Atlanta flight was canceled.
- 12/31/2016
- For the 2015/16 school year, the eighth graders will be taking technology education for the first time.
- 1000 km/hour
- 1/2 = 1/4 + 1/4

38

Numerals

Words or Figures?

Your main concern with numbers is whether to spell them out in words or to express them in figures. As so often happens with matters of English usage, there are many times when both forms are correct, and you will regularly come across variations not covered in a book of rules, so use your discretion. Clarity is always your strongest guideline.

Printed Text and Prose Text

Generally, in prose text, numbers under 101 are spelled out, and the numbers 101 and over are shown in figures. The more formal the text is, the greater is the tendency to express the number in words.

In printed text, a number used for comparison with other numbers in the same section should be in numerical form.

- An excavation of 500 feet can be finished as rapidly as 200 feet if the right equipment is used.

At the Beginning of a Sentence

A number appearing at the beginning of a sentence, if it can be expressed in one or two words, should be spelled out:

- Sixteen new cars were delivered.

- Thirty or forty bushels were needed.

- *NOT:* 2,746,892 copies were purchased.

The last example should be rewritten so that the figure appears later in the sentence:

- The company purchased 2,746,892 copies.

Legal Documents

In legal documents, numbers are written in both words and figures to prevent misunderstanding, and the same is true in papers that transfer land title:

- The west thirty (30) feet of Lot Nine (9) in Block Four (4) . . .

Round Numbers

Approximate round numbers are spelled out:

- The station is about fifty blocks away.
- He found nearly two thousand dollars.

Sets of Numbers

To differentiate two sets of numbers occurring in the same sentence, use words for one and figures for the other:

- Three of the men drove 2,000 miles each; four drove 3,000 miles each; and only one drove the complete 3,000 miles.

If the sentence cannot be rewritten, use a comma or dash to separate the numbers:

- During the year 2014, twenty million people visited the park.
- We received 1,213—of which 113 . . .

Large Numbers

As a general rule, write out numbers up to and including one hundred, and use figures for numbers over one hundred. But for large numbers, if a number can be written as one or two words, do so:

- four hundred
- five million
- two billion

Use the short form for writing numbers over a thousand not pertaining to money:

- fourteen hundred
- *NOT:* one thousand four hundred

Large, even amounts may combine figures and words:

- Production of 38 million paper clips and a budget of $146 billion . . .

If a figure or the word *several* precedes *hundred, thousand, million, billion*, and so on, the singular form is used. After *many*, the plural form is used:

- six hundred pages
- several million years
- many hundreds of pages

Separating Digits

All numbers above 999 are written with commas to separate every group of three digits, counting from the units place:

- 1,001
- 123,000
- 1,436,936

Exceptions: Commas are omitted in long decimal fractions, page numbers, addresses, telephone numbers, room numbers, and form numbers:

- 0.10356
- Page 3487

■ 1467 Wilshire Boulevard

■ 201-555-9088

■ Room 2630

■ Form 2317-A

Commas are also omitted in four-digit year numbers, but they are added for years with five or more digits:

■ The company began in 1992.

■ The pottery shards were dated at about 14,000 B.C.

■ This science fiction novel takes place in the year 27,345 A.D.

Patent numbers are written with commas:

■ Patent No. 3,436,987

Serial numbers are written without commas:

■ Motor Number 245889954

■ Policy Number 894566

Dollars and Cents

Use figures for money:

■ 1 cent

■ 20 cents

■ $20,000

However, as with other numbers, amounts of money are always written out when beginning a sentence:

■ One cent was contributed by each child.

■ *NOT:* 1 cent was contributed by each child.

A series of prices is written in figures only:

■ These shoes were priced at $50, $60, and $85.

Dollar and Cent Signs

Use the dollar sign before the number, not the word *dollar* or *dollars* after the number.

■ The duplex rents for $700 per month.

If a large number combines figures and words, use the dollar sign before the figure:

■ The budget calls for $850 billion.

■ *NOT:* The budget calls for 850 billion dollars.

Repeat the dollar sign with successive numbers:

■ The bonds could be purchased in denominations of $10,000, $12,000, $15,000, and $20,000.

Exception: Omit all but the first dollar sign when numbers are in tabulated form:

▪ The bonds could be purchased in denominations of the following amounts:

▪ $10,000

▪   12,000

▪   15,000

▪   20,000

The dollar sign is not used when the figure given is in cents alone. Use the cent sign ¢ after amounts less than one dollar, but never use the cent sign with a decimal point:

▪ 25¢

▪ *NOT:* .25¢, for that would mean one-fourth of a cent

Exception: The only time the dollar sign is used when the figure is in cents alone is in statistical work when the part of the dollar is carried out to more than two decimal places:

▪ $0.3564

Decimal Points

Decimal points are another way of writing fractions, especially large fractions. When a decimal occurs with no unit before it, use a cipher (a zero) for quick interpretation:

▪ a 0.75-yard measurement

▪ rainfall of 0.356 inch

Sometimes the fraction is part of a dollar. When the amount of dollars given is not followed by cents, omit the decimal point and the ciphers:

▪ $3

▪ $1,200

▪ *BUT:* $17.75

The decimal point and ciphers are not used with even amounts of money unless in tabulated form. If tabulated, and some amounts contain cents and some do not, the even amounts should contain ciphers:

▪ $19.36

▪   5.00

▪   2.14

▪   38.00

▪   1.23

▪   .19

▪   .02

Time

When a figure and a word come together as an adjective to express time, connect the two with a hyphen:

- a 24-hour day
- *BUT:* a day of 24 hours
- two 2-year 12-percent notes
- *BUT:* two notes for two years at 12 percent

Hours, minutes, and seconds are separated by a colon:

- 10:05:02 a.m.

Never use "this a.m." instead of "this morning." With *a.m.* or *p.m.*, the word *o'clock* should not be used:

- I will meet you at 4 p.m.
- I will meet you at four o'clock this afternoon.

Ciphers after the number of the hour are unnecessary. For exact noon and midnight, it is correct to use the words:

- I will meet you at noon.
- The horn blew at midnight.

Dates

The day is written in numerals, without *th, st,* or *d,* unless the day is written before the name of the month:

- May 1, 2015
- *NOT:* May 1st, 2015
- *BUT:* On the 2d of June 2015
- In the August 21 and September 3 editions (*NOT* 21st or 3d)

In legal documents, dates are spelled out:

- the twelfth day of May, A.D. Two Thousand and Eight

The Hyphen

Written-out numbers below one hundred are hyphenated:

- thirty-three
- ninety-nine
- twenty-seven

Hundreds and thousands are not hyphenated:

- six hundred thousand
- three hundred million

When modifying a noun, numbers are hyphenated, as are any compound adjectives:

- five-thousand-foot mountain
- three-foot rule

Fractions of less than one are hyphenated:

- one-third
- three-quarters
- *BUT:* one twenty-third

Mixed numbers are not hyphenated between the whole number and the fraction, both when written as words and figures:

- one and one-half
- 1 1/2

Do not write one part of the fraction as a numeral and the other as a word:

- one-fourth-inch bolt
- *NOT:* 1 fourth-inch bolt

When a mixed number is the subject of a sentence, the noun is plural. However, the verb is singular because the quantity is considered as a single unit:

- 1 5/8 inches is needed
- 2 1/4 miles is the length of the track

Ages

Use the general rule in giving the age of a person or a period of time (write out up to and including one hundred; use figures over one hundred):

- She is twelve years old.
- He has held the same position for twenty-six years.
- She is now 105 years of age.
- The company has been in this city for 102 years.

In compound adjectives denoting age, the words designating time may be used before *old*, but in that event the words *year* and *day* must appear in the singular:

- 12-day-old baby elephant
- 6-month-old pony
- 200-year-old building
- 3-day-old kitten

Dimensions

The signs reserved for technical writing are ′ for feet, ″ for inches, and × for by.

- 9′ × 12′ (9 feet by 12 feet)
- 8″ × 10″ (8 inches by 10 inches)

In regular prose text, write out the word "by" for "×."

Ciphers can be used to indicate exact measurement if they improve clarity:

- 9′0″ × 12′0″ × 20′6″

Weights and Measures

Abbreviations are used without capitalization:

- 6 lb. 3 oz.
- *OR* 6 pounds 3 ounces
- 192 lbs
- *OR* 192 pounds

In a compound adjective showing a weight or a measure, the numeral is hyphenated to a singular noun:

- 600-mile-an-hour speed
- *BUT:* speed of 600 miles an hour
- a 40-hour workweek
- *BUT:* a workweek of 40 hours

Percentages

The numeral is retained whether or not a percentage sign is used:

- 5% price reduction
- loss of 10 percent
- almost 30 percent of the population

For percentages in succession, use the sign after each numeral:

- 30% to 50%
- 6%, 8%, and 10%

Numbers

Page Numbering

For all page numbering, use figures to show the numbers. Commas are not used in page numbers greater than 999.

On legal documents, a page number is centered at the bottom of each page; on other papers, it is usually shown at the top. Manuscripts and briefs are numbered in the upper right corner; papers that are to be bound at the left are numbered in the lower right corner. In each case, all numbers should appear at exactly the same place on all pages. Title pages are not numbered. A first page of a work or of a chapter is not marked with a number, although the numbering of the following pages takes into consideration the number of the first page.

It is acceptable to use a short dash before and after the page number, -3-, without a period. Never use quotation marks and never type the word *page* before the number. Frequently, the number stands alone—2—without a period.

The Abbreviation for Number

The abbreviation for *number—no.—*or the number sign—#—is usually omitted:

- Building 38
- *NOT:* Building No. 38
- Invoice 3457
- *NOT:* Invoice #3457
- Page 92
- *NOT:* page no. 92

In text, however, it may be convenient to use the abbreviation:

- When he came to No. 16, he halted.
- The only houses to be painted this year are Nos. 16, 17, and 18.

Plurals of Numbers

Form the plural of a numeral or other character by adding *s* or *es* to the word. If the number is a figure, use *s* or *es* as your boss prefers:

- 5s and 6s *OR* 5's and 6's *OR* fives and sixes
- the 1890s *OR* the 1890's
- MD88s OR MD88's

Roman Numerals

Roman numerals are often used in outlines and some dates. Table 38-1 lists the most commonly used Roman numerals. Use the forms listed in Table 38-2 for dates.

TABLE 38-1   Most Commonly Used Roman Numerals

Arabic	Roman	Arabic	Roman	Arabic	Roman
1	I	15	XV	150	CL
2	II	16	XVI	200	CC
3	III	17	XVII	300	CCC
4	IV	18	XVIII	400	CD
5	V	19	XIX	500	D
6	VI	20	XX	600	DC
7	VII	30	XXX	700	DCC
8	VIII	40	XL	800	DCCC
9	IX	50	L	900	CM
10	X	60	LX	1,000	M
11	XI	70	LXX	1,500	MD
12	XII	80	LXXX	2,000	MM
13	XIII	90	XC	3,000	MMM
14	XIV	100	C		

TABLE 38-2   Roman Numeral Dates

1900	MCM	1960	MCMLX	2020	MMXX
1910	MCMX	1970	MCMLXX	2030	MMXXX
1920	MCMXX	1980	MCMLXXX	2040	MMXL
1930	MCMXXX	1990	MCMXC	2050	MML
1940	MCMXL	2000	MM		
1950	MCML	2010	MMX		

Numerals

Financial Activities

39

Bookkeeping and Accounting

Financial Record Keeping

Bookkeeping and accounting are fields requiring special training. Smaller companies may assign these duties to the administrative assistant, especially with today's new computerized accounting programs. Larger companies typically have an in-house accounting department or contract for the services of an accountant to prepare tax statements and other important records. Even so, it's useful to familiarize yourself with the simple mechanics of bookkeeping and accounting no matter what size company you work for. The more informed you are, the more valuable you are to the company.

Assets

Property owned by a business organization and used in its operation is known as *assets*. The proprietor or owner of the business may be one person, two persons (in a partnership), half a dozen persons, or numerous persons operating a corporation. The interest of the owner or proprietor in the assets of the business is called *proprietorship, net worth*, or *capital*. If the business is free of claims against these assets, except for those of the proprietor, then assets equals proprietorship. For example, if John King purchased a stationery store for $10,000, his financial condition would be expressed in this way: assets $10,000 equal proprietorship $10,000.

Liabilities

A business owner may obtain additional property by borrowing money to purchase the property needed or by purchasing the property with a promise to pay for that property at some future date. Those from whom business owners borrow are known as *creditors*. The creditor has a claim on the property until the proprietor pays in accordance with an agreement. This claim is known as the *liabilities* of the business.

For example, Mary Brown borrows $5,000 from a bank to enlarge the building used for her dry cleaning establishment. The bank thus becomes her creditor. This $5,000 increase in Brown's assets is accompanied by the bank's corresponding claim on her assets until the borrowed $5,000 is repaid. To fill the newly enlarged building, Brown purchases additional equipment and merchandise from the American Dry Cleaning

451

Equipment Company amounting to $5,000; the American Dry Cleaning Company thus becomes another creditor. If Brown fails to pay this $5,000, the company can enforce its claim by legal action; this potential claim of the company on Brown's assets is another liability.

Assets of a business are, therefore, subject to two kinds of claims: (1) those arising from the rights of creditors, and (2) those arising from the rights of the proprietor. The sum of these rights is equal to the value of the assets. Thus, assets equal liabilities plus proprietorship.

Effect of Business Transactions

The proprietor must know the effect of all business transactions on his or her assets, liabilities, and proprietorship in order to make decisions regarding future operations. Accounts furnish the proprietor with a record for this purpose, which is why it's critical that accounts be concrete, precise, and accurate.

For example, if the proprietor is considering hiring additional sales associates, he or she should know the results of the existing sales force to be able to estimate the probable results of hiring additional personnel. If the proprietor is considering purchasing additional merchandise, equipment, or space, attention should be given to the results from existing facilities.

The efficient proprietor is always seeking information concerning the effect of past operations in order to plan future operations. Such plans are known as *budgets*. Therefore, the primary purpose of accounting records is to give the proprietor information concerning the nature of his or her liabilities and proprietorship, as well as to furnish a concrete record of the effect of the business operation on them.

The purposes of accounting are to (1) record, (2) analyze and classify, and (3) summarize the activities of the business and their effects on each enterprise. Accounting simply reduces to writing the activities of a business.

Accounting Statements

Accounting statements (1) list a description of and amounts of property, together with ownership rights; and (2) report the effects of the operations on the owner's equity.

The first statement is known as the *balance sheet* (Figure 39-1). The balance sheet shows the assets, together with the rights of the creditors and the rights of the proprietor. The second statement is known as the *income statement* or *profit and loss statement* (Figure 39-2). It shows income and costs of operation, with the resulting increase or decrease in proprietorship. The balance sheet shows the financial condition of the business at a given time; the income statement covers the periods between any two balance sheets.

These summaries are interesting to persons other than the proprietor. When the owner of the business wishes to borrow money from a bank, the bank officers, in order to judge the owner's ability to repay the loan, ask for information concerning the assets and liabilities and the profits earned in previous periods. Creditors request the same information before selling merchandise on account. The Internal Revenue Service (IRS) also requires a similar statement to be assured that the income tax for the coming year is being estimated properly.

FIGURE 39-1   A balance sheet.

BALANCE SHEET
November 30, 2016

Current Assets

Cash on hand and in the bank	$ 4,000	
Merchandise inventory	90,000	
Accounts receivable	6,000	
Total Current Assets		$100,000

Fixed Assets

Real estate—land		18,000
Real estate—building original cost	$64,000	61,000
Less depreciation	3,000	
Furniture, fixtures and equipment—original cost	$12,000	11,400
Less depreciation	600	

Total Assets $190,400

Current Liabilities

Accounts Payable	$32,000	
Notes Payable	16,000	

Total Current Liabilities	$ 48,000
Long-Term Debt	22,000
Capital	120,400
Total Liabilities & Capital	$190,400

FIGURE 39-2   Profit and loss statement.

PROFIT AND LOSS STATEMENT
November 30, 2016

Sales		$200,000
Cost of Sales		140,000
Gross Income		60,000
Selling Expenses	$25,000	
General Expenses	10,000	
Operating Expenses		35,000
Operating Income		25,000
Interest Expense		1,200
Net Income Before Taxes		23,800
Income Taxes		6,600
Net Income		$17,200

A large business has hundreds and even thousands of assets to list; these are classified as current assets, fixed assets, and deferred charges to expenses.

Current assets appear in the form of cash or items that may reasonably be expected to be converted into cash in the near future by the regular operation of the business. This includes stocks, bonds, mutual funds, and other negotiable financial instruments. When listed on the balance sheet, these assets are arranged in the order in which they will be converted. Columns are also provided to show the quantity, description, price, and extensions. When all these sheets are extended and totaled, their sum is entered on the balance sheet as merchandise inventory.

Fixed assets are those of a permanent (or fixed) nature that will not be converted into cash as long as they serve the needs of the business. They are not intended for resale but are expected to wear out in the course of the business. They include store equipment, office equipment, delivery equipment, building, and land.

Deferred charges to expenses are assets purchased for use in the business that will be consumed in the near future—for example, store supplies, office supplies, and prepaid insurance.

The classification commonly used for liabilities is similar to that for assets: current liabilities, fixed liabilities, and deferred credits to income.

Current liabilities are those that will be due within a short time. For example, if John King purchases equipment on account with the agreement that he will pay for it within thirty days, this transaction results in a current liability. A liability is considered to be a current one if it comes due within one year after the balance sheet date. Under this heading are notes payable, accounts payable, and accrued liabilities.

Notes payable are promises given by the proprietor to someone to whom he or she owes money. The proprietor may give these to a creditor from whom he or she has purchased equipment or merchandise, or to a bank when borrowing money. *Accounts payable* are the financial obligations of a business, usually arising from a purchase on account, when the buyer has given his or her promise to pay at some future time for the goods received. *Accrued liabilities* are amounts owed to the government on taxes, to employees on wages, or to creditors on interest. If one of these is unusually high, it may be set up singly under some designation such as "taxes payable," "wages payable," and so forth.

Fixed liabilities are those that will not be due for a comparatively long time after they are contracted. They usually arise in the purchase of fixed assets and include liabilities that will not be liquidated within one year from the date of the balance sheet—for example, mortgages payable or bonds payable.

A *mortgage payable* represents a debt owed by a business for which the creditor possesses a mortgage on a particular asset. *Bonds payable* are long-term obligations of corporations commonly evidenced by bonds without referencing a particular asset.

Deferred credits to income are the unearned portion of a payment when a business is paid in advance for a service. For example, an insurance company receives in one fiscal period a payment for insurance that extends over a future fiscal period. The unearned portion of the premium is a deferred credit to income and would usually be listed as unearned premium income.

The Balance Sheet

Usually the purpose of any business is to increase its proprietorship—that is, to make money. The amount of profit or loss incurred during a given period is the most important single fact.

A *balance sheet* (Figure 39-1) shows the proprietor the amount of his or her proprietorship to help determine whether the proprietorship is increasing or decreasing; it does not, however, show the cause of the increase or decrease.

The Income Statement

At various intervals, the proprietor has to plan to increase profit and eliminate future losses. For this, a report is needed to show the amount of sales, the cost of procuring and selling the goods that are sold, and the difference between the two, which is the profit or loss. The *income statement* (Figure 39-2) gives such information, as well as the gross profit on sales, operating expenses, and depreciation. The period it covers is known as the *fiscal period*.

Income Statement Terms

There are a variety of important terms included on an income statement that need some explanation.

- *Sales*—The gross return from operations. Different businesses use different terms for their sales, depending on whether the business sells commodities or services. For example, sales in a mercantile business are the total amount of money customers have paid or agreed to pay for merchandise sold to them. Airlines have passenger revenue or freight revenue, whereas professional men and women have fees. Investment trusts have interest income and dividend income.

- *Cost of goods sold*—The purchase price paid by a business for the goods it has sold, as distinguished from the sales price. Cost of goods sold is made up of (1) the price charged by the seller as shown on the invoice of sale, and (2) the shipping and handling charged for the delivery of the goods.

- *Gross profit on sales*—Derived by subtracting the cost of merchandise sold from the total sales, representing the profit that would be made if no expenses were incurred in conducting the business. Because expenses are always incurred, they must be considered in determining profit. The expenses of operating the business must be deducted to obtain the net profit.

- *Operating expenses*—Includes all commodities and services expended in the operation of a business: services of personnel, paper, electricity, fuel, postage, and so forth.

- *Depreciation*—The cost arising from the decrease in value of the fixed assets. Not only are supplies and services used to operate a business, but fixed assets, such as office equipment and store equipment, are gradually worn out through use.

The income statement shows the result of the operations of a specific business during a particular period of time. It lists the income from sales and subtracts from this the expenses of the business in making such sales. The last figure is the net profit from operations.

The Account

Each time a business performs a transaction, a change is made in one or more elements of the equation "assets equal liabilities plus proprietorship." Regardless of the number of transactions, the results of all changes must be ascertained in order to prepare an accurate balance sheet and an accurate income statement at the end of the fiscal period. To accomplish this, each transaction must be recorded as it occurs. The *account* is the method used to record these individual transactions, and it is from this word that the subject of accounting receives its name.

The Account Record

The account is the record of each item entered on the balance sheet and on the income statement—that is, the increases and decreases that occur. In its simplest form, the account provides (1) the name of the customer, (2) transactions decreasing the amount of proprietorship, and (3) transactions increasing the amount of the same item.

Trial Balance

If the bookkeeper has correctly recorded each transaction, the total of all the debits in all the accounts will equal the total of the credits in all the accounts. A test is made at intervals, usually at the end of the month, to check whether the debits do equal the credits; this test, known as a *trial balance*, summarizes the ledger information. If the sum of the debits does not equal the sum of the credits, an error has been made, and then the bookkeeper has the job of reconciling.

Mixed Accounts

If all transactions recorded in the accounts coincide with the accounting period as shown on the balance sheet and the income statement, the trial balance is a satisfactory check. But it is impossible to arrange transactions so that there will be no carry-overs between accounting periods. A means must therefore be provided to meet this condition; this is called a mixed account—an account with a balance that is partly a balance sheet amount and partly an income statement amount.

For example, the trial balance amount for the account called Office Supplies summarizes all office supplies purchased plus those on hand at the beginning of the period covered. To find out how many office supplies have been used during the accounting period, an inventory of office supplies is taken. The office supplies on hand are a balance sheet entry; the office supplies used are an income statement entry. Therefore, the account Office Supplies is a mixed account.

The adjustment of mixed accounts must determine the correct balance sheet amount and the correct income statement amount for any trial balance entry that is mixed. For example, a typewriter is recorded as an asset at the time of purchase and appears in the trial balance. The depreciation of the typewriter is not recorded each day and must, instead, be recorded by an adjustment at the end of the accounting period.

Other types of business operations continually affect accounts—for example, as insurance expires and wages and salaries accrue. It's necessary to record all such mixed accounts. A purchase of office supplies is debited to the asset account Office Supplies, or it can be debited to the expense account Office Supplies Used. By means of an account for Office Supplies Used or Expired Insurance, the adjustment can be made. This is an asset adjustment. A liability adjustment is made similarly.

Adjusted Trial Balance

The *trial balance* summarizes only transactions during the accounting period. Insurance has expired, supplies have been used in operating the business, office and other salaries

Bookkeeping \ Accounting

FIGURE 39-3 Sample payroll form.

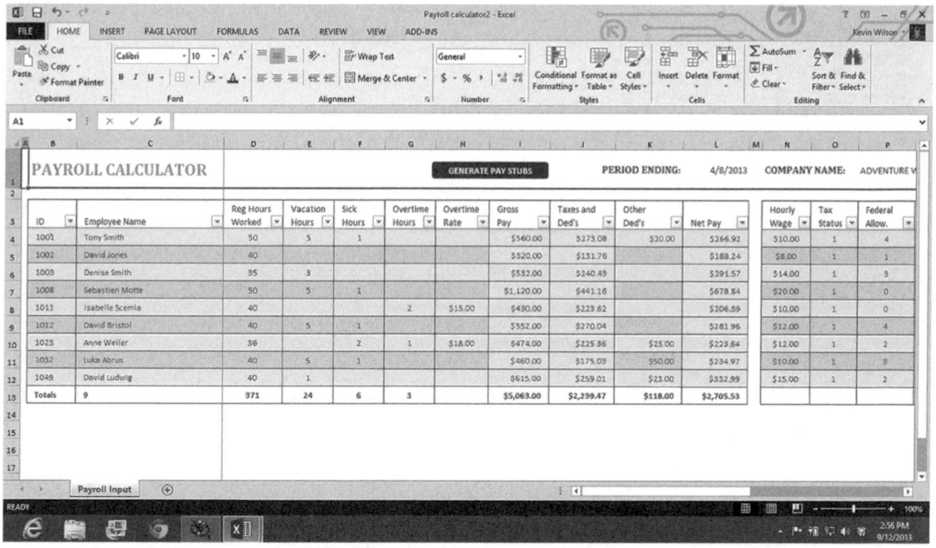

PAYROLL CALCULATOR — GENERATE PAY STUBS — PERIOD ENDING: 4/8/2013 — COMPANY NAME: ADVENTURE W

ID	Employee Name	Reg Hours Worked	Vacation Hours	Sick Hours	Overtime Hours	Overtime Rate	Gross Pay	Taxes and Ded's	Other Ded's	Net Pay	Hourly Wage	Tax Status	Federal Allow.
1001	Tony Smith	50	5	1			$560.00	$273.08	$20.00	$266.92	$10.00	1	4
1002	David Jones	40					$320.00	$131.76		$188.24	$8.00	1	1
1003	Denise Smith	35	3				$532.00	$240.43		$291.57	$14.00	1	3
1008	Sebastien Motte	50	5	1			$1,120.00	$441.16		$678.84	$20.00	1	0
1011	Isabelle Scemla	40			2	$15.00	$430.00	$223.62		$206.39	$10.00	1	0
1012	David Bristol	40	5	1			$552.00	$270.04		$281.96	$12.00	1	4
1025	Anne Weiler	36		2	1	$18.00	$474.00	$225.36	$25.00	$223.64	$12.00	1	2
1032	Luka Abrus	40	5	1			$460.00	$175.03	$50.00	$234.97	$10.00	1	3
1049	David Ludwig	40	1				$615.00	$259.01	$23.00	$332.99	$15.00	1	2
Totals	9	371	24	6	3		$5,063.00	$2,239.47	$118.00	$2,705.53			

Screen shot used with permission from Microsoft.

are incomplete, and equipment has depreciated. The adjustments must be combined with trial balance amounts by means of an adjusted trial balance.

Payroll

A good bookkeeping system must provide accurate information concerning the *payroll* (Figure 39-3). Because of Social Security laws, income-tax–withholding laws, and other state and federal regulations, any and all of this information must be instantly available. Therefore, an individual payroll record book should be maintained. The following information is needed for accurate and complete payroll accounting:

- Name of employee, with address and personal data
- Social Security number
- Company number (if any)
- Department number (if any)
- Date employment began and ended (and reason for separation)
- Dates worked, rate of pay, hours per day worked, regular and overtime status
- Regular salaries paid if not on hourly basis
- Deductions (federal withholding tax, Social Security taxes, state and local taxes, medical insurance premiums, union dues, retirement plan contributions, etc.)
- Totals by month, quarter, and year

Travel and Entertainment and Auto-Expense Records

If your boss travels as part of the job, he or she may ask your help in maintaining a record of travel and entertainment expenses. If the boss uses his or her personal vehicle for business travel, you'll need to maintain a vehicle expense record as well. The IRS requires detailed records with documentary evidence for each, especially for expenses over the "standard amounts" it specifies. Such records should be accurate.

Travel and Entertainment Expenses

Records for all travel and entertainment expenses should show:

- Expenditure amount
- Date of departure and date of return for every trip
- Number of days spent on business versus days spent on pleasure
- Business purpose of the expenditure
- Place of travel or place of entertainment (if clients were entertained)
- Relationship to the business of the person or persons being entertained by the taxpayer

Evidence for these expenses is required, such as credit card charge copies and receipts of all bills paid for lodging and meals while traveling. In addition, travel expense report forms are useful to keep track of out-of-pocket expenses, such as tolls, taxies, tips, and telephone calls. These forms are obtainable from any office supply store.

Figures 39-4 and 39-5 show samples of expense report forms that can be created using the Task Wizard in Microsoft Excel.

Automobile Expenses

Anyone who uses a personal automobile for business purposes (other than commuting) is entitled to deduct such expenses on his or her income tax return, according to IRS

Bookkeeping \ Accounting

FIGURE 39-4   Sample travel expense record.

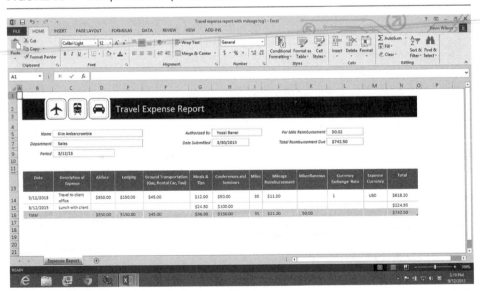

Screen shot used with permission from Microsoft.

FIGURE 39-5   Sample expense report.

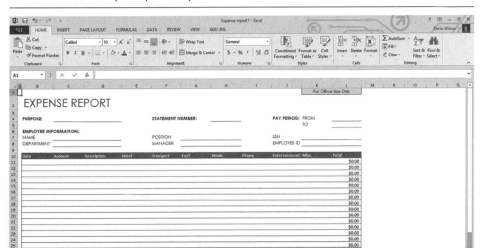

Screen shot used with permission from Microsoft.

rules. If the personal vehicle is used entirely for business, all expenses can be deducted; if the vehicle has both business and personal use, its expenses may be deducted in part. A printed form, Record of Automobile Expenses, is obtainable in most office supply stores. So is a pocket-size booklet that can be handily kept in a briefcase or automobile glove compartment.

You can also use a Smart Phone to record automobile mileage and expenses. A sample of an automobile expense record that can be created using one of the Task Wizards available in Microsoft Excel is available in Figure 39-6.

If the boss does not want to keep detailed records of automobile expenses, an optional deduction method is allowed. Instead of deducting a vehicle's actual fixed and operating expenses with a separate deduction for depreciation (for an individual), the boss could deduct a standard mileage rate for annual business miles traveled. State and local taxes (not including gasoline tax) and interest payments on loans to purchase business vehicles are deductible as well.

These laws change frequently, and it would be wise for you or your employer to secure up-to-date IRS booklets for rules on required record maintenance and reporting to make sure you're keeping adequate records. But even with these booklets, your employer should also utilize the services of a competent accountant.

Cash Budgets

A *cash budget* is an estimate of expected cash receipts and expenditures. It is necessary for any business, especially a small business where every dime counts. Cash budgets should be prepared six months ahead or, if possible, twelve months ahead with revision as needed.

FIGURE 39-6   Sample automobile expense record in Microsoft Excel.

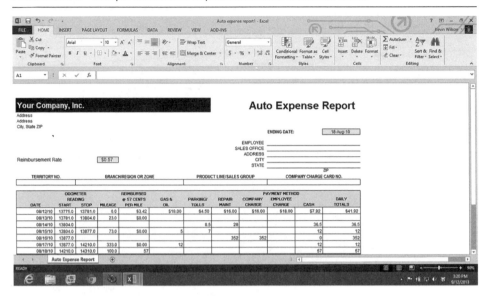

Screen shot used with permission from Microsoft.

FIGURE 39-7   Cash flow statement.

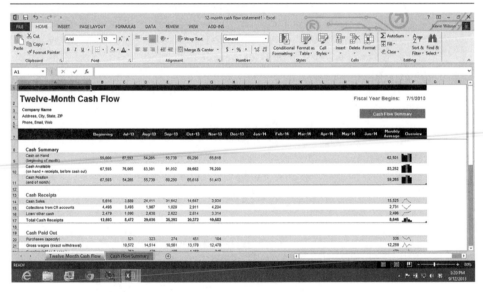

Screen shot used with permission from Microsoft.

When you help your boss develop a cash budget, it must be a realistic estimate. A cash budget is completely useless unless it is based on realistic, sober judgment springing entirely from experience.

Figure 39-7 shows a cash flow statement that can be created using one of the many Task Wizards available in Microsoft Excel software.

Records for Lenders

If your employer is just starting a business, a lender is likely to request a specific list and total estimate of the business's start-up costs. Table 39-1 shows a sample. You might help your employer gather the necessary information.

As with a start-up estimate, a lender is likely also to request an estimate of probable monthly expenses, which when multiplied by twelve will be an estimate of first-year expenses. Table 39-2 shows a suggested form to use.

TABLE 39-1   An Estimate of Start-Up Costs for a Retail Shop

Description	Cost
Inventory	$50,000
Fixtures and equipment	7,000
Decoration	9,000
Legal and professional fees	2,000
Utility deposits	100
Pre-opening promotions	1,800
Cash contingency fund	2,000
Insurance	500
Supplies and equipment	1,500
Security	2,000
Miscellaneous	500
Total	$76,400

TABLE 39-2   An Estimate of Monthly Expenses for a Retail Shop

Description	Cost
Salaries	$2,000
Rental	800
Utilities and telephone	200
Inventory replenishment	4,000
Advertising	100
Supplies and postage	200
Insurance	125
Maintenance	70
Professional fees	100
Delivery expense	250
Interest on loan	80
Subscriptions and dues	40
Miscellaneous	250
Monthly total	$8,215

Bookkeeping \ Accounting

40

Weights and Measures

U.S. Weights and Measures

Tables 40-1 through 40-7 list standard U.S. weights and measurements.

TABLE 40-1 Linear Measure

1 inch	=	0.0083 foot
12 inches (in)	=	1 foot (ft)
3 feet	=	1 yard (yd)
5½ yards	=	1 rod (rd), pole, or perch =16½ ft
40 rods	=	1 furlong (fur) = 220 yds = 660 ft
8 furlongs	=	1 statute mile (mi.) = 1,760 yds = 5,280 ft
3 land miles	=	1 league
5,280 feet	=	1 statute or land mile
6,076.11549 feet	=	1 international nautical mile

TABLE 40-2 Area Measure

144 square inches	=	1 sq ft
9 square feet	=	1 sq yd = 1,296 sq in
30¼ square yards	=	1 sq rd = 272¼ sq ft
160 square rods	=	1 acre = 4,840 sq yds = 43,560 sq ft
640 acres	=	1 square mile
1 mile square	=	1 section (of land)
6 miles square	=	1 township = 36 sections = 36 square miles

TABLE 40-3   Cubic Measure

1,728 cubic inches (cu in)	=	1 cu ft
27 cubic feet	=	1 cu yd

TABLE 40-4   Liquid Measure

1 gill (gi)	=	4 ounces (oz)
4 gills	=	1 pint (pt) = 28.875 cu in
2 pints	=	1 quart (qt) = 57.75 cu in
4 quarts	=	1 gallon (gal) = 231 cu in = 8 pts = 32 gills

TABLE 40-5   Dry Measure

2 pints	=	1 qt = 67.2006 cu in
8 quarts	=	1 peck (pk) = 537.605 cu in = 16 pts
4 pecks	=	1 bushel (bu) = 2,150.42 cu in = 32 qts

TABLE 40-6   Units of Circular Measure

Second (")	=	—
Minute (')	=	60 seconds
Degree (°)	=	60 minutes
Right angle	=	90 degrees
Straight angle	=	180 degrees
Circle	=	360 degrees

TABLE 40-7   Troy Weight

24 grains	=	1 pennyweight (pwt)
20 pennyweights	=	1 ounce troy (oz t) = 480 grains
12 ounces troy	=	1 pound troy (lb t) = 240 pennyweights = 5,760 grains

Weights and Measures

The International System (Metric)

Tables 40-8 through 40-12 list various metric measurements.

TABLE 40-8 Linear Measure (Metric)

10 millimeters (mm)	=	1 centimeter (cm)
10 centimeters	=	1 decimeter (dm) = 100 millimeters
10 decimeters	=	1 meter (m) = 1,000 millimeters
10 meters	=	1 dekameter (dam)
10 dekameters	=	1 hectometer (hm) = 100 meters
10 hectometers	=	1 kilometer (km) = 1,000 meters

TABLE 40-9 Area Measure (Metric)

100 square millimeters (mm²)	=	1 sq centimeter (cm²)
10,000 square centimeters	=	1 sq meter (m²) = 1,000,000 sq millimeters
100 square meters	=	1 are (a)
100 ares	=	1 hectare (ha) = 10,000 sq meters
100 hectares	=	1 sq kilometer (km²) = 1,000,000 sq meters

TABLE 40-10 Volume Measure (Metric)

10 milliliters (ml)	=	1 centiliter (cl)
10 centiliters	=	1 deciliter (dl) = 100 milliliters
10 deciliters	=	1 liter (l) = 1,000 milliliters
10 liters	=	1 dekaliter (dal)
10 dekaliters	=	1 hectoliter (hl) = 100 liters
10 hectoliters	=	1 kiloliter (kl) = 1,000 liters

TABLE 40-11 Cubic Measure (Metric)

1,000 cubic millimeters (mm³)	=	1 cu centimeter (cm³)
1,000 cubic centimeters	=	1 cu decimeter (dm³) = 1,000,000 cu millimeters
1,000 cubic decimeters	=	1 cu meter (m³) = 1 stere = 1,000,000 cu centimeters = 1,000,000,000 cu millimeters

TABLE 40-12   Weight Measure (Metric)

10 milligrams (mg)	=	1 centigram (cg)
10 centigrams	=	1 decigram (dg) = 100 milligrams
10 decigrams	=	1 gram (g) = 1,000 milligrams
10 grams	=	1 dekagram (dag)
10 dekagrams	=	1 hectogram (hg) = 100 grams
10 hectograms	=	1 kilogram (kg) = 1,000 grams
1,000 kilograms	=	1 metric ton (t)

Conversion Table

Table 40-13 can be used to convert various U.S. measurements into metric. In the table, "×" means multiply, "/" means divide, and "#" means the value is exact. All other values are approximate.

TABLE 40-13   Conversion Table

From	To	Formula
acres	hectares	× 0.4047
acres	sq. kilometers	/ 247
acres	sq. meters	× 4047
acres	sq. miles	/ 640
barrels (oil)	cu. meters	/ 6.29
barrels (oil)	gallons (UK)	× 34.97
barrels (oil)	gallons (US)	× 42
barrels (oil)	liters	× 159
centimeters	feet	/ 30.48
centimeters	inches	/ 2.54
centimeters	meters	/ 100
centimeters	millimeters	× 10
cubic cm	cubic inches	× 0.06102
cubic cm	liters	/ 1000
cubic cm	milliliters	× 1
cubic feet	cubic inches	× 1728
cubic feet	cubic meters	× 0.0283
cubic feet	cubic yards	/ 27
cubic feet	gallons (UK)	× 6.229
cubic feet	gallons (US)	× 7.481
cubic feet	liters	× 28.32
cubic inches	cubic cm	× 16.39
cubic inches	liters	× 0.01639

(*continued*)

Weights and Measures

TABLE 40-13   (*continued*)

From	To	Formula
feet	centimeters	× 30.48
feet	meters	× 0.3048
feet	yards	/ 3
fl. ounces (UK)	fl. ounces (US)	× 0.961
fl. ounces (UK)	milliliters	× 28.41
fl. ounces (US)	fl. ounces (UK)	× 1.041
fl. ounces (US)	milliliters	× 29.57
gallons	pints	× 8 #
gallons (UK)	cubic feet	× 0.1605
gallons (UK)	gallons (US)	× 1.2009
gallons (UK)	liters	× 4.54609
gallons (US)	cubic feet	× 0.1337
gallons (US)	gallons (UK)	× 0.8327
gallons (US)	liters	× 3.785
grams	kilograms	/ 1000
grams	ounces	/ 28.35
hectares	acres	× 2.471
hectares	square km	/ 100
hectares	square meters	× 10000
hectares	square miles	/ 259
hectares	square yards	× 11 960
inches	centimeters	× 2.54
inches	feet	/ 12
kilograms	ounces	× 35.3
kilograms	pounds	× 2.2046
kilograms	tonnes	/ 1000
kilograms	tons (UK/long)	/ 1016
kilograms	tons (US/short)	/ 907
kilometers	meters	× 1000
kilometers	miles	× 0.6214
liters	cu. inches	× 61.02
liters	gallons (UK)	× 0.2200
liters	gallons (US)	× 0.2642
liters	pints (UK)	× 1.760
liters	pints (US liquid)	× 2.113
meters	yards	/ 0.9144
meters	centimeters	× 100
miles	kilometers	× 1.609
millimeters	inches	/ 25.4
ounces	grams	× 28.35
pints (UK)	liters	× 0.5683
pints (UK)	pints (US liquid)	× 1.201
pints (US liquid)	liters	× 0.4732
pints (US liquid)	pints (UK)	× 0.8327

From	To	Formula
pounds	kilograms	× 0.4536
pounds	ounces	× 16
square feet	sq. inches	× 144
square feet	sq. meters	× 0.0929
square inches	square cm	× 6.4516
square inches	square feet	/ 144
square km	acres	× 247
square km	hectares	× 100
square km	square miles	× 0.3861
square meters	acres	/ 4047
square meters	hectares	/ 10 000
square meters	square feet	× 10.76
square meters	square yards	× 1.196
square miles	acres	× 640
square miles	hectares	× 259
square miles	square km	× 2.590
square yards	square meters	/ 1.196
tonnes	kilograms	× 1000
tonnes	tons (UK/long)	× 0.9842
tonnes	tons (US/short)	× 1.1023
tons (UK/long)	kilograms	× 1016
tons (UK/long)	tonnes	× 1.016
tons (US/short)	kilograms	× 907.2
tons (US/short)	tonnes	× 0.9072
yards	meters	× 0.9144

41

Business Math

There are a variety of business-related math formulas that may be used by administrative assistants when preparing documents or correspondence. While it is not difficult to calculate these formulas manually, most likely you will use a calculator or spreadsheet such as Microsoft Excel.

In addition to calculations, numerical data in a spreadsheet can be easily converted to attractive graphs and charts for use in your documents and presentations.

Using a Calculator

Calculators are fairly simple to use except when working with negative numbers and more complex formulas involving exponents. Whether you use a physical calculator or a software calculator on your computer, all calculators have four basic operations and each has its own button. The + (plus) button is for addition, while the – (minus) is for subtraction. The × (times) or * (asterisk) is for multiplication, while the ÷ (division sign) or / (slash) is for division.

Simple Arithmetic

To add numbers, enter the first number, then press the + button followed by the second number. Some calculators will automatically add the two numbers at that point; however, some units require that you press the = (equals) button or an ENTER button.

Subtraction works the same way. If you want to subtract one number from another number, enter the number you want to subtract from first, then press the – button.

Multiplication is handled just like addition. To multiply two numbers, enter the first number, then press the × or * button, followed by the second number.

When you want to divide one number by another, enter the number you want to divide, press the ÷ or /, and then enter the number you want to divide by.

For more complex calculations, most calculators also have a memory function that will save the result of your first calculation and allow you to recall it later.

Calculations Involving Negative Numbers

The subtraction symbol (–) is used for operations on a calculator. When working with formulas that involve negative numbers (such as –5), a calculator can get confused if you use the subtraction symbol to designate a negative number. To solve this problem, many calculators have a negative key in addition to the subtraction symbol.

Using a Spreadsheet

Computer spreadsheets like Microsoft Excel allow you to perform calculations on large groups of numbers with relative ease. With a spreadsheet, you can do everything you can with a calculator. For example, you can easily add a column of numbers and create complex formulas with variables in parentheses. You can also copy and paste data and formulas to repeat the same operations over and over without having to rekey the data or the formulas.

Summing a Row or Column of Numbers

There is an automatic feature built into Microsoft Excel 2010 that will allow you to add a row or column of numbers. Just place your cursor in the cell where you want the sum to appear, and then from the Home tab ribbon bar, click AUTOSUM and then press ENTER on your keyboard. If you need to enter a more complex formula, start by adding the command =SUM (, followed by the formula, and then close the parentheses. The following is an example:

$= sum(A1+B2)$

Fractions, Decimals, and Percentages

Fractions, decimals, and percentages are closely related. For example, every fraction can also be written as a percent. To convert from a fraction to a percent, you first must convert the fraction to a decimal. To convert a percent to a fraction, you must first convert the percent to a decimal.

Converting Fractions to Decimals

Converting from a fraction to a decimal is fairly simple. Divide the top number of the fraction by the bottom number. For example:

$¼ = 1 \div 4 = 0.25$

If the result of the division is a repeating decimal, such as 0.3333, you can round the decimal to the nearest decimal point depending on the accuracy desired.

Rounding Decimals

Sometimes when converting a fraction to a decimal, you may end up with a repeating decimal such as .03333 whereby the 3's go on forever. Or, you may not need the accuracy of a decimal that goes beyond one hundredth-thousandth.

You can round off decimals to the nearest tenth, hundred, thousandth, and so forth. The best rule for rounding up or down is based on which method will create a decimal ending in 0, 2, 4, 6, or 8.

Decimal Places

The decimal places to the right of a decimal point can be described according to the following list:

0.1	one tenth
0.01	one hundredth

Business Math

0.001	one thousandth
0.0001	one ten-thousandth
0.00001	one hundred-thousandth
0.000001	one millionth
0.0000001	one ten-millionth
0.00000001	one hundred-millionth

Converting Decimals to Fractions

To convert a decimal into a fraction, use the descriptions above to create a fraction in words, then convert that fraction to numbers. For example, 0.25 is 25 hundredths because it is two places to the right of the decimal. You can then write that as the fraction 25/100. To reduce the fraction to its lowest terms, divide both the top number (numerator) and the bottom number (denominator) by the same number. In this case:

$25 \div 25 = 1$

$100 \div 25 = 4$

So the resulting fraction is ¼.

Percent and Decimals

A percent is a number that describes how much something is compared to 100. A percent is often easier to understand than a fraction, although the two may be equal. For example, ½ and 50% are the same amount.

To change a percent to a decimal, move the decimal point in the percent two places to the left and remove the percent sign. For example:

25% would be 0.25

To change a decimal to a percent, move the decimal point two places to the right and add a percent sign. For example:

0.50 would be 50%

Adding and Subtracting Fractions

You can add or subtract fractions only when they have the same denominator (bottom number). Thus, in order to perform the calculation you must first convert the fractions so they have the same denominator. This is done by converting a fraction to the equivalent multiple. For example, the multiples of ¼ are ⅛, ⁴⁄₁₆, ⁸⁄₃₂, and so on.

When adding or subtracting fractions, once the fractions have been converted so they all share the same denominator, perform the calculation on the numerator (top number) and keep the denominator the same. For example:

⅔ + ½ would be ⁴⁄₆ + ³⁄₆ = ⅞

Converting Whole Numbers to Fractions

Whole numbers like 1, 2, 3, and so forth can be converted to fractions by just placing them over 1 as the denominator. For example:

1 is ⅟₁, 2 is ²⁄₁, and 3 is ³⁄₁

Adding or Subtracting Mixed Numbers

Mixed numbers are whole number/fraction combinations. For example, 1½ is a mixed number.

To add or subtract mixed numbers, first convert the mixed number to a fraction and then follow the normal rules for adding or subtracting fractions. For example:

1½ is the same as 3/2

Multiplying and Dividing Fractions

When multiplying fractions, you do not need to convert the fractions so they have the same denominator. Instead, you can perform the calculation across the top and then across the bottom. For example:

⅔ × ½ = 2/6 or, 2 × 1 = 2, 3 × 2 = 6

When dividing fractions, you convert the problem to a multiplication problem and flip the second fraction. For example:

¾ ÷ ½ is converted into ¾ × 2/1 = 6/4

Graphs and Charts

Graphs and charts can convert tables of numbers into meaningful images that are easy to interpret. The most common types of graphs are scatter plots, line graphs, bar graphs, and pie charts.

The simplest way to create a graph or chart is to use a spreadsheet such as Microsoft Excel. For information on how to create these visual aids, see Chapter 22, Using Microsoft Excel.

Scatter Plot

With a scatter plot, the numbers are represented as dots distributed on a graph with two measurement axes. Scatter plots often involve measurements taken over time. For example, the number of sales per hour or day, the output of machines over time, or the number of defects per day, can all be represented as scatter plots. Figure 41-1 shows a sample scatter plot.

Line Graph

A line graph consists of a series of connected data points that show the number of occurrences over a period of time. The lines in a line graph make it easy to see trends in the data. A line graph has two axes that use different numbering systems, so that two values can be compared. For example, the value of a business over time could be measured using a line graph. One axis would be the value, while the second axes would be time. Figure 41-2 shows a sample line graph.

Bar Graphs

Bar graphs are often called *histograms*. They are used to measure the frequency of different categories of data. For example, a bar graph could be used to show the sales of a group of different products. A bar graph usually has just one axis for the particular thing being measured, while the other axis is for the different categories. A bar graph

FIGURE 41-1   Sample scatter plot.

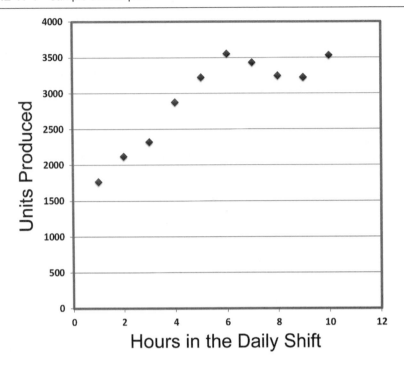

FIGURE 41-2   Sample line graph.

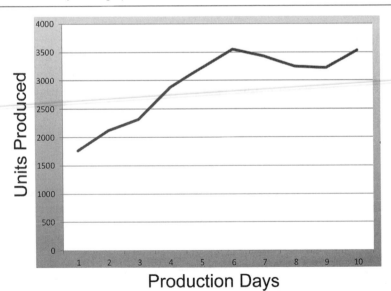

FIGURE 41-3 Sample bar graph.

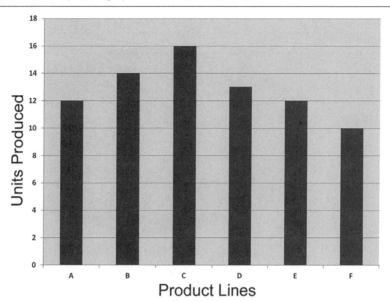

makes it easy to see the relationships between the individual categories being compared. Figure 41-3 shows a sample bar graph.

Pie Charts

Pie charts are used to show how much a particular category is compared to the whole. The whole is represented as a circle and each category is a wedge-shaped piece of the circle. For example, the various products or services offered by a business could be compared using a pie chart to see how much each contributes toward total sales. Figure 41-4 shows a sample pie chart.

Business Calculations

There are a variety of calculations that an administrative assistant may need to perform while preparing business documents. These include simple calculations involving statistics, financial calculations, payroll-related formulas, and measurements.

Averages

The average of a group of numbers is the sum of the numbers divided by the number of numbers that have been added together. For example, the average of 1, 2, 3, 4, 5, 6 is $1 + 2 + 3 + 4 + 5 + 6$ divided by 6.

Simple Interest

The formula for computing simple interest earned on a particular amount of money is as follows: Simple interest equals the principal (the amount of money invested) times

FIGURE 41-4   Sample pie chart.

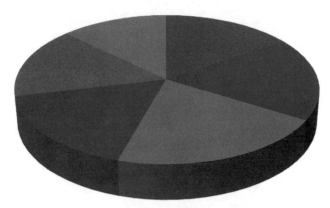

Sales Breakdown By Division

- Eastern Division
- Central Division
- Gulf Coast Division
- Western Division
- Southern Division
- Northern Division

the rate of the interest (written as a decimal), times the amount of time (usually in years if the interest rate is a yearly rate). The formula for this is:

I = Principle × rate × time.

For example, the simple interest earned on $150,000 at 5% is $7500.

150,000 × .05 × 1 = 7,500

Paycheck Calculation

Salaried employees receive a set amount of money each pay period, in addition to the potential for bonuses that may be paid in one particular pay period. To calculate the monthly gross pay before deductions, first determine the number of pay periods in the year. For example, if someone is paid twice a month, that is twenty-four pay periods. Then, divide the total yearly salary amount by the number of pay periods to determine the gross pay per pay period. For example, Joanne earns $50,000 per year at a company with 24 pay periods.

50,000 ÷ 24 = 2083.33

Commissions

Commissions are amounts earned by sales people based on the amount of their sales. Usually, a commission is a percentage of the total amount sold. Thus, to calculate a commission payment for a salesperson, take the amount of the sales and multiply it times the commission percentage, written as a decimal. For example, Laura sold $28,000 this month and earns a 12% commission. Therefore:

$28,000 \times .12 = 3360$

Markup Pricing

For retail stores or stores that resell parts to customers, the cost of the product is marked up by a certain percentage or amount to determine the selling price. The calculation for this is:

Cost + markup in dollars = selling price.

If the markup is a percentage, then calculate the markup by multiplying the cost times the markup percentage expressed as a decimal. For example, a part costs $32 and the markup is 25%:

$32 \times 0.25 = 8$ (the markup in dollars).

thus, the retail price would be $32 + 8 = 40$.

Discount Pricing

Sometimes prices are discounted for special customers or when the business has a sale. To determine the discounted amount, take the retail price and multiply it times the discount percentage expressed as a decimal. Then, subtract the discount amount from the retail price to determine the discount price.

For example, customer A gets a 25% discount on all his purchases. If the customer wants to purchase a product that retails for $64, then the discount is $64 \times 0.25 = 16$ (discounted amount). The discount price would be:

$64 - 16 = 48$.

Profit

A company's *profit* is the amount of money the business has left over after paying for goods or services and other expenses related to running the business. To calculate profit, take the total revenue and subtract the cost. For example, a business earns $125,000 in revenue and has $82,000 in expenses that include salaries, cost of products purchased for resale, and other expenses. Profit would then be:

$125,000 - 82,000 = 41,000$

Area

Area is a measurement of space. The most common area formula is:

Area = length × width.

For example, suppose the area of a piece of land is 200 feet by 100 feet. The area is:

$200 \times 100 = 20,000$ square feet

Acreage

Acreage is calculated similarly to area, with one acre being 41,560 square feet.

Career Advancement

42

Your Future

Growing as the Company Grows

As you begin or continue your career, you have numerous choices regarding type and size of companies. Which is better to work for: a large or a small one? You'll find as many answers as there are administrative assistants. A large company often offers the best available salary and benefits, as well as steady advancement within its corporate structure. Yet small companies, too, offer growth potential. They may not always be able to afford as generous a salary or benefit package, but they often provide a wider range of experience than would otherwise be possible to get. And when a small company successfully expands, the administrative assistant has the excitement of getting in on the ground floor and moving higher as the business grows. In many instances, the small-business administrative assistant can inherit as much responsibility as he or she wants.

Learn About the Business

It's important that no matter what type of business you work for, what size it is, or where it's located, you should do your best to learn as much about it as possible. This learning process should never stop. Even if your duties are strictly defined and fairly routine, you should do your best to discover how the business is managed, how customers or clients are obtained, and how the products or services provided are produced. Although you may see no immediate need for this knowledge, it can be invaluable in a later emergency, as you advance, or if you seek work with a different company.

Upgrade Your Skills

No matter what type or size of company you work for, focus on acquiring essential business skills, whether or not you need any one of them now. Make sure your skills are top-notch in such office-related areas as keyboarding, maintaining a filing system, handling incoming and outgoing mail, setting appointments, answering telephones, taking dictation, and using office machines. Try to acquire proficiency in correspondence, research, customer service, purchasing, budgeting, bookkeeping, invoicing, training new employees, and supervising an office staff. You should learn how to write and speak effectively and be able to plan and organize your work. And finally, you must be computer literate. Having all these skills will give you the most flexible preparation to meet any challenge you face—either an on-the-job crisis or a career opportunity.

As proof of the level of quality of your skills, you may want to investigate being certified by the International Association of Administrative Professionals (formerly the National Secretaries Association) as a Certified Professional Secretary (CPS) or Certified Administrative Professional (CAP). This certification is granted only upon the successful completion of examinations in various aspects of secretarial/administrative procedures and skills. Serious secretaries and administrative assistants may find it worthwhile to inquire about the activities of this outstanding association. Being certified can be a tremendous boost to your career.

Recognizing a Time for Change

One of the trends in modern business is the changing nature of administrative work. Today in businesses of all sizes, more managers are doing work on their own desktop computer systems that in the past would have been handled by a secretary. As these trends continue, there will be fewer and fewer secretaries and more office and information specialists. It's up to you to create a place for yourself in this changing world.

Learning new skills and improving your old ones is the best professional insurance you can acquire, and it can put you in the position of being a better secretary than your current position demands. If you cannot expand your current role but are capable of much more than you're doing, your dissatisfaction may lead you to want to change your direction in life and seek out a new job. Your new skills will help you get the best possible situation.

These skills will also prove invaluable if change is forced upon you. Gone are the days when a secretary might work forty-five years for the same company, many of those years for the same boss. This is true of both large and small companies. A large company used to provide stability, but no longer. Corporate restructurings, which have affected hundreds of thousands of people over the past years, have been a mixed blessing for administrative assistants. In the wake of restructuring, some assistants have to leave their position when their boss leaves, but others are asked to take on greater responsibility, to "take up the slack" as middle managers are phased out. Either situation could be professionally devastating if it was not what the administrative assistant would have chosen himself or herself.

On the other hand, small businesses have their own dangers, particularly in the first eighteen months of operation, though knowing that doesn't make it easier for the secretary who faces possible job loss. Rather than restructure, a small business may just fold completely, perhaps without giving you adequate notice, perhaps even without giving you a final paycheck.

Always be alert to conditions or changes that could affect your job, no matter what size company you work for. In a large company, be wary if your boss is excluded from meetings he or she used to attend, is dropped from routing lists, or is told to cut back on budget and staff. Do people who used to lunch or chat with your boss no longer do so? These warning signs can also signal that your own position might be in jeopardy.

In a small business where you work directly for the owner, pay attention to details. Has business been slipping lately? Is it just a temporary slump or something more serious? Has the boss paid vendors and other creditors, or are you starting to receive dunning letters and telephone calls? Of critical importance to you is whether the boss has paid payroll taxes and health insurance premiums. If your boss has not and the business folds, the Internal Revenue Service will look to the individual worker to pay the overdue taxes even though the money was already withheld from earlier paychecks. You may have no health care coverage even though deductions for premiums may have been taken from your paycheck. And you might not even be able to collect unemployment benefits though taxes for that were deducted, too.

What should you do if something like this should happen? Your best bet is to consult an attorney; however, be advised that though you might file and win a lawsuit against your former employer, collecting your judgment may prove to be difficult and costly.

The better advice is to be aware of the financial health of your employer so you can take action before it's forced on you. These events are the exception, but it's better to be employed and equipped with this knowledge than to experience it unexpectedly when you can least afford it.

Finding a New Job

When, for whatever reason, you feel the need to find a new job, explore all possible ways. Don't simply look in the paper or sign up at an employment agency for a position as a secretary, administrative assistant, or office manager. A more aggressive search can find you a more satisfying position.

Start by researching companies you might want to work for or areas where you might like to work. With newspapers and trade journals in hand, read about companies that were voted "family friendly," or instituted company-wide training programs in computers or second languages, or have a strong policy of promoting from within. One company might be known for its laid-back atmosphere and flexible hours. Another might be known for its hard-driving excellence. Which interests you more? Which do you need more? These are the companies to target.

Locally, drive around office or industrial parks or anywhere else businesses are located. Stop in and talk and ask questions. Find out what the business does and if there are any job openings. These cold-call, in-person visits are not as difficult as they might sound. If you are friendly and don't take up too much time, you can gain much valuable information.

You can also conduct research by looking through directories available in larger public libraries. The Better Business Bureau and the Chamber of Commerce of the town or city you're interested in can give you lists of local businesses. Both organizations are also good sources for checking the reputation of a particular business you may be interested in.

Tap your network of relatives, friends, neighbors, and professional associates for information. That insurance agent who calls, that vendor you talk to so frequently, that secretary you met at an office skills conference—these are just some of the people to tell when you're looking for a new position.

Also check job postings on Internet job sites such as Monster.com and HotJobs.com. You can conduct searches by key word, city, or date. These websites also allow you to post your résumé for perspective employers.

Finally, don't overlook temporary placement services. One benefit is that many agencies provide free training on new equipment and software packages, which can make you more desirable to a prospective employer. A second benefit is that temporary work allows you to experience different companies as an insider; once you find a company you like, apply for full-time work. Yet another benefit is that temporary work allows you maximum flexibility in scheduling your personal time.

Your Résumé

No matter which path you take to look for a new job, you will need a professional-looking résumé, the document describing your work history and skills to a potential employer. There are two basic formats to follow. One focuses on a history of where you've worked (Figure 42-1) and the other on particular skills you have (Figure 42-2). All résumés should include:

- Your name, address, and telephone number
- Your educational background: schools attended; degrees, diplomas, or certificates awarded; special training received or courses attended
- A listing of all previous employment
- Your current job

FIGURE 42-1   Sample résumé in a chronological format.

Evelyn Flo Boyd
12345 Heartside Drive
Western Branch, GA 31234
404-555-1234

Experience

2014–Present   Lyon's Still Photography
                   Acworth, Georgia
                   Office manager and assistant to business owner

                   Maintained files and records, accounts receivable, and
                   customer database. Assisted photographer with photo
                   subjects, as well as sales of proofs and prints. Handled
                   scheduling of business activities, all correspondence, and
                   travel arrangements.

1997–2014   Third Coast Video, Inc.
                   Austin, Texas
                   Office assistant

                   Scheduled clients and facilities for video production and
                   postproduction facility. Scheduled freelance crews and
                   equipment rentals. Arranged for shipping of equipment and
                   travel for crews. Also handled invoicing and correspondence.

Education

1993–1997   B.A., English
                   University of Texas
                   Austin, Texas

FIGURE 42-2   Sample résumé in a skills format.

Evelyn Flo Boyd
12345 Heartside Drive
Western Branch, GA 31234
404-555-1234

Experience

ADMINISTRATION—Maintained files and records, accounts receivable, and customer database. Handled scheduling of business activities, all correspondence, and travel arrangements.

SALES—Worked with customers to set appointments and to sell photography services.

VIDEO PRODUCTION—Coordinated scheduling of crews and facilities. Hired freelance crews and outline equipment rentals.

TECHNICAL SKILLS—Complete understanding of IBM-compatible software including: Windows, Word for Windows, Excel, and WordPerfect. Also, some understanding of Apple Macintosh computers including Microsoft Word and Excel. Good typing skills (50 wpm). Working knowledge of most office equipment, copiers, fax machines, and typewriters.

Work History

2014–Present
Office Manager and Assistant to Business Owner
Lyon's Still Photography
Acworth, Georgia

1997–2014
Office Assistant
Third Coast Video, Inc.
Austin, Texas

Education

1993–1997 B.A., English
University of Texas
Austin, Texas

One mistake many people make on a résumé is attempting to explain why they left one job and moved on to another. This is not the place to discuss it. You may be asked this question in an interview, so be prepared with an answer, but don't volunteer it in your résumé.

It can be very useful to prepare several versions of a résumé, adapting the basic facts to emphasize the different skills required for different jobs. Suppose the administrative assistant were applying for a position in a sales department. She might want to rewrite the skills-format version of her résumé, putting her sales experience as the first item and enlarging upon it wherever possible. Did she work with sales representatives? Did she handle objections or close calls herself? Did she find new prospects for the salespeople? Emphasizing this side of her experience could make her more attractive to the interviewer.

This in no way means you should make up qualifications. If you do, it could prove disastrous if you are called on to perform a task you claim to be experienced at doing.

The Cover Letter

Along with your résumé, you should also include an application or cover letter that states your interest in a particular job, briefly lists your qualifications, and explains why you might like to work for this particular employer (Figure 42-3). When you apply for a job online, include the cover letter as an email and attach the resume to the message.

The Interview

If your résumé and letter are successful, your next step will be an interview with the prospective employer. There are several ways you can prepare for it and techniques you can use for conducting yourself during it:

- Examine your image. How do you look to the outside world? Consider the way you dress, the way you talk, even the way you stand. Can you talk to someone and look that person in the eye, rather than glance around or stare at your feet?

- How about your skills? Can you do anything that someone would want to hire you to do?

- What about experience? Have you ever practiced these skills in an employment situation?

- How much money do you want? What are employers in your area willing to pay for your skills? Find this out before you go to the interview by asking people and checking resources at the library, Chamber of Commerce, or Better Business Bureau.

- What do you know about the company where you're going to interview? How does it make money? What does its success depend on?

If you can find out this information, you'll be prepared to show how you can help make the business better. And that's what an employer wants to hear.

FIGURE 42-3   Job application cover letter.

12345 Heartside Drive
Western Branch, GA 31234
December 2, 2015

Mr. Kevin Wilson
President
Videologies, Inc.
10 North Main St.
Atlanta, GA 30303

Dear Mr. Wilson,

I am very interested in applying for the job of office assistant listed in the *Atlanta Constitution* on December 1.

As you can see from my enclosed résumé, I have worked for both a still photographer and a small video production company. I enjoyed working at both of these companies, and I feel this past experience qualifies me for the position described in your advertisement.

I have a good understanding of the visual medium and the many details you must handle in your work. I believe I can help take responsibility for some of these details with little additional training.

I would appreciate the opportunity for a personal interview. You can reach me at 555-1234.

Thank you for your consideration.

Sincerely yours,

Evelyn Boyd

43

Presentation Skills

Why Make Presentations?

As you grow in your career, one way to demonstrate your knowledge and abilities is by making presentations. Perhaps you won't be making presentations at a board of directors meeting, but there will be opportunities to make presentations to your coworkers. For example, your boss may ask you to present a new company policy, or you volunteer to host a lunch-and-learn where you share some of your knowledge in the form of a presentation. You might make presentations on behalf of your boss at regular company meetings.

A formal presentation is a planned event where one or more people speak, visual aids such as PowerPoint or handouts are used, and the purpose is to pass along information that will be useful to the audience.

One key aspect in making a presentation is that it involves public speaking. Many people rate public speaking as their number-one fear. Essentially, they are afraid the audience won't accept them; however, this is not true. The audience wants the speaker to succeed. They're glad you are the one speaking and not them. All you need to do in order to be a successful presenter is be prepared, confident, and relaxed. Good preparation will calm your nerves and help you avoid making mistakes.

Good Preparation

Whenever you are faced with giving a presentation, you should start by focusing on the purpose. Ask yourself: Why am I speaking? What do I want to achieve? What should the audience get from the presentation? What are their needs and expectations? What will be their attitude toward my ideas? What do they already know? Do they need to hear the presentation in a particular order?

Good presenting is about entertaining as well as conveying information. Your audience will remember more if they enjoy themselves.

You'll have approximately ten to fifteen seconds at the start of your presentation to make a positive first impression, so make sure your opening is strong and well rehearsed. Don't start with a joke, since jokes are risky. And, if something goes wrong, don't apologize for anything.

The average attention span of your audience is only about five to eight minutes, so you'll need to spice up your material to help keep your audience interested. For example, you might include stories, questions, pictures, cartoons, video clips, sound clips, graphs, audience participation, quotes, and props.

Structure

No matter how interesting your material is, your audience will have a difficult time following your presentation if it is carelessly assembled. The structure of your presentation should be simple, clear, and logical.

Start by breaking your main topic into three to five ideas. Then, present each idea along with supporting materials and evidence. Make sure you cite any sources for your data. Some common presentations structures include:

- Problem and solution
- Comparisons
- Chronological order
- Theory and practice
- Desire and action

If your presentation will be longer than forty-five minutes, you'll need to plan on giving your audience a break. You need to let everyone get up and stretch their legs, otherwise they'll fade out on you regardless of how engaging your presentation is. After ninety minutes, you'll need to schedule a break to allow your audience to use the restrooms.

One thing you can do to take the pressure off yourself is to not talk the entire time. Plan your presentation to include audience participation. Have the audience work together to communicate and solve problems.

Starting and Ending Your Presentation

Before you begin your presentation, you will have gathered some ideas about who your audience is and how they will receive your message. As you begin speaking, your audience will be deciding whether you are worth listening to. Are you interesting? Are you energetic, enthusiastic, and sincere?

The first words out of your mouth must get your audience's attention. You must entice them to listen to you. There are several suggestions for how to start your presentation, including the following:

- Ask the audience a question.
- Quote from someone famous.
- Tell a story.
- Provide some historical background.
- Talk about a current issue in the news.
- Shock your audience with statistics, announcements, and warnings.

Whatever you decide to do, the opening must naturally lead into the body of your presentation. In addition to getting your audience's attention, your introduction should

Presentation Skills

also provide a statement about the purpose of your presentation. You should include an agenda of topics that will be covered.

To conclude your presentation, you should give your audience something they can take with them by summarizing key points, calling for action, asking a question, telling another story, or using a prop or visual aid.

Visual Aids

Visual aids improve the retention of the spoken word by up to 70 percent. Therefore, if you can include printed visual aids (such as handouts) or a projected PowerPoint presentation, you will improve your audience's memory.

When creating PowerPoint presentations, follow these guidelines:

- Keep your slides uncluttered and simple.
- Don't have more than five words to a line.
- Don't have more than seven lines per slide.
- Don't overuse PowerPoint animations and sound effects.
- Use a readable serif font, such as Times, for your headlines.
- Use 14- to 16-point fonts for headlines.
- Use sans serif fonts for your body text. Arial is a popular sans serif font.
- Use no more than two different fonts on each slide.
- Use no more than two size/bold/italic combinations.
- Use 12- to 14-point fonts for body text.
- Avoid all uppercase (capital letters) for the body text.
- All uppercase is okay for headings.

In addition to PowerPoint presentations, your visual aids can include overhead transparencies, flip charts, photographs, illustrations, maps, graphs, and diagrams.

Handouts

Handouts can also be useful in reinforcing the concepts of your presentation. You can use handouts to provide background material or additional reading material. You can distribute handouts before your presentation or make them available afterward. Handouts should be simple and directly related to the presentation.

For many business presentations that use PowerPoint slides, a copy of the slides is printed in handouts view, with two or three slides per printed page. This gives the audience a place to take notes. One key thing to watch for with handouts is distracting your audience. If you want the audience to pay attention to you rather than having their noses buried in your handouts, distribute the handouts when you are finished.

Solid Delivery

There are several ways you can deliver your presentation. For example, you can read your notes, memorize your speech, or speak extemporaneously. Free-flowing or extemporaneous speaking is usually the most effective style of delivery, since you will be able to connect with your audience, make eye contact, and be sincere. While it is unnecessary to write out the entire script of your presentation, many presenters prefer doing so. The process of writing helps them remember the presentation later. If you must, you can use cue cards to help jog your memory with key bullet points.

Always rehearse your presentation. Never go into an important presentation without giving yourself time to practice. Some people practice while driving to work. Others practice at home in front of a mirror. The more you practice, the more effective you'll be. As you refine your delivery, you'll be able to focus on body language, movement, use of hands, and eye contact. You'll also be more comfortable using your visual aids.

Always check the room where you'll be delivering your presentation. Give yourself enough time to rearrange the room if necessary. Try to get comfortable in the room before anyone else arrives.

While it is natural to feel nervous before a presentation, your job as a presenter is to harness that anxiety and use it to energize your presentation. Without this energy, your presentation can be lifeless.

You can control your nervousness by rehearsing, visualizing a successful presentation, and using positive thinking. Yogic breathing techniques are also helpful. By exhaling completely and holding your diaphragm tightly, you can squeeze out the nervousness. Deep breathing also helps.

As you begin delivering your presentation, speak naturally and loudly enough so you can be heard. Enunciate clearly and vary the pitch and the pace.

Pausing between thoughts is sometimes as important as the thoughts themselves. It gives the audience time to digest what you've just said.

Be aware of your body language, since the way you use your body enhances or weakens your message. Use your hands, your posture, and facial expressions to emphasize your message. Audiences are generally impressed by enthusiasm, energy, and sincerity. Your audience will see you this way if you stand tall, smile, act confident, keep eye contact, gesture when appropriate, and look as if you are enjoying yourself.

For most presentations, people will want to ask questions; therefore, it is important that you anticipate the kind of questions you'll get and be prepared to answer them. One good way to manage your presentation is to hold audience questions until the end of the presentation. In many cases, a question someone asks at the beginning is covered later in the presentation itself.

As your audience asks questions, listen carefully and make sure you understand the question. It's a good idea to rephrase the question in your own words, so that everyone can hear it and to confirm that you understood the question correctly. Your answer should be concise and refer to any visuals or slides in your presentation.

If a person asks a long and rambling question, paraphrase only part of it and give it a short answer. Usually, this will satisfy the person.

If people in your audience begin to talk among themselves, stop and look at them. You don't have to say anything, just look at them. They'll soon get the point. This technique can work with an entire unsettled audience, too.

Don't be defensive when answering questions. Keep your body language open and be as pleasant as possible. Don't make up an answer. If you don't know the answer, be honest and tell your questioner you'll follow up with an answer later. Don't get into arguments with an individual in the audience. And, if you need time to think about a question, take your time and pause.

Don't end your presentation with a "thank you." Your audience should be thanking you; you shouldn't be thanking them. The same goes for "any questions" or "that's it."

Presentation Skills

If you plan time for taking questions, always have a final presentation summary ready that truly concludes your presentation. Inspire your audience. Energize them to follow your ideas and take action. End with a statement or a question that summarizes your presentation in one sentence. If there's only one thing your audience should do or re-members when you are finished, now is the time to make sure you communicate it.

Group Presentations

Sometimes business presentations are made by teams. The same principles apply whether you are delivering a presentation alone or in a group; however, you need to pay attention to the roles of the team members, plan the transitions between individual team member speeches, and provide each other with support and feedback.

Make an assessment of the team's strengths and weaknesses with regard to speaking skills. The strongest speakers should introduce and close the presentation.

The first speaker should introduce the group and try to capture the attention of the attendees, motivate them, and give them a preview of the main ideas that will be covered in the presentation. The last speaker needs to summarize the presentation so that the key concepts are reinforced from a different perspective.

The transitions between speakers that occur in group presentations can sometimes be problems because the speakers are working on their speeches by themselves. Some attention needs to be given to the entire presentation as a whole and how each person contributes to the common purpose. Therefore, each person adds value to the group. So, rather than just announcing the next person to talk, you can introduce the important concepts the next speaker will cover.

While other members of the team are speaking, make sure you support the speaker. Don't fiddle with your notes or look off into space. Keep your attention on the speaker. If anyone in the audience looks at you, he or she should see that all your attention is focused intently on what the current speaker is saying.

After you finish your group presentation, spend some time reviewing what happened and learn how to make improvements in the future. Did you achieve your objective? Were your visual aids effective? Did the schedule and transitions work out OK? Did anything unexpected happen? What could you do differently next time?

The team members in a group presentation should coach each other throughout the process, from researching and writing to rehearsing and refinement. Then, when you've completed your presentation, you work together as a team of coaches, providing positive and constructive feedback as well as congratulations. By having everyone involved and contributing, a successful group presentation can be a very rewarding work experience.

44

Communications Skills

Good communications skills are critical to your success in business. You have to be able to communicate your ideas as well as respond to ideas from others. You have to be able to respond to questions, handle conflict, and listen.

Communication starts when two or more people need to exchange information. Perhaps one of your coworkers wants to ask you a question. Perhaps you want to ask your boss something. Perhaps you want someone to do something for you. Each of these situations involves communication.

Talking is not the same thing as communicating. Communicating is more complicated; it often involves listening and speaking skillfully as you interact with people who are fearful, angry, or frustrated. Miscommunication occurs when we fail to communicate clearly. Many times it is the cause of the conflict in the first place.

Giving Feedback

Feedback means giving information back to someone. When we think about feedback, most of us think of it as an opportunity to give someone our opinion about something he or she did. But the main purpose of the feedback is to make the situation better next time.

When you offer feedback in business, think about the following:

- Be clear about what you want to say to the person.

- Focus on the positive rather than the negative aspects of the performance.

- Be specific and use people's names and project names rather than pronouns like *him, her, it, that*, and *them*.

- Focus on the behavior, not the person.

- Explain what should be changed about the behavior.

- Be descriptive about the change you desire, rather than evaluating the behavior as good or bad.

- Give your own feedback, not someone else's.

- Avoid generalization words like *always, never*, or *all*.

Listening Well

Only about 25 percent of listeners grasp the ideas being communicated. To be a more effective listener, mentally summarize what a speaker is saying. Listen between the lines to the tone of the person's voice. Weigh any evidence the person provides in stating his or her position. As you listen, think about what's in the message for you. How can you benefit from what the speaker is saying? Fight distractions and concentrate on the person and the message. Avoid judging speakers until they have finished offering all the evidence that supports their position.

Don't get distracted by a speaker's poor communications habits. Skip over the delivery errors and focus on the message. Look for central ideas that are the main point of the conversation. Try to keep eye contact with the speaker and help the speaker along by showing an active body posture. Good listeners listen with their faces as well as their ears.

To help remember what was said, take notes during the talk or immediately after the speaker has finished.

Nonverbal Communications

Nonverbal communications include facial expressions, tone of voice, speaking style, gestures, eye contact, posture, touch, and movement. In the case of nonverbal communications, it's not what you say; it's how you say it. Nonverbal messages are an essential part of the communications process.

Your awareness of nonverbal behavior will allow you to better understand what a speaker really means. You'll become a better communicator yourself if you learn how to use nonverbal signals that reinforce your point.

Some of the major nonverbal communication behaviors are:

- Eye contact
- Facial expressions
- Gestures made with the arms and hands
- Posture
- Body position in relationship to the listener
- Closeness between the speaker and listener
- Paralinguistics

Eye contact is an important aspect of interpersonal communication because it helps regulate communication. It's like saying "uh-huh" on the telephone, which acknowledges that the listener is still there and tuned in. Eye contact shows you are interested in the speaker. Eye contact by a speaker helps increase the speaker's credibility and shows interest, concern, warmth, and credibility.

Perhaps the most powerful facial expression is the smile. Smiling shows happiness, friendliness, and warmth. If you want to come across as likable and approachable, smile when you speak or listen.

If you don't use your hands while speaking, you come across as boring and stiff. The use of gestures animates your communication as a speaker, capturing your listener's attention and making the material more interesting. As a listener, you can nod your head to indicate that you are listening.

The way you walk, stand, or sit also communicates information about yourself. Standing tall and leaning slightly forward indicates that you are approachable, receptive, and friendly.

Cultural norms dictate maintaining a certain distance between communicators. You should look for signs of discomfort from others, including rocking, leg swimming, finger tapping, and averting one's gaze. Typically, in a group meeting, being too close is not an issue. In fact, there is usually too much distance. To counteract this, arrange your meeting rooms so presenters can interact with their audience and make eye contact with everyone in the group.

Paralinguistics is an aspect of nonverbal communication that involves the tone, pitch, and rhythm of your voice. The idea is to avoid speaking in a monotone and being boring. Good communicators learn to modulate their voices, use pauses, vary the pitch, raise and lower the loudness, and use inflection as additional communications tools.

Customer Service

Because an administrative assistant may often be a point of contact with the customers of a business, it is important that the customers have a great customer experience whenever they speak with an administrative assistant, whether on the phone or in person.

The word *customers* also applies to people within your own organization with whom you have interactions. They may request information, leave messages, or ask for your assistance. It is important that you treat every interaction as an opportunity to deliver exceptional customer service.

Delivering good customer service is everyone's job. Good customer service means satisfying the customers and fulfilling their needs. The key to understanding what that signifies is to think about your interaction from the customer's point of view. Is the person having a great customer experience? Customer experience is how customers feel about the interaction they have with you. It is an emotional feeling. It goes beyond just meeting customers' expectations to exceeding their expectations and wowing them.

Think about the times you've had a great customer experience. They were probably situations where you got something more than you expected. And it usually came not from the product or service itself but from the people who you interacted with as part of doing business. You remember those places where you had a great customer experience and you tend to want to shop there or eat there again.

So in your own work, you goal should be to create that emotional experience with all of your customers. Whether it is on the telephone, in a meeting, or via email, there are countless opportunities to practice good customer service every day.

Customer Services as a Value Proposition

There are many different ways to develop a relationship with your customers, but the most important is to hear them, see them, to learn about them, and to be able to respond to them in a way that makes them feel that you know who they are and what they are trying to achieve.

One popular term used in business today is *value proposition*. A value proposition is the value a company offers its customers in exchange for their time and money. That value consists of three things: product, process, and price. Some organizations make their products the biggest piece of the pie. Think about Nike shoes or Apple computers or Bentley cars. Other organizations don't have products. Instead, they offer a process, as does a bank, airline, or hotel. A third group focuses on price as their value proposition. Walmart is a good example of a business that offers value to customers based on price.

Those businesses that focus on a process or service put the biggest emphasis on customer service. Two examples of businesses that are famous for their customer service are Starbucks and Disney.

Regardless of the value proposition a business relies on to be competitive, customers demand that service be the biggest part of the pie; that is the way the business tries to ensure customer loyalty. A mega-store like Walmart may attract customers based on price, but it takes friendly employees to keep customers coming back. The same is true for Southwest Airlines. In order for the airline to save money, customers don't get assigned seats; they board based on when they checked in, choosing their seats at that time.

Today, customers assume they are getting a good product at a fair price. Companies that have poor products or high prices don't survive very long. With that in mind, customers now look at their customer experience as one of the key reasons they choose to do business with one company over another. The customer's standards for service are rising, too. With email, the Web, and overnight delivery, customers now expect instant results. They don't want to wait. Administrative assistants should keep this in mind when responding to requests from customers on behalf of their managers.

Likewise, customers cannot tolerate a one-size-fits-all process any longer. In order to know the specific needs of their customers, many organizations maintain customer profiles in computer databases. If your organization keeps such records, make sure you have access to it. Otherwise, you should keep your own database in order to learn about the customers with whom you have interactions, so that you'll better be able to respond to their needs again in the future.

High service standards from companies like Disney, FedEx, and Amazon influence customer expectations for all other companies. If Amazon can get a purchase to you tomorrow, why can't you send something from your business just as quickly? If FedEx can answer the phone on two rings, why can't you? And if USAA Insurance Company knows everything about your case regardless of who you talk to, why can't you respond the same way?

Similarly, whether or not you have personal contact with the company's customers, you still have customers. One way or another, every action you take on the job has some impact on the folks who contribute the money to pay the bills. The best way to have customer service on the outside is to have great employee service on the inside. The way you serve your business associates who interact with customers affects how effectively they serve their customers. Everyone in your organization is either directly serving a customer or serving someone who does. Therefore, great customer service is everyone's job.

Customer Service Fundamentals

Many companies survey their customers to get their opinions on things like customer service. One of the factors that comes up frequently in these surveys is the need for *consistency*. Also, the number-one attribute that customers value in the service they receive is *reliability*—an organization's providing what was promised, in a dependable, consistent, and accurate manner. Customers expect that the experience they receive at one operating location will be similar to other operating locations for the same business. Therefore, the customer service you provide can have a ripple effect across the entire company.

Here are some specific actions and behaviors that you can use to help provide great customer service:

- *Use the customer's name.* Whenever you have contact with a customer, make sure you get the person's name; write it down in order to remember it, and use it when addressing the individual.

- *Be pleasant.* When meeting with customers in person, proactively address them and welcome them. Offer an energetic and genuine greeting, make eye contact, and wear a smile or pleasant expression.

- *Be trustworthy.* Whenever you agree to do something for a customer, follow through and deliver. Honesty, integrity, and keeping promises are the foundations of customer service. Being able to do this even under difficult circumstances is even more important.

- *Be responsible.* If a customer has a problem and you are contacted about it, you should own the problem until it is resolved. Don't just pass it off onto someone else and forget about it.

- *Be grateful.* Always thank your customers for their business, offer a pleasant good-bye, and invite them to contact you again in the future.

Interviews

One form of communication that is very common in business is the interview. Whether you are interviewing for a job or interviewing someone else, it's important to understand the proper way to conduct an interview. As your business grows and as your role in the business changes, you will likely be involved in conducting interviews of prospective candidates for new positions.

Interviews are a form of communication used for getting the story behind someone's résumé. If you are the interviewer, you can pursue in-depth information about a topic. For example, you could use an interview as a follow-up to certain answers given on an application. Usually, open-ended questions are asked during interviews. If you are the person being interviewed, knowing the fundamentals of interviewing will only increase your chances of success.

Basic to the interview process is developing and asking good questions. But before you design your interview questions, you need to make sure you have a clear purpose for gathering the information. This helps you focus on the answers given and select follow-up questions.

Here are the basic steps for preparing for and conducting an interview. Knowing the process and being clear on your objectives will help you develop those questions.

Getting Started

Select a setting for the interview that won't be distracting. Try to find a quiet, private place where the interviewee will feel comfortable.

When you will meet the interviewee, you will explain the purpose of the interview and any issues surrounding confidentiality. You will let the person know who will get access to information and how the answers will be analyzed.

Communications Skills

Then, you will explain the format of the interview and how it will be conducted. If you want the person to ask questions, let him or her know that questions are welcome, or else ask the person to hold any questions until the end of the interview. You can also invite questions at the start of the interview.

Types of Interviews

There are two basic styles of interviews, with varying degrees of application. The informal, conversational interview has no predetermined questions. The interview remains as open and adaptable as possible, depending on the interviewee. The formal, guided approach has a set group of questions; this ensures that the same general information is collected from each interviewee. There's still a degree of freedom for the interviewer, but there's more focus on obtaining specific information in each interview.

A hybrid approach is to use a set of open-ended questions that are asked of all interviewees. With an open-ended interview, the respondents are free to decide how they want to answer. A fixed-response interview involves asking all interviewees the same questions via a questionnaire, with the same set of multiple-choice answers. This approach results in faster interviews that are easier to analyze and compare.

Types of Interview Questions

There are six categories of interview questions commonly asked. Any of these questions can focus on the past, the future, or present. The categories are the following:

1. Behavior—what a person has done or is currently doing in his or her life
2. Opinions and values—what a person thinks about a particular topic
3. Feelings—how a person feels about a particular topic or situation
4. Knowledge—what a person knows about work-related topics
5. Sensory—what a person has experienced in life
6. Background—standard questions about a person's education, work history, and hobbies

Question Sequence and Wording

Try to get the interviewee involved in the interview as soon as possible. Don't start out by giving a long speech. Before asking about things such as feelings and opinions, however, start by asking about some facts. Using this approach, you can get the person involved in the interview before having to talk about personal matters.

Avoid long lists of fact-based questions. Instead, sprinkle them throughout the interview. Ask questions about the present before you explore the past or future. It is usually easier for interviewees to talk about what is happening right now than to recall past events or project themselves into an imaginary future. Your last question should give interviewees a chance to provide any other information that they would like to add, as well as provide their impressions of how the interview went.

Ask your questions one at a time, and be sure they are clear and easily understood. For example, avoid using company- or industry-specific terms or acronyms.

For best results, make your questions open-ended, so that interviewees can answer in their own, unique way, rather than giving simple yes or no responses. Also, be sure your questions are neutral, so that they avoid expressing an opinion that might sway a person's answers. For example, asking, "You wouldn't want to work in a loud, crowded office, would you?" assumes you'll be seeking a negative response.

Finally, avoid asking, "Why?" Questions that ask why something happened or why something was done imply a cause-and-effect relationship that may be more complex than a single answer can explain. "Why" questions also put interviewees on the defensive, as they feel they have to justify their responses.

Conducting the Interview

No one can remember everything that is covered during an interview, so you need either to take notes or to use a recording device. Make sure you discuss the use of a recorder with the interviewee ahead of time and explain its purpose. Check the status of the recorder from time to time to make sure it is still functioning.

As you move through the interview, focusing on one question at a time, don't show strong emotional reactions to the person's responses. Act as if you've heard these same answers before. Be matter-of-fact.

Provide encouragement by nodding your head and saying, "Uh-huh." If you are taking notes, be careful when you break away from the person to write something down. This breakaway signals that you were surprised or pleased with an answer, which may influence the answers for future questions.

When you move from one topic to another, provide transitions. For example, you can say, "We've been talking about your past work history. Now let's talk about where you want to go in your career."

Keep control of the interview. If the interviewee strays over into another topic and takes a long time to answer a question, the time may run out before you've completed everything on your list. Refocus the person on the topic with additional targeted questions.

After the Interview

When the interview is completed, thank the person for attending the interview and say your good-byes. Then, check the recorder and turn it off. If it is a digital recorder, transfer the file to your computer.

If you've written notes during the interview, check the notes and make sure they make sense to you. If you need to clarify something or rewrite anything that may be difficult to read later, do it now. Write down any observations you made during the interview, as well. How did the person come across? Was the person confident or nervous? Were there any surprises?

In many cases, a job candidate will be interviewed by several people in a business or department before being hired. The interview you conduct may be only one of many. Be prepared to share your observations in the form of a report or as part of a future meeting with other members of the hiring team.

45

Office Management and Supervision

As your career evolves over time, it may naturally lead to a role as an office manager or supervisor. In a small office, you may run the overall operations of the office while your boss focuses on business relationships. You may be responsible for interviewing prospective employees and filtering out the best for your boss to meet in follow-up interviews. (See Chapter 44 for information on interviewing skills.)

Organizational Structure

The way the business you work for is organized will vary depending on its business objectives, what tasks it must accomplish, and how those tasks are allocated, coordinated, and supervised. The most common organizational structure is hierarchical, with a top-down structure of managers and direct reports. The organizational structure may include different business entities, such as branches, departments, and workgroups.

The organizational structure of a business provides a foundation for its operating procedures and determines which individuals participate in the decision-making process.

- *Small business structure:* Many small businesses rely on a strategic leader who makes all key decisions. Most communication is handled by one-on-one conversations. This type of organizational structure gives the founder of a business control over growth and development.

- *Hierarchy structure:* Some large businesses rely on a bureaucracy that has a strict hierarchy of managers and with subordination of their direct reports. The organizational structure of a large business may include divisions or subsidiaries that are further divided into departments. Departments are further divided into functional teams, each with its own manager.

- *Division structure:* The divisions of a business usually are structured around a particular product or service. Each division includes all the necessary resources and functions to operate as if it were an independent business. Sometimes divisions are further subdivided geographically to better serve customers of a particular country or region.

■ *Matrix structure:* A matrix structure groups employees by both their function and the product or service offered. Teams of employees work together to take advantage of strengths and to make up for weaknesses.

In one type of matrix structure a project manager oversees the functional aspects of the project and maintains control over employee resources assigned to the project. Another type of matrix structure includes both project managers and functional managers.

■ *Work team:* One of the newest structures is the work team. In a small business, the work team may be the entire organization. Teams may include a variety of employees who perform different functions or a group of employees who perform the same function. For example, a work team may be all the employees of a particular store within a much larger company. Another example would be all of the employees working together on a software development project.

■ *Network:* Another new organizational structure is the ad-hoc network, where managers hire vendors or teams of contractors to perform services or supply products. The managers spend their time coordinating these external resources. An example of this structure is a company that has outsourced various aspects of its service or manufacturing business to outside vendors. In some cases, the network may include vendors from all over the world.

■ *Virtual team:* With the availability of email and Web conferencing software, some organizations use virtual teams that rarely meet together face to face. Sometimes a virtual team consists of a manager and various contractors or suppliers that form a network structure. Other times, the members of the virtual team may be employees who work at various offices scattered around the country or in their homes. The virtual team structure is common in software development and consulting services.

The Role of the Office Manager

Office managers often hold one of two jobs in a company. They may supervise people or they may be involved in getting a product or service out the door in order to generate revenue for the business. In a small business, you are likely to be involved in both.

In a small business, the office manager may also provide the services of human resources. You may be responsible for coordinating employee benefits, creating personnel policies, furnishing training and development, conducting performance appraisals, and providing career development. You may also have to handle personnel and performance problems.

Regardless of whether you are running the office in a small business or supervising a department in a large business, the supervisor is usually responsible for making sure the employees follow the organization's policies and procedures for things like vacation time, sick time, leaves, and overtime. You may also have responsibilities of hiring, firing, and promotions.

Supervisors must review the career needs of the employees and the staffing needs of the organization. Supervisors are often the first to recognize the need for a new position, and they may open a new role by getting authorization from management. This

Office Management

will likely require communication in order to justify the new role. The supervisor could then be involved in advertising for job candidates, reviewing résumés, and conducting interviews. You may recommend candidates for a job, then handle all the new-hire paperwork if the candidate is hired, including benefits, payroll, and tax forms. Finally, your job may involve making sure the new employee has the necessary workspace, office equipment, and supplies.

A supervisor will likely make sure that new employees get an orientation about the business, including the personnel policies, facilities, and work schedule. You may develop a training plan with the employees to make sure they have the skills needed for the job. At various times throughout the year, you may provide ongoing guidance in the form of coaching and counseling. The goal here is to help the employees take responsibility for their own development and to assist them when they need company approval to take classes or take time away from work for training.

Employee performance management may be a responsibility for an office manager or supervisor. The supervisor maintains job descriptions with responsibilities and qualifications for each position. The supervisor sets the performance standards for each job role and ensures that employees have appropriate and realistic goals. Throughout the year, they give the employees feedback on their performance. Performance reviews are then conducted throughout the year to assess how the employees have performed and what they can do to improve their performance.

A good supervisor is also a good coach. Coaching involves working with employees to create realistic goals, action plans, and time lines. The supervisor provides ongoing guidance as the employees work toward their goals. There are five aspects of goal setting that can best be remembered by using the acronym SMART:

- Specific
- Measurable
- Attainable
- Realistic
- Timely

A good coach also acts like a mentor to the employee. Since a supervisor will likely understand the organization better than the employee, the supervisor can serve as a mentor offering advice about the job and career. The employee can look to the supervisor as a role model.

Since the supervisor is the first person to share news about new policies and programs, the supervisor must be an advocate for the organization. Employees get confused and fearful whenever change is involved; however, in the rapidly changing business world, change is evitable. The supervisor must be a supporter of the organization's change initiatives to help reduce the anxiety. You must be authentic in how you present your feelings about new programs and organization change, yet tactful in how you present it.

At the same time, a supervisor must also be an advocate for employees and represent employee requests to management. For example, if an employee deserves a promotion, the supervisor must often justify the reason to management.

It's not unusual for a supervisor to be seen by employees as being one of them and a part of management at the same time. It's a unique combination that has both pluses and negatives.

Building Trust with Your Team

Trust is important in the relationship between a supervisor and an employee. Teams whose members trust one another are more productive and have fewer personnel issues. With trust, you learn to depend on one another. There's really no substitute for trust; your team either has it or it doesn't.

Trusting the people on your team means that your employees are willing to take your word for it when you tell them they need to do something they don't really want to do. Trust means you're willing to be influenced. Trust elevates performance because team members are willing to do things without debate.

A conversation is a relationship. Each person influences the other. A supervisor can't build trust with employees without being able to listen. In addition, you must share important information about yourself. You must be vulnerable in order to build trust. There must be a certain amount of interdependence in order to build trust. We must depend on others and they must depend on us. Fulfilling your promises and being fair helps build trust.

Acceptance is the key to trust, so avoid office humor that belittles people. Avoid putdowns or conversations that show disrespect. Trust is built over time as it is demonstrated. Disrespect erodes the trust that has been established.

Some people are more likely to trust than others. It depends on their history of experience. It also depends on their character in general. If they've learned not to trust people in the past, or they can't even trust themselves, then they will not trust you either.

Key aspects of trust include the following:

- Ability—The employees have knowledge skills and competencies, so that they perform in a way that meets your expectations.

- Integrity—You maintain accepted behavior based on past actions, credibility of communications, and fairness.

- Benevolence—You are concerned about the welfare of others; you would like to advance your employees rather than impede them.

- Open communication—You share control and delegate decisions.

Ethics in Business

Ethics as it relates to business involves the principles and moral problems that an individual or an organization follows in the course of conducting business. Competition between companies and even among coworkers can lead to unethical decisions. Fear of losing a job or a client, or the drive to succeed at any cost, often results in unethical corporate practices. It has several facets, as explored below.

Corporate Social Responsibility

Business ethics overlaps with business philosophy. While some businesses still focus solely on the financial return to shareholders or owners, many have expanded their focus to include corporate responsibilities to the rights and interests of everyone else. Corporate outreach programs that involve volunteering and donations often benefit the company with positive public relations. These programs also enrich the lives of employees who get involved, help improve morale, and assist other people and organizations that are in need.

Office Management

Decision-Making Styles

There are several decision-making styles that you may encounter throughout your career that go to the heart of business ethics, although there are parallels to what we all consider acceptable societal behavior. One style is to make decisions based on one's personal needs and fears while ignoring the needs of others. Another style is to be concerned primarily for others and for what will benefit everyone. A third style is to be concerned about the current situation and not about oneself or others. The fourth style is to be guided by principles and rules.

Typical Ethical Issues in Business

Some of the most common business ethics issues that appear in the news from time to time include creative accounting practices, insider trading, securities fraud, excessive executive compensation, bribery, and kickbacks.

Many ethnical issues involve human resource management in such areas as recruitment, hiring, performance management, training and development, union relations, and safety. Perhaps the most important of these is safety, since safety is sometimes weighed against profit when making decisions. A variety of workplace laws have been enacted to help ensure fairness in human resource–related activities. These laws are summarized later in this chapter.

Ethics in sales and marketing involves being responsible to consumers. For example, it is unethical to target vulnerable sections of the population for consumption of unnecessary or dangerous products and services. There are currently laws that attempt to control ethical matters in sales and marketing, such as product labeling, health and safety warnings, and financial risk.

Other related areas where unethical behavior is sometimes demonstrated include price fixing, price discrimination, anti-competitive practices, bait and switch, email spam, attack ads, and pyramid schemes. Ethics in property rights involves such matters as theft of copyright, illegal software and music copying, real estate property rights, patent infringement, and trademark infringement.

Company Policies on Ethical Behavior

Many companies have created policies that govern the ethical conduct of employees. These policies detail what is expected from workers and offer guidance on ethical decision making. Ideally, implementing these policies will help companies avoid future lawsuits.

These policies are written documents that are supported and monitored by top management. They explain what conduct is sanctioned and state the consequences for failure to adhere to the rules. Additionally, some companies have appointed compliance or business conduct officers whose job is to search for instances of fraud, corruption, and abuse. These officers report to the CEO and are responsible for assessing the ethical nature of the company's activities and making recommendations.

Conflict Management

Another aspect of being an office manager or supervisor is handling conflict management. Conflict occurs when two or more values, perspectives, or opinions are opposite in nature. You may experience personal conflict when you don't live up to your own values. You experience conflict with someone else when your values or points of view are threatened. You may experience conflict because of fear of the unknown or a lack of fulfillment. Conflict is inevitable and is a natural phase in the team-building process. When you have a diversity of ideas, it often leads to contradictory opinions.

Conflict often helps raise important issues. It causes us to work on the most important questions and it motivates people to participate in solving problems. Conflict management helps people learn to recognize differences in opinion and to learn from those differences. Therefore, conflict isn't the problem. The problem is when conflict is managed poorly. When this happens, conflict hampers productivity, lowers employee morale, mushrooms into larger conflicts, and causes people to react inappropriately.

A supervisor can cause workplace conflict by communicating poorly with employees. If employees are constantly surprised by new programs and policies without having their supervisor explain the situation, the employees don't understand the reasons for the decisions and feel left out of the process and disrespected. As a result, people will resort to getting information from the rumor mill.

Conflict can be caused by poor leadership, such as when a manager or supervisor passes the buck rather than dealing with issues head on. If decisions are inconsistent, or are made uniformly, or are not made at all, leaving an issue undecided, then conflict is evitable. Workplace conflict can also occur when there are not enough resources to go around or there is a disagreement about who does what. Conflict can occur because of personal chemistry between coworkers or between managers and employees. Strong personalities may clash. Opposite opinions may collide.

Minimizing Conflicts

There are several things you can do to minimize conflict at work. Start by reviewing the job descriptions of your team. Set up meetings with your employees and discuss the job descriptions together. Are they still accurate? Do they need to be revised? Make sure that the job roles for your team don't conflict with one another.

Take time to build relationships with each of your employees. Meet with them one-on-one at least once a month. Talk about accomplishments and any problems. You should also hold regular management meetings with your entire team to discuss initiatives and the status of major projects. Ask your team to provide regular status reports and include accomplishments, current issues, needs from management, and plans for the upcoming period.

You can minimize conflict by training your team on conflict management, delegation skills, and interpersonal communications.

Document the procedures and processes in your department so employees have job aids that describe how to perform routine tasks. Have the employees write the procedures when possible. Distribute the procedures to your team and train the team, so that team members can back one another up for business continuity purposes.

Difficult People

One unpleasant part of being an office manager or supervisor is that from time to time you have to work with difficult people. Difficult people are unhappy people. They are working from the negative side of their personality. They don't intentionally wake up each morning and decide to be difficult. They are often unaware of themselves and how their attitude affects others. They don't realize how their attitude is harmful to the team and to their own careers. As a supervisor, you will constantly be faced with situations where people challenge your decisions and make it difficult to get things done. It's important to be able to understand other people's viewpoints and why they act a certain way.

One well-recognized personality type, especially with technical people, is the *know-it-all*. This type is often seen with computer programmers, software developers, engineers, doctors, and attorneys. You might ask a know-it-all a simple question and get the response, "How dare you question me." Or, you might make a suggestion for how to do a task and get a multitude of reasons your idea won't work. Eventually, you give up trying to work with the know-it-all.

This trait is a manifestation of arrogance. People act arrogantly to avoid feeling vulnerable or insecure. They are afraid of being seen as unworthy or incompetent, so they throw up a defensive shield of arrogance. The result of this behavior is that people refuse to work with them, no one believes what they say, people don't think they really know what they're doing, and they lose credibility and respect.

Another common trait of difficult people is the *my-way-or-the-highway* attitude. This trait seems prevalent in management positions. No matter what anyone else thinks, these people force their ideas on everyone. There is no open discussion about issues. Things must be done the way these people want, or else. As an example, if you were in a meeting with this type of person and offered a suggestion, the my-way-or-the-highway person would make it clear your suggestions were not wanted. Eventually, no one wants to contribute, and the added value that comes from having a diversity of ideas is lost.

This trait is an aspect of dominance. Working with this type of person is like living under a dictatorship. When you combine dominance with power, this person becomes king of the planet. The positive side of dominance is leadership, though. When such people focus on the positive side of their personality, they can be effective and charming. But in a stressful situation they quickly jump to the dark side.

As a result of their being domineering, the team refuses to interact with these individuals. People won't tell them the truth or provide them with enough information that might help them make better decisions. People try to ignore the domineering characters and avoid implementing their ideas.

How to Handle Difficult People

When you are working with people who go into attack mode or become extremely defensive, don't try to argue with them. These people are very insecure and the more you push, the worse it will get. Since these people are probably under stress, wait until another time to pursue the discussion. If they are always this way, the only alternative is to find someone else with whom to work. Keep your self-confidence and don't allow yourself to be attacked verbally. If your boss is one of these difficult people, it's probably time to find another job.

When supervising difficult people, try to help them see how their behavior is damaging their career. Set goals that help them learn to work better with others, and then monitor their behavior closely to see if it improves. If their attitude doesn't improve, you'll have to terminate their employment.

If you find that you are becoming a difficult person yourself, learn to recognize the signs. Try not to react so quickly, and realize that you are not being attacked personally. Learn to listen when someone else asks a question or makes a suggestion. Repeat what someone has said to confirm that you understand. Ask the person to restate the question or comment if you are still unclear about what was intended. Take some time before you respond. This will help reduce the stress, so you can make a decision without feeling under pressure.

Realize that other people have good ideas that are just as valid as your own. Look for courses or workshops that teach listening skills or team building. Look for someone in the organization who can help you work on the situation. Ask him or her to let you know when you're being a jerk, to call your attention to your behavior. You have to realize that this learned behavior may take years to overcome, but don't give up on yourself.

As you prepare to work with difficult people on the job, you should do the following:

- Confront difficult people face-to-face and by yourself.
- Write down the issue that needs to be handled and your goal for the outcome of your conversation.
- Write down a list of points you need to make to support your goal.
- Write down the objections or reactions the other person may have to your view.
- Organize your notes and gather supportive documents and evidence.
- Arrange a meeting in a private place where you will not be disturbed.
- Hold the meeting and share your view.
- Stay on target by describing your points.
- Listen to the other person's side.
- Communicate and be persistent.

The more frequently you confront and deal directly with difficult people, the easier it becomes. The amount of time it takes to prepare for these types of meetings will decrease. The result is that you will become stronger and tougher.

When you confront and handle these types of situations, people will respect you for your courage and control. Taking positive action in the face of fear is an important trait shared by successful people.

Workplace Law

There are a wide variety of workplace laws that govern the relationship between businesses and employees. Many of these laws were enacted to help prevent employer abuse of employees and to control working conditions. Workplace laws vary from state to state, so it is important that you consult the Department of Labor website for your state in order to familiarize yourself with what the legal requirements are for your business and your employer.

Industrial Home Work

Many states have laws that control manufacturing activities in the home. A company may not require workers to take home components for assembly of products or to repair company equipment unless a special permit has been approved. When a permit has been received, workers must be paid the same wage as that paid in the factory or other place of business. One of the key elements in getting approval for industrial home work involves the safety of employees and whether dangerous equipment or substances are used in the manufacturing process.

Smoking in the Workplace

Some states and localities have antismoking laws that prohibit smoking in the workplace. These laws pertain to smoking in a business location, such as an office building or factory. Most of these laws do not restrict smoking outside in public areas, such an exterior break area, loading dock, or grounds. Antismoking laws also protect employees who assist in the supervision or enforcement of these laws from retaliation by the employer.

Some companies have extended their antismoking policies to include no smoking in company vehicles and no outdoor smoking on their campuses.

Regarding smoking at home, outside of the workplace, most states have laws that say that an employer may not require an employee to refrain from smoking or using tobacco products as a condition for employment. An employer may not discriminate against smokers in regard to hiring practices or compensation.

Breast-Feeding in the Workplace

Some states have laws that allow mothers to breast-feed or pump breast milk during a meal or break period. Employers are supposed to provide a room near the work area where the employee can produce milk in private. Employers are prevented from discriminating against or taking any disciplinary action against employees who exercise this right.

Electronic Surveillance

While employers may have electronic surveillance systems that involve video and audio monitoring of employee activities, there are laws that prevent electronic monitoring in break rooms, locker rooms, rest rooms, and lounges. In addition, electronic monitoring is prohibited during employment contract negotiations between managers and employees.

Employers who do engage in electronic monitoring of employee activities must inform employees in writing. This includes direct observation as well as monitoring of computers and telephones. Whenever an employer has reasonable grounds to suspect that an employee may be engaged in illegal conduct, then the employer may monitor the employee's activities without providing written notice.

Polygraph Testing

Many states have laws that prevent employers from requiring polygraph testing as a condition for employment or require a current employee to take a polygraph examination in order to continue employment. Employers may not dismiss or discipline an employee who voluntarily takes a polygraph test and fails the test.

Criminal Records

Employer inquiries about erased criminal records are prohibited. An employer may not ask about whether someone was arrested or charged if the records have been erased. This applies mainly to youthful offenders whose criminal records are erased when they become an adult, as well as people who have a criminal charge dismissed, are charged of a criminal offense but not convicted, or who are pardoned.

Whistleblowing

Employees who disclose illegal activities or unethical practices in the workplace are protected from retaliation from their employers. This not only applies to employees who report misconduct but also those who are required to testify as part of an investigation into corporate behavior on behalf of a state or federal agency. Regardless of what an employee discloses or reports, an employer may not fire, discipline, or otherwise penalize the employee.

Plant Closing Laws

Whenever a business must close a location, the business must continue to provide health insurance coverage for a certain period of time.

Drug Testing

Drug testing is allowed as a condition for employment if the employer provides written notice of the requirement at the time of the employment application. The results of any drug test must be kept confidential and should not be disclosed to any person other than the person tested.

Drug testing is also allowed for current employees if the employer has a reasonable suspicion that the employee is under the influence of drugs or alcohol, which would adversely affect job performance or threat safety. Employers are not allowed to directly observe an employee in the process of providing a urine sample.

If an employee or applicant tests positive for drugs or alcohol, the employer must allow for a second test which is separate and independent from the first. If an employee tests positive twice, then the employer may terminate an employee, deny promotions or raises, or take other disciplinary action.

Meal Periods

Generally, most state workplace laws require that employees be given a meal period at some point within an eight-hour workday. Meal periods are generally thirty minutes and are required to be given sometime after the first two hours of work or before the last two hours of work.

Blacklisting

It is illegal to publish the name of any employee for the purpose of preventing the person from securing employment.

Emergency Phone Calls

Employers must inform employees of any phone call the employer receives in which the caller states that there is an emergency that involves members of the employee's family. All reasonable efforts must be made to notify the employee of the emergency phone call.

Family and Medical Leave

The Family and Medical Leave Act (FMLA) entitles eligible employees to take unpaid, job-protected leave for specific family and medical reasons. Employers must continue to provide group health insurance coverage under the same terms and conditions as if the employee had not taken a leave.

Eligible employees are entitled to a take a leave of up to twelve workweeks within a 12-month period for the following:

- Birth of a child and the care for the newborn child within one year of birth.
- Adoption of a newly placed child or foster care of a newly placed child within one year of the placement.
- Care of the employee's spouse, child, or parent who has a serious medical condition.
- Serious health condition that makes the employee unable to perform the essential functions of his or her job.
- Issues related to the employee's spouse, child, or parent who is a member of the military engaged in active duty.

Personnel File Laws

Employees may submit a written request to their employer for access and inspection of any personnel files, if such files exist. The inspection of the files must be made during regular business hours at the place of employment. Each employer who has personnel files should keep such files for at least one year after the termination of an employee.

Work Schedule

Some states have laws that limit the number of workdays within the calendar week. In most cases, the limitation for a work schedule is no more than six days per week. Employees who observe a religious day each week may not be dismissed for refusing to work that day.

Index

About the Authors

James Stroman has served as a private professional secretary, administrative assistant, and executive assistant to a wide range of individuals including an army general, a governor, a university president, and the owner of an NFL football team (the Dallas Cowboys). He lives in Woodstock, Georgia.

Kevin Wilson is a writer, instructional designer, training consultant, and Vice President of Videologies, Inc., a company that specializes in training development for Fortune 500 companies. He is the author of *The AMA Handbook of Business Writing*, and *The AMA Handbook of Business Documents*. He lives in Acworth, Georgia.

Jennifer Wauson is a training consultant, video producer and director, project manager, and President of Videologies., Inc. She has managed multimillion-dollar projects, feature films, produced a national television series, and produced award-winning multimedia, training programs for companies like IBM, Sony, Chevron, and Verizon. She is the co-author of *The AMA Handbook of Business Writing* and *The AMA Handbook of Business Documents*. She lives in Acworth, Georgia.